PRAGMATISM AND AMERICAN EXPERIENCE

Pragmatism and American Experience provides a lucid and elegant introduction to America's defining philosophy. Joan Richardson charts the nineteenth-century origins of pragmatist thought and its development through the twentieth and twenty-first centuries, focusing on the major first- and second-generation figures and how their contributions continue to influence philosophical discourse today. At the same time, Richardson casts pragmatism as the method it was designed to be: a way of making ideas clear, examining beliefs, and breaking old habits and reinforcing new, useful ones in the interest of maintaining healthy communities through ongoing conversation. Through this practice we come to perceive, as William James did, that thinking is as natural as breathing, and that the essential work of pragmatism is to open channels essential to all experience.

Joan Richardson is Distinguished Professor of English, Comparative Literature, American Studies, and Liberal Studies at The Graduate Center of The City University of New York (CUNY). She is the recipient of a 2012 Guggenheim Fellowship, a National Endowment for the Humanities Senior Fellowship, and a Woodrow Wilson Fellowship. Her book, *A Natural History of Pragmatism: The Fact of Feeling from Jonathan Edwards to Gertrude Stein*, was published by Cambridge University Press in 2007 and nominated for the 2011 Grawemeyer Award in Religion.

PRAGMATISM AND AMERICAN EXPERIENCE

An Introduction

JOAN RICHARDSON

The Graduate Center, CUNY

CAMBRIDGE
UNIVERSITY PRESS

CAMBRIDGE
UNIVERSITY PRESS

32 Avenue of the Americas, New York, NY 10013-2473, USA

Cambridge University Press is part of the University of Cambridge.

It furthers the University's mission by disseminating knowledge in the pursuit of
education, learning, and research at the highest international levels of excellence.

www.cambridge.org
Information on this title: www.cambridge.org/9780521145381

First published 2014

Printed in the United States of America

A catalog record for this publication is available from the British Library.

Library of Congress Cataloging in Publication data
Richardson, Joan, 1946–
Pragmatism and American experience : an introduction / Joan Richardson.
pages   cm
Includes bibliographical references and index.
ISBN 978-0-521-76533-6 (hardback) – ISBN 978-0-521-14538-1 (pbk.)
1. Pragmatism.   2. Philosophy, American – 20th century.   I. Title.
B832.R53 2013
144'.30973–dc23   2013036433

ISBN 978-0-521-76533-6 Hardback
ISBN 978-0-521-14538-1 Paperback

Contents

Preface

> If this life be not a real fight, in which something is eternally gained for the universe by success, it is no better than a game of private theatricals from which one may withdraw at will. But it *feels* like a real fight – as if there were something really wild in the universe which we, with all our idealities and faithfulnesses, are needed to redeem; and first of all to redeem our own hearts from atheisms and fears. For such a half-wild, half-saved universe is our nature adapted. The deepest thing in our nature is ... this dumb region of the heart in which we dwell alone with our willingnesses and unwilling-nesses, our faiths and fears. As through the cracks and crannies of caverns those waters exude from the earth's bosom which then form fountain-heads of springs, so in these crepuscular depths of personality the sources of all our outer deeds and decisions take their rise. Here is our deepest organ of communication with the nature of things ... here possibilities, not finished facts, are the realities with which we have actively to deal.

This famous passage near the closing of William James's 1895 address, "Is Life Worth Living?" lies at the heart of pragmatism and of American experience. The address was collected in a volume published two years later entitled *The Will to Believe and Other Essays in Popular Philosophy*, which James dedicated to his "Old Friend, Charles Sanders Peirce," whom he had named as the founder of pragmatism, and of whom Ian Hacking has said, "He finished nothing, but began everything." Pragmatism springs from the realization that each of us has a real stake in what the world is to become, "that our own reactions on the world, small as they are in bulk, are integral parts of the whole thing, and necessarily help to determine the definition."[1] James stressed *feels* in his address because of all he had come to know over the previous quarter-century from his investigations and experiments in the nascent field of psychology. "The mind feels when it thinks," Jonathan Edwards, one of James's studious ghosts, had observed a century and a half earlier. In *The Principles of Psychology* (1890), James's monumental contribution to the field he helped establish, he offered the evidence confirming Edwards's perception. James's *Principles* continues today to be the source of material animating the researches of neuroscientists, cognitive scientists, philosophers, linguists, and language theorists, as well as psychologists. Alfred North Whitehead called James "that adorable genius" with good reason, as the pages here devoted to him will amply demonstrate.

Barack Obama is a direct inheritor of the pragmatism of Peirce and James, grounded as it is in the realization that "possibilities ... are the realities with which we have actively to deal." It is the story of pragmatism and American experience that has brought Obama to understand where he and we find ourselves, a situation Ralph Waldo Emerson adroitly captures in the opening of "Experience," arguably his most important essay:

> Where do we find ourselves? In a series of which we do not know the extremes, and believe that it has none. We wake and find ourselves on a stair; there are stairs below us, which we seem to have ascended; there are stairs above us, many a one, which go upward and out of sight .... Sleep lingers all our lifetime about our eyes, as night hovers all day in the boughs of the fir-tree. All things swim and glitter. Our life is not so much threatened as our perception.[2]

The genius of these lines informs all that American pragmatism as understood by its founders and its later practitioners, like Obama, means and offers. As the pages here given to Charles Sanders Peirce will make clear, this meaning and offering have as their aspiration the idea of society conceived as – in the words of Peirce's friend and mentor, father of his friend William, Henry James, Sr. – "the redeemed form of man," redemption understood to be the condition of individuals working, "all mean egotism vanishe[d]," in and as a community in ongoing conversation with contemporaries as well as with the shades inhabiting our histories. As Obama observed in *The Audacity of Hope* (2006), the Constitution is an instrument "designed to force us into a conversation," offering "a way by which we argue about our future" by making explicit what is at stake in acting one way or another, in, for example, en*acting* the passage of a law or the repeal of an amendment. As political theorists have shown, pragmatism is ideally suited to the process of democracy. Being a method devised in response to what I call "the Darwinian information," grounded in the knowledge that we inhabit a universe of chance, pragmatism offers the tools needed to take account of where we find ourselves in this ever-changing "environment of fact," examining our beliefs as we set aims. *A New Name for Some Old Ways of Thinking*, James subtitled *Pragmatism*, his 1907 framing document, a secular sacrament naturalizing grace for the spirit continuing the pluralist experiment in the aftermath of Darwin's news.

It was John Dewey among the first-generation pragmatists who made the lines connecting the method with democracy and with Darwin most explicit. It was also Dewey who named Emerson a philosopher, a designation still resisted by many within the profession. It has been Stanley Cavell's almost singular effort among philosophers to justify Dewey's naming. In lecturing and writing over the past several decades Cavell has shown Emerson not only to have influenced pragmatism but also, through Nietzsche – Emerson's strongest European reader – to have anticipated both Heidegger and the later Wittgenstein. As I discuss in Chapter 4, Dewey, in his 1903 essay, "Emerson – The Philosopher of Democracy," contextualized Emerson's enlarged understanding of "logic" – evidenced in the idiosyncratic, variously disjunct and aleatory nature of his style – presenting it as a necessary recalibration of this most basic instrument of thought, adequate to what Emerson evocatively described as "this new yet unapproachable America," "America" realized *un*exceptionally, not as a "place" but as an "event," an idea unfolding in time, an "extended duration" in Whitehead's phrase, a new name for an old idea, democracy. The work of the pragmatists, following Peirce, was and is to map and implement this new logic, stretching the logic of sequence inherited from Aristotle to accommodate both probability – the engine of our universe of chance – and the different shapes and tempos thought might take once the open, random nature of our habitation and being is admitted; non-linear geometries and algebras were born out of the same accommodations. Dewey, who had studied logic with Peirce, was exemplary in taking on this work, explicating and illustrating in everything he wrote the whys and hows of the new method's selective breeding of ideas in its application to the various fields of human endeavor: politics and political theory, education, art, and aesthetics.

Moving on from Dewey, Cavell and Richard Rorty abundantly illustrate in their work, each in his distinctive way, what happens to the idea of philosophy when it opens itself to "the use of a little imagination," as William James had urged. Cavell and Rorty set themselves to use imagination to expand the grammar and syntax of philosophical language in order to make room for what they both describe as a "therapeutic" purpose, creating a virtual space in which the texture of thinking itself can be observed. "Therapeutic" derives from a Greek word that means healing by giving attention, as a physician does, by listening – not only to what is said but to what is felt, sensed by palpation, by observing gestures and even fleeting moods as they register in pauses, punctuations of breath. Within the movement of Cavell's sentences we experience him wrestling with expression itself: stopping, listening for echoes, straining to capture words in their sites, turning around them, examining them to find whether they can render adequately the various moods prompted by his thinking about thinking. It is as though his sentences stage dramas in which the characters performing are words themselves. Rorty's experimentation, in turn, extends the range of philosophical engagement by trying out different vocabularies, multiplying the possibilities of adaptation somewhat in the manner of the evolutionary process itself. Both Cavell's and Rorty's methods aim to heal the rift between thought and language. They know at the same time that a perfect match is impossible, that we are all immigrants in language, but that this irony – another way of describing skepticism – belongs to the human condition: "Life itself is a bubble and a skepticism, and a sleep within a sleep," as Emerson went on to observe in "Experience." To become aware of this actuality of our condition frees us from the collective neurosis of believing that there is a one-to-one correspondence between words and things, words and ideas, and so of the repetition compulsion, as it were, of persisting to think that we will eventually get things absolutely right and see *the truth*. As A. O. Lovejoy observed in 1908, of what he characterized as the thirteen varieties of pragmatism then on offer, the common feature of all was to cultivate "the habit of self-analysis."[3] Pragmatism is a cure of the mind. Emerson had given the clue, the thread leading out of the labyrinth: if we conceive our habitation in language, the condition of human life, as only "a tent for the night," then the very sense of habitation, of abode, changes to become the sense of being always on the road – experience itself.

As I outline in the first chapter, my involvement with and understanding of pragmatism began many years ago when I was an undergraduate majoring in philosophy. I am indebted to those I mention and to others, then contemporaries, whose contributions to class discussions and later conversations around cafeteria tables stimulated and sharpened my thinking. In more recent years, leading graduate seminars in pragmatism together with Jack Diggins and Luke Menand while they were both at The Graduate Center (CUNY) refocused my early preparation and more than brought me up to speed in the late-twentieth-century currents charging the method. Jack's death in 2009 saddened me more than I could have anticipated – we were and continue to be diminished by his loss. Luke's move to Cambridge figures as an equal, if not final, loss. More immediately, I am especially indebted to the participants in the graduate seminars I have been conducting over the last several years at the Center. Running under the rubric of "American Aesthetics," these seminars have had as their content, in varying combinations and with different additions, the work of the figures who are the subjects here. My sense of the significance and effectiveness of pragmatism as the precising instrument it was devised to be has been consistently reinforced by the ways I have seen my students put the method to work in the streams of their own experience. Their thinking and their writing have greatly enriched my own. To name only a few of them would be to misrepresent the unfinished symphony of our engagement. They will, I know, recognize themselves individually in these pages.

Also contributing to shaping the ideas presented here has been my participation at various conferences and symposia to which I had the good fortune to be invited, as well as the singular and stirring experience of spending a day in February 2010 interviewing and simply talking with Stanley Cavell at his home in Brookline, Massachusetts. This meeting with Cavell was pivotal in allowing me to revisit aspects of his work that I had been addressing over the previous few years; the results of this encounter were presented as a lecture under the title of "Return of the Repressed: Cavell and Emerson" at a conference in his honor held in Edinburgh in 2008 and as a paper, "Emerson and Cavell," at the American Literature Association meeting in 2009. I was later to put this material in conversation with the longer history of Cavell's development as it was offered in his autobiography published in August 2010 under the title of *Little Did I Know: Excerpts from Memory*. The chapter here given to Cavell was seeded by these experiences as well as by what I learned in framing an essay for James Loxley and Andrew Taylor's *Stanley Cavell: Philosophy, Literature and Criticism* (2011); this piece, "Thinking in Cavell: The Transcendentalist Strain," grew out of the "Return of the Repressed" talk. My chapter is also informed by the essay on Cavell and his autobiography that appeared in the Winter 2012 issue of *Raritan*, "It's About Time: Stanley Cavell's Memory Palace."

Similarly, the shape of the first chapter, as well as features of the chapter given to Richard Rorty, developed from talks I was asked to give at Modern Language Association meetings in 2008 and 2009: the first, "Pragmatism and Moral Perfectionism: Emerson, William James, and Barack Obama," at a Pragmatism Round-Table; the second, "'Conversation is a game of circles,' or, Thirteen Ways of Looking at Richard Rorty" at a special session – Richard Rorty, Pragmatism, and Criticism. Exchanges with fellow panelists and comments offered by members of the audiences for these sessions that I recorded on the reading copies of my presentations have inflected what I offer in the pages following.

Even more directly, the chapter devoted to William James grew from three talks on James and pragmatism that I was invited to give: the first, "The Varieties of American Religious Experience," was a keynote lecture at the meeting of the European Association of American Studies held in Oslo, Norway, in May 2008; the second, "'Pragmatism ... she widens the field of search for God,'" also a keynote lecture, was delivered at the William James Commemorative Conference held in Hamburg, Germany, in June 2010; and the third, a lecture from which the chapter here draws its subheading, "Into the cosmic weather," was presented at "The Uses of Pragmatism" symposium held at the University of Illinois at Urbana-Champaign in September 2010. A version of "'Pragmatism ... she widens the field of search for God'" appeared in Susanne Rohr and Miriam Strube's volume, *Revisioning Pragmatism: William James in the New Millennium* (2011).

Conversations with colleagues during these various gatherings, many prompted by the responses to my talks and by the question and answer sessions on these occasions and others – with Norton Batkin, Gregg Crane, Herwig Friedl, Russell Goodman, Gordon Hutner, Heinz Ickstadt, James Kloppenberg, Sami Pihlstrom, Susanne Rohr, and Miriam Strube, among others – and ongoing conversations in New York and at other meetings with Ann Lauterbach, Steven J. Meyer, and Ross Posnock have textured what appears in these pages. I am, in addition, especially indebted to Ross Posnock for the invaluable combination of his acuity and critical generosity as a constant reader of my work.

In connection with continuing to increase the depth of field surrounding James as a subject, I am also grateful to John Irwin for inviting me to contribute an essay to the resurrected *Hopkins Review*. He asked for a piece on *Deadwood*, the three-season (12 episodes each) HBO series created by David Milch (of *Hill Street Blues* and *NYPD Blue* fame) set in the Black Hills of South Dakota during the late 1800s; the series was wildly successful and ran from March 2004 through August 2006. I was a fan of the series and had known about Milch's deep involvement with William James and with the James family; he had during the 1980s worked with R. W. B. Lewis on what they conceived as a television series but ended up instead as Lewis's volume, *The Jameses: A Family Narrative*, published in 1991 – cable broadcasting being still in its toddler stage. I had not realized, however, until carefully reading the scripts for all the *Deadwood* episodes together with Milch's detailed commentary on each episode as I prepared to write the piece for the *Review* how directly Jamesian pragmatism, permeated as it is by Emerson's spirit, informed the Milchian experience of *what-was-not-yet-but-aspired-to-be America*, as presented in the series. Aspects of what I came to understand about pragmatism as I composed my essay, "*Deadwood*: Unalterable Vibrations,"[4] have found their way into this volume. (I should also add that with this piece as credential, on the happy occasion of first meeting and speaking with David Milch in 2010, I had the good luck of being invited to spend some time at his Red Board Productions studio, where I began to learn the ropes of script-writing. I nurse the hope that cable might now be ready for something about "the James boys," as Emerson called them.)

Finally, I thank Ray Ryan for his persistence in urging me to undertake this volume and for his abiding appreciation of my work. I have been immensely rewarded by all I have learned on this adventure; I would not have had the experience were it not for him. I am, of course, grateful to the Cambridge editorial and production crews: here in New York City, particularly Louis Gulino, Marielle Poss, and Caitlin Gallagher; and in Chennai, India, the beautifully named Jayashree Prabhu, who was consistently prompt, attentive, and kind. My thanks, too, to The Graduate Center, CUNY, for a subvention that helped defray some of the costs of permissions; and to my research assistants: Amelia Greene, who negotiated the permissions for the Wallace Stevens material, and Justin Van Wormer, who aided me in compiling the index.

Abbreviations

The following works have been abbreviated for convenience. Quotations from them are identified by abbreviated title and page number. Complete citations can be found in the Bibliography.

AE   John Dewey, *Art as Experience*
CPP   Wallace Stevens, *Collected Poetry and Prose*
EL   Ralph Waldo Emerson, *Essays and Lectures*
EN   John Dewey, *Experience and Nature*

CHAPTER I

Introduction: Thirteen ways of looking at pragmatism

"All things converge on feelings," the Buddha says.... Feeling is the past being taken up into the present. It is the vector character of many things being synthesized as the fulfilled reason.

NOLAN PLINY JACOBSON, Understanding Buddhism

There is still an air of provincialism about pragmatism.... [But Donald] Davidson may have been right when he wrote that "a sea change" is occurring in recent philosophical thought – "a change so profound that we may not recognize that it is occurring." If the change of which Davidson spoke is someday recognized as having occurred [then] Peirce, James, and Dewey may cease to be treated as provincial figures. They may be given the place I think they deserve in the story of the West's intellectual progress.

RICHARD RORTY, "Pragmatism as Anti-Representationalism"

Pent in, as the pragmatist more than anyone else sees himself to be, between the whole body of funded truths squeezed from the past and the coercions of the world of sense about him, who so well as he feels the immense pressure of objective control under which our minds perform their operations? If any one imagines that this law is lax, let him keep its commandments one day, says Emerson. We have heard much of late of the uses of imagination in science. It is high time to urge the use of a little imagination in philosophy.

WILLIAM JAMES, Pragmatism

I. WHAT'S IN A WORD?

Early in January 2012, National Public Radio in New York City (WNYC) reported that *pragmatic/pragmatism/pragmatist* were the terms most searched on engines and most used in the various national media during 2011. While the commentator did not extrapolate, I think it is clear to most that this broad interest and appearance are connected with the fact that Barack Obama and his agenda have consistently been described, from the time of his first campaign for the presidency, as "pragmatic" or "pragmatist."[1] Indeed, one of Obama's deeply valued guides on how to live, what to do is the work of Reinhold Niebuhr, perhaps the purest second-generation inheritor of the aspirations and practices of William James and John Dewey – though, importantly, he unsettled the Deweyan faith in progress with his foregrounding of human limitation and imperfection. During a famous 2007 interview with then-Senator Obama, *New York Times* columnist David Brooks asked Obama whether he had ever read Niebuhr. Obama replied, "I love him. He's one of my favorite philosophers." Brooks followed up by asking what Obama had "taken away" from the pragmatist theologian. Obama responded, as Brooks described, "in a rush of words":

> I take away the compelling idea that there's serious evil in the world, and hardship and pain. And we should be humble and modest in our belief that we can eliminate those things. But we shouldn't use that as an excuse for cynicism and inaction. I take away the sense we have to make these efforts knowing they are hard, and not swinging from naïve idealism to bitter realism.[2]

Reflecting this indebtedness, *The New York Times Magazine* printed on its cover early on in Obama's presidency (May 3, 2009) a photo of him holding the same pose in which Niebuhr is figured on the cover of the reissued 2008 paperback edition of his *The Irony of American History* published by the University of Chicago Press, which features Obama's aforementioned response to Brooks on its back cover. (The portrait of Niebuhr originally appeared as the "Man of the Year" cover of the March 8, 1948 issue of *Time* magazine; see illustrations.)[3] Niebuhr's 1952 incisive meditation on America's coming of age as a world power during the turbulent but triumphant post–World War II years is an eloquent modern jeremiad warning against the "arrogance of virtue" and unexamined idealism. This warning is coupled with a reminder of the pragmatist understanding of beliefs as platforms for action; that is, of the necessity of considering as carefully as possible effects that will and might ensue from our beliefs. *Washington Post* columnist E. J. Dionne, remarking recently on Niebuhr's importance and centrality, has suggested that the following quotation from Niebuhr "should hang over all seminars": "We must always seek the truth in our opponents' errors and the error in our own truth." It has been noted that Obama – having learned important lessons from Niebuhr – wants politicians, including Democrats, to accept "the possibility that the other side might sometime have a point."[4]

In addition to voicing his admiration for Niebuhr, Obama has also noted Ralph Waldo Emerson, for whom his maternal great-grandfather was named, as inspiration. In his response to a question about his vision for America just before the closing statements of the second presidential debate in October 2012, Obama named "self-reliance" as the quality he would want each citizen to embody. Emerson has been claimed variously, as will be discussed in the chapters following, as a source or influence for American pragmatists. Obama also appointed to his cabinet Cass Sunstein, self-described as a pragmatist, to lead the Office of Information and Regulatory Affairs (OIRA), a post he held until August 2012.

The American Heritage Dictionary lists as the first sense of "pragmatism": "*Philosophy*. A movement consisting of varying but associated theories, originally developed by Charles S. Peirce and William James and distinguished by the doctrine that the meaning of an idea or proposition lies in its observable practical consequences." But it is the second sense – "A practical, matter-of-fact way of approaching or assessing situations or of solving problems" – that is almost without exception taken to be the meaning whenever one of the variants is used in connection with the Obama administration's practice or program.[5] This is most unfortunate, especially since Obama's education and experience – including his teaching at the University of Chicago, identified as it is with the inheritance of Dewey, George Herbert Mead, and other distinguished pragmatists – abundantly illustrate how profoundly he has understood the grounds and aspiration of the philosophy developed by Peirce and James and the other first-generation pragmatists.

As Obama knows, pragmatism was designed and practiced by its founders in response to the Darwinian information: realizing ourselves to be accidental creatures inhabiting a universe of chance. As Freud famously observed, there have been three great blows to our ideas about ourselves: (1) Copernicus's discovery that the earth is not at the center of the universe and so human beings do not necessarily enjoy a privileged place in the cosmos; (2) Darwin's uncovering of our descent from "a hairy, tailed quadruped, probably arboreal in its habits" and so not created "in the image" of an anthropomorphic "God"; and (3) Freud's own contribution to the continuing disturbance of our ideas of selfhood: that we are motivated largely by unconscious drives, making the question of the sixth-century monk of Sinai, John Climacus – "What is this mystery in me?" – part of the common experience of twentieth- and twenty-first-century Westerners. Emerson's often-quoted opening to his essay "Experience" perfectly captures the tenor and mood of modern human being, the spiritual landscape out of which pragmatism grew:

> Where do we find ourselves? In a series of which we do not know the extremes, and believe that it has none. We wake and find ourselves on a stair; there are stairs below us, which we seem to have ascended; there are stairs above us, many a one, which go upward and out of sight.... Sleep lingers all our lifetime about our eyes, as night hovers over day in the boughs of the fir-tree. All things swim and glitter. Our life is not so much threatened as our perception.[6]

While pragmatists, of course, yield both the notion of special creation and the idea of an anthropomorphic God, they nonetheless, for the most part, remain curious about the great order beyond us and remain intent on honoring the possibility of perceiving ourselves "part or particle" of that order – to borrow a phrase from Emerson. As William James explicitly described pragmatism's function, figuring the new method as female and as "democratic" and "flexible" as "mother nature," "she widens the field of search for God."[7] In spite of this announcement, however, there is no mention of an idea of God or of any variety of religious experience in the work of the latest "new pragmatists."[8] This is surprising. As James noted in "The Present Dilemma in Philosophy" – the first lecture/chapter of *Pragmatism* (1907) – the following observation is as true today as it was then: "Our children, one may say, are almost born scientific. But our esteem for facts has not neutralized in us all religiousness. Our scientific temper is devout."[9] To my mind, this volume – one meant to serve as an introduction to pragmatism – would not be adequate to its task if it did not include in the story of how this method came to be an account of the ways that the residues of God were preserved and naturalized into James's expanded conception of the empirical, into Peirce's conception of community, and into Dewey's idea of democracy.

2. WHAT'S THE STORY?

When Cambridge University Press editor Ray Ryan asked me to undertake a second volume about American pragmatism, I was, of course, honored, but also especially pleased since, as I indicated in the Preface to the previous volume (*A Natural History of Pragmatism: The Fact of Feeling from*

Jonathan Edwards to Gertrude Stein [2007]), I could not there cover all I had come to see and understand about this signally important philosophical method. *A Natural History of Pragmatism* traced the emergence of this form of thinking from the accidental combination of the theological impulse motivating the Puritan "errand into the wilderness" with the actuality of that wilderness, where the language brought by the settlers to this "new world" was inadequate to describe all they found and felt. I did not have space there to provide the "backstory" – or, better, to use Henry James's famous phrase, *the story of the story* – of pragmatism, a "redescription" or "renarration" that, it is to be hoped, will provide a handle with which to grasp the slippery nature of this most protean subject.[10]

A recent review of Simon Schama's *The American Future: A History* (2009) recalled Jacques Barzun's observation that "of all the books it is impossible to write, the most impossible is a book trying to capture the spirit of America."[11] Even more than democracy, our inherited political ideal and practice, pragmatism, America's defining philosophy, breathes this spirit. And the first thing to remark about this philosophy is that its name belies it, as it is not an *-ism* in any sense, but a *method* – a tool, an instrument, a way of thinking about thinking that gets us from where we find ourselves to somewhere we want to go, even if only a step closer to "this new yet unapproachable America," as Emerson so powerfully described the aspiration for a society envisioned by his friend Henry James, Sr. as "the redeemed form of man." The important part played by the elder James not only in the thinking of William James, but also in that of Charles Sanders Peirce, belongs to the story of the story of pragmatism that unfolds in the pages of this volume.

3. METHOD

A recent translator of one of Martin Heidegger's texts comments on the philosopher's reminding us of the derivation of the word "method" from the Greek *methodos* – literally, "with(in)-a-path" – and notes that the word means more particularly "to-be-on-the-way ... not thought of as a 'method' man devises but a way that already exists, arising from the very things themselves, as they show themselves through and through."[12] As William James put it in one of his many lucid descriptions of the method that would come to be identified with his name:

> New truth is always a go-between, a smoother-over of transitions. It marries old opinion to new fact so as ever to show a minimum of jolt, a maximum

of continuity. We hold a theory true just in proportion to its success in solving this "problem of maxima and minima." But success in solving this problem is eminently a matter of approximation.... The point I now urge you to observe particularly is the part played by the older truths. Failure to take account of it is the source of much of the unjust criticism leveled against pragmatism.[13]

James's complete title for his defining 1907 volume is *Pragmatism, A New Name for Some Old Ways of Thinking*, and it is comprised of what he called in his subtitle "Popular Lectures on Philosophy" (of which there are eight), which were originally delivered in Lowell, Massachusetts and at Columbia University in 1906 and early 1907, respectively. As indicated by his title, James's aim was to foreground that the method he was delineating was nothing other than *thinking* itself and that what he was doing was making explicit what the Greeks first conceptualized in their word for "thinking": *stochasmos* – literally, preparing for and taking aim at a target. What does this mean as a figure for thinking?

James would have known that *stochasmos*, the "old way of thinking" of the Classical and Hellenistic Greeks, inherited by the Romans, designates "conjecture," its form expressed in the questions it poses: "Does the thing at issue exist?" "Is there an act to be considered?" "Is there evidence for the case?" And as James would have known from his study of medicine, *stochazesthai* – the reflexive verbal form of *stochasmos* – in the Hippocratic corpus means the search for "the right measure" as an "individual" measure, and that a shift in the meaning of *stochazesthai* to "the right *mean*" was first made by Aristotle. James also would have known that it was Galen (ca. 130 CE–ca. 210 CE), the most famous doctor of the Roman Empire, who, out of attempts to define pain, made conjecture (*stochasmos*) "a conceptual tool in its own right along with reason and experience."[14] Finally, framing all of these uses is Plato's observing in his dialogue *Philebus* (56a) that harmony is discovered by "conjecture [*stochasmos*] through skillful practice." In connection with this passage, a recent commentator, drawing on the etymology of *stochasmos*, observes:

> One hits upon harmony like an archer hits his mark. The path leading to the actual success of the archer remains in the final analysis mysterious and elusive. There can be no comprehensive account why and how an archer hits the mark; there can be no comprehensive account how harmony is established between things at variance except to say that the *homologos* [shared logos, agreement] is aimed at, guessed and established through skillful practice.[15]

In a piece collected in Cheryl Misak's *New Pragmatists* reader (2007), titled "On Our Interest in Getting Things Right: Pragmatism without Narcissism," Jeffrey Stout uses the figure of the archer once again to clarify both what is at issue for pragmatists and what is at stake in thinking:

> It may be true … that the goal of getting something right should not be considered *apart* [Stout's emphasis] from – in complete abstraction from – the goal of holding beliefs one is entitled to hold. Return to the case of the archer [which he uses earlier in his essay]. Surely somewhere in the list of things she is expected to do, if she is to count as an excellent archer, is to take dead aim at her target. This aim is embedded, so to speak, in the standards of competence and excellence that have arisen in the practice of archery. Trying to shoot well involves adopting this aim. Archers who generally fail to take aim, who do not have hitting the bull's eye as one of their goals, are not excellent archers. But putting the point in this way allows us to see how important it is to continue referring to this goal if we want to capture the target-directedness of the practice. If we let this goal slip out of the picture, we are bound to lose track of one dimension of success and failure that matters to anyone actually participating in the activity.[16]

Grounded in the knowledge that we belong to a universe of chance and accordingly relinquish any notion of foundational or *un*-changing truth, pragmatists use "getting something right" in the place of an explanation of what truth is. Truth remains instead, in the felicitous phrasing of Donald Davidson (one of the important second-generation pragmatists),[17] *an unexplained primitive*, like the word for "truth," *a-letheia* in the "old way of thinking" of the Greeks, which literally means "what is not or cannot be forgotten"; it is a constantly renewed activity of perception, not dogma or an *-ism*. The title of a late poem by Wallace Stevens beautifully captures this sense: "Reality Is an Activity of the Most August Imagination." As Stout explains, borrowing from Davidson, with truth conceived in this way, "the approach to [it] is 'to trace its connections to other concepts' that are equally basic, not to define it." Or, quoting Richard Rorty – perhaps the most prominent of the second-generation pragmatists – Stout adds, "There is no such thing as Reality to be gotten right – only snow, fog, Olympian deities, relative aesthetic worth, the elementary particles, human rights, the divine right of kings, the Trinity, and the like."[18] As James established in "What Pragmatism Means," the second lecture/chapter of *Pragmatism*, using one of the phrases that was to become intrinsically associated with the method: "[I]f you follow the pragmatic method, you cannot look on any such word [such as 'God,' 'Matter,' 'Reason,' 'the Absolute,' 'Energy'] as closing your quest. You must bring out of each word its practical cash-value, set it at work within the stream of your experience."[19]

It is easy to see that if the aim of thinking about truth is "to trace its connections to other concepts" – a nutshell description of James's "radical empiricism," where the *relations between* things are as "real" as the things themselves – then the larger the sample of "other concepts" of what is "true," of what has not been, or cannot be forgotten leads to a greater chance of "getting something right." This takes us back once more to Aristotle, who observed that "the best thing by far is to be master of meta-phor" as he is the one most able to see the *homologues* (the agreements or shared features) among things. Borrowing a term from today's cultural lexicon, we could describe pragmatism's method as beginning in what I will call *intellectual sampling* – or, perhaps better, *perceptual sampling* – where we relax stringent conceptual boundaries and/or prescribed formats to allow for and attend to associative, metaphorical firings to create *a field of search* for whatever it is we have set as target or aim, ranging from an idea of God to the Higgs boson. This relaxation is the intellectual equivalent of an archer's releasing tension from the body as she focuses attention on the target, takes a stance, draws in breath as she stretches the bow before – finally – releasing the arrow. Feeding that relaxation are "the standards of competence and excellence that have arisen in the practice of archery." In the case of thinking, it is "the part played by the older truths" that feeds the opened field of perception. Into this space of relaxed mental vigilance come – as, in fact, *in-spiration*, in drawing breath – perceptions associ-ated with the end held in mind: the target. This particular "way of think-ing" James learned from Emerson, who described it in *Nature* (1836), the anonymously published azure-covered volume that sparked the revolution in thinking about thinking that James's *Pragmatism* would complete sev-enty years later. In his "Language" chapter, Emerson offers the following in describing the aim of communicating our thoughts in conversation:

> The moment our discourse rises above the ground line of familiar facts, and is inflamed with passion or exalted by thought, it clothes itself in images. A man conversing in earnest, *if he watch his intellectual processes* [emphasis added], will find that a material image, more or less luminous, arises in his mind, cotemporaneous with every thought, which furnishes the vest-ment of the thought.... This imagery is spontaneous. It is the blending of experience with the present action of the mind. It is proper creation. It is the working of the Original Cause through the instruments he has already made.[20]

Henry David Thoreau, following Emerson, describes how "With thinking we may be beside ourselves in a sane sense":

> By a conscious effort of the mind we can stand aloof from actions and their consequences; and all things good and bad, go by us like a torrent.... I only know myself as a human entity; the scene, so to speak, of thoughts and affections; and am sensible of a certain doubleness by which I can stand as remote from myself as from another. However intense my experience, I am conscious of the presence and criticism of a part of me, which, as it were, is not a part of me, but spectator, sharing no experience, but taking note of it; and that is no more I than it is you.[21]

It is not difficult to recognize in these observations anticipations of what Sigmund Freud would devise as the psychoanalytic method in the next half-century. And we will see in Chapter 5 that Stanley Cavell has aligned these early lessons from Emerson and Thoreau with psychoanalytic procedures to enlarge through his style in writing and speaking the scope of philosophy's practice – one of the prime reasons for considering Cavell a pragmatist, in spite of his demurrals about being so designated. Contemporary psychoanalyst Christopher Bollas calls the kind of mental activity described by Emerson and Thoreau and characterizing the "free association" informing analytic sessions "grazing," noting that it is "a very different form of thinking from cognitive thought" and provides "food for [cognitive] thought that only retrospectively could be seen to have a logic."[22] In any case, it is important to register pragmatism's birth alongside that of psychology; their coming into being at the moment when the nature and behavior of mind had, in the absence of God in his heaven, to be looked at and accounted for in themselves. What once would have been attributed to divine inspiration, these methods search for in the answers we provide to the question "Where do we find ourselves?" – taking our stance, after "grazing" or "sampling," to ground our aim for the future in all we've learned or found. Just as Isaac Newton made the invisible nature and behavior of light – our most constant and necessary element – visible to the mind's eye through his meticulous experimental accounting of its process, breaking it into its spectrum with a prism, pragmatism breaks our invisible train of thought, making us stop to *watch our intellectual processes*, and so *find ourselves beside ourselves in a sane sense*, understanding where we are, taking a stance on our "platforms for action," our beliefs, before we act: "only an attitude of orientation is what the pragmatic method means," James noted;[23] and elsewhere, "Thinking is the only morality." Having made thinking the subject of thinking, pragmatism brought

philosophy into the field of high modernism. It has, since, taken as many
forms as there are minds using it.

4. EXAMPLE

THIRTEEN WAYS OF LOOKING AT A BLACKBIRD

I

Among twenty snowy mountains,
The only moving thing
Was the eye of the blackbird.

II

I was of three minds,
Like a tree
In which there are three blackbirds.

III

The blackbird whirled in the autumn winds.
It was a small part of the pantomime.

IV

A man and a woman
Are one.
A man and a woman and a blackbird
Are one.

V

I do not know which to prefer,
The beauty of inflections
Or the beauty of innuendoes,
The blackbird whistling
Or just after.

VI

Icicles filled the long window
With barbaric glass.
The shadow of the blackbird
Crossed it, to and fro.
The mood
Traced in the shadow
An indecipherable cause.

VII

O thin men of Haddam,
Why do you imagine golden birds?
Do you not see how the blackbird

Walks around the feet
Of the women about you?

VIII

I know noble accents
And lucid, inescapable rhythms;
But I know, too,
That the blackbird is involved
In what I know.

IX

When the blackbird flew out of sight,
It marked the edge
Of one of many circles.

X

At the sight of blackbirds
Flying in a green light,
Even the bawds of euphony
Would cry out sharply.

XI

He rode over Connecticut
In a glass coach.
Once, a fear pierced him,
In that he mistook
The shadow of his equipage
For blackbirds.

XII

The river is moving.
The blackbird must be flying.

XIII

It was evening all afternoon.
It was snowing
And it was going to snow.
The blackbird sat
In the cedar-limbs.

WALLACE STEVENS

5. RENTING A HOUSE

Stevens's poem is an excellent example of the sampling or grazing that is one of the ways of thinking, and readers will have realized by now that sampling is the manner in which I am presenting material in this introduction. In a draft of an introduction left in manuscript late in his life, 1910 (MS 678), Charles Sanders Peirce offers that an introduction seeks a reader for the book to follow, like the description given by a house-holder who wants to let his house out to rent.[24] An item not generally included on the checklist advertising a house's features, but that should be added to improve the chances of securing a lessee, is noting how and why one came to live in this house and why one loves it. In the case of this book, it is Wallace Stevens's work with its many wondrous rooms that occasioned my original entry (now more than forty years ago) and my continuing residence in all that pragmatism means.

I learned early on in my investigations into Stevens's sources and influ-ences that his father had read – as they appeared – the articles Peirce published in *Popular Science Monthly* in 1877–8 under the heading of "Illustrations in the Logic of Science" that became the core of what would come to be called "pragmatism" – "The Fixation of Belief," "How to Make Our Ideas Clear," "The Doctrine of Chances," "The Probability of Induction," "The Order of Nature," "Deduction, Induction, and Hypothesis."[25] (William James would characterize this group of articles as the "birth certificate" of pragmatism.[26]) Later, in letters to his son Wallace studying at Harvard, Garrett Stevens would offer paraphrases of what he had gleaned from his reading Peirce about "how to make our ideas clear" or to "look not *at* facts, but *through* them." Finding these indications, I began my own careful reading of Peirce and went on, in tracing the line-aments of Stevens's imagination, to follow pointings to William James, to Emerson, to Jonathan Edwards, and so, eventually, to become myself a pragmatist. On coming across in those first years of explorations A. O. Lovejoy's "The Thirteen Pragmatisms," describing in 1908 the varieties already then on offer, I could not help but think that Stevens, from his wanderings in imagination, had, among other samplings, this article in mind in titling his poem. Of course, there is no way of knowing, as there is no hard evidence concerning the Lovejoy piece remaining in the poet's papers, but I am not alone in drawing lines of connection between Stevens and pragmatism. In *Poetry and Pragmatism* (1992), Richard Poirier made eminently clear that Stevens, who in a late letter remarked that during his years at Harvard the spirit of William James hung over everything, had internalized and incorporated the lessons of pragmatism into his manner and method.

I have used Stevens's poem as an example here – as well as other poems, lines, phrases, and titles from his work in the chapters following – because it is in his corpus that I first found and continue to find answers to "Where do we find ourselves?" in this extended moment, still so powerfully inflected by the discovery of what Stevens called our "bond to all that dust."[27] Stevens's work is centered in what "already exists, aris[es] from the very things themselves, as they show themselves through and through." In a review of Stevens's *Selected Poems* (2009), James Longenbach captures this aspect in writing about the "incandescent plainness" of Stevens's rendering of the dithering relation between "Nothing that is not there and the nothing that is":

> Stevens stands simultaneously among the most worldly and the most otherworldly of American poets, and it is paradoxically through his otherworldliness – through poems whose plain-spoken diction feels spooky – that his respect for the actual world is registered.... [T]he consolation of "The River of Rivers in Connecticut" feels enticingly complex because the poem's diction is so eerily generalized, its syntax quietly declarative. The poem's celebration of human limitation would not feel convincing if its tone did not make small means feel magical.... This tone is Stevens's great achievement, his most enduring response to the world.[28]

Reading or hearing Stevens's lines in memory always puts me in mind simultaneously of the limitation and the wonder of knowing anything at all. It is in and out of this "in-between" that pragmatism was conceived. As William James wrote in closing the Preface to *Talks to Teachers on Psychology: and to Students on Some of Life's Ideals* (1899), where we see the seeds of the method germinating in the practical advice he offers:

> [T]he truth is too great for any one actual mind, even though that mind be dubbed 'the Absolute,' to know the whole of it. The facts and worths of life need many cognizers to take them in. There is no point of view absolutely public and universal. Private and uncommunicable perceptions always remain over.... The practical consequence of such a philosophy is the well-known democratic respect for the sacredness of individuality.[29]

My aim in the chapters following is to open the conversation about pragmatism to a wider circle, remembering that it was "How to Make Our Ideas Clear" that began it all, Peirce laying out for a popular audience the first steps of the method. Peirce, James, and Dewey grounded their experiments in thinking about thinking in what they had distilled from British empiricism filtered through Emerson's alembic to be naturalized back into *experience*, the literal meaning of "empiricism" (from the Greek *empeiria*) – a meaning all but forgotten in the English *–ism*. *Empeiria*, as Emerson and the first-generation pragmatists knew, contains in its various forms an array of meanings – trial, experiment, test, attempt, endeavor, scrutinize, entice, discipline, assay, examine, go about, prove, tempt – all linked "through the idea of piercing": "Once, a fear pierced him...." As William James made explicit, the "fact of feeling" is intrinsic to experience. We cannot describe or relate what has not in some way touched us. Or, as Ludwig Wittgenstein, who acknowledged a great debt to James and recognized in his own work a variety of pragmatism, famously expressed, "Whereof one cannot speak, thereof one must be silent."[30] I offer the sampling in this introduction to familiarize readers with the range of experience from which I draw in telling this story of the story of pragmatism. James once observed that one should know the biography of a philosopher in order to understand his work. I have in the pages to come provided those biographical details for each of my subjects that I feel illuminate the varieties of their philosophical experience.

Complementarily, because all of these figures were, by their own accounts, experimenting in "bring[ing] out of each word its cash-value, set[ting] it at work within the stream of [their] experience," I have provided extended samplings of their writing to give the flavor of that very process, to allow the witnessing of their thinking as they "bec[a]me beside [them]selves in a sane sense," making notations of interior dialogues and conversations. Without these samplings, "the fact of feeling" always accompanying and feeding thought would be lost. I have also along the way repeated lines and sections of earlier quoted passages in illustration of the actuality of the ongoing conversation through time that each of the writers discussed here, beginning with Emerson, understood thinking to be: a thread of meaning unwoven from an earlier text, taken up to be rewoven and color a new fabric of ideas. As Peirce clearly understood, the process by which thinking changes is like music: "Music is thinking, then, not sound," Stevens would announce as the major chord of "Peter Quince at the Clavier," one of his most cryptically revealing of poems where thinking is both form and content. Peirce had provided the score in "How to Make Our Ideas Clear": "Thought is a thread of melody running through the succession of our sensations.... And what, then, is belief? It is the demi-cadence which closes a musical phrase in the symphony of our intellectual life."[31] The symphony will continue as long as we have life on the planet, themes being played out in their varieties of belief. Following the movements of the composers who are the subjects here, I have attempted to mark some of the demi-cadences, echoing re-statements of old ideas touching new minds. The repetitions, in other words, are not evidence of bad editing, but fully intended to embody a central aspect of the method of pragmatism itself.

6. INTERLUDE

> There is a process in the mind very analogous to crystallization in the mineral kingdom. I think of a fact of singular beauty & interest. In thinking of it I am led to many more thoughts which show themselves first partially and afterwards more fully. But in the multitude of them I see no order. When I would present them to others they have no beginning. There is no method. Leave them now, & return to them again. Domesticate them in your mind, do not force them into arrangement too hastily & presently you shall find they will take their own order. And the order they assume is divine. It is God's architecture.
>
> EMERSON, *Journals and Miscellaneous Notebooks* (3: 316)

7. CONVERSATION IS A GAME OF CIRCLES

Conversation is the heart of pragmatism. After all, to have a conversation, "in earnest," one has to know, or *should* know, what one is talking about or looking for – "Whereof one cannot speak, thereof one must be silent." As Anne Freadman, an astute reader of Peirce – who himself valued conversation above all else – has observed of what she has learned from him:

> Conversation with neighbors is a practice of the fence. We recognize, and can learn, or learn about, practices that are not "ours." What constitutes "we" changes as a result. Practices are conversations that confer membership on particular groups and distinguish those groups from others, but they are not exclusive, and no human individual engages in only one kind of conversation.[32]

In describing conversation as "a game of circles," Emerson compared it as well to the "cloven flame" of Pentecost, where each speaker, "another redeemer" in the exchange of ideas, "strikes a new light,"[33] adds another voicing of experience from a particular extended moment in space-time – "The facts and worths of life need many cognizers to take them in." It was in the early meetings during the 1870s of the group Peirce would ironically call "The Metaphysical Club," where the ideas that would crystallize to become the method of pragmatism began to be talked about. Louis Menand and Paul Jerome Croce, as well as Philip Weiner and others before and after them, have provided comprehensive accounts of the historical context and concerns of this group, shadowed as it was by the Civil War and committed to giving close attention to the complex interplay between science and religion in light of the Darwinian event. Within this group it was Chauncey Wright – like Peirce, a mathematical prodigy – who made conversation central. As I offered in *A Natural History of Pragmatism*:

> Wright's untimely death in 1875 precluded the possibility of his formally working out and publishing, in the manner of Peirce and James, the ideas germinal to the conversations, which he seems most often to have instigated during the early meetings of the circle, about the "new intellectual style" necessary to the changed environment of uncertainty, the "cosmic weather," as he put it; indeed, in true Emersonian spirit, invoking the "original relation" offered to inquiry by the Socratic model, Wright believed in practicing "philosophy as conversation," [a] habit James would methodically cultivate.[34]

The model of conversation as practiced by the Greeks was one of the "old ways of thinking" that pragmatism revitalized, its aim to make our ideas clear by drawing on individual experience, looking for the illustration, comparison, metaphor, story, or aphorism to translate what is held in mind into what Stevens described as "the language of fact ... [b]ut fact not realized before."[35] "[A]ll language is vehicular and transitive," Emerson observed,[36] and in this its exquisite value. Given the change in the "cosmic weather" brought with Darwin's news, the conversations of the first-generation pragmatists circled around developing a new logic – a logic of probability to supersede the logic of sequence that had been in place, with modifications, since Aristotle. This new logic was the subject of manuscript lectures Peirce – "Charles Sanders Peirce was the greatest philosopher of probability whom we have known," observes Ian Hacking[37] – distributed to members of the Metaphysical Club during the 1870s. Out of the conversations generated by these lectures developed the method that would be given the "new name" of "pragmatism":

> Much like Ralph Waldo Emerson's reading of "Nature" at the Transcendentalist Club in the middle 1830s, Peirce's logic papers were a thunderbolt that generalized and highlighted the implications of the perspectives on philosophy and scientific method the group had been grappling with for years.... Peirce remembered that "it was there that the name and doctrine of pragmatism saw the light."[38]

Of course, as Peirce made explicit, thinking is "talking" with oneself, and so also conversation,[39] even if the language of this talk consists not of words, but of numbers or diagrams. (Indeed, Peirce recognized his own "diagrammatic thinking" together with his left-handedness as key to what he was able to perceive; thinking "out of the box," as it were.) The singular feature of conversation is the *conversion* of *the shape of an idea from one form into another.* "Truth *happens* to an idea"[40] (James's emphasis) in an ongoing conversation through time. "We must not begin by talking of pure ideas," Peirce said, " – vagabond thoughts that tramp the public roads without any human habitation, – but must begin with men and their conversation."[41]

8. PRAGMATISM AND COMMON SENSE

"Pragmatism and Common Sense" is the title of the fifth lecture/chapter in James's *Pragmatism*. He offers there additional brilliantly useful figures central to keep in mind in the ongoing conversation that this method is:

> To begin with, our knowledge grows in spots. The spots may be large or small, but the knowledge never grows all over: some old knowledge always remains what it was. Your knowledge of pragmatism, let us suppose, is growing now. Later, its growth may involve considerable modifications of opinions which you previously held to be true. But such modifications are apt to be gradual....
>
> Our minds thus grow in spots; and like grease spots, the spots spread. But we let them spread as little as possible: we keep unaltered as much of our old knowledge, as many of our old prejudices and beliefs as we can. We patch and tinker more than we renew. The novelty sinks in; it stains the ancient mass; but it is also tinged by what absorbs it. Our past apperceives and co-operates; and in the new equilibrium in which each step forward in the process of learning terminates, it happens relatively seldom that the new fact is added raw. More usually it is embedded cooked, as one might say, or stewed down in the sauce of the old.
>
> New truths thus are resultants of new experiences and of old truths combined and mutually modifying one another. And since this is the case in changes of opinion to-day, there is no reason to assume that it has not been so at all time. It follows that very ancient modes of thought may have survived through all the later changes in men's opinions. The most primitive ways of thinking may not yet be wholly expunged. Like our five fingers, our ear-bones, our rudimentary caudal appendage, or our other "vestigial" peculiarities, they may remain as indelible tokens in our race-history. Our ancestors may at certain moments have struck into ways of thinking which they might conceivably not have found. But once they did so, the inheritance continues....
>
> [O]ur fundamental ways of thinking about things are discoveries of exceedingly remote ancestors, which have been able to preserve themselves throughout the experience of all subsequent time. They form one great stage of equilibrium in the human mind's development, the stage of common sense. Other stages have grafted themselves upon this stage, but have never succeeded in displacing it.[42]

9. A NEW NAME FOR SOME OLD WAYS OF THINKING

As William James reminded his various audiences throughout his career, the way of thinking that took on the new name of "pragmatism" was engrafted not only on the old way of thinking of the Greeks or the more recent old way of thinking of the empiricists, but also deeply inflected by some of the oldest ways of thinking embodied in what Stanley Cavell has characterized as the "Eastern longings" of Emerson and Thoreau, the ancient forms of wisdom contained and expressed in the Sacred Books of the East – the *Vedas*, the *Upanishads*, the *Bhagavad Gita*. These texts began to have their effect in America during the early part of the nineteenth century, and the history of these influences has been widely discussed, but Cavell has pointed to a particular account that was significant as well to Gershom Scholem, to Freud, and to Wallace Stevens: French novelist Romain Rolland's biographies of Ramakrishna and Vivekananda.[43]

In *The Life of Vivekananda and The Universal Gospel* (1929), Rolland devotes three chapters to accounting for America's readiness for and receptivity to "Vedantic thought ... [which] did not escape any of the Emerson group, beginning with Emerson himself"; he describes Emerson, together with Thoreau and Whitman, as the "Anglo-Saxon forerunners of the spirit of Asia."[44] Rolland is excellent in detailing "the revolutionary character of [America's] spiritual and social movement" in the nineteenth century "and the impression of 'Bolshevism' which it produced on the minds of the governing classes and on middle class opinion" in the shape of experiments such as Brook Farm. Referring to an article published in February 1929 in *The Bookman* by Harold D. Carey, Rolland reminds readers that it was Emerson who was accused by the conservative constituency "of being chiefly responsible for the spirit of revolt"[45]; it is pertinent to remind today's readers of the continuing resistance in professional philosophy to admitting Emerson as a philosopher and that the varieties of nineteenth-century Transcendentalism triggered by his anonymously published 1836 volume all had in common a revolutionary, political intent directed against the increasing materialism of the culture. Notably, it has been Cavell's singular effort within the academy to establish Emerson as the "philosopher of democracy" John Dewey was the first to name him. The connection of democracy and the transformation of values with what Vivekananda brought to America of the spirit of India belongs to what I have called the "transcendentalist strain" that Cavell identifies as characterizing Emerson's voice and motivating his "moral perfectionism."[46] As will be discussed in Chapter 5, it is this aspect of Emerson that to Cavell's mind is not represented in "calling Emerson a pragmatist." This issue is a knot that needs to be untied, and it is part of my purpose in and with the chapters collected here to do just that: attempt squaring the circle, showing pragmatism itself to be as "transcendentalist as it is pragmatist" – to borrow Cavell's words describing Emerson.

One of the reasons for Cavell's wish to distinguish Emerson's and his own varieties of philosophical practice from pragmatism is the tendency of the Continental and analytic schools to regard pragmatism as a provincial and consequently inferior expression of philosophy's purpose; a prejudice that serves to maintain hierarchy and European authority within the tradition. This, as it were, Old World attitude completely occludes the importance of William James and his direct inheritance from Emerson; yet those maintaining this attitude at the same time acknowledge Nietzsche's indebtedness to the Sage of Concord. One of the consequences of erasing James from the picture is losing a central feature of the context in which Jamesian pragmatism was born – a context vibrantly colored by the spiritual and social aims epitomized by Vivekananda's visits to the United States between 1893 and 1900, events pointed to by James not only in *The Varieties of Religious Experience* (1902) but also, importantly, in the last lecture/chapter of *Pragmatism*, "Pragmatism and Religion," where he directs his audience and later readers to "Remember Vivekananda's *use* [emphasis added] of the Atman: it is indeed not a scientific use, for we can make no particular deductions from it. It is emotional and spiritual altogether."[47] During 1907, James not only published *Pragmatism*, but also an article in *The American Magazine* titled "The Energies of Men." After quoting a passage from the January 1907 issue of the *Philosophical Review* written by his friend the Polish philosopher Wincenty Lutoslawski about Hatha Yoga and Yoga practices generally "unlocking what would otherwise be unused reservoirs of individual power," James gives a vivid description of turn-of-the-century America's thirst for spiritual regeneration, remarking of Yoga that it is "the most venerable ascetic system and the one whose results have the most voluminous experimental corroboration":

> We are just now witnessing a very copious unlocking of energies by ideas in the persons of those converts to "New Thought," "Christian Science," "Metaphysical Healing," or other forms of spiritual philosophy who are so numerous among us today. The ideas here are healthy-minded and optimistic; and it is quite obvious that a wave of religious activity, analogous in some respects to the spread of early Christianity, Buddhism, and Mohammedism, is pouring over our American world....

> How far the mind-cure movement is destined to extend its influence, or
> what intellectual modifications it may yet undergo, no one can foretell....
> But no unprejudiced observer can fail to recognize its importance as a
> social phenomenon today, and the higher medical minds are already trying
> to interpret it fairly, and make its power available for their own therapeutic
> ends.[48]

It is in this climate that James offers *Pragmatism* as a method that enables
finding "ideas which unlock our hidden energies"; a process of thinking as
conversion, conversation, and *contradiction* – testing the possibilities offered
to find what will work best to move us if only one step closer to our aim
in our time.[49] "Both our personal ideals and mystical experiences must
be interpreted congruously with the kind of scenery which our thinking
mind inhabits. The philosophic climate of our time inevitably forces its
own clothing on us"[50]:

> [F]or there never can be a state of facts to which new meaning may not
> truthfully be added, provided the mind ascend to a more enveloping point
> of view. It must always remain an open question whether mystical states
> may not possibly be such superior points of view, windows through which
> the mind looks out upon a more extensive and inclusive world.[51]

"Pragmatism and Religion" provides a final summation of "What
Pragmatism Means" – the title of James's second lecture/chapter – by
exemplifying the method at work in dealing with the ultimate question
of how to conceive our relation to the universe, picking up on the aim
described in closing that second lecture/chapter:

> In short, she widens the field of search for God. Rationalism sticks to logic
> and the empyrean. Empiricism sticks to the external senses. Pragmatism is
> willing to take anything, to follow either logic or the senses and to count
> the humblest and most personal experiences. She will count mystical expe-
> riences if they have practical consequences. She will take a God who lives in
> the very dirt of private fact – if that should seem a likely place to find him.
>
> Her only test of probable truth is what works best in the way of leading us,
> what fits every part of life best and combines with the collectivity of experi-
> ence's demands, nothing being omitted. If theological ideas should do this,
> if the notion of God, in particular, should prove to do it, how could prag-
> matism possibly deny God's existence? She could see no meaning in treat-
> ing as "not true" a notion that was pragmatically so successful. What other
> kind of truth could there be, for her, than all this agreement with concrete
> reality?
>
> In my last lecture I shall return again to the relations of pragmatism with
> religion. But you see already how democratic she is. Her manners are as

various and flexible, her resources as rich and endless, and her conclusions as friendly as those of mother nature.[52]

James's drawing specifically on "Vivekananda's use of the Atman" in that last lecture is highly significant as it was Vivekananda's singular mission to adapt Vedantism to the actualities of the present, taking the developments in science and evolutionary theory in particular into full account. Vivekananda came from a high-caste family, was deeply educated and cosmopolitan, and was active in introducing Western ideas and "evolutionism" into Hinduism, for which he was accused of blasphemy by Hindu representatives of rival societies at the Parliament of Religions held as part of the 1893 Columbian Exposition in Chicago, where Vivekananda's ideas were first presented to the West. Over the next several years, he would lecture and teach widely in the United States; in New York, for example, meeting and sharing ideas with Sir William Thomson (later Lord Kelvin), Hermann von Helmholtz, and Nikola Tesla. His lecture at Harvard on "The Philosophy of the Vedanta" that he delivered at the invitation of William James in March 1896 was especially influential, sparking vigorous responses generally as well as ongoing conversations with James, "who called his new friend 'an honor to humanity.'" So impressive was Vivekananda's talk that he was offered the chairmanship in Eastern philosophy at Harvard, which he declined, "noting his vows as a monk." (It is reported that Gertrude Stein, then a student of James's at Radcliffe, was also one of the members of the distinguished audience.)[53] And most importantly in connection with what would emerge in *Pragmatism* was what James learned about Raja-Yoga and Jnana-Yoga – the Yoga of the mind – from Vivekananda. James not only talked about these varieties of yoga with his new friend, but also studied Vivekananda's *Raja-Yoga* and learned its practice, which has the transformation of energy into will as its focus.[54]

Vivekananda set the idea of Atman in an evolutionary frame, as in the following passage where, as noted by Margaret Elizabeth Noble (who was to become one of his most devoted disciples), he describes the growth of the religious idea and the relation of its various forms to one another:

> At first the goal is far off, outside Nature, and far beyond it, attracting us all towards it. This has to be brought near, yet without being degraded or degenerated, until, when it has come closer and closer, the God of Heaven becomes the God in Nature, till the God in Nature becomes the God who is Nature, and the God who is Nature, becomes the God within this temple of the body, and the God dwelling in the temple of the body becomes the temple itself, becomes the soul of man. Thus it reaches the last words it

can teach. He whom the sages have sought in all these places, is in our own hearts. Thou art He, O Man! Thou art He![55]

As significant as the content of his message was his practice. Vivekananda energized Vedanta, exemplifying in his own career and directing in his followers a shift in understanding the Eastern religious attitude from passivity to ongoing activity aimed at improving oneself and others in moving toward greater freedom and democracy; as Rolland describes, he "shattered" the idea of religion as "contemplative inaction" and stressed that thought was to be expressed in action: "Religion, if it is true religion, must be practical."[56] He taught his "Practical Vedanta" as a version of Emersonian self-reliance: "It is a man-making religion that we want," he proclaimed; "it is man-making education all around that we want.... Truth ... must be invigorating.... Give up these weakening mysticisms ... the greatest truths are the simplest things in the world, simple as your own existence."[57] He acknowledged the imperfection and evil in the world, and constantly urged the union of East and West, adjusting the ways of teaching to different individuals and circumstances: "Her manners are ... various and flexible, her resources ... rich and endless." Phrases from Vivekananda's lectures appear in James's *Pragmatism*: the subject of "the one and the many"; the shift in "centre of gravity" from the empyrean to the earth.[58] And in preemptive response to the common negative criticism of pragmatism that it is simplistically optimistic and Pollyannaish, ignoring suffering and evil, we have James voicing in his fourth lecture/chapter that "the scale of the evil actually in sight defies all human tolerance; and transcendental idealism, in the pages of a Bradley or a Royce, brings us no farther than the book of Job did – God's ways are not our ways, so let us put our hands upon our mouth."[59]

Vivekananda adapted Vedanta for the reality of his moment, incorporating the Darwinian information into that system of belief to urge as great a variety as possible of actions directed toward improving individual and societal conditions. Similarly, in the final lecture/chapter of *Pragmatism*, James details what he means by *meliorism* – a concept adapted to understanding that the universe is not fixed, but evolving and that humans have "a stake" in the manner of its development. James makes a crucial distinction between the "rational unity of things" and "possible empirical unification." The "rational unity of all things" corresponds to the idea of Brahman – the Absolute – as fixed, an idea belonging to traditional Hindu cosmology; "possible empirical unification," in contrast, takes account of evolutionary process and corresponds to Vivekananda's realization of Brahman as constant yet changing. As we have witnessed most recently with the discovery of the Higgs boson, we move ever closer to seeing the truth of Vedanta: that Atman is Brahman; indeed, the mass of everything in the universe – stars, planets, and we ourselves – *becomings* of motion through that invisible field, shapes of space-time. "[I]n the language of physics," as Alfred North Whitehead would describe, "the aspects of a primate are merely its contributions to the electro-magnetic field"; "individuality ... the transmission of a definite train of recurrent waveforms."[60]

As James details, these *becomings* on the human scale depend on our platform of belief being *in between* the optimist's – who believes moral progress inevitable – and the pessimist's – who believes no moral progress is possible and remains indifferent and passive. The in-between position – *not*, significantly, the optimism of mind-cure or New Thought – is *meliorism*, the method of pragmatism: "Where do we find ourselves? In a series of which we do not know the extremes, and believe that it has none": "... on the way." "Meliorism treats salvation [or moral progress of any kind] as neither inevitable nor impossible. It treats it as a possibility, which becomes more and more of a probability the more numerous the actual conditions of salvation [or improved societal conditions] become."[61] In spite of imperfection and evil, to act well – "to give relief to no matter how small a fraction of the world's mass. This is living reason" – improves the chances of the world we inhabit becoming a better place:

> Our acts, our turning-places, where we seem to ourselves to make ourselves and grow, are the parts of the world to which we are closest, the parts of which our knowledge is the most intimate and complete. Why should we not take them at their face-value? Why may they not be the actual turning-places and growing-places which they seem to be, of the world – why not the workshop of being, where we catch fact in the making, so that nowhere may the world grow in any other kind of way than this? ...
> I find myself willing to take the universe to be really dangerous and adventurous, without therefore backing out and crying 'no play.'[62]

And so, we are where we began, with Barack Obama's response concerning his "take-away" from Niebuhr, now understanding the full sense of his pragmatism:

> I take away the compelling idea that there's serious evil in the world, and hardship and pain. And we should be humble and modest in our belief that we can eliminate those things. But we shouldn't use that as an excuse for cynicism and inaction. I take away the sense we have to make these efforts knowing they are hard, and not swinging from naïve idealism [optimism] to bitter realism [pessimism].

David Brooks's column on July 19, 2012 titled "Where Obama Shines" praises the president's "nimbleness" in having "created a style of [foreign] policy making that is flexible, incremental and well adapted to the specific circumstances of this moment." Brooks goes on to comment that Obama's "record is impressive," noting his ability not only to manage "ambiguity" and "uncertainty," but also "the tension between multilateral and unilateral action"[63] – the many and the one. These accomplishments and skills are those of someone who has heeded and practiced well the method Peirce, James, Dewey, their fellows and inheritors devised to address the conditions of life in a universe of chance. Obama's nimble performance, with his aspiration and simultaneous acknowledgment that "the imperfect is our paradise,"[64] is "as transcendentalist as it is pragmatist," perfectly illustrating the Emersonian "moral perfectionism" that Stanley Cavell has kept at the center of our conversations about "this new yet unapproachable America."

10. THE MEANING NOT THE NAME I CALL[65]

On several occasions, William James described pragmatism as continuing the work of the Protestant Reformation, loosening the ties of orthodoxy and outworn habit of any kind to admit all the possibilities of belief belonging to a pluralistic universe. In the penultimate paragraph of *Pragmatism*, he writes: "[W]e do not yet know which type of religion is going to work best in the long run. The various overbeliefs of men, the several faith-ventures, are in fact what is needed to bring the evidence in."[66] Just as nature described by Darwin produced a superabundance of varieties in each species, offering thereby the possibility of fit and so continuity within the constantly changing order of things, so the varieties of religious experience offer possibilities for our continuing relation to a universe beyond our understanding, of "vital conversation with the unseen divine"[67]:

> [T]he Absolute has nothing but its superhumanness in common with the theistic God. On pragmatistic principles, if the hypothesis of God works satisfactorily in the widest sense of the word, it is true. Now whatever its residual difficulties may be, experience shows that it certainly does work, and that the problem is to build it out and determine it, so that it will combine satisfactorily with all the other working truths. I cannot start upon a whole theology at the end of this last lecture; but when I tell you that I have written a book on men's religious experience, which on the whole has been regarded as making for the reality of God, you will perhaps exempt my own pragmatism from the charge of being an atheistic system. I firmly disbelieve,

myself, that our human experience is the highest form of experience extant in the universe. I believe rather that we stand in much the same relation to the whole of the universe as our canine and feline pets do to the whole of human life. They inhabit our drawing-rooms and libraries. They take part in scenes of whose significance they have no inkling. They are merely tangent to curves of history the beginnings and ends and forms of which pass wholly beyond their ken. So we are tangents to the wider life of things. But, just as many of the dog's and cat's ideals coincide with our ideals, and the dogs and cats have daily living proof of the fact, so we may well believe, on the proofs that religious experience affords, that higher powers exist and are at work to save the world on ideal lines similar to our own.[68]

"Pragmatism ... she widens the field of search for God."

In discussing Vivekananda's mission in coming to the West, Margaret Noble stresses repeatedly his embodying the crucial distinguishing feature of Hinduism – "the idea that the path of the soul is to be chosen by itself" – "making [Hinduism] not only tolerant, but absorbent, of every possible form of faith and culture": "The vast *complexus* of systems which made up Hinduism, was in every case based upon the *experimental* realization of religion, and characterized by an infinite inclusiveness" (emphases in original).[69] Pragmatism's method, too, was bringing the wisdom of this "old way of thinking" to the West in its own language. As Vivekananda reminded his audiences, according to Hindu *savants*, "the whole universe is only *the meaning of words* [emphasis in original]. After the word comes the thing. Therefore, the idea is all!":

> Orthodox Hinduism makes *sruti*, the sound, everything. The *thing* is but a feeble manifestation of the pre-existing and eternal Idea. So the *name* of God is everything: God Himself is merely the objectification of the idea in the eternal mind. Your own name is infinitely more perfect than the person, you! Guard you your speech! [Emphases in original]

"As he talked," Noble observes, "one saw that the whole turned on the unspoken conviction, self-apparent to the Oriental mind, that religion is not a creed, but an experience; a process, as [he] said, of being and becoming."[70] Repeatedly, Cavell in his practice of what I call "transcendentalist pragmatism,"[71] has reminded his audiences and readers that "in philosophy it is the sound which makes all the difference."

II. THE THING IS, OR IT'S ABOUT TIME

In telling a story of the story of pragmatism, one learns many new things and deepens understandings of others. These findings, or, better, *seeings*, naturally affect what had been projected – the plan – somewhat in the way one plots a course before one sets out to sail, but always finds that adjustments, course corrections, and unplanned stops in certain ports because of the weather have to be made. Thus, the actual route comes to resemble the meander of a river or stream. Evolution meanders in its "progress," more complex forms growing and making new designs, like crystals; "knowledge grows in spots," as James described; or, as Wallace Stevens observed of the processes of mind, "Thought tends to collect in pools."[72] Indeed, allowing thinking to shape itself as it moves toward the end held in mind characterizes the method of pragmatism itself. As Richard Rorty observed in the Introduction to *Philosophy and the Mirror of Nature* (1978), a seminal text for the second-generation, "neo-" pragmatists, the method plays by a completely new set of rules; it is purposely not "systematic," like the practice of analytic philosophers, but, rather, "therapeutic." Of his volume, Rorty writes:

> The aim of this book is to undermine the reader's confidence in "the mind" as something about which one should have a "philosophical" view, in "knowledge" as something about which there ought be to a "theory" and which has "foundations," and in "philosophy" as it has been conceived since Kant.[73]

Rorty shares what he calls this "therapeutic" aim with Cavell, both making explicit their debt to Nietzsche in this ambition. Rorty clarifies what "therapeutic" means by explaining how Wittgenstein, Heidegger, and Dewey in their later works deconstructed their earlier efforts to retain a certain traditional conception of philosophy by questioning their motives for "philosophizing" and so questioned where they found themselves and the nature of the work "philosophy" could, in fact, do. The work of philosophy for pragmatists new and old is, simply, to help us understand why and how the practice has come to be what it is in our moment and to demonstrate its usefulness. This is the work I hope to continue within the space of these chapters. It has been intensely challenging to wrestle with the highly articulate figures who are my subjects, themselves wrestling with material that is in the most actual sense "unhandsome," "lubricious," slippery, as they struggle to make adequate distinctions, to make their ideas clear:

> I take this evanescence and lubricity of all objects, which lets them slip through our fingers then when we clutch hardest, to be the most unhandsome part of our condition. Nature does not like to be observed, and likes that we should be her fools and playmates. We may have the sphere for our cricket-ball, but not a berry for our philosophy. Direct strokes she never

gave us power to make; all our blows glance, all our hits are accidents. Our relations to each other are oblique and casual.[74]

I have focused on the main figures in the first- and second-generation pragmatists, all of whom exemplify in the evolution of their practice the method itself, their address to the changing environment of fact in which they found themselves. While, for example, I have learned from Ruth Anna and Hilary Putnam, they remain within the "systematic" frame Rorty describes, as does Donald Davidson. I have also not taken up the technical conversations that would remain opaque to those outside the profession. At the same time, these are important discussions, and there are several collections available that will provide interested readers a comprehensive survey of the field. These include, in addition to Cheryl Misak's *New Pragmatists*, Russell B. Goodman's *Pragmatism: A Contemporary Reader* (1995); Louis Menand's *Pragmatism: A Reader* (1997); John J. Stuhr's *Pragmatism and Classical American Philosophy: Essential Readings and Interpretive Essays* (1999), as well as his *100 Years of Pragmatism: William James's Revolutionary Philosophy* (2010); Stuart Rosenbaum's *Pragmatism and Religion* (2003); Susan Haack and Robert Lane's *Pragmatism Old and New: Selected Writings* (2006); Robert B. Talisse's *A Pragmatist Philosophy of Democracy* (2007); Robert B. Talisse and Scott F. Aikin's *Pragmatism: A Guide for the Perplexed* (2008), as well as their *The Pragmatism Reader: From Peirce through the Present* (2011); and Joseph Margolis's four volumes, the latest of which – *Pragmatism Ascendent, A Yard of Narrative, a Touch of Prophecy* (2012) – examines pragmatism particularly in relation to analytic philosophy. Balancing these, Richard Westbrook in *Democratic Hope: Pragmatism and the Politics of Truth* (2005) offers what is considered by many to be the best current intellectual history of pragmatism. In addition, there are two issues of *Contemporary Pragmatism* edited by Mitchell Aboulafia and John R. Shook that are particularly useful for current debates (Volume 6, Number 1 [June 2009] and Volume 8, Number 2 [December 2011], the latter devoted to Obama's affiliation with and practice of pragmatism). Most recently, as the typescript of this text was circulating for the publisher's readers' reports, Philip Kitcher's *Preludes to Pragmatism: Toward a Reconstruction of Philosophy* appeared, promising with his "pragmatic naturalism" to renew the pragmatism of James and Dewey.[75] And, a few months before this volume will be released, Cheryl Misak's newest volume, *The American Pragmatists* will be published.

Complementarily, there are other texts not specifically addressed to pragmatism that together constitute a set of required readings for those interested in the larger cultural conversation inflecting the evolving concerns of pragmatism. At the top of this list is, of course, Darwin's *On the Origin of Species*, followed by James's *The Principles of Psychology* and *The Varieties of Religious Experience*, Henri Bergson's *Creative Evolution*, Freud's work generally, Alfred North Whitehead's *Science and the Modern World*, Wittgenstein's *Philosophical Investigations* and *On Certainty*, J. L. Austin's *Sense and Sensibilia*, Thomas Kuhn's *The Structure of Scientific Revolutions*, Ian Hacking's *The Taming of Chance* – and encompassing all, the work of, in James's phrase, "the divine Emerson." Without these anchorages of thought, I could not have understood what I have nor been able to tell the story that unfolds in this volume. In addition, a vast body of scholarship exists focused on pragmatism itself as well as on each of the subjects of these chapters. Simply listing those titles to which I am indebted over the years of my engagement with the method and its practitioners would at least quadruple this volume's already lengthy bibliography; in Stevens's words, "the catalogue is too commodious." In short, what I offer is neither comprehensive nor definitive, but having been asked to undertake this project, I have responded as clearly as I can to the questions opened in the "conversations" about pragmatism/of pragmatism in which I have participated. If Emerson has taught us anything, it is the central lesson of the pragmatist method: that we can only speak of what belongs to our experience – indeed, the "classic American tradition's sense of experience," as distinct from "the empiricisms of European philosophy," that is,

> for the American tradition, experience is not perception, nor the act of description, nor like the interpretation of texts, but rather is an engagement with things such that one learns more about them. Experience is an activity that corrects and teaches, that changes habits so as to be less parochial or mistaken ... experience as a learning activity, not as a window, a filter or a translator.[76]

I cannot from my experience alone address all the modes and issues involved with pragmatism, but I can draw from what I have learned to illuminate certain contours.

12. THE MEETING OF EAST AND WEST

It happens that I was an undergraduate student majoring in philosophy at Queens College during the period when it was the aspiration of the department there to foster participation in what was then known as the Pluralist movement. Following the model of the department at Yale chaired by John Edwin Smith – where Richard Rorty studied and served as research assistant for Smith – Queens, together with Hunter College and City College in the City University of New York system, and other institutions such as Fordham, Vanderbilt, Emory, Pennsylvania State University, Stony Brook, New York University, and Boston University were not (unusual in America at the time) dominated by analytic philosophy. Moreover, Smith's influence extended through his teaching and writing to explore American pragmatism's function as a "go-between," bringing together West and East, pursuing the affiliations between what Cavell has called Emerson's and Thoreau's "Eastern longings" in the nineteenth century into Peirce's and James's preoccupations with Buddhism and Vedantism in the early twentieth. Indeed, one of Smith's colleagues at Yale – the philosopher of science, F. S. C. Northrop – published in 1946 *The Meeting of East and West*, a volume that remains, as described by Robert Cummings Neville, "what might turn out to be the most symbolic and prescient book of that period [at Yale after Smith assumed the chair] ... because the students of the 1950s, 1960s, and 1970s, led by Smith, mainly have been instrumental in bringing Chinese and Indian philosophies into the mainstream of discussion in America."[77] My own reading of Northrop's text sometime in the 1970s primed me to be alert to the various superpositionings of ways of thinking and epistemic mood I found in American writers and Eastern texts – ancient and modern (particularly the commentaries of D. T. Suzuki); at the same time, Smith's work grounded me in a broadened cultural historicism for philosophical reflection. Moreover, at Queens, Ralph W. Sleeper – in classes I took with him – was working through the ideas about pragmatism and Dewey that he would later publish. And John McDermott was teaching his classes in American Philosophy and Aesthetics to over-tallied students sitting cross-legged on the floor and draped on the windowsills of his classrooms, "eating and sleeping and talking McDermott," who was himself delivering Emersonian experience and James's "secular liturgy" powerfully and purely while all the time underscoring "the Stevensian doctrine of 'the imagination as social form' as the entering wedge into a liberatory human future."[78] My readings reflect these background accidents of time and place, as well as the many more impinging on me over the years that will inevitably reveal themselves between the lines of my text.

13. ENVOI: THE FACT OF THE MATTER

> To any one who has ever looked on the face of a dead child or parent the
> mere fact that matter *could* have taken for a time that precious form, ought
> to make matter sacred ever after. It makes no difference what the *principle*
> of life may be, material or immaterial, matter at any rate cooperates, lends
> itself to all life's purposes. That beloved incarnation was among matter's
> possibilities. [James's emphases][79]

Finally, it was to the fact of this mystery so exquisitely expressed by James
that pragmatism addressed itself. In the absence of any account of origin or purpose, a concern with the nature and behavior of our particular formal possibility – protoplasm, "man's glassy essence," shaped by the
accidents of the cosmic weather, became paramount – "Where do we find
ourselves? In the middle of a stair...."

CHAPTER 2

Context: William James, Into the cosmic weather

When we think about the future of the world, we always have in mind
its being at the place where it would be if it continued to move as we
see it moving now. We do not realize that it moves not in a straight
line, but in a curve, and that its direction is always changing.

LUDWIG WITTGENSTEIN, *Culture and Value*

THIS NEW YET UNAPPROACHABLE AMERICA

Even before the moment of first arrival in the New World, John Winthrop
offered his fellow passengers on the *Arbella* in delivering his lay sermon,
"A Model of Christian Charity" (1630), a vision of their projected community as a body. His words fashioned a proleptic covenant with the
God whose Providence could ensure him and his accidental congregation
safe landing on the threatening shore. We could, without much stretching, see this gambit as the first move in the American language game that
would come to be called "pragmatism": that is, the projection of a belief
convincing enough to serve as a platform for action. For Winthrop and
his hungry listeners, the body offered as "model" – the image anchoring the belief – was that of Christ. Within this conception, all the *many*
members were to imagine themselves performing throughout their lives
and into the generations following them – if God's promise were to be
kept on their "errand into the wilderness" – the multifarious functions
necessary to the ongoing life of the *one* great spiritual body. Doing so
would fulfill their continuing part in the covenant secured with their successful landing. Thus, the idea later to be inscribed as the motto of the
pointedly secular republic, *E pluribus unum*, had already been articulated
in the theological motive that gave birth to this variety of "American"
experience. It should be noted that in this body the collectivity of minis-
ters would serve as the "head."

Of course, by the time the Founding Fathers of the republic gave what would become, literally, *currency* to the Latin phrase, Enlightenment values had begun to re-inflect the nature of God; the anthropomorphic image yielding somewhat to the more abstract Deistic notion of Godhead; the eye of Providence eerily suspended as above the top of an unfinished pyramid of thirteen steps – perhaps another image flickering in Stevens's sampling in his titling of "Thirteen Ways of Looking at a Blackbird." The idea of active participation in the larger body, translated into "separate but equal," informed the population of the growing nation through the years of the continuing secularizing impulses of the nineteenth century. This translation was epitomized in the person and work of Ralph Waldo Emerson, who pronounced "the sentence [as] the unit of democracy." His vision was of a naturalized Pentecost wherein the Holy Spirit became iden-tified with an intrinsically processual political principle, realized by him as an organism, ever-renewing itself and being modified in a changing envir-onment of fact. Shaped early in his career by the same readings in geology, botany, natural history, and philosophy that prepared Charles Darwin's imagination while on the voyage of the *Beagle* to begin formulating what would eventually be spelled out in *On the Origin of Species* (1859), Emerson, as was first noted by Oliver Wendell Holmes, anticipated the evolution-ary process, even before Robert Chambers's 1844 *Vestiges of the Natural History of Creation*. This anticipation crystallized during his famous 1833 visit to the Jardin des Plantes in Paris, after which he vowed to himself, "I will be a naturalist." After this experience, preserving his ministerial purpose to foster community in the new nation, Emerson directed him-self "to annul that adulterous divorce which the superstition of many ages ha[d] effected between the intellect and holiness."[1] To this end, through the rhetorical structures of his lectures and essays, the "model" of Christ's body was gradually refigured as the abstract *activity of* "divinity" – divin-ing, questioning, uncovering the evolving "method of nature" beneath the transient forms of appearance, the function of the all-seeing "transparent eyeball." In this dispensation, "Man thinking" rather than "man inhabited by thought" – inhabited by ideas inherited from authority, scriptural or otherwise – was to recognize his participatory responsibility in "creation"; that responsibility was to describe for each generation "an original relation to the universe,"[2] a relation informed by developments in the different "sciences" as they precipitated out of natural history. The "one" was to be conceived not as a static body, but as what Francis Bacon called in the *Novum Organum* (1620), "the law of continuity"; Bacon explained how experience could be employed to arrive at a true assessment of the forms and natures of things and provided a classification of different kinds of experiences and instances according to how they contributed to under-standing. For Emerson, in what he described as "this new yet unapproach-able America" (as he closed what is perhaps his most unsettling essay, "Experience"), this pursuit meant that every man and woman, from farmer to teacher, soldier to president, by examining the varieties of their experience – announcing and recording their performances as necessary activities within the larger scope of establishing a viable polity – would issue their own sentences, so to speak, self-consciously and freely voice their bondage, their participation in community, through recognizing the relation of each of their individual and different parts to the whole: "The sentence is the unit of democracy." Religious conversion was converted to participatory democracy.[3]

William James, who described himself as Emerson's "spiritual heir," was particularly disposed to consider the idea and reality of democracy by his father, a friend of Emerson's, who was a frequent visitor to the James household in its various residences on this side of the Atlantic. In New York City on a lecture tour in 1842, months after the death of his five-year-old son Waldo from scarlet fever, Emerson, between engagements, visited Henry James, Sr. – then resident with his wife and infant son William at their new home on Washington Place – and asked to be "taken upstairs" to see the babe, on whom he bestowed a blessing. The benefi-cence was realized. William James took on most seriously his role as his godfather's spiritual heir. The legacy was a true one in passing on the most valuable items from a past lived in a particular place to a future imag-ined, *of if.* The value of the conversations overheard and participated in by both William and Henry James as boys and young men on the continuing occasions of Emerson's visits to the James households (where, in one of the more permanent residences there was, even, "Mr. Emerson's room"[4]) and of the many visits made later, during the 1860s and 1870s by William to the Emerson family in Concord, was to show itself in the use to which William put his legacy, in what he was "to lecture or teach or preach" as Henry, early on, described his brother's vocation – the necessity of taking into full account *feeling* in the ongoing activity of describing "an original relation to the universe."[5] As William James pointedly described in *The Varieties of Religious Experience* (1902): "Individuality is founded in feel-ing; and the recesses of feeling, the darker, blinder strata of character are the only places in the world in which we catch real fact in the making, and directly perceive how events happen, and how work is actually done."[6] This understanding derived in large measure from Henry James, Sr. who, throughout his life, investigated the nature of individuality and attempted to resolve the tension between individual feeling and communal needs. His interest in the ideas of Charles Fourier and his lifelong study of what he called *The Secret of Swedenborg* (the title of the volume he published in 1869) translated into the necessity of acknowledging feeling as spirit, spirit and the spiritual as actual.

William James was especially attentive both to his father's and to Emerson's lessons. After exploring fully the implications of "Man thinking" in his monumental *The Principles of Psychology* (1890) – a volume he composed over more than a ten-year period – wherein, following Emerson's direction, the Darwinian information replaced God as the origin of our "bond to all that dust," James continued in *The Varieties of Religious Experience* (delivered first in 1901–02 as a series of ten lectures – the Gifford Lectures on Natural Religion in Edinburgh) to demonstrate religious experience itself, rather than the content of the experience, as an aspect of human nature serving as successful adaptation to changing environments.[7] James articulated, to borrow Wallace Stevens's later phrasing, that "It is the belief and not the god that counts."[8] In the "Postscript" to *Varieties*, he suggested a recuperative conceptual revolution to complete the political revolution that had established the republic, nothing less than a return to polytheism as an appropriate platform for a pluralistic society. In his words:

> The ideal power with which we feel ourselves in connection, the "God" of ordinary men, is both by ordinary men and by philosophers, endowed with certain of those metaphysical attributes which in the lecture on philosophy I treated with such disrespect. He is assumed as a matter of course, to be "one and only" and to be "infinite"; and the notion of many finite gods is one which hardly any one thinks it worth while to consider, and still less to uphold. Nevertheless, in the interests of intellectual clearness, I feel bound to say that religious experience, as we have studied it, cannot be cited as unequivocally supporting the infinitist belief. The only thing that it unequivocally testifies to is that we can experience union with *something* larger than ourselves and in that union find our greatest peace....
>
> It need not be infinite, it need not be solitary. It might conceivably even be only a larger and more godlike self, of which the present self would then be but the mutilated expression, and the universe might conceivably be a collection of such selves, of different degrees of inclusiveness, with no absolute unity realized in it at all. Thus would a sort of polytheism return upon us ...
>
> Upholders of the monistic view will say to such a polytheism (which, by the way, has always been the real religion of common people, and still is

today) that unless there be one all-inclusive God, our guarantee of security is left imperfect. In the Absolute, and in the Absolute only, *all* is saved. If there be different gods, each caring for his part, some portion of some of us might not be covered with divine protection.... The ordinary moralistic state of mind makes the salvation of the world conditional upon the success with which each unit does its part. Partial and conditional salvation is in fact a most familiar notion when taken in the abstract, the only difficulty being to determine the details.... I think, in fact, that a final philosophy of religion will have to consider the pluralistic hypothesis more seriously than it has hitherto been willing to conceive it. For practical life at any rate, the *chance* of salvation is enough. No fact in human nature is more characteristic than its willingness to live on a chance. The existence of the chance makes the difference ... between a life of which the keynote is resignation and a life of which the keynote is hope. [James's emphases][9]

His "pragmatism," as framed in his 1907 volume, informed by his "radical empiricism," would provide the method, in his words, for a "final philosophy of religion" – a method revitalizing an ancient system, "a new name for some old ways of thinking" for the *variety* epitomized by the American experience, a nation of immigrants, common people. The method James described in and as *Pragmatism*, pointed its connection, by his emphasizing its "look[ing] *forward* into facts themselves" (emphasis added) as "the seat of authority," to the continuation of the "protestant reformation"; he even called the pragmatist method "philosophic protestantism" – a method, as noted in Chapter 1 of this volume, that "widens the field of search for God."[10] The gradual transformation of religious experience into ongoing revelation of the ordinary *as* extraordinary was James's project, looking not *at* facts, but *through* them "to find" – in Wallace Stevens's phrasing – "the good, which in the Platonic sense, is synonymous with God."[11] This chapter will fill in some of the details of the background I have traced here in opening as part of a discussion of pragmatism in the context of the evolution of "[t]he thought of what America would be like if...."[12]

CONVERT, CONVERT, CONVERT

As Henry James, the novelist, recorded late in his life in *A Small Boy and Others* –reflecting on what had prepared his imagination, what had contributed to making him "one on whom nothing [was] lost" – the most "constantly repeated" injunction Henry James, Sr. voiced to his children was: "Convert, convert, convert ... to convert and convert ...

everything that should happen to us, every contact, every expression, every experience."[13] And underlying these injunctions was the most constantly repeated theme of freedom of thought, the birthright of each being, intrinsically intertwined with the accidents of time and place. As I have detailed in *A Natural History of Pragmatism*, one of the lessons taught by Henry James, Sr. that neither Henry nor William would ever forget was "that the 'feeling' mind is measured ... by the verbal style that it invents for itself"; a lesson grounded in the belief expressed by Socrates in the *Phaedo* that "to express oneself badly ... does some harm to the soul."[14]

In his review of Robert Richardson's magisterial biography of William James, Michael Wood, underlining James's relevance for us today, adroitly places him "in a curious double time, that of the late 19th century and our early 21st-century moment: a time when Darwin is the enemy, religion is the answer, wizards, cranks and conversions are everywhere, and an ageing American empire repeats the raw interventionist international politics of its youth. James is enormously helpful here." As Wood also observes:

> The point of pragmatism is that it is local and essayistic, you can always have another go. James is not laying down the law, he is trying to unsettle the leveling law we keep thinking we need. [We recall Emerson, "People wish to be settled; only as far as they are unsettled is there any hope for them."[15]] "Dogmatic philosophies," [James] says, "have sought for tests of truth which might dispense us from appealing to the future. Some direct mark, by noting which we can be protected immediately and absolutely, now and for ever, against all mistake." He cites Kierkegaard's maxim that we live forwards but understand backwards and offers radical empiricism as a new turn, a philosophy that "insists on understanding forwards." "The true is what works" doesn't mean success breeds success or might is right, it means truth is in transit, *can't be taken out of time* [emphasis added], and waits for us only in an as yet unsettled future ... [T]he future will always require revisions of us, or – better – *may* [Wood's emphasis] always require revisions of us; and doubts about possibilities have no automatic privilege over beliefs in those same possibilities.... William James's thought becomes clearest in his provisional accounts of belief, which he wants to associate both with faith and with scientific theory, allowing for a range of estimates and acts of trust in between. The effect is to demystify faith quite a bit, and to make science, or at least the undogmatic science that ultimately interests James, into a set of wagers.... Belief just might work and a cool contemplation of probabilities almost certainly wouldn't [to save oneself, to act].[16] [We recall here the situation of John Winthrop and the passengers on the *Arbella*.]

Wood provides the key to James's importance for us: "he wants to associate *both* with faith and with scientific theory," having realized belief itself, not the content of belief, as "the necessary angel of reality." In Wallace Stevens's beautiful phrasing: "...believe,/ Believe would be a brother full/ Of love, believe would be a friend,/ Friendlier than my only friend."[17] The essential tension James set himself to resolve, then, was how to preserve the *feeling* of believing, the confidence attendant on being in place in a determined and protected universe while recognizing, at the same time, that, in *fact*, we inhabit a universe of chance, that we are neither in a privileged relation nor protected on a planet spinning at 66,660 mph (that is, 107, 279 km/h or 30 km [18.5 miles] per second) around a dying star while simultaneously spinning on our axis at approximately 795 mph or 1279 km/h in New York at about 40 degrees north latitude (1040 mph or 1669.8 km/h at the equator). Again, as Stevens (James's spiritual heir as James was Emerson's) put it: "The final belief is to believe in a fiction, which you know to be a fiction, there being nothing else. The exquisite truth is to know that it is a fiction and that you believe in it willingly."[18] In this situation, taking full account of "the local and the essayistic" phrased in a "verbal style" that will do no "harm to the soul" is central.

A FEELING OF IF

It is important to recall here James's pointing out the connection between pragmatism and the Protestant Reformation, calling his method "philosophic protestantism" and its goal to "widen the field of search for God." It cannot be stressed enough that the Jamesian project was a response to a new world situation even more threatening than the physical facts of seventeenth-century settlement in "the howling wilderness" of the North American continent. Indeed, the new world situation that Charles Darwin began to describe in *On the Origin of Species* continues until this very moment in America to threaten so violently the possibility of communal belief that rational discourse on the subject is not an option for those who wish to maintain that they are specially created in the image of their maker and set here to fulfill their destinies in this "one nation under God." James's purpose, as he reminded his audiences in lecturing and in print, was "to embrace the darwinian facts."[19] "[W]iden[ing] the field of search for God" would acknowledge the *fact of feeling* the need expressed by religious experience for individuals throughout human history, to recognize themselves as "part or particle of God" – in Emerson's immemorial words – but to redescribe "God" so as to accommodate the "varieties" of response to the new world situation in which human beings have found themselves since the discovery of our descent from "a hairy, tailed quadruped, probably arboreal in its habits." The dust from the explosion of the Darwinian information has not yet settled. We live in a universe of chance in which the optimal operational mode, following "the method of nature," is, indeed, to optimize chances, even about belief itself, "allowing for a range of estimates and acts of trust in between."

James realized that each individual is differently prepared to accept "the stubborn facts"[20] being continually uncovered by natural historians and scientists, and can only "by degrees" accommodate and adapt to a new habit of mind; we recall his words: "the universe might conceivably be a collection of such selves, of different degrees of inclusiveness, with no absolute unity realized at all." The continuing Reformation project, James understood, meant and means breaking not only the physical but also the verbal icons that inhibit us from making our own individual wagers with the universe. James also realized that the project would be ever ongoing and gradual, again following the "method of nature." A habit of mind practiced for more than 2,000 years cannot be abruptly replaced with another program; a habit of mind practiced for more than 2,000 years has for all practical purposes become part of the hard wiring. As the eminent historian of ancient philosophy Pierre Hadot astutely observed in describing the intrinsic connection between "the forms of life and forms of discourse" in Greek and Roman philosophy, where individual and idiosyncratic interpretations, *conversions*, of older texts were understood to be necessary to healthy spiritual life, "We must formulate the rule of life *to ourselves* [emphasis added] in the most striking and concrete way." This requires a kind of selective breeding of the ideas that can help us know "how to live, what to do." Hadot continues:

> Thought evolves by incorporating prefabricated and pre-existing elements, which are given new meaning as they become integrated into a rational system. [The idea itself holds less interest than the prefabricated elements in which the writer believes he recognizes his own thought, elements that take on an unexpected meaning and purpose when they are integrated into a literary whole. This sometimes brilliant reuse of prefabricated elements gives an impression of "bricolage," to take up a word currently in fashion, not only among anthropologists but among biologists.] It is difficult to say what is most extraordinary about this process of integration: contingency, chance, irrationality, the very absurdity resulting from the elements used,

or, on the contrary, the strange power of reason to integrate and systematize these disparate elements and give them a new meaning.[21]

William James grasped that the winding cloth preserving the body of Christian monotheism had to be undone, the body exposed, turned back to dust as the culture would, he hoped, turn back to its pre-Christian ground, "an original relation to the universe." As he opined, "... in that 'theory of evolution' which, gathering momentum for a century ... we see the ground laid for a new sort of religion of Nature."[22] James knew that this decreation, this deconstruction, would take time. In the meantime, he brilliantly allowed, following Kant, as he indicates in one of the central passages in *The Varieties of Religious Experience*, one could, according to one's situation, act *as if* there were a God. We do, after all, act *as if* the earth is still and flat:

> Immanuel Kant held a curious doctrine about such objects of belief as God, the design of creation, the soul, its freedom, and the life hereafter. These things, he said, are properly not objects of knowledge at all. Our conceptions always require a sense-content to work with, and as the words "soul," "God," "immortality," cover no distinctive sense-content whatever, it follows that theoretically speaking they are words devoid of any significance. Yet strangely enough they have a definite meaning *for our practice*. We can act *as if* there were a God; feel *as if* we were free; consider Nature *as if* she were full of special designs; lay plans *as if* we were to be immortal; and we find that these words do make a genuine difference in our moral life....
>
> The sentiment of reality can indeed attach itself so strongly to our object of belief that our whole life is polarized through and through, so to speak, by its sense of the existence of the thing believed in, and yet that thing, for purpose of definite description, can hardly be said to be present to our mind at all. It is as if a bar of iron, without any touch or sight, with no representative faculty whatever, might nevertheless be strongly endowed with an inner capacity for magnetic feeling; and as if, through the various arousals of its magnetism by magnets coming and going in its neighborhood, it might be consciously determined to different attitudes and tendencies. Such a bar of iron could never give you an outward description of the agencies that had the power of stirring it so strongly; yet of their presence, and of their significance for its life, it would be intensely aware through every fibre of its being.
>
> It is not only the Ideas of Pure Reason, as Kant styled them, that have this power of making us vitally feel presences that we are impotent articulately to describe. All sorts of higher abstractions bring with them the same kind of impalpable appeal. Remember those passages from Emerson which I read at my last lecture. The whole universe of concrete objects, as we know them, swims, not only for such a transcendentalist writer, but for all of us,

in a wider and higher universe of abstract ideas, that lend it its significance.
[James's emphases][23]

The "wider and higher universe of abstract ideas" is what lends significance
to "the whole universe of concrete objects." The "ideas" moving through
us in the manner of magnetic currents determine how we understand the
nature of our reality. James, as a man of science, had full confidence in its
method, as did Charles Sanders Peirce, Chauncey Wright, and the other
members of the Metaphysical Club; they all trusted that over time, those
"ideas," those guesses/hypotheses, wagers, that "paid-off" statistically, that
repeatedly worked in helping us survive in nature, would win out. Peirce
spelled this out over and over again in various lectures and essays, as we
shall have occasion to discuss in Chapter 3.

Alfred North Whitehead called James "that adorable genius" and placed
him in exalted philosophic company: "In Western literature," Whitehead
observed, "there are four great thinkers, whose services to civilized thought
rest largely upon their achievements in philosophical assemblage; though
each of them made important contributions to the structure of philosophic
system. These men are Plato, Aristotle, Leibniz, and William James."[24]
Whitehead realized "assemblage" – an earlier, philosophical descriptive for
what I have characterized as "sampling" in Chapter 1 here – as an essential mode of representing the actuality of experience as an animate being,
an organism; flattening this actuality into a system or into a "systematic" philosophy is to ignore the prime and primal aspect of existence, its
multiplicity and simultaneity of functions. It is also highly significant that
Niels Bohr credited James with having prepared his own thinking about
the nature of quantum reality, particulary the central concepts of complementarity and superpositioning. "In 1962 Bohr ... remembered definitely
having read James before 1912, i.e., long before complementarity appeared
in 1927.... We know that at this time ... the young Bohr was struggling
to come to to grips with the problems of describing the contents of psychological processes, an interest common to both his father [Christian Bohr,
a prominent physiologist] and [Harald] Hoffding [one of his preceptors]
as well." "As those who knew Bohr best have testified, the ideas which he
later used in quantum theory were all with him from boyhood ... from his
earliest studies of William James in 1904."[25] The consensus of those who
have studied the development of Bohr's thinking is that James essentially
discovered quantum theory thirty-five years before the physicists did.[26]

Whitehead and Bohr realized in James's descriptions of the superpositioning of *many* different sets of behaviors and awarenesses coexisting

within *one* personality a model both for the simultaneity of development of different parts from the same germ in an organism and for the multiplicity of quantum states all existing at once until one is selected for observation. As James described in the central "Stream of Thought" chapter of *The Principles of Psychology*: "the mind is at every stage a theater of simultaneous possibilities"; and in the pages just before, in the chapter entitled "The Relations of Minds to Other Things": "It must be admitted … that in *certain persons*, at least, *the total possible consciousness may be split into parts which coexist but mutually ignore each other*, and share the objects of knowledge between them. More remarkable still, they are *complementary*. Give an object to one of the consciousnesses, and by that fact you remove it from the other or the others" (James's emphases).[27] James's model is, Bohr and Whitehead recognized, the "law of continuity" sought by Bacon and later elaborated as "synechism" by Peirce, continuity operating all the way up and all the way down. (Peirce's *synechism* will be discussed in the following chapter.) As Bohr translated the Jamesian paradigm in his *Atomic Theory and the Description of Nature* (1925, 1927, 1929; first published as a volume 1931):

> The epistemological problem under discussion may be characterized as follows: For describing our mental activity, we require, on the one hand an objectively given content to be placed in opposition to a perceiving subject, while, on the other hand, as is already implied in such an assertion, no sharp separation between object and subject can be maintained, since the perceiving subject also belongs to our mental content. From these circumstances follows not only the relative meaning of every concept, or rather of every word, the meaning depending on the arbitrary choice of point of view, but also that we must, in general, be prepared to accept the fact that a complete elucidation of one and the same object may require diverse points of view which defy a unique description.[28]

The view that includes the subject is complementary to the one that does not: *both/and* not *either/or*. The one is an inner view, an introspection into the implicate order; the other is an outer view in the context of the explicate order. We again recall James in "The Stream of Thought": "What appeals to our attention far more than the absolute quality or quantity of a given sensation is its *ratio* to whatever other sensations we may have at the same time" – a statistical situation – "the right *mean*." And this now famous passage:

> If there be such things as feelings at all, *then so surely as relations between objects exist in rerum natura, so surely, and more surely, do feelings exist to*

which these relations are known. There is not a conjunction or a preposition, and hardly an adverbial phrase, syntactic form, or inflection of voice, in human speech, that does not express some shading or other of relation which we at some moment actually feel to exist between the larger objects of our thought. **If we speak objectively, it is the real relations that appear revealed; if we speak subjectively, it is the stream of consciousness that matches each of them by an inward coloring of its own.** In either case the relations are numberless, and no existing language is capable of doing justice to all their shades. [James's italics; boldface emphasis added][29]

Consider now Bohr's parallel observations:

[T]he apparent contrast between the continuous outward flow of associative thinking [James's stream of consciousness] and the preservation of the unity of personality exhibits a suggestive analogy with the relation between the wave description of the motions of material particles, governed by the superposition principle, and their indestructible individuality. The unavoidable influence on atomic phenomena caused by observing them here corresponds to the well-known tinge of the psychological experiences which accompanies any direction of the attention to one of their various elements.[30]

This is not the place to detail the enormous debt that both William James and Niels Bohr owed to the work of Hermann von Helmholtz, a fact accounting to the greatest degree for their common apprehension of the continuity between the nature and behavior of consciousness and the nature and behavior of light that permitted their singularly monumental contributions to our understanding.[31] Indeed, Dame Gillian Beer has remarked that in spite of the fact that "[b]y the end of the 1870s Helmholtz is, with Darwin, the recurrent point of reference for writers in *Nature* and *Mind*," the prevalence of his ideas has received singularly little attention from scholars.[32] I have begun, in my chapter on William James in *A Natural History of Pragmatism,* to mind that gap, but much more needs to be done. Suffice it here simply to note James's and Bohr's common debt to Helmholtz, as well as, of course, Bohr's to James. What Bohr came to describe as intrinsic to the structure of our relationship to nature – "that the separation required for ontological existence and quantum measurement theory in the quantum explicate order cannot be maintained as an absolute"[33] – James had expressed abundantly in his descriptions of consciousness. The same understanding underpinned his rejection of the "Absolute," as a "one and only" idea of "God."

A "new sort of religion of Nature" would have to take account of the first and foremost of the "darwinian facts": the profligacy of forms and the extravagance of varieties superpositioned and ready to fill the accidental niches made available by the ever-changing conditions of the planet. In this new world dispensation, with the continuity of matter and spirit acknowledged – "Spirit is matter reduced to an extreme thinness: O *so* thin!" as Emerson had already offered in 1844[34] – the individual variation of each mind has equally to be taken into account. Moreover, given the continuity of all forms, organic through inorganic, visible to invisible, a "new sort of religion of Nature" would have to extend the possibilities of imagining, of populating a new heaven/haven, with stardust itself: something, in fact, that Emanuel Swedenborg had elaborately attempted in his angelology – where the habits and behavior of the different ranks of angels are metaphors for the activity and behavior of the different crystalline structures comprising the universe (an avenue currently being explored in the extraordinary art work of Olafur Eliasson) – and that Jonathan Edwards had begun to incorporate into theology by converting what he learned from Newton's *Opticks* about the nature and behavior of light into his descriptions of grace and the soul.[35] William James had been a most attentive reader of both Swedenborg and Edwards; a new mythology was necessary, a new kind of imagining, a new kind of spiritual exercise, following what Edwards had begun to teach, for example, in this exquisite lesson:

> When we go to expel body out of our thoughts, we must be sure not to leave empty space in the room of it; and when we go to expel emptiness from our thoughts we must not think to squeeze it out by anything close, hard and solid, but we must think of the same that the sleeping rocks dream of; and not till then shall we get a complete idea of nothing.[36]

Stretching, then, from those able to "think of the same that the sleeping rocks dream of" – identifying, as Wallace Stevens did, with the planet itself moving year after year around its sun – to those unable, for whatever reasons, to let go, to imagine themselves as what Whitehead describes, no more than a temporary disturbance in the electromagnetic field, are our various beliefs, "assemblages," functioning variously in different contexts to get us from here to there: "we must ... be prepared to accept the fact that a complete elucidation of one and the same object may require diverse points of view which defy a unique description." "Thus would a sort of polytheism return upon us." "Our conceptions always require a sense-content to work with...." " [I]n the general problem of the quantum theory, one is faced ... with an essential failure of the pictures in space and time on which the description of natural phenomena has hitherto been based."[37] We need new, moving pictures. "The river is moving./ The blackbird must be flying."

> As we take … a general view of the wonderful stream of our consciousness [James observes], what strikes us first is [the] different pace of its parts. Like a bird's life, it seems to be made of an alternation of flights and perchings. The rhythm of language expresses this, where every thought is expressed in a sentence, and every sentence closed by a period. The resting-places are usually occupied by sensorial imaginations of some sort, whose peculiarity is that they can be held before the mind for an indefinite time, and contemplated without changing; the places of flight are filled with thoughts of relations, static or dynamic, that for the most part obtain between matters contemplated in the periods of comparative rest.[38]

We need *time* as a culture to wean ourselves from the "sensorial imagin[ings]" that have nurtured us for so long before our remembering. It will take *time* to complete the task to which Emerson directed us, "to annul that adulterous divorce which the superstition of many ages has effected between intellect and holiness," to make our "forms of discourse" match more closely the "forms of life," and to extend our notion of the body of which we are a part into the inorganic and invisible. We need to repair the breach between what C. P. Snow now more than half a century ago called the "two cultures," attend most assiduously to those poets, writers, artists, musicians, and filmmakers who have themselves attended, like Emerson, to the developments in the science and technology of their moments: Henry David Thoreau, Emily Dickinson, George Eliot, Thomas Hardy, Henry James in the nineteenth century; in the twentieth – in addition to Stevens – Paul Valery, Gertrude Stein, Robert Frost (who even sought out Niels Bohr for conversations), Thomas Pynchon, J. M. Coetzee, Richard Powers, Marianne Wiggins, Susan Howe, Christian Bok, Jorie Graham, Werner Herzog, Terrence Malick, James Turrell, Olafur Eliasson, Tomas Saraceno, among others. These are individuals who, like James and Whitehead, have not only taken Darwin fully into account, but who have realized, as well, that Darwin's discoveries depended on what Richard Rorty in an important essay on Whitehead, published forty-seven years ago, described as "taking time seriously."[39]

I was reminded of this phrase by Steven Meyer in a paper he presented at the "Modernism: The Time of the Unconscious" conference held at the University of Pennsylvania in the spring of 2008. Meyer ultimately tracked the source of the phrase back through Stuart Hampshire's 1951 volume, *Spinoza,* and eventually to Samuel Alexander's *Space, Time and Deity* (1926). "Samuel Alexander's pertinent criticism of Spinoza," Hampshire wrote, "was that, in common with most metaphysicians before Whitehead and Alexander himself, he had failed to 'take time seriously,' through no fault of his own other than his having had the misfortune of living in a pre-Darwinian, pre-Einsteinian age."[40] Alexander's 1921 lecture "Spinoza and Time" begins: "If I were asked to name the most characteristic thought of these last twenty-five years, I should answer, the discovery of Time. I do not mean that we have waited until today to become familiar with Time; I mean that we have only just begun, in our speculation, to take Time seriously, and to realize that in some way or other Time is an essential ingredient in the constitution of things."[41] As Whitehead would further explain, "Alexander enforces the precept that we should take time seriously. No philosopher takes time seriously who *either* conceives of a complete totality of all existence *or* conceives of a multiplicity of actual entities such that each of them is a complete fact, 'requiring nothing but itself in order to exist'."[42] Or, as William James put it quite pointedly in connection with his description of a pluralistic universe in a 1908 letter to Henry Adams, "unless the future contains genuine novelties, unless the present is really creative of them, *I don't see the use of time at all*" (emphasis added).[43] We recall Michael Wood's reminding us that James conceived of his pragmatism, inflected by his radical empiricism, as a method that "insists on understanding forwards," that "truth is in transit, can't be taken out of time, and waits for us only in an as yet unsettled future." "Understanding forwards" in our terrible moment, if we do not wish the next generations to perish – at best, suffocating and thirsty – demands that we in the United States invent mythologies for our body politic that will teach identification with "all things bright and beautiful" rather than with the restricted notion of the body of Christ, originally emblematized for the culture by Winthrop's "Model of Christian Charity," a model that violently precludes and perverts understanding the human place in nature. "Understanding forwards," explicating our implication in nature, happens through time, as time. Meyer reminds us that Whitehead modeled his conception of an actual entity or occasion on James's "specious present," thereby generalizing from consciousness to experience. In this experience of superpositioned "manys," the ego is collapsed, even for limited duration, into an experience of an "eternal present," into "the open of a vivid sensory present," an "altered temporal sense" that involves suspending "merely functional time."[44] This is, in other words, religious experience, "momentary existence on an exquisite plane," as Stevens so exquisitely described, the "imperfect" that is our "paradise," the paradise of creatures endlessly dissolving in time.[45]

INTO THE COSMIC WEATHER

In his contribution to John J. Stuhr's recent collection, *100 Years of Pragmatism: William James's Revolutionary Philosophy* (2009), Ross Posnock focuses on one of the most crucial passages from James's 1907 text (referred to in passing earlier in this volume): "the dramatic image that ends his third lecture: pragmatism requires rotating the axis of philosophy," Posnock observes, "from the vertical to horizontal, as it 'shifts the emphasis' – in James's words – from exalted first principles, abstractions such as God and Free Will. This shift means that" – continuing with James's words – "the centre of gravity of philosophy must therefore alter its place. The earth of things, long thrown into shadow by the glories of the upper ether, must resume its rights.... It will be an alteration in the 'seat of authority' that reminds one almost of the protestant reformation."[46] Earlier in this lecture/chapter, entitled "Some Metaphysical Problems Pragmatically Considered," James sets the stage on which this dramatic shift will play out:

> According to the theory of mechanical evolution, the laws of redistribution of matter and motion, though they are certainly to thank for all the good hours which our organisms have ever yielded us and for all the ideals which our minds now frame, are yet fatally certain to undo their work again, and to redissolve everything that they have once evolved....
>
> That is the sting of it, that in the vast driftings of the cosmic weather, though many a jewelled shore appears, and many an enchanted cloud-bank floats away, long lingering ere it be dissolved – even as our world now lingers, for our joy – yet when these transient products are gone, nothing, absolutely *nothing* [James's emphasis] remains, to represent those particular qualities, those elements of preciousness which they may have enshrined. Dead and gone are they, gone utterly from the very sphere and room of being. Without an echo; without a memory; without an influence on aught that may come after, to make it care for similar ideals. This utter final wreck and tragedy is of the essence of scientific materialism as at present understood. The lower and not the higher forces are the eternal forces, or the last surviving forces within the only cycle of evolution which we can definitely see.[47]

(James borrowed the phrase "cosmic weather" from Chauncey Wright, who, as noted here in Chapter 1, believed in practicing "philosophy as conversation," a premise that would conceptually underpin the pragmatic method as articulated by James.[48])

Posnock astutely connects James's stance and stake as a philosopher with that of "the Ancients, for whom philosophy was above all a spiritual exercise, a way of life." He continues, drawing on and quoting from the work of Pierre Hadot, to comment that philosophy as a "way of life" is a "mode of existing-in-the-world.... For real wisdom does not merely cause us to know: it makes us 'be' in a different way."[49] For Posnock, it is Diogenes the Cynic, "content to call himself a citizen of the world," who "shameless and self-reliant ... presides over a 'tramp and vagrant world,' to borrow James's words," who is "a supreme emblem of the philosopher as unassimilable" and James's "tutelary deity."[50] While I clearly agree with Posnock that "some of the old ways of thinking" James wanted to revitalize under the banner of pragmatism include the manners and methods of the Ancients, I would suggest that an equally effective model for him was offered by the Stoics. I was struck by this realization as I read a review not too long ago entitled "Stoicism and Us" by Emily Wilson in *The New Republic* (a review of two recently published volumes, one a biography of Marcus Aurelius and the other a more general study of Stoicism). I reflected as I was reading particularly on the parallels between the pragmatist emphasis on philosophy as conversation and the methodology of the Stoic philosophers as detailed by Hadot. In *Philosophy as a Way of Life*, Hadot repeatedly underscores the intrinsic connection between "the forms of life and forms of discourse" in ancient Greek and Roman philosophy, where individual and idiosyncratic interpretations, *conversions*, of older texts were understood to be necessary to healthy spiritual life. "We must formulate the rule of life to ourselves in the most striking and concrete way," we recall Hadot observing. This practice requires what I have earlier called a kind of *selective breeding of ideas* to make them come alive – the same kind of engagement, it is to be remarked, that characterizes the Protestant Reformation.

A salient difference between the dispositions of the Cynic and the Stoic is captured by, on the one hand, Diogenes, a "citizen of the world," repelled and disaffected by the political and social corruption evident in the marketplace, and, on the other, Marcus Aurelius, who urges himself in his *Meditations* to act as a "citizen of the universe" and to "live *as if you were on a mountain*"[51](emphasis added). For the Stoic, it is within this enlarged frame of being, taking account of the "cosmic weather" rather than simply taking the temperature of the world's marketplaces, where the human mind is to orient itself and navigate its way – an attitude James and his contemporaries were reminded of by the teaching of Vivekananda. It is pertinent to recall in this context that it was during William James's July 1898 hiking trip in the Adirondacks, on the night of the 7th, after having climbed that morning to the top of Mount Marcy, at 5,334 feet the highest point in New York State – which he reached, after a five-hour ascent, at noon –, that he experienced, in his words, "a state of spiritual alertness of the most vital description ... one of the most memorable of all my memorable experiences," as he wrote to his wife Alice. While he went on to observe that he could not describe the full significance of what he had undergone, what he did offer reveals precisely the contours of the Stoic's perspective of understanding oneself as a "citizen of the universe": "The intense human remoteness of its inner life," James wrote, "and yet the intense *appeal* [James's emphasis] of it, its everlasting freshness and its immemorial antiquity and decay ... all whirled inextricably together.... It was one of the happiest lonesome nights of my existence." Projecting the illumination to convert it to use – as though recollecting his father's repeated injunction to his children: "Convert, convert, convert ... to convert and convert ... everything that should happen to us, every contact, every expression, every experience" – James continues, "and I understand now what a poet is. He is a person who can feel the immense complexity of influences that I felt and make some partial tracks in them for verbal statement"[52] – someone, in other words, who can transcribe the record of his "habits of conversation with nature."[53]

In his biography of James, Robert Richardson properly underscores that this illumination – James's "transparent eyeball" moment, I would add – was the catalyst for what would become *The Varieties of Religious Experience*. Seminal in this connection, but not teased out by Richardson (or, as far as I know, by anyone else) is the inextricable link James, in describing his epiphany, articulated between "the immense complexity of influences" he felt and "verbal statement." It is this relation that crystallized not only *Varieties,* but also – as this chapter will spell out – his understanding of pragmatism. As James writes in the sixth lecture/chapter of *Pragmatism*, "Pragmatism's Conception of Truth" and quoted as one of the epigraphs to Chapter 1:

> Pent in, as the pragmatist more than any one else sees himself to be, between the whole body of funded truths squeezed from the past and the coercions

of the world of sense about him, who so well as he feels the immense pressure of objective control under which our minds perform their operations? If any one imagines that this law is lax, let him keep its commandment one day, says Emerson. We have heard much of late of the uses of the imagination in science. It is high time to urge the use of a little imagination in philosophy.[54]

James took the first steps leading to this realization during childhood, guided by his father's "Convert, convert." As noted earlier, Henry James, Sr. believed, following Socrates's admonition in the *Phaedo*, that not using words properly does some harm to the soul. One of the ways James Sr. reinforced his conviction was by transforming into the idiom of everyday life the work of Emanuel Swedenborg, whose primary focus had been to redeem the language of the Bible for ready use, translate theology into currency. The novelist Henry James recalled in *A Small Boy and Others* that the one constant in the family's ongoing peregrinations in America and Europe was his father's multivolume, red morocco-bound set of the writings of the Swedish mystic. While after the death of James Sr., William James would come to his own appreciation of Swedenborg as he compiled *The Literary Remains of Henry James Sr.* (1884), memorializing his father's spirit, earlier in his own life, he was drawn more strongly to other "doers of the word," concerned equally with the transfigurations of spiritual force into commonplace effects – the conversation between the invisible and the visible.

In 1863 James found himself moving back and forth for the second time in his life between the Stoics, particularly Epictetus and Marcus Aurelius, and Jonathan Edwards – the latter, besides Swedenborg, one of the few religious writers James Sr. approved of by name. (James's first engagement with these writers had been in 1859.) Now, as his two younger brothers were off to fight in the Civil War, the twenty-one-year-old William was coming to share Edwards's and his father's sense that evil is real.[55] He was especially compelled by Edwards's *Great Christian Doctrine of Original Sin Defended*, moved as much by its style as by its content. He filled eleven closely written notebook pages with observations, commenting variously on Edwards's excellent use of "concrete examples" and his verbal power. (Robert Richardson observes that James's style in these notebook entries surpasses even Edwards's.) At the same time, Epictetus and Marcus Aurelius, whose *Meditations* James reread frequently, offered him their apothegmatic remarks as ways to freedom.[56] Three years later, James was again steeped in Marcus Aurelius. In June of 1866 he was reading George Long's translation of the *Meditations* very slowly and carefully, at the rate of two-to-three pages a day. He came to regard the emperor's text as a model for his own working philosophy, with Stoicism grounding his "beliefs," following Alexander Bain's definition: beliefs are "that upon which a man is prepared to act." Before returning to Marcus Aurelius, however, James had had his firsthand experience of the "cosmic weather," having accompanied Louis Agassiz on the expedition to South America, undertaken by the Harvard naturalist with the aim of showing Darwin's revolutionary theory to be "wholly without foundation in fact."[57] James's coming of age during the moment of impact of *On the Origin of Species* was productively complicated for him by his travels with Agassiz. He was already practiced in being unsettled by his family's constant moving from one place to another (the explicit motive for these repeated dislocations being Henry James, Sr.'s desire to cultivate a variety of educational experience for his children[58]). These new accidents combined with the young man's already highly developed verbal skills to make him the perfect figure to negotiate the breach in reality occasioned by the Darwinian event. "People wish to be settled; only as far as they are unsettled is there any hope for them" – William James might have heard this lesson taught by Emerson,[59] his spiritual godfather, echoing in his mind as he lost his bearings and found them again both at sea with Agassiz and then back home in Boston, where not long after his return he would abandon his practical study of medicine to explore more speculative regions.

It is interesting to note in this context that like Charles Darwin on the *Beagle*, William James was terribly seasick for the greater part of his outward journey, forced to remain horizontal as days gave way to nights and nights to days. In "Four Bodies on the *Beagle*," Gillian Beer has insightfully elaborated how Darwin's extended experience of horizontality contributed significantly to an embodied sense of his own creatureliness, priming his intelligence for the discovery he would make concerning our growth out of the common ground of life on the planet.[60] Her observations can be applied equally to William James "rotating the axis of philosophy from the vertical to horizontal," shifting the emphasis: "The centre of gravity of philosophy must therefore alter its place. The earth of things, long thrown into shadow by the glories of the upper ether, must resume its rights." That James further envisaged this "alteration in 'the seat of authority'" to be equivalent to the current dispensation of "the protestant reformation" connects his new/old way of knowing with the ongoing work of converting what remained for him – as it continues to remain for us in our post-postmodern moment – a sacred text, the Christian

Bible, into available personal and secular use. In doing this, James was
following the guiding principle of "the divine Emerson" – as he referred to
him in writing to his brother Henry[61] – that "Each individual soul is such
in virtue of its being a power to translate the world into some particular
language of its own."[62] This reminder of the continuing Reformation project comes from Emerson's 1841 oration, "The Method of Nature"; this is
where he describes his "office ... to annul that adulterous divorce which
the superstition of many ages has effected between the intellect and holiness." Emerson here lays the groundwork for the "new intellectual style"
that would become the method of pragmatism, a method allowing "the
earth of things ... [to] resume its rights." He described the necessary shift
away from verticality: "The crystal sphere of thought is as concentrical as
the geological structure of the globe. As our soils and rocks lie in strata,
concentric strata, so do all men's thinkings run laterally, never vertically."[63]
As noted earlier, Emerson had been tracking the change in the "cosmic
weather" as early on, if not earlier, than Darwin. Emerson's prescience in
turn prepared William James, returned from his voyaging, "to embrace
the Darwinian facts" without hesitation.[64]

Perhaps from moving so long "up and down between two elements"[65]
during his time at sea, William James came to experience himself as a
needle on a compass, constantly oscillating, drawn by the very force of
the earth itself suspended in its magnetic field, feeling "infinitesimal
attraction ... yield[ing] to a current so feeble as can be felt only by a
needle delicately poised."[66] (James expressed this sense of himself often
enough so that Alice Gibbens, his future wife, would, during one of the
up-and-down periods of their courtship, give him a small compass, which
James almost always carried with him from then on.) Rereading Marcus
Aurelius after having felt himself aboard a pitching vessel, "merest minuscule in the gales,"[67] and after nosing into the immense unknowns of the
Amazon and its tributaries in small open canoes – James covered more
than 4,000 miles in this way during the expedition – he tingled in recognition of the Stoic's perspective as "a citizen of the universe." The
words had been made real in his flesh – a secular incarnation. As Robert
Richardson records, James wrote to his friend Tom Ward, who had trav-
elled with him in Brazil:

> "every man's life ... is a line that continually oscillates on every side of its
> direction." Ward was in similar straits. James offered his newly compact
> Stoicism as advice to Ward.... "Much of your uneasiness comes from ...
> your regarding each oscillation as something final," James told Ward. "I

think we ought to be independent of our moods, look upon them as external for they come to us unbidden, and feel if possible neither elated or depressed, but keep our eyes upon our work, and if we have done the best we could in that given condition, be satisfied."

Marcus Aurelius "certainly had an invincible soul," he went on, "and it seems to me that any man who can, like him, grasp the love of a 'life according to nature' ie [sic] a life in which your individual will becomes so harmonized to nature's will as cheerfully to acquiesce in whatever she assigns you, knowing that you serve some purpose in her vast machinery which will never be revealed to you, any man who can do this will, I say, be a pleasing spectacle, no matter what his lot in life."[68]

WE LIE IN THE LAP OF AN IMMENSE INTELLIGENCE

This early physical experience of the Stoical attitude was powerfully renewed during James's Adirondack hiking trip about which he wrote to his wife of "the immense complexity of influences that [he] felt" and of his desire to "make some partial tracks in them for verbal statement." It was, in fact, in the months immediately following that James composed "Philosophical Conceptions and Practical Results" – the talk he would deliver at Berkeley in August of 1898 that came to be regarded as "the beginning of the pragmatist movement"; major portions of it were later incorporated both into the 1901–02 Gifford Lectures that would become *The Varieties of Religious Experience* and into the 1906–07 lectures that would be published as *Pragmatism: A New Name for Some Old Ways of Thinking*. Indeed, the passages quoted here in opening from *Pragmatism's* third lecture/chapter, "Some Metaphysical Problems Pragmatically Considered," come directly out of this 1898 talk. Worth noting about this moment in James's life is that it was in the days just after the revelatory *Walpurgisnacht*, as he called it, when he felt himself isolated, but joyfully "whirled inextricably" as "part or particle" of the universe's "intense … remoteness" – "it seemed as if the gods of all nature, mythologies were holding an indescribable meeting in my breast with the moral gods of the inner life"[69] – that he began experiencing (because of the overexertion of climbing to the altitudes he did on that day and days following, carrying weighty packs) the cardiac strain that was a sharp reminder of his mortality. There was an urgency, then, for him to set down as clearly as possible the premises of the way of thinking and being that he had begun to suggest as far back as twenty years earlier in "The Sentiment of Rationality."

He regarded his present purpose both as personal necessity and moral responsibility. It was important not only to describe the "new intellectual style," but also to plot its history and name it, as well as its name-giver. The first heartbeats of pragmatism's life sounded as James felt – "in my breast" – the "queer cardiac symptoms" that with increasing frequency signaled his own heart's weakening.⁷⁰

James opened his talk at Berkeley drawing from the combined experiences of exploring the tropical Amazonian forests and trekking in the Adirondacks the figure he used to anchor what he offered as the inadequacy of words ever to capture "truth":

> I have come across the continent to this wondrous Pacific Coast – to this Eden, not of the mythical antiquity, but of the solid future of mankind ... to help cement our rugged East and your wondrous West together in a spiritual bond, – and yet, and yet, and yet I simply cannot. I have tried to articulate it, but it will not come. Philosophers are after all like poets. They are path-finders.... They are, if I may use a simile, so many spots, or blazes, – blazes made by the axe of the human intellect on the trees of the otherwise trackless forest of human experience. They give you somewhere to go from. They give you a direction and a place to reach. They do not give you the integral forest with all its sunlit glories and its moonlit witcheries and wonders. Ferny dells, and mossy waterfalls, and secret magic nooks escape you, owned only by the wild things to whom the region is a home. Happy they without the need of blazes! But to us the blazes give a sort of ownership. We can now use the forest, wend across it with companions, and enjoy its quality. It is no longer a place merely to get lost in and never return. The poet's words and the philosopher's phrases thus are helps of the most genuine sort, giving to all of us hereafter the freedom of the trails they made....
>
> No one like the path-finder himself feels the immensity of the forest, or knows the accidentality of his own trails. Columbus, dreaming of the ancient East, is stopped by poor, pristine simple America, and gets no farther on that day; and the poets and philosophers themselves know as no one else knows that what their formulas express leaves unexpressed almost everything that they organically divine and feel. So I feel that there is a center in truth's forest where I have never been: to track it out and get there is the secret spring of all my poor life's philosophic efforts; at moments I almost strike into the final valley, there is a gleam of the end, a sense of certainty, but always there comes still another ridge, and so my blazes merely circle towards the true direction; and although now, if ever, would be the fit occasion, yet I cannot take you to the wondrous hidden spot today. To-morrow, it must be, or to-morrow, or to-morrow, and pretty surely death will overtake me ere the promise is fulfilled.

> Of such postponed achievements do the lives of all philosophers consist.
> Truth's fullness is elusive; ever not quite, not quite! So we fall back on the
> preliminary blazes – a few formulas, a few technical conceptions, a few ver-
> bal pointers – which at least define the initial direction of the trail.[71]

James then continues to indicate that "the most likely direction in which
to start upon the trail of truth" was offered by "Mr. Charles S. Peirce ...
one of the most original of contemporary thinkers," and goes on, "the
principle of practicalism – or pragmatism, as he called it, when I first
heard him enunciate it at Cambridge in the early '70's – is the clue or
compass by following which I find myself more and more confirmed in
believing we may keep our feet upon the proper trail."[72]

Finding one's way, finding the right words – pragmatism, the compass;
James the needle oscillating around its center, offering "verbal *pointers*,"
moving to articulate within the limitation of language the "direct experiences of a wider spiritual life with which our superficial consciousness
is continuous, and with which it keeps up an intense commerce ... the
primary mass of direct religious expression."[73] Seeing philosophy as an
instrument, an aid to navigation, rather than as a vessel carrying passengers to a safe haven resets the game of philosophy to be played once
again in what Peirce called "a universe of chance" – a setting familiar to
the Stoics whose mode of being was to negotiate uncertainty by making constant adjustments, necessary course corrections as changes in the
weather of life required. While the security offered by the idea of a determined universe ordered by an Unmoved Mover dissolved under the pressure of the evolutionary information, the fact of human connection with
a realm of being incomprehensible in its extension was, ironically, con-
cretized. "We lie in the lap of an immense intelligence," Emerson beautifully put it,[74] an intelligence we glimpse in quivering stillnesses as we
continue in our "habits of conversation with nature" to quiz all sounds,
all sense, all everything for what seems, from our limited perspective,
the music and manner of chance – at our best, as James, adopting the
Stoics' attitude, realized: "so harmonized to nature's will as cheerfully
to acquiesce in whatever she assigns you, knowing that you serve some
purpose in her vast machinery which will never be revealed to you."[75] A
parallel instance voiced against the same background noise of cosmic suspense was expressed by Soren Kierkegaard in his *Concluding Unscientific
Postscript*: "An objective uncertainty held fast in an appropriation process
of the most passionate inwardness is the truth, the highest truth attainable for an existing individual."[76]

COSMIC COMMITMENT

In addition to what William James came to learn from Emerson, from his father, from Swedenborg, from Edwards, from the Stoics, from his own sense of the evolutionary drift, there were other early pointings that had prepared him to assume an attitude appropriate to inhabiting a universe of chance. Primary among these was the direction offered by Bishop Joseph Butler in his 1736 defense of religion, *The Analogy of Religion Natural and Revealed to the Constitution and Course of Nature*. James's attraction to Butler began during the same period when he first read Epictetus and Edwards, in the fall of 1859, when he was seventeen and the family had moved back to Europe, on this occasion to Geneva where James would study anatomy, osteology, and math at the Geneva Academy. His note-book for this time exhibits an extraordinary range and depth of interests, and while it is not clear that he read all of the titles he lists, what is clear is that in addition to those texts where there is evidence that he did read and profit from what he read, he was also especially drawn into Indic lit-erature and religion during this span – an interest that would be actively renewed during the last decade of the century with Vivekananda's visits to the United States.[77] There was, then, a climate of religiosity about the young man's curiosities rather than a specific involvement with religion or *a* religion.

In 1888, matured and well-established in his career at Harvard, his interests having found the nascent discipline of psychology as the center around which they would hiss and spin, James reread Butler with renewed attention as he also reread Plato's *Republic*, selections from Aristotle, Adam Smith, William Paley, and Baruch Spinoza in preparation for a philosophy course he was to teach during the fall semester on recent English contribu-tions to theistic ethics.[78] This was also the period when James was finally completing *The Principles of Psychology*. His return to Butler was richly productive. The theme of Butler's *Analogy* is the famous phrase, "probabil-ity is the very guide of life," his concern being neither mathematical nor statistical probability, but finding a way to extend or transcend traditional rational modes of argument for the existence of God. He opened his work with a discussion of immortality, which he summarized pointedly in his conclusion at the end of Part I. There he says that it is "contrary to experi-ence" to suppose that "gross bodies" are ourselves. In *Religious Language: An Empirical Placing of Theological Phrases*, Ian T. Ramsey, one of the last generation's foremost investigators of the nature of religious experience, underscored Butler's very useful and beautiful conception of religion as "an odd discernment" coupled with "a total commitment"[79]; a compound notion that Ramsey adopted and fruitfully developed. Outlining Butler's argument for immortality, Ramsey writes:

> Belief in immortality is thus founded in an awareness that as "living agents" we are more than our public behaviour. Here, I suggest, is the discernment without which no distinctive theology will ever be possible; a "self-awareness" that is more than "body awareness" and not exhausted by spatio-temporal "objects." Such a discernment lies at the basis of religion, whose characteristic claim is that there are situations which are spatio-temporal and more. [Here we think of James's "fringe," the nimbus of "faint brain-process upon our thought, as it makes us aware of relations and objects but dimly perceived."[80]] Without such "depth"; without this which is "unseen" no religion will be possible.[81]

"But more needs to be said about this characteristic situation than has so far been covered by calling it a 'discernment,'" Ramsey observes, and goes on to point out the intrinsic connection between discernment and realizing "probability [as] the guide of life." In a passage from Butler that he quotes, we find the prototype for William James's argument in *The Will to Believe* (1897), famously emblematized by the two climbers facing an abyss whose only chance of survival depends on believing a leap across will be successful:

> "In questions of difficulty," says Butler, "where more satisfactory evidence cannot be had, or is not seen; if the result of the examination be, that there appears on the whole, any ... presumption on one side, though in the lowest degree greater; *this determines the question*, even in matters of speculation; and *in matters of practice, will lay us under an absolute and formal obligation*, in point of prudence and of interest, to act upon that presumption or low probability, though it be so low as to leave the mind in very grave doubt which is the truth.... For numberless instances might be mentioned respecting the common pursuits of life, where *a man would be thought, in a literal sense, distracted, who would not act, and with great application too, not only upon an even chance, but upon much less, and where the probability or chance was greatly against his succeeding.* [Ramsey's emphases][82]

Ramsey goes on to clarify the relation between discernment and commitment:

> Now it is ... a total commitment, appropriate to a "question of great consequence," a commitment which is based upon but goes *beyond rational considerations* [emphasis added] which are "matters of speculation"; a commitment which sees in a situation all that the understanding can give

us *and more* [emphasis added]; a commitment which is exemplified by conscientious action building on "probabilities," which Butler thinks to be characteristic of a religious attitude."[83]

Ramsey further illuminates Butler's insight by particularizing the nature of the relation between discernment and commitment: that a response of total commitment to the visionary glimpses that constitute discernment cannot be contained or elicited in "impersonal" object language. Since the experiential "situation is *more* [Ramsey's emphasis] than 'what's seen,' it has taken on 'depth'; there is something akin to religious 'insight,' 'discernment,' 'vision.'"[84] We recall what James observes of "Vivekananda's use of the Atman": "It is emotional and spiritual altogether." The *more* always belongs to authentic religious experience and is characterized by the breakdown of the subject-object distinction – what is experienced is what Ramsey calls a creature's "cosmic commitment" – and requires language to be used in a way that maximizes the possibility for continuing, albeit periodic, discernment and for the action appropriate to such insight. Language used in this way *points* rather than defines. As Ramsey astutely observes, "In this respect ... they [words registering the *more*, James's "fringe"] may be compared with mathematical operators which themselves 'mean' nothing, but are directives of procedure if we want to discover what the mathematical writer has in store for us."[85] (This comparison is useful, as well, in thinking about John Dewey's description of philosophy as simply a "set of operations" and what is later detailed by J. L. Austin as the "performative" aspect of ordinary language.) It is in this context that C. S. Peirce's crucial contribution to pragmatism, as William James abundantly appreciated, sets the rules of play. Peirce was first and foremost a mathematician, but a mathematician, like Lewis Carroll, fascinated, even to the edge of obsession, with the permutations of syntax, grammar, and semantics on which successful human being in the world depends.

Peirce's theory of signs, his original and grounding contribution to what has come to be known as "semiotics," is generally thought of in terms of a logical system, closer to the abstraction of symbolic logic than to anything else. Obscured by this take is that what Peirce – as avid a reader of Swedenborg as Henry James, Sr. – was pursuing was a religious purpose; we recall that he was attempting to preserve in what he called "agapism" the basis of Christianity's ethic. Moreover, his mathematical imagination had prepared him to conceive of the "I" as nothing more than a cipher – that extraordinary concept introduced to the West with the notation of zero. While Emerson had intuited this realization, offering "I – this thought which is called I,"[86] Peirce would, as it were, back up its paradoxical reality with mathematical *proof,* demonstrating it to be an open center, an "axis of vision," in Emerson's words,[87] around which elements of lived experience are drawn as to a magnetic pole. "One is immediately conscious of his or her feelings," Peirce writes, "but not that they are feelings of an ego – the self is only inferred; there is no time in the present for any inference at all."[88] Many will be familiar with Peirce's "existential graphs," his pages and pages of sentences and parts of sentences repeating with minor variations in inflection and/or syntax, these accompanied by a sign system of lines, shading and boxes scoring the changes in nuance and meaning. These exercises in what he called "diagrammatic reasoning" were experiments in his theory of signs –actually a "sign language" with which to express an orientation, a relation of *firstness,* experienced *concretely* by what John Dewey would call "the live creature" in a spatio-temporal environment; Peirce's "graphical system of logic (his existential graphs) improves on other logics for the representation of discourse, and the study of language generally."[89] In the closing chapter of his *Essay Concerning Human Understanding,* John Locke suggested the extension of "'the doctrine of signs' beyond a simple analysis of words or the relation of ideas to the study of the order by which thought itself is possible." Pointing toward this extension, Locke invokes *semiotike,* which, most interestingly, as a term, derives from the art of musical notation as used by Locke's friend John Wallis in his 1682 edition of Ptolemy's *Harmonics.* Locke notes that in this expanded sense, semiotics is "aptly termed also *Logike,* logic: the business whereof it is to consider the nature of signs the mind makes use of for the understanding of things or conveying its knowledge to others." To understand ideas and words in the context of such a doctrine "would afford us another sort of logic and critic, than what we have been hitherto acquainted with."[90] Peirce knew Locke's *Essay* well and had taught it. As though following Locke's direction, Peirce developed his own *semiotike,* using his signs to modulate the movement of mind from one key to another. As Gregory Bateson would detail almost 100 years later, this kind of scored, as it were, *performative* language is necessary if human beings and the societies they create are to avoid or escape the "double bind" situations resulting from confusions of call and response in inadequate and incompatible linguistic codes.[91]

Nolan Pliny Jacobson's work on the affinities between America's defining philosophy and Buddhism is particularly useful concerning Peirce's major significance in this context. It is also useful to note here that Vivekananda

repeatedly reminded his audiences that the Buddha was Hindu, the first
to bring Vedanta out of India. Here, then, is Jacobson:

> For Peirce … all thinking is dialogic in nature, extending the feelings
> of the thinker into the feelings of others – this is what he means by the
> "outreaching identity" of the self.* What distinguishes the human mind
> is not that it is unextended – nothing really is, Gilbert Ryle's "ghost in the
> machine" notwithstanding.** What distinguishes the mind is the acuteness
> of its sensitivity to the shared processes of feeling and the equally distinct-
> ive ability to extend the range of our awareness by *high-level sign language*
> [emphasis added], "by knowing which," Peirce says, "we know *something
> more*" [emphasis added] and engage in dialogue with private and public
> moments in our experience. This is crucial for Peirce's philosophy of sci-
> ence, as well as an access road into profound dialogue with the Buddhist
> orientation. "There is an immediate community of feeling between parts of
> mind infinitesimally near together, between the self at one moment and the
> oncoming self of the next; without this," Peirce writes, "it would have been
> impossible for minds external to one another ever to become coordinated
> in the search for public truth to which even the most prejudiced persons
> will come if they pursue their inquiries far enough."*** The alternative is
> that each person will be the victim of narrowness, as Peirce says, a "little
> prophet," a "crank," a "victim" of the "ghost in the machine."**** …
>
> Peirce is one of the few philosophers, East or West, who has been utterly
> clear on the concreteness compared with which everything else is abstract.
> With amazing persistence, he argues that a linguistic system does the very
> opposite of what most philosophers and members of the lay public assume:
> language does *not* [Jacobson's emphasis] bring together in fellow-feeling
> and compassion what has been split, or for all practical purposes evacuated
> by cultural metaphor and myth.[92]

Following Jacobson's insights helps us to see that what James recognized
in Peirce's method was the practical grounding for religious experience. It
was after integrating what he learned from Peirce that James returned to
Butler and began to braid their strands of thinking and feeling with his
own. Over the course of the next decade, as he completed *The Principles*
and then concentrated more and more intensely on the central aspects laid
out therein – perception, attention, will, belief – this braiding would issue
in "The Psychology of Belief," an article he sent to *Mind* in November
1888 that became the keystone chapter of *The Principles of Psychology* and
forecast of *Pragmatism*. In this decisive offering, James drew not only
on his reading but also – as he would again in his 1898 talk at Berkeley,
"Philosophical Conceptions and Practical Results" – on his experience in
the Amazon, exposed to the "cosmic weather," in order to articulate certain

identities central to negotiating successfully as creatures in a universe of chance. Using the example of an Amazonian girl who *believed* a cucumber to be alive and cared for it accordingly, James identifies belief as a feeling; an emotion intrinsically connected with "habits of attention." He then observes, "Our own activity of attention will thus determine what we are to know and what we are to believe." By the time he revised his talk for inclusion in *Principles*, he was explicit in grounding attention and belief in the primacy of action. "How can we believe at will[?]" he asks, and then provides a "method": "*we need only in cold blood* ACT *as if the thing in question were real, and keep acting as if it were real, and it will infallibly end by growing into such a connection with our life that it will become real*" (James's emphasis and capitalization).[93] The chapter, appropriately retitled from "The Psychology of Belief" to "The Perception of Reality," ends: "*Will and Belief, in short, meaning a certain relation between objects and the self, are two names for one and the same* psychological *phenomenon ... our belief and attention* are the same fact" (James's emphasis and capitalization).[94] Here was James *realizing* yet another of Emerson's lessons: "A man should know himself for a necessary *actor* [emphasis added]. A link was wanting between two craving parts of nature, and he was hurled into being as the bridge over that yawning need, the mediator betwixt two else unmarriageable facts."[95] "The Method of Nature" was being rephrased as the method of pragmatism. The next announcement would be the 1898 Berkeley talk, and an even more explicit articulation was to come that would focus, significantly, on activity – the nature of nature in relation to "this thought which is called I."

THE BODY IS THE STORM CENTER

This articulation came in a 1904 address to the American Philosophical Association entitled "The Experience of Activity" where James outlined the prehistory of pragmatism against the background of Darwin's universe of chance: "No philosophic knowledge of the general nature and constitution of tendencies, or of the relation of large to smaller ones, can help us predict which of all the various competing tendencies that interest us in this universe are likeliest to prevail."[96] James noted that there was a "certain systematic way of asking questions" emerging that was "known sometimes as the pragmatic method, sometimes as humanism, sometimes as Deweyism, and in France, by some of the disciples of Bergson, as the Philosophie nouvelle," and continued, "almost any day a man with a

genius for *finding the right word for things* [emphasis added] may hit upon
some unifying and conciliating formula that will make so much vaguely
similar aspiration crystallize into more definite form." He then announced,
"I myself have given the name of 'radical empiricism' to that version of
the tendency in question which I prefer."[97] He particularized the heart
of his version of the method: "'Change taking place' is a unique content
of experience, one of those 'conjunctive' objects which radical empiricism
seeks so earnestly to rehabilitate and preserve. The sense of activity is thus
in the broadest and vaguest way synonymous with the sense of 'life.'"[98]
And it is only as "part or particle" of "life" that "the individualized self"
exists, most notably experienced and vividly described by James in terms
of what Wallace Stevens would later superbly phrase as "Nothing that is
not there and the nothing that is"[99] – Peirce's cipher, the "I" as zero, "origin of all coordinates":

> The individualized self, which I believe to be the only thing properly called
> self, is a part of the content of the world experienced. The world experi-
> enced (otherwise called the "field of consciousness") comes at all times
> with our body as its center, center of vision, center of action, center of
> interest. [We think of Emerson, "The eye is the first circle ...."[100]] Where
> the body is is "here"; when the body acts is "now"; what the body touches
> is "this"; all the other things are "there" and "then" and "that." These words
> of emphasized position imply a systematization of things with reference
> to a focus of action and interest which lies in the body; and the system-
> atization is now so instinctive (was it ever not so?) that no developed or
> active experience exists for us at all except in that ordered form. So far as
> "thoughts" and "feelings" can be active, their activity terminates in the
> activity of the body, and only through first arousing its activities can they
> begin to change those of the rest of the world. *The body is the storm center,*
> *the origin of coordinates, the constant place of stress in all that experience-*
> *train. Everything circles round it, and is felt from its point of view. The word*
> *"I," then, is primarily a noun of position* [like a compass needle, we should
> add], *just like "this" and "here." Activities attached to "this" position have*
> *prerogative emphasis, and, if activities have feelings, must be felt in a peculiar*
> *way. The word "my" designates the kind of emphasis* [emphasis added]. I see
> no inconsistency whatever in defending, on the one hand, "my" activities
> as unique and opposed to those of outer nature, and, on the other hand,
> in affirming, after introspection, that they consist in movements in the
> head. The "my" of them is the emphasis, the feeling of perspective interest
> in which they are dyed.[101]

It is from the ground of experiencing human being at this fully
embodied level that James will go on to say that "the earth must resume

her rights." In foregrounding the intrinsic connection between the body and the earth, James, echoing the Advaitaic premises of the lessons of Raja-Yoga, underscores the Necker-cube quality of our perception of the relation:

> Our body is itself the palmary instance of the ambiguous. Sometimes I treat my body purely as a part of outer nature. Sometimes, again, I think of it as "mine," I sort it with the "me," and then certain local changes and determinations in it pass for spiritual happenings. Its breathing is my "thinking," its sensorial adjustments are my "attention," its kinesthetic alterations are my "efforts," its visceral perturbations are my "emotions."[102]

The realization of being always *in-between* – knowing in "flashes," "blazes," growing in "spots" around a "more" that is never still nor fully known – underwrites accepting the imperfect as our paradise and that the method appropriate to this condition is approximate, at best offering only "guesses at the riddle," in Peirce's phrase. Charles Hartshorne, a preeminent scholar of Peirce and of Whitehead, carried this knowledge to the second-generation pragmatists through his student Richard Rorty. As Nolan Pliny Jacobson, himself aligning pragmatism with Buddhism, observes, quoting Hartshorne: "The unity of any person or thing through time covers 'an ultimate multiplicity of momentary states or "flashes" of reality.'"[103] The use of the pragmatic method is to navigate from where we are to where we want to go, plotting a course into the cosmic weather, at the most extreme allowing us to believe we can leap across an abyss. *Intention* is central = "I" = the "storm-center." Just as it is necessary to have a destination in order to plot a course, it is necessary to have an intention, an aim, to direct activity; a knowledge that repeats the primal scene of instruction of the West's foundational myth where it is God's words that implement intention and effect creation. In closing "The Experience of Activity," James recuperates this knowledge, but dresses it in ordinary language:

> If we take an activity-situation at its face-value, it seems as if we caught *in flagrante delicto* the very power that makes facts come and be. I am now eagerly striving ... to get this truth which I seem half to perceive, into words which shall make it show more clearly. If the words come, it will seem as if the striving itself had drawn or pulled them into actuality out from the state of merely possible being in which they were. How is this feat performed? How does the pulling *pull*? How do I get my hold on words not yet existent, and when they come by what means have I *made* them come? Really it is the problem of creation; for in the end the question is: How do I make them *be*? Real activities are those that really make things be, without which things are not, and with which they are there....

Sustaining, persevering, striving, paying with effort as we go, hanging on and finally achieving our intention – this *is* action, this *is* effectuation in the only shape in which, by a pure experience-philosophy, the whereabouts of it anywhere can be discussed. Here is creation in its first intention, here is causality at work. To treat this offhand as the bare illusory surface of a world whose real causality is an unimaginable ontological principle hidden in the cubic deeps, is, for the more empirical way of thinking, only animism in another shape.[104]

It is easy to understand from this description what James elsewhere observed: "Thinking is the only morality." And it is within this understanding that he offered the "way of thinking" outlined by his version of pragmatism as continuing the work of the Protestant Reformation – now circling back to recover the originary Eastern strains of religious experience in the West.

In *The Great Code: The Bible and Literature* (1981), Northrop Frye provides a lucid and concise analysis of the Reformation project. It begins, he says, with "the conception of a transcending of the Church within history." What this meant was that "the Church's role was to enter into a dialogue with the Word of God and not to replace it as the source of revelation." Frye goes on to comment that "Milton ... being a poet, understood that changes in metaphor were far more important than changes in doctrine" and so "remarked that this involved thinking of the Church not as a 'mother,' but as a young bride about to be instructed in her duties." "*The analogy between this conception of reformation and the growth of a descriptive approach to language is clear enough,*"[105] Frye notes (emphasis added). Entering "into a dialogue," a *conversation*, "with the Word of God" is the defining activity of the Reformation. Moreover, the specific nature of the linguistic activity is that it will become instructive, persuasively effective in examples chosen. Frye also observes:

> Metaphors of unity and integration take us only so far, because they are derived from the finiteness of the human mind. If we are to expand our vision into the genuinely infinite, that vision becomes decentralized. We follow a "way" or direction until we reach the state of innocence symbolized by the sheep in the twenty-third Psalm, where we are back to wandering, but where wandering no longer means being lost. There are two senses in which the word "imperfect" is used: in one sense it is that which falls short of perfection; in another it is that which is not finished but continuously *active*, as in the tense system of verbs in most languages. It is in the latter sense that "the imperfect is our paradise," as Wallace Stevens says, a world that may change as much as our own, but where

change is no longer dominated by the single direction toward nothing-
ness and death.[106]

In discussing the accidental fact of our being born into a particular society and language – "within a pre-existing social contract" – Frye observes
that "as the individual develops within his society, all the essential aspects
of thought and imagination and experience take place in him. Social freedom, however essential, is general and approximate;" but "real freedom is
something that only the individual can experience," and that "the sense
of an individuality that grows out of society ... is infinitely more than
a social function." Frye continues brilliantly, by way of naturalizing the
Pauline model, to explain how it is that the only way an individual can
effectively experience true individuality is by "acquir[ing] the internal
authority of the unity of the Logos, and it is this unity that makes him an
individual."[107] Introducing the way he will follow to this illumination, in
his first chapter, "Language I," of Part One, "The Order of Words," Frye
suggests:

> [W]e might come closer to what is meant in the Bible by the word "God"
> if we understood it as a verb, and not a verb of simple asserted existence
> but of a verb implying a process accomplishing itself. This would involve
> *trying to think our way back to a conception of language in which words were*
> *words of power, conveying primarily the sense of forces and energies rather*
> *than analogues of physical bodies* [emphasis added]. To some extent this
> would be a reversion to the metaphorical language of primitive commu-
> nities, as ... to a cycle of language and the "primitive" word *mana*....
> But it would also be oddly contemporary with post-Einsteinian physics,
> where atoms and electrons are no longer thought of as things but rather
> as traces of processes. God may have lost his function as the subject or
> object of a predicate, but may not be so much dead as entombed in a dead
> language.[108]

In his study of the spiritual universe of the Persian sages and mystics
of the twelfth century, the great French Islamist scholar Henry Corbin
speaks of the motive animating their "prophetic philosophy"; this motive
"is denoted by the word *ta'wil*, which literally means to 'reconduct something to its source.'"[109] Frye's aspiration to have us "think our way back
to a conception of language in which words were words of power" echoes this impulse as does Ludwig Wittgenstein's description of the work
of the philosopher of the future: "What *we* do is bring words back from
their metaphysical to their everyday use." Wittgenstein voices this after
noting that,

[Philosophical problems] are not empirical problems; they are solved, rather, by looking into the workings of our language, and that in such a way as to make us recognize those workings.... The problems are solved, not by giving new information but by arranging what we have always known. Philosophy is a battle against the bewitchment of our intelligence by means of language.[110]

This is the work of pragmatism. Wittgenstein's lifelong preoccupation with James was clearly in play in his language game.

CHAPTER 3

Method: Charles Sanders Peirce, The call of the wild

Refinement is what characterizes our intellectualist philosophies....
But I ask you in all seriousness to look abroad on this colossal universe of concrete facts, on their awful bewilderments, their surprises and cruelties, on the wildness which they show, and then to tell me whether "refined" is the one inevitable descriptive adjective that springs to your lips.

Refinement has its place in things, true enough. But a philosophy that breathes out nothing but refinement will never satisfy the empiricist temper of mind. It will seem rather a monument of artificiality. So we find men of science preferring to turn their backs on metaphysics as on something altogether cloistered and spectral, and practical men shaking philosophy's dust off their feet and following the call of the wild.

WILLIAM JAMES, Pragmatism

Wherefore, I say, let everyone be of good cheer about his soul who, after having renounced the insatiable hungers of the self, and the indefinite postponement of life, as working harm rather than good; has employed *the claws of wisdom*, not to increase the mind's distinctive power to hate, nor to seek dominion over others, but to *foster that higher tropism to the light still hidden below the rim of the world....* Thus adorned in the soul's most perfect jewel, enjoying the beauty and loving the variousness of life, he is ready to enter at last into the *silent almost secret bond of fellow-feeling that holds the world together.*

PLATO, Phaedo

The rapt saint is found the only logician.

EMERSON, The Method of Nature

BEGAN IN THE TWILIGHT[1]

It came, literally, as a moment of "seeing the light." I heard myself say, "Oh, yes! Of course!" In addition to his work measuring gravity for the United States Coast and Geodetic Survey after graduation from Harvard (with the first Bachelor of Science degree, in 1863, awarded summa cum laude), Charles Sanders Peirce spent years early in his career turning his attention "to the light still hidden below the rim of the world." Among the texts I had gathered to prepare for writing this chapter was one I had never read, *Photometric Researches*, a descriptive survey covering measurements of the light from distant stars that he took and recorded – still as an Assistant in the Coast Survey, but for this project under the direction of the Harvard Observatory – over a three-year period from 1872 to 1875. The study was published in 1878, the only volume of his work to see press during his lifetime, and one of which he remained, with good reason, quite proud.[2] In *Photometric Researches*, Peirce "proposed an original use of the relative brightness of stars as a means of determining an approximate shape for the solar galaxy and a mode of distribution of stars within it, based both on the observations he had made ... and on existing star catalogues, such as those by Ptolemy and Tycho Brahe."[3] The first of its five chapters is entitled "The Sensation of Light" and begins with the observation that while an indefinite number of numbers is required to define light comprised as it is of "heterogeneous undulations" (different wave lengths) emitted from a point, "*just three numbers* [emphasis added] are in every case requisite to define the sensation produced" upon the human retina. "In other words," the paragraph concludes, "*light is a triple sensation*" (emphasis added) for the creatures we happen to be. In addition to his famous division of experience into *Firstness, Secondness,* and *Thirdness,* triads of different kinds characterize all aspects of Peirce's later work.[4] His understanding of the nature of the human registration of light – the primary and constant condition of being – was the physical analogue anchoring his priming in other triadic relations, a structure truly overdetermined in our relation to our universe: syllogisms, dimensions of objects, the three persons of the Trinity and grammar, the kingdoms – animal, vegetable, mineral. Peirce himself commented on this basic fact of life as we know it: "The problem of how genuine triadic relationships first arose in the world is a better, because more definite, formulation of the problem of how life first came about."[5] A recent explicator of the importance of Peirce's work in the investigations into signs, processes, and language games in their relation to ontology offers a useful gloss on Peirce's observation:

> In every living being, from bacteria to humans and perhaps beyond, semiosis is the crucial Thirdness that enables the organism to respond to signs by taking actions that serve to further its goals of getting food, avoiding harm, and reproducing its kind. For most life forms, these goals are unconscious, and most of them are built into their genes. But there is no difference in principle between the evolutionary learning that is encoded in genes and the individual learning that is encoded in neurons. Understanding at every level and in every kind of organization from colonies of bacteria to human businesses and governments requires an understanding of signs, goals, communication, cooperation, and competition – all of which involve aspects of Thirdness.[6]

In connection with the fact of being the creatures we are, with sensory capacities and limitations evolved through hundreds of thousands of years of life on our planet, it is instructive to consider that along the electromagnetic spectrum that scales currently observed and *useable* wave frequencies (of frequencies extending infinitely), visible light waves – the range within which we can actually *see*, in other words, the range that is our habitat – stretches only from 0.4 to 0.7 micrometers (4,000–7,000 angstroms); an atom, by comparison, is a few angstroms in size. (One of the analogies used to give a more concrete sense of the astonishing *difference* in scale between the visible range available to human sensation and the invisible realm, nonetheless pulsing and flowing around and through us continuously, is to imagine this latter instrumentally observable and useable range as a length stretching from New York to California on which our visible range would be the span of a pinky fingernail.) As the son of a noted mathematician and astronomer, Benjamin Peirce, Charles Sanders Peirce was from childhood aware of our being – to borrow Stevens's phrase again – "merest minuscule[s] in the gales" of the cosmic weather. So extended into the invisibilities of being was Benjamin Peirce that his teaching "about functions and infinitesimal variables seemed," at least to one of his advanced students, "to be theories or imaginations rather than facts or realities."[7] But for his son Charles, the exquisite plane where his father resided and that he described in all its detail was the "environment of fact … but of fact not realized before."[8]

In Chapter 2, it was noted that William James's and Charles Darwin's embodied experiences of horizontality (being confined for long periods, because of seasickness, to their bunks aboard the ships in which they each traveled early in their respective careers to South America) intrinsically informed their perception and the subsequent theoretical development of what they had realized in having shifted ordinary point of view. We recall, for example, in James's case, his announcing: "The centre of gravity of philosophy must therefore alter its place. The earth of things, long thrown into shadow by the glories of the upper ether, must resume its rights." Similarly, Peirce's protracted experience of working with the instruments he did— measuring the varying force of gravity on the planet, observing aberrations of starlight and the perturbations of the earth's movement through the heavens – established habits of minding that he would develop and apply as a new tripartite logic that would become the basis of his epistemology and of his theory of signs. Peirce realized through repeated computations of varying measurements over time and his statistical projections from them – activities that together constituted his practices as a calculator of changing terrestrial mass and as a celestial observer – what those working half a century later would only then begin to develop as the field of quantum mechanics, the field describing "the natural history of matter and energy making their way through space and time."[9] The key permitting entry into the strange new world imaginatively inhabited and mapped by Peirce – later theoretically described by quantum mechanics – was and is the understanding that "just as ambivalence holds more information than any single emotion,"[10] the effect of swinging thought, like a pendulum, between the extremes of probabilities opens *truth* to compass the *consequences* to be considered in projecting one possibility or another: "I will say ... that while in practical matters nothing is more unwise than to carry an idea to extreme lengths, yet in speculative thought, this is the greatest of locomotives for advancing upon the road to truth. Indeed, it is the extreme cases which alone teach you anything new."[11] Peirce internalized this habit of mind from recording the orbits of pendulums used to measure variations in gravitational pull and the movement of the earth in relation to the sun and other stars, and from observing through telescopes the light of stars long extinct just then reaching earth. Expressing his realization about what is called "truth" in *its* most extreme form, that is, including all of future time in his calculation, Peirce observed in closing "How to Make Our Ideas Clear," the lecture/essay that was the spark igniting the ideas that would come to be framed as "pragmatism," that truth, like reality, is an *activity* – "the activity of the most august imagination" – of "investigation carried sufficiently far." "The very origin of the conception of reality," Peirce observed already as early as 1868, "involves the notion of a community without definite limits, and capable of a definite increase in knowledge."[12] And again, more expansively, later, in 1878:

> And then, after the universe is dead (according to the prediction of some scientists), and all life has ceased forever, will not the shock of atoms continue though there will be no mind to know it? To this I reply that, though in no possible state of knowledge can any number be great enough to express the relation between the amount of what rests unknown to the amount of the known, yet it is unphilosophical to suppose that, with regard to any given question (which has any clear meaning), investigation would not bring forth a solution of it, if it were carried far enough. Who would have said, a few years ago, that we could ever know of what substances stars are made whose light may have been longer in reaching us than the human race has existed? Who can be sure of what we shall not know in a few hundred years? Who can guess what would be the result of continuing the pursuit of science for ten thousand years, with the activity of the last hundred? And if it were to go on for a million, or a billion, or any number of years you please, how is it possible to say that there is any question which might not ultimately be solved?

> But it may be objected, "Why make so much of these remote considerations, especially when it is your principle that only practical distinctions have a meaning?" Well, I must confess that it makes very little difference whether we say that a stone on the bottom of the ocean, in complete darkness, is brilliant or not – that is to say, that it *probably* makes no difference, remembering always that that stone *may* be fished up to-morrow. But that there are gems at the bottom of the sea, flowers in the untraveled desert, etc., are propositions which, like that about a diamond being hard when it is not pressed, concern much more the arrangement of our language than they do the meaning of our ideas. [Peirce's emphases][13]

There are several details important to remark in this brilliantly prescient and beautiful passage. One of the most striking of Peirce's insights, in light of current findings about "dark energy," is his understanding that "in no possible state of knowledge can any number be great enough to express the relation between the amount of what rests unknown to the amount of the known." This is precisely the way in which cosmologists today describe the relation between what is known and/or can be observed in the universe and "dark energy" – the nature of which we do not now know, although we *do* know that it comprises approximately 78 percent of the universe. Against what Peirce offered in his 1878 projection, we have this description from physicist and quantum mechanical engineer Seth Lloyd concerning the present state of our situation in relation to what we can know:

The part of the universe about which we can have information is said to be "within the horizon." Beyond the horizon we can only guess as to what is happening....

As time passes, the horizon expands, at three times the speed of light. When we look through a telescope, we also look backward in time, and the most remote objects we can see appear as they were a little under 14 billion years ago. In the intervening time, because of the expansion of the universe, those objects have moved even farther away, and right now they are 42 billion light-years away from us. As the horizon expands, more and more objects swim into view, and the amount of energy available for computation within the horizon increases. *The amount of computation that can have been performed within the horizon since the beginning of the universe increases over time.* [Lloyd's emphasis][14]

Entrained by the alternating currents of his combined habits of observation, reading – "Real reading consists in putting oneself into the author's position, and assimilating his ways of thinking"[15] – and study, Peirce's manner of thinking had to process induction and deduction almost at once, yet with his attention as interpreter constant. The habit of attending through telescopes to the aberrations of starlight, recording variations while *simultaneously integrating imaginatively*, projecting how that shape would work as a theory describing scintillations of starlight falling to earth, prepared him to conceive of an ever-expanding universe decades before there was evidence that, indeed, this is the case. And so, in the second half of his observation about the "amount of what rests unknown to the amount of the known, he continued: "yet it is unphilosophical to suppose that, with regard to any given question (which has any clear meaning), investigation would not bring forth a solution of it, if it were carried far enough." What Peirce expresses in this conclusion is a secular form of faith. This brings us to the second detail important to remark about the passage.

The faith expressed by Peirce in the power of mind extending to infinite potentiality is the same kind of faith expressed by Ralph Waldo Emerson in opening *Nature* (1836) – the volume, as noted earlier, that sparked what was to become known as "transcendentalism" in the same way that "How to Make Our Ideas Clear" was to spark "pragmatism." Here is Emerson:

Undoubtedly, we have no questions to ask which are unanswerable. We must trust the perfection of the creation so far, as to believe that whatever curiosity the order of things has awakened in our minds, the order of things can satisfy. Every man's condition is a solution in hieroglyphic to those inquiries he would put. He acts it as life, before he apprehends it as truth.

In like manner, nature is already, in its forms and tendencies, describing its own design. Let us interrogate the great apparition that shines so peacefully around us....

...to a sound judgment, the most abstract truth is the most practical. Whenever a true theory appears, it will be its own evidence. Its test is, that it will explain all phenomena.[16]

As Emerson well knew, "as large a demand is made on our faith by nature, as by miracles."[17]

TO DO WHAT IN ME LIES[18]

It was also noted in Chapter 2 that it was Peirce's critical insight in applying mathematical operations to processes of thinking and language that set the rules of play for pragmatism. As Kenneth Laine Ketner and Hilary Putnam have similarly observed in their introduction to *Reasoning and the Logic of Things*, the series of lectures Peirce gave at Harvard in 1898 under the urging of William James that he present his ideas as lucidly as possible to a popular audience:

> Because it explored the consequences of pure hypotheses by experimenting upon representative diagrams, mathematics was the inspirational source of the pragmatic maxim, the jewel of the methodological part of semeiotic, and the distinctive feature of Peirce's thought. As he often stated, the pragmatic maxim is little more than a summarizing statement of the procedure of experimental design in a laboratory – deduce the observable consequences of the hypothesis.[19]

And, indeed, it was Peirce's skill as a calculating mathematician and logician – in the language of the nineteenth century, *he was a "computer"* – that shifted the ground from Emerson's "transcendentalist" faith to the "pragmatist" faith, a faith that justifies the incorporation of the hypothetical and interpolating practices of scientific method, *guessing*, to expand what we know and practice as "rationality." Peirce's term for this additional "type" or "figure of reasoning" is "Retroduction," to be added as the second– mediate – mode between "Deduction" and "Induction."[20] Peirce's Retroduction is a formalization of the process of trial and error for which he provided not only definition, but also a symbolic language following the manner of mathematical notation. (We shall have occasion a bit further on to discuss this centrally important amplification to thinking about thinking.) It is also important to note that James persuaded Peirce to offer this series of lectures spelling out his method – "Monday and Thursday Evenings in February and March, 1898, at eight o'clock" – in the months just before he would himself in August give the talk at Berkeley, "Philosophical Conceptions and Practical Results," where he spoke for the first time of "pragmatism," attributing the term to Peirce and calling him, as noted earlier, "one of the most original of contemporary thinkers," and adding that "the principle of practicalism – or pragmatism, as he called it, when I first heard him enunciate it at Cambridge in the early '70's – is the clue or compass by following which I find myself more and more confirmed in believing."[21]

It was remarked as well in Chapter 2 that Peirce was a deep reader of Emanuel Swedenborg, following, in his devotion, Henry James, Sr.[22] Indeed, during the almost two years that William James went off to Germany to continue his scientific studies (1867–8), his friend Charles virtually took the place of the eldest son of the James household, keen to learn as much about the Swedish polymath as he could from James Sr. for whom Swedenborg's work had become sacred scripture. (William James and Peirce met and began their friendship in 1861 as students in the Lawrence Scientific School, both studying under Louis Agassiz during the period when the controversy over Darwin's theory was at its peak. It was during the period of William's going off to Brazil with Agassiz on the Thayer expedition – April 1865–February 1866 – that Peirce began having extended conversations with Henry James, Sr. about Swedenborg.) As Eugene Taylor has noted, "[i]n the mid-nineteenth century ... no one could call himself educated who had not read Swedenborg's works or come into contact with the various Swedenborgian ideas that permeated the transcendentalist atmosphere of the day." We know, of course, of the significance of Swedenborg, "or, the Mystic," for Emerson, who observed: "The moral insight of Swedenborg, the correction of popular errors, the announcement of ethical laws, take him out of comparison with any other modern writer, and entitle him to a place, vacant for some ages, among the lawgivers of mankind." His aim, "the highest end" for Emerson, was "to put science and the soul, long estranged from each other, at one again."[23] Emerson – as Taylor, following Perry Miller observes— "had taken his Swedenborg mainly from Sampson Reed between 1826 and 1844, while thereafter he relied mainly on the interpretations of Henry James Sr. and the biography and translations of James John Garth Wilkinson, English physician and translator of Swedenborg's scientific and medical writings."[24] Peirce's exposure to the work of the Swedish mystic was more constant and extended than Emerson's – indeed, he remained occupied with Swedenborg's work throughout his life. Peirce, like Emerson, was motivated to give careful attention to the Book of Nature by the kind of religious impulse that had prompted Swedenborg. As Peirce expressed, "Nature is something great, and beautiful, and sacred, and eternal, and real, – the object of [science's] worship and admiration."[25] And for both Emerson and Peirce, religious experience had already begun to be loosened from orthodoxy though preserving the sense of the divine as *the activity of divining*, of looking not simply *at* facts, but *through* them.

Peirce had been prepared in his attitudes and habits by his father. In addition to being an eminent mathematician and astronomer, Benjamin Peirce was also, like Emerson, a Unitarian and one of the members of the "Saturday Club," the group – also including Louis Agassiz, Asa Gray, and Oliver Wendell Holmes – that met monthly in the years from 1855–70 to discuss the latest discoveries and speculations of their moment. (Benjamin Peirce held a professorship at Harvard while also serving, for a time, as superintendent of the United States Coast and Geodetic Survey.) Because, like Emerson, Benjamin Peirce separated theism from the *mythos* of Christ, many of his contemporaries thought him an atheist. In his acutely insightful intellectual biography of Charles Sanders Peirce, Joseph Brent underscores the spiritual aspect of Benjamin Peirce's work, in spite of its unorthodoxy: "Benjamin Peirce taught mathematics as a kind of Pythagorean prayer. He proclaimed the mystical doctrine that, however the supernatural might be, it existed in the natural world and was experienced there." Brent goes on to draw the line connecting the father's to the son's projects:

> In 1889, in the *Century Dictionary*, Charles, under the heading of "ideal-realism," described his father's position (essentially his own in time as well) as "...the opinion that nature and the mind have such a community as to impart to guesses a tendency toward the truth, while at the same time they require the confirmation of empirical science."[26]

The abiding nature of the spiritual impulse for the younger Peirce, particularly as expressed in the work of Swedenborg, is evidenced as late as 1897 when he wrote to William James expressing his gratitude for James's continuing efforts in his behalf. (James had been for several years contributing substantially to his friend's support as well as having organized what amounted to a pension fund for Peirce, to which others also gave.) In this letter, as again observed by Ketner and Putnam in their introduction to *Reasoning and the Logic of Things*, Peirce gave a brief outline of this course of lectures that he had originally proposed to call "On the Logic of Events,"[27] concluding with:

> I am all alone in the house here ["Arisbe," the farmhouse in Milford, Pennsylvania – "the wildest part of the Eastern States," as Peirce described

in a letter to George Cantor in 1900[28] – rebuilt and named by Peirce after an ancient Greek colony in Asia Minor that was a center of cosmology, philosophy, and science. Peirce lived in Arisbe with Juliette Froissy, his second wife, from 1888 until his death in 1914; he had hoped to establish a contemporary summer colony following the Greek model.] and have spent some of the quiet hours over Substance and Shadow [Henry James Sr., *Substance and Shadow: or, Morality and religion and their relation to life* (1863)] and in recalling your father. My experiences of the last few years have been calculated to bring Swedenborg home to me very often.

In the "experience of the last few years," so much in solitude – "[t]o go into solitude, a man needs to retire as much from his chamber as from society ... if a man would be alone, let him look at the stars"[29] – Peirce was able to renew and be invigorated by the "habits of conversation with nature"[30] enjoined by Emerson. Peirce had early in his life recognized these habits as essential to developing a method of thinking adequate to our inhabiting what he had realized to be, following his first reading *On the Origin of Species* shortly after its publication, "a universe of chance" – a realization of the basic fact of the all-important Darwinian information. Combining what he internalized through his reading of Darwin with what he projected mathematically, Peirce was able, already in the 1860s, to imagine the universe as it is currently described by quantum mechanics:

> Every galaxy, star, and planet owes its mass and position to quantum accidents of the early universe. But there's more: these accidents are also the source of the universe's minute details. *Chance is a crucial element of the language of nature* [emphasis added]. Every roll of the quantum dice injects a few more bits of detail into the world. As these details accumulate, they form the seeds for all the variety of the universe. Every tree, branch, leaf, cell, and strand of DNA owes its particular form to some past toss of the quantum dice. Without the laws of quantum mechanics, the universe would still be featureless and bare.[31]

Just after his appointment as a regular aide in the Coast Survey in 1859, during an extended period aboard the schooner *Twilight* surveying the coastal areas of Mississippi, Peirce, not yet twenty-one, wrote in his journal of the value of, as he put it, "drawing nigh unto the personality in nature" and of solitude. He continued in the same entry to offer in counterpoint the necessity, too, of "intercourse" with others:

> Positively, everybody knows it is drawing nigh unto the personality in nature, and that it is, in an humble sense, walking with God. It is a calmness preparatory to enthusiasm on those things worthy of enthusiasm &

the enthusiasm it makes is of calm and noble, unpartisan [*sic*] nature. Thus, rightly used, Solitude has a reference to the world, and if it is rightly used, the mind grows under its climate....

The Important [*sic* capitalization] portion of this earth consists of variegated land, with inland seas (the Atlantic, the Mediterranean, the Indian, the Arctic) all made for the promotion of intercourse. This is man's workshop. But a full half the globe is nothing but Polynesian ocean – all isolation – with nothing out of the monotony, either to think of or to care for. Thus we see that the idea that man should sometimes be solitary is expressed in the very contour and face of the planet.[32]

About Peirce's experience on the perfectly named – given his sense of the mediate, the "in-between" – *Twilight*, Kenneth Laine Ketner in his "autobiography" of Peirce observes: "Indeed, his location on the *Twilight* surrounded often by raw nature, placed him in the ideal venue to receive the lessons of solitude, to draw nigh to the personality in nature through his own experience instead of through descriptions of the experiences of others."[33] Somewhat qualifying this characterization of the relationship between Peirce and "the experiences of others," Anne Freadman in her lucid study of Peirce's semiotic, *The Machinery of Talk: Charles Peirce and the Sign Hypothesis* (2004), rightly underscores the centrality of "intercourse," of conversation, for Peirce and for pragmatism. Freadman notes that conversation "makes its first appearance in public" as a significant figure very early on, in his "so-called cognition series of 1867–68, the series of papers that immediately followed the publication of [his] 'New List'" – "On a New List of Categories" (1867), Peirce's first published paper in which he offered the first formulation of his sign hypothesis, revising the earlier lists of categories offered by Aristotle and Kant. Freadman underscores that the idea or *figure* of "conversation" remains thereafter a "constant" in Peirce's thinking and that it is intrinsic to his concept of semiosis. Following Max Fisch's introductions to the first and second volumes of his chronological edition of Peirce's writings (Fisch was one of the preeminent first-generation Peirce scholars), Freadman describes the manner in which Peirce solved the problem of the binary relation of world and mind by introducing a "three-term relation that is, moreover, dynamic." She continues:

The third term is the "interpretant." The issue turns on the status accorded to any particular act of cognition, which for Peirce is not the nub of the problem. He objects to the "individualism" of modern philosophy since Descartes and turns to a collective account. It is not that any particular judgment, made at any particular point of time, is "true," but that truth is arrived at over time, by people working together. A number of influences came together for Peirce as he formulated this idea, but perhaps the clinching one was his own experience of international teamwork in astronomical research (W 2, p. xxxi ff.) and his engagement in the very precise work that corrected for error the measurements arrived at by previous "pendulum swingers" (W 1; introduction, passim). Reality is something essentially involving the notion of "community" (W 2, p. xxviii); true statements about it are arrived at gradually, in "conversation."[34]

Peirce's unusual ability to engage in conversations with nature in all its aspects as if actually engaging in conversation with other human beings began in his childhood as he observed the behavior of animals in the household, which prompted him to speculate about the nature of reason. As he recorded late in his life:

> Some seventy years ago, my beloved and accomplished school-ma'am taught me that humankind, being formed in the image of a Maker, were [*sic*] endowed with the power of Reasoning, while "animals," lacking that power (which might have made them dissatisfied), receive, each kind, certain "instincts" to do what was generally necessary for their lives. At least, so I understood her. But when I subsequently came to observe the behaviours of several big dogs and little birds and two parrots, I gradually came to think quite otherwise. For ... I gradually amassed a body of experiences which convinced me that many animals, perhaps all the higher ones, do reason.[35]

While David Hume had earlier suggested that animals shared basic forms of observation and induction with humans, Peirce went further. In addition to Hume, a few rare individuals in the generations preceding Peirce, like Erasmus Darwin (who primed the sensibility of his grandson with early lessons about plants and creatures) and Emerson (who early in his career vowed to himself to become "a naturalist"), felt that humans shared *instinct* with animals, but not even Hume had ventured to describe what animals do in their negotiations with their environments as *reasoning with signs*. Peirce repeatedly observed the favorite amusement of a family parrot of calling the dog: on seeing it arrive with its tail wagging and looking for its master, the bird would laugh mockingly at the obvious confusion of the dog. Reading the behavior of the bird as he had learned to read books, Peirce put himself in the position of the parrot to imagine its ways of thinking. He realized that the creature was using the name of the dog as a sign, creating thereby a stage where something would happen in the place of nothing. Meditating on and extending the ramifications of his observations into other forms of life as well, Peirce eventually came to describe a revolutionary conception of mind, a conception he was able to detail and map, though only recently has the monumental significance of his contribution started to be recognized, as developments in philosophy, mathematics, and philosophy of science, following technological advances and instrumentation, have begun to reproduce the activity and shape of what he *could see in his imagination.*

WE ARE NEVER TIRED, SO LONG AS WE CAN SEE FAR ENOUGH[36]

It must be remembered that Peirce's ability to *see the invisible* was a direct result of the habits of mind he had from childhood been taught to practice by his mathematician/astronomer father – habits he continued to cultivate throughout his life, projecting infinitesimals and multitudes into invisibilities, often and understandably beyond the point of strain into "that realm of imaginary quantities which lies on the other side of infinity."[37] Straining even beyond physical extremes had been inculcated by Benjamin Peirce, who sometimes kept the young Charles up all night in mental exercises to develop his concentration.[38] Benjamin Peirce also supervised his son's study of Kant's *Critique of Pure Reason*, over the course of three years before he was sixteen![39] But the later compensations of pushing beyond limits were myriad, the younger Peirce having been among the few – following Carl Gauss and his student, Johann Listing – to demarcate and explore further not only the field of topology, but also (within what Peirce called his "logic of relatives") systems theory, both areas opened to him from his groundbreaking work on signs. There was nothing Peirce valued more than the power of vision. Later in his life when he found that days of enforced fasting (because of financial troubles) had the welcome effect of allowing him to think more clearly, he afterwards imposed periods of fasting on himself. An even greater instance of his wildly prescient vision is his having come to entertain the "many worlds" or "multiverse" theory currently being investigated by cosmologists at the cutting edge. Peirce's ability to project this possibility – venture this immense guess – derived from his having formally explicated and deployed the step of retroduction into logic. This addition forecasts precisely the mechanism now recognized and mapped in cognition as feedback–feedforward looping, following the theorizing of recursion done in the mid-twentieth century by Alonzo Church, Alan Turing, and Kurt Godel; work that engaged the problems Peirce began grappling with in the 1860s and that he continued to wrestle with throughout his life. Peirce was able to arrive at his "many worlds" speculation because he understood, first, the operation of topology, the continuous deformation of shape, as *the* fundamental mathematical operation: numbers and equations describe shapes and periodicities, as the Pythagoreans laid out, though they had not projected, as did Peirce, an *endlessly moving continuum* in which the shapes would undergo constant permutation – *morphing* in today's computational vocabulary. Even beyond this understanding, however, Peirce realized that this operation applies equally to the process of evolutionary change; or, more precisely, that *evolution is itself an instance of topology*, the invisible itself, shape-shifting time or time-shifting shape – the mediating, retroductive term, the "objective interpretant," we could say – in its relation with matter: "my kind of objective logic," Peirce called it.[40]

In his comments on the eighth and last of Peirce's lectures from *Reasoning and the Logic of Things*, "The Logic of Continuity," Hilary Putnam foregrounds the centrality of topology in Peirce's vision and the identity Peirce realized between the continuity of process common to topology and evolution, which, if theoretically extended to infinity, generates the possible existence of many universes. Here are the relevant passages from Putnam's gloss:

> We shall not comment in detail on Peirce's explanations of projective geometry and topology, since it is the metaphysical part of the lecture that will most interest present-day readers. Suffice it to say that like many mathematicians, Peirce regarded the projective properties of space as more fundamental than the metrical properties, and the topological properties as more fundamental still ... the topological properties invariant under the widest class of continuous transformations.... Peirce held, contrary to the opinion of his time, that the human mind *can* visualize non-Euclidean spaces and spaces with strange topologies. (To do so, we just have to *imagine the experiences we would have in such a space* [Putnam's emphases].)

And in commenting about the crucial question Peirce poses for himself and rehearses for his audience concerning *how a continuum could evolve* – "Has it, for example, been put together? Have the separated points become welded, or what?" – Putnam, drawing directly from Peirce, offers that all of his explorations concerning evolution ("All the evolution we know of proceeds from the vague to the definite") had convinced him that,

> "however it may be in special cases ... we must suppose that as a rule the continuum has been derived from a more general continuum, a continuum of higher generality." In other words, every evolutionary development is

the realization of one of continuously many possibilities, and therefore, if a continuum is to evolve, *the whole* continuum must itself be one of *continuously many possible continua* [Putnam's emphases], an actualization of one of the potentialities in a "continuum of higher generality."

Those potentialities, the "world of ideas" of which "the existing universe with all its arbitrary secondness" is an offshoot, or "an arbitrary determination," may also be thought of as a logical space, a space of possible worlds (in present-day metaphysical language) of which the actual world is just one. It is not that we look at the impoverished actual world and project the "world of ideas" with "our superior logic" (as we like to imagine), but that the world of ideas was ontologically prior, and our actual world evolved as one of its determinations. And ... Peirce went on to say, "If this be correct we cannot suppose the process of derivation, a process which extends before time and from before logic, we cannot suppose that it began elsewhere than in the utter vagueness of completely undetermined and dimensionless potentiality."

"The evolutionary process is, therefore, not a mere evolution of the *existing* [Putnam's emphasis] universe, but rather a process by which the Platonic forms themselves have become or are becoming developed." The whole logical space, the whole space of possible worlds, and of possible attributes and relations and possible continua as well, is the product of cosmic evolution![41]

I observed earlier that Peirce extended the ramifications of his observations concerning the rationality of animals to other forms of being and in so doing came to be able to articulate a revolutionary conception of mind. I say "came to be able to articulate," rather than "discovered," because it is crucial to emphasize that for him, and equally for our understanding the profound significance of his work in its complex relatedness, what he had come to realize did not belong to his "individuality." As Anne Freadman notes in the passage quoted earlier, "It is not that any particular judgment, made at any particular point of time, is 'true,'" for Peirce, "but that truth is arrived at over time, by people working together" and "Reality ... something essentially involving the notion of 'community'... true statements about it ... arrived at gradually, in 'conversation.'" Freadman perceptively observes that a number of influences predisposed Peirce to formulate this idea – which he would eventually name *synechism* (from the Greek meaning "to have or hold together," as the activity of rowers on a bi- or trireme) – and sees the "clinching" experience to have been Peirce's participation in the "teamwork" involved over centuries in astronomical research. And, indeed, when we imagine the work of the young man who, in preparation for his own observations, spent months at the *Bibliothèque nationale* in Paris translating the star catalogues of Ptolemy, Tycho Brahe, and later celestial observers – *imagining himself in their positions* – before undertaking the correction of errors in their charts, we begin to get a sense of the *intrinsic relation between practice and mind,* an understanding which is, *essentially, the basis of the pragmatic method.*

In giving the name "pragmatism" to the method, Peirce was keen to preserve Immanuel Kant's distinction between *praktisch* and *pragmatisch*. As Sami Pihlstrom, among others, has noted, "The former ... is concerned with a priori moral laws established through practical use of reason; the latter, instead of being concerned with morality, relates to the purposive nature of cognition in relation to sensibility and is closer to what Peirce had in mind in discussing the experimental procedures of inquiry." While, as Pihlstrom goes on to observe, William James saw no effective difference between the two modes, believing that moral (practical/*praktische*) issues "are always already at work in our pragmatic assessments of the conceptions of reality we operate with in our practices, scientific conceptions included,"[42] Peirce was and remained adamant about the difference in habits of mind and practice required to address moral/practical concerns as against those required to address the cosmic weather – we could say, to borrow one of Stevens's titles, that Peirce's concern was with "the manner of addressing clouds."[43] It was because of this difference that after James's August 1898 talk at Berkeley, when it became clear to Peirce that James's view did not preserve the central distinction and that the Jamesian offering had, moreover, all but overtaken the identity of "pragmatism," Peirce distinguished *his* understanding of the method as "pragmaticism." Exploring Peirce's insistence about this difference will illuminate some of the shadow still obscuring the substance of this extraordinary man and underscore, at the same time, a singularly important aspect concerning the dynamic animating the triangulated relationships of Peirce, James, and Henry James, Sr. In a word, what William James found himself resisting – in the familiar drama of fathers and sons – Peirce, as acolyte, was open to receiving. This web of relations is another part of the story of the story of pragmatism.

OF THE MANNER OF ADDRESSING CLOUDS

Ralph Barton Perry, in his 1936 Pulitzer Prize-winning biography of William James, was the first to comment on Peirce's role in the James family dynamic and on the connection between the differences in

temperament and training of Peirce and James that issued in their different manners of interpreting pragmatism:

> There were intellectual as well as moral differences. Peirce both by aptitude
> and by training, was an exponent of exact science, where a man might be
> sure of his ground, and where inaccuracy was the deadliest of sins; whereas
> James was at home in literature, psychology, and metaphysics, where accur-
> acy is likely to be pretentious or pedantic, and where sympathy, insight,
> fertility, and delicacy of feeling may richly compensate for its absence. It is
> commonly said that James did not understand Peirce. James himself said
> so, and Peirce agreed. It seems to be generally assumed that Peirce under-
> stood James. But it is to be noted that James rarely claimed to understand
> anybody, whereas it was characteristic of Peirce to feel that he understood
> everybody – only too well.... To this it must be added that James most
> eagerly desired to be understood, while Peirce was sometimes playfully or
> maliciously obscure.
>
> At the same time it must be recognized that James was comparatively
> defective in that formal or symbolic of statement which Peirce, as a trained
> mathematician and logician regarded as the acme of clearness.[44]

Indeed, as Perry observes, Peirce himself, late in his own life, had offered
the earliest observations concerning the differences in temperament
and intellectual predisposition between himself and his friend. "Having
referred to James's 'almost unexampled incapacity for mathematical
thought, combined with intense hatred for logic'," Peirce went on to say:

> After studying William James on the intellectual side for half a century, –
> for I was not acquainted with him as a boy, – I must testify that I believe
> him to be, and always to have been during my acquaintance with him
> about as perfect a lover of truth as it is possible for a man to be....
>
> In speaking of William James as I do I am saying the most that I could of
> any man's intellectual morality; and with him this was but one of a whole
> diadem of virtues. Though it is entirely out of place in this connexion, and
> I must beg the reader's pardon for so wandering from the point under con-
> sideration, I really lack the self-command to repress my reflexions when I
> have once set down his name. Though his lectures were delightful, they not
> at all exhibited the man at his best. It was his unstudied common behav-
> iour that did so by the perfection of his manners, in their perfect freedom
> from expressing flattery or anything else false or inappropriate to the occa-
> sion. He did not express himself very easily, because rhetoric was his antip-
> athy and logic an inconvenience to him. One always felt that the pencil,
> not the pen, was the lever with which he ought to have moved the world;
> and yet no! it was not the externals of things but their souls he could have
> pictured.

His comprehension of men to the very core was most wonderful. Who, for example, could be of a nature so different from him as I. He so concrete, so living; I a mere table of contents, so abstract, a very snarl of twine. Yet in all my life I found scarce any soul that seemed to comprehend, – naturally, [not] my concepts, but the mainspring of my life, better than he did. He was even greater in practice than in theory of psychology.[45]

Eugene Taylor has reminded us in his own consideration of the relations among Henry James, Sr., Peirce, and William James, that William James believed that there can be no philosophy without autobiography and that "to understand a person's philosophy it is necessary to capture the center of his vision."[46] In this context, and drawing on the aforementioned passages, it is important to emphasize the salient parts played in the story of the story of pragmatism by "habit," "conversation," and their conjoined form of "habits of conversation." Beginning at the beginning, it is crucial to imagine as fully as possible the primary difference in the childhoods of Peirce and James. As "a native of the James family,"[47] William James and his siblings were encouraged by their father from the time they began speaking to engage in lively conversations around the dinner table as part of their daily habit. As noted not as fully in Chapter 2, Henry James recalled in *A Small Boy and Others*, the first part of the autobiography he composed near the end of his career, the single direction guiding these exchanges and the development of their personalities generally was, simply, to "Convert, convert, convert!" – *convert* impressions and experience into the currency of *conversation* as a *social* activity, "social" having attached to it "a splendid meaning":

As I reconsider both my own and my brother's early start – even his too, made under stronger propulsion – it is quite for me as if the authors of our being and guardians of our youth had virtually said to us but one thing, directed our course by but one word, though constantly repeated: Convert, convert, convert! With which I have not even the sense of any needed appeal in us for further apprehension of the particular precious metal our chemistry was to have in view.... We were to convert and convert ... and simply everything that should happen to us, every contact, every impression and every experience we should know, were to form our soluble stuff; with only ourselves to thank should we remain unaware, by the time our perceptions were decently developed, of the substance finally projected and most desirable.... Our father's prime horror was of *them* [prigs] – he only cared for virtue that was more or less ashamed of itself; and nothing could have been of a happier whimsicality than the mixture in him, and in all his walk and conversations, of the strongest instinct for the human and the liveliest reaction from the literal. The literal played in our education as small a part as it perhaps ever played in any, and we wholesomely breathed inconsistency and ate and drank contradictions. The presence of paradox was so bright among us – though fluttering ever with as light a wing and as short a flight as need have been – that we fairly grew used to allow, from an early time, for the so many and odd declarations that we heard launched, to the extent of happily "discounting" them; the moral of all of which was that we need never fear not to be good enough if we were only social enough: a splendid meaning indeed being attached to the latter term.[48]

Contrast *this* habit of conversation with that cultivated from his earliest childhood in Charles Peirce by his father, keeping him up through the night musing the obscure, learning the language of stars – a vocabulary of infinitesimal measurements and calculations of the silent light reaching him from eons before even the planet's crystallizing out of spinning dust. For Peirce, inhabitant of this radiant and productive atmosphere, conversation, like that enjoyed by Milton's angels, was silent, though extended through human time in exchanges with those who had also recorded in *startalk* what they learned: analemmas, ellipses, spirals, vortices, "amazing mazes" – "a moving picture of thought"[49] following light, enjoying "the silent almost secret bond of fellow-feeling that holds the world together." Having learned this language and practiced this habit of mind from childhood, when on reading, under Henry James, Sr.'s tutelage, Swedenborg's *The Economy of the Animal Kingdom* and finding the following description, Peirce would recognize his own experience and delight:

> To find the causes of things from the study of given phenomena certainly requires a talent of a peculiar kind. It is not every one that can confine his attention to one thing, and evolve with distinctness all that lies in it.... This is a peculiar endowment into which the brain must be initiated from its very rudiments, and which must afterwards by a gradual process be made to acquire permanence by means of habit and cultivation.... When, after a long course of reasoning, they [those so endowed and trained] make a discovery of the truth, straightaway there is a certain cheering light, and joyful confirmatory brightness, that play around the sphere of their mind; and a kind of mysterious radiation, – I do not know whence it proceeds, – that darts through some sacred temple in the brain. Thus a sort of rational instinct displays itself, and in a manner gives notice that the soul is called into a state of more inward communion, and has returned at that moment into the golden age of its intellectual perfections.[50]

Unlike Peirce, William James had not traveled out into the extremes of the cosmic weather, did not know the language of stars. For him, as for the greater number of others who read his father's *The Secret of Swedenborg*, the secret would remain so, though also like many others, he did appreciate

Swedenborg's social message and Henry James, Sr.'s desire to extend it. But while William could not move through the levels of abstraction familiar from boyhood to Peirce from climbing invisible ladders to the stars, he did recognize the rarity and richness of his friend's "'atmosphere' of thought."[51] In describing his response to Peirce's 1898 lectures, for example, he wrote to Paul Carus (editor of the *Monist*) of "the whole thing leaving you with a sense that you had just been in the place where ideas are manufactured."[52]

Writing of Henry James's tantalizingly difficult novelistic style, Ross Posnock describes James's "mimetic logic" that "transforms feeling into a kind of doing and thereby imperils 'simplification' – the propensity for sharply distinguishing 'parts of any adventure.'"[53] Our way of learning anything, as we know, begins in somehow feeling our way and mimicking. And whatever it is that is given the most repeated and constant attention will, to an astonishing – even seemingly uncanny – degree, establish neuronal patterning in the brain that is mimetic of the unconscious processes that follow or track what is claiming attention and occupying consciousness. Evidence of something like this kind of mapping, though primitive by comparison since it deals with the large-scale exchange of sense and motor information rather than abstract thinking, is what is known as "Penfield's homunculus." From his work studying the brains of epileptics, Wilder Penfield (1891–1976) discovered that the amount of cerebral tissue or cortex devoted to given body regions is proportional to how much that body part or region is used and that the "cortical homunculus" changes over time and is different for each person, so that the map of the tissue innervated by an infant's hand, for instance, is much smaller than that of a concert pianist's. Penfield published his work on this subject with examples of his "maps" in 1951; they are still used today. The signally important finding is that there are "neuron concepts" of which we are not directly conscious that nonetheless are at work in processing perception and thinking. In the phrasing of one of our foremost contemporary neuroscientists, Gerald Edelman, "Neurons that fire together wire together." These "neuron concepts," which result from habituation, process at speeds too quick to be articulated in any ordinary language, but to the largest degree *they* direct *or are* whatever it is we call "thinking."[54] The shapes and rhythms of these different neuronal processes, however, do correlate (as can be tracked today in functional magnetic resonance imaging – fMRI) through "mimetic logic" with what excites mental activity. Most recently, for example, researchers recording neural population responses in the non-primary auditory cortex of individuals listening to spoken words have been able to reconstruct the original spoken words from the population activity.[55] And, again, those objects that claim the greatest attention will have their representations inscribed to become "neuron concepts" – the lenses shaping what we perceive. Emerson, a practiced introspective voyager, variously described the effects of this process: "By obeying each thought frankly, by harping, or, if you will, pounding on each string, we learn at last its power. By the same obedience to other thoughts, we learn theirs, and then comes some reasonable hope of harmonizing them."[56]

A discussion and illustration of the differences in mental levels and function being pointed to here was offered recently by Francis Crick (not long before his death) and Christof Koch as they were reviewing work in this area by Ray Jackendoff – a cognitive neuroscientist with a background in linguistics, who is also a performing musician and who has extensively attended to and elaborated parallel operations in linguistics, the structure of music, and the visual system.[57] In their review, Crick and Koch note that Jackendoff is investigating experimentally speculations offered earlier, notably by Kant and Sigmund Freud, who, for example, in his essay on "The Unconscious" published in 1915, observed: "In psychoanalysis there is no choice but for us to assert that mental processes are in themselves unconscious, and to liken perception of them by means of consciousness to the perception of the external world by means of sense-organs."[58] It should be added here that William James had, before Freud, richly explored this area in *The Principles of Psychology*, most specifically in the chapters on "The Relations of Minds to Other Things," "The Consciousness of Self," and "Hypnotism." But while James had recognized the "different pace of [the] parts" of the mind – "Like a bird's life, it seems to be made of an alternation of flights and perchings. The rhythm of language expresses this" – and understood and had himself inhabited the space of "the vague," "the fringe," the numinous "margins," associated with the varieties of religious experience, he did not have direct experience of this space as anything but unsettling and terrifying. John Banville in a review essay of Robert Richardson's recent selection of James's writing emphasizes this aspect as well:

> After this glimpse into the *horror rerum* [James's vision during his most serious breakdown as described in *The Varieties of Religious Experience*], James writes, "the universe was changed for me altogether" and he was left with "a sense of the insecurity of life that I never knew before, and that I have never felt since." Somewhat surprisingly, perhaps, he concluded by professing to believe that "this experience of melancholia had a religious bearing."[59]

James's early experience of terror, combined with an understandable resistance to his father's proselytizing about "The Buddha of the North," as Swedenborg came to be known, during the same extended moment when James was establishing his legitimacy as a man of science, sheds light on a certain mental blindness he had to the Swedish mystic's vision. In contrast, the space of the numinous for Peirce was plotted and scaled, as ordered as a garden. For him, voyaging into strange seas of thought was second nature; he had learned to chart these spaces and was prepared – like sailors heading for Cape Horn – for the heavy weather as he approached the polar extremes of perception and of *human* being.[60] It is this kind of charting, moving in the latitudes of God's architecture, that comes under the heading of *pragmatisch*.

IT IS GOD'S ARCHITECTURE[61]

The current state of theorizing about the mind's life, as summarized by Crick and Koch, bears directly on Peirce's insistence that the difference between *praktisch* and *pragmatisch* be preserved in his description of "pragmaticism." Here, then, the summary from Crick and Koch:

> Jackendoff remarks that common sense seems to tell us that awareness and thought are inseparable and that introspection can reveal the contents of the mind. He argues at length that both these beliefs are untrue. They contrast strongly with his conclusion that thinking is largely unconscious. What is conscious about thoughts is visual or other images, or talking to oneself. He maintains that visual and verbal images are associated with intermediate-level sensory representations, which are in turn generated from thoughts *by the fast processing mechanisms in short-term memory. Both the process of thought <u>and its content</u> are not directly accessible to awareness.*
>
> An example may make this clearer. A bilingual person can express a thought in either language but the thought itself, which generates the verbal activity or imagery, is not <u>directly</u> accessible to him *but only in these sensory forms.*
>
> Another way of stating these ideas is to say that most of what we are directly aware of falls under two broad headings:
>
> 1. a *representation* of the outer world (including our bodies), and
> 2. a *representation* of the inner world; that is, of our thoughts.
>
> This implies that we are neither <u>directly</u> aware of the outer world nor of the inner world, although we have the persistent illusion that we are. *Curiously enough, this idea, which seems very appealing to us, has attracted rather lit-*

tle attention from brain scientists though it dates back to at least as early as Immanuel Kant.

In addition:

> 3. <u>both</u> of these representations are expressed solely in sensory terms. [Emphases added; underlinings Crick and Koch][62]

Reenter Charles Sanders Peirce. There are several details to note. First, Peirce clearly understood that for him, Kant held a distinctive place: "[Chauncey] Wright, James, and I were men of science, rather scrutinizing the doctrines of the metaphysicians on their scientific side than regarding them as very momentous spiritually. The type of our thought was decidedly British. I, alone of our number, had come through the doorway of Kant, and even my ideas were acquiring an English accent."[63]

Secondly, practiced as he was in what I have called *startalk* and his father's forms of "Pythagorean prayer," Peirce enjoyed a range of reference naturally extended to the harmonies of the universe, hidden to those whose experience and language were more "humanly" and mundanely circumscribed. So, for example, William James, having suffered serious nervous crises in his late twenties and knowing of his father's similar early "vastation," was understandably interested in the salvific varieties of religious experience allegorically described by Swedenborg. But Peirce was attuned, rather, to hear and recognize, beyond these spiritual strains, the higher-pitched accuracy of the Swedish mystic's scientific descriptions that gave shape to his later religious parables. These included not only descriptions of the formation of planets and the sun, of light and cosmic atoms, of molecular magnetism, of the formation of crystals, but also, amazingly, in attempting to understand the relation of the finite to the infinite and of the soul to the body – as described in *The Economy of the Animal Kingdom* and *The Animal Kingdom*, texts carefully studied by Henry James, Sr. – an understanding of brain function 150 years before any other scientist. As observed by Charles Gross in *Brain, Vision, Memory: Tales in the History of Neuroscience* (1999) in connection with this last aspect:

> In 1901, Swedenborg's extraordinary anticipations on the brain were finally publicized by the great historian of neuroscience Max Neuberger, professor of the history of medicine in Vienna. [Originally published in English beginning with two volumes in 1882 and continuing until 1887, Swedenborg's *The Brain* received "rave reviews" in the journal *Brain*, where the reviewer called it "one of the most remarkable books we have seen." But Swedenborg's writings on the brain then disappeared from sight until Neuberger's recuperation.] As a result, they became the subject of further

accounts by neuroanatomists and historians. . . . In 1910 a conference of 400 delegates from 14 countries was held in London in honor of his many contributions to science, philosophy and theology.[64]

Among those in attendance at this July 1910 "conference" (The International Swedenborg Congress commemorating the 100th anniversary of the founding of the Swedenborg Society in London) were Henry James (the novelist and a vice president of the congress) – Henry James, Sr. had died in 1882, the year the first volume of *The Brain* was published in English – William Dean Howells, and D. T. Suzuki (also a vice president of the congress). During the opening session the great Swedish chemist J. J. Berzelius was quoted commenting variously on Swedenborg's astonishing powers of imaginative projection and prescience. In letters to J. J. Garth Wilkinson, Berzelius wrote of how "in all he [Swedenborg] undertook, he was in advance of his age," and of his surprise at finding "how the mind of Swedenborg has anticipated the present state of knowledge," adding, "I hope the anatomists and physiologists of our day will profit by this work, both for the sake of extending their ideas, and of rendering justice to the genius of Swedenborg."[65]

During the afternoon session of the congress, Henry James, Howells, and Suzuki would have heard the chairman of the science section of the congress, the Reverend J. R. Rendell, in his address, speak of Swedenborg's extraordinary inventions and discoveries and quote liberally from various of Swedenborg's works. Among the inventions were a "flying machine" that anticipated the "petrol engine," the conveyor belt, and the first mercurial air pump. And more than 100 years before Irish physicist John Tyndall's authoritative *Heat as a Mode of Motion* (1870), Swedenborg in 1740 realized that heat was not a subtle fluid (caloric), but simply a product of motion, of vibration:

> What is heat? The rational mind, educing principles out of pincipiates [*sic*], knows of heat as no other than a vibration (*tremiscentia*) and gyration of the active parts of the body. It may thus be seen that nothing real exists in heat, fire, or cold, since they are only the affections and qualities of trembling and gyrating substances, or, on the contrary, of such as are quiescent.[66]

And in connection with light (Peirce's abiding object of observation and study), Swedenborg, who was equally fascinated – writing in a letter, "I read Newton every day" – found that Newton's corpuscular theory of its transmission was inadequate, and in his own *Miscellanea Observata* anticipated wave theory: "Light is nothing more than the undulation of rays, or the vibration of the ether." Further, in his *Principia,* Swedenborg observes:

"Motion diffused from a given centre through a contiguous medium or volume of particles of ether, produces light. The rays from the sun will undulate through the whole sky," adding, "I am not aware that there is any impropriety in assuming that sight or vision consists in the undulation of rays in the membrane of the eye."[67] In concluding his remarks, Chairman Rendell, offered:

> To-day, physical science, which seems to be absorbing chemistry, is tending to establish the theory that all the chemical elements and the multifarious combinations are but wonderful assemblages and coalitions of one primal element, a *materia prima*, perhaps, of what is now called the electron. This electron, by its movements, fashions the atom, and the atom the various substances of the universe; the fundamental idea being that all the varieties of substance and changes of form and property are due to motion. Swedenborg enunciated the conception long ago. In the brief introduction to the work *On Chemistry*, he asks, "What are physics and chemistry? What is their nature if not geometrical? What is the variety of experiments but a variety of position figure, weight and motion in particles?" Indeed, this conception of motion being the fundamental fact of all phenomena runs right through all his scientific work. In this respect, so far as I am able to judge, he was far ahead of his contemporaries.[68]

Rendell closed noting that even before knowing of electric current, Swedenborg had described and illustrated the theory of magnetism that Michael Faraday would detail decades later. In addition to all these extraordinary anticipations were Swedenborg's work on the brain and spinal cord, his realization of the pituitary as the "master" gland, and his descriptions of "automatism" – the remarkable feats recalled to attention by Professor Max Neuberger, who concluded his own contribution to the congress, "Swedenborg on the Spinal Cord," by saying:

> We must therefore regard it as a most remarkable phenomenon that Swedenborg, without the necessary aids, simply by means of his mental vision, so correctly recognized some of the fundamentals of the tectonics of the spinal cord, a power not given to any of his contemporaries.

> Thus also in this department he is proved to have been a Seer.[69]

To all these aspects of Swedenborg's achievement, Peirce was not only responsive but indebted, recognizing his own best thoughts elaborated by "the Swedish Aristotle" into a cosmic design of infinite detail and scope and depending on the infinite conversation through time that Peirce had so early in his life joined. Attending to the cosmic landscape, becoming familiar with the neighborhood of stars was the work of *pragmatische* reason, as Kant described. Peirce understood the necessity of learning and practicing its logic. This is not to say that the "moral law" – the *praktische* aspect as understood and developed by William James – loses the least bit of its value, but that the Peircean aspect offers a complement and completion not yet adequately realized in pragmatism's method. That this addition to pragmatism had yet to be developed and theorized was noted as long ago as 1986 by Eugene Taylor. My offering in these pages takes up this task, if only in preliminary mapping.

A poem from Wallace Stevens's first volume, *Harmonium* (1923) provides an access of a different kind to what is being addressed here. As noted in Chapter 1 Stevens had been early in his career influenced by Peirce's ideas, communicated to him initially in letters from his father written to him while he was a student at Harvard (1897–1900). These lessons were not lost on the poet who had been constantly aware of the spirit of William James in the Harvard Yard and who late in his life characterized what had been "the problem of his age" as "the will to believe."

A High-Toned Old Christian Woman

> Poetry is the supreme fiction, madame.
> Take the moral law and make a nave of it
> And from the nave build haunted heaven. Thus,
> The conscience is converted into palms,
> Like windy citherns hankering for hymns.
> We agree in principle. That's clear. But take
> The opposing law and make a peristyle,
> And from the peristyle project a masque
> Beyond the planets. Thus, our bawdiness,
> Unpurged by epitaph, indulged at last,
> Is equally converted into palms,
> Squiggling like saxophones. And palm for palm,
> Madame, we are where we began. Allow,
> Therefore, that in the planetary scene
> Your disaffected flagellants, well-stuffed,
> Smacking their muzzy bellies in parade,
> Proud of such novelties of the sublime,
> Such tink and tank and tunk-a-tunk-tunk,
> May, merely may, madame, whip from themselves
> A jovial hullaballoo among the spheres.
> This will make widows wince. But fictive things
> Wink as they will. Wink most when widows wince.[70]

Stevens's "disaffected flagellants" recall the beings who have glimpsed the cosmic order in Swedenborg's *Animal Kingdom*, their heads bathed in the shining air of seeing, understanding a part of this order so magnificently greater than the order described by "the moral law." We recall here from the passage quoted earlier from Nolan Pliny Jacobson what he observed in pursuing what Peirce characterized as his "Buddho-Christian" aspiration. "Thinking is not a process that takes place 'behind' or 'underneath' bodily activity," we are told by researchers working today in the microanalysis of mathematics learning, "but is the bodily activity itself."[71] Bees, as Peirce knew, create perfect habitations, their bodies shaping the hexagonal cells that optimize spatial economy and efficiency: "Indeed, what reason may not go to school to the wisdom of bees, ants, and spiders?"[72]

IN THY BRAIN THE GEOMETRY OF THE CITY OF GOD[73]

Peirce recognized and admitted Swedenborg's gifts as "a Seer" because he knew them in himself and, as he wrote to William James in the 1897 letter quoted earlier, his "experiences … ha[d] been calculated to bring Swedenborg home to [him] very often." What Emerson had drawn from Swedenborg and what Henry James, Sr. had made it his life's work to communicate and broadcast was that it is through receptive and interrogative attention to "the wisdom of bees, ants, and spiders," to rocks and minerals, considering even "what the sleeping rocks dream," that "all mean egotism vanishes" in the exhilarated understanding and witnessing of oneself as "part or particle of God," "God" realized to be but a name, a *sign*, for the spirit animating all, a *sign-language* one could read: "Thus adorned in the soul's most perfect jewel, enjoying the beauty and loving the variousness of life, he is ready to enter at last into the silent almost secret bond of fellow-feeling that holds the world together." As Emerson described in "The Poet," listing Swedenborg among those epitomizing the class:

> As the eyes of Lyncaeus were said to see through the earth, the poet turns the world to glass, and shows us all things in their right series and procession. For, through that better perception, he stands one step nearer to things, and *sees the flowing or metamorphosis; perceives that thought is multiform*.... All the facts of the animal economy, sex, nutriment, gestation, birth, growth, are symbols of the passage of the world into the soul of man.... He uses forms according to the life, and not according to the form. This is true science. The poet alone knows astronomy, chemistry, vegetation, and animation, for he does not stop at these facts, *but employs them as signs*. He knows why the plain, or meadow of space, was strown with these flowers we call suns, and moons, and stars....

This insight, which expresses itself by what is called Imagination, is a very high sort of seeing, which does not come by study, but *by the intellect being where and what it sees, by sharing the path, or circuit of things through forms, and so making them translucid to others. The path of things is silent.* [Emphases added][74]

Heeding Emerson's call voiced later in his powerful exhortation, "Let us have a little algebra, instead of this trite rhetoric, – universal signs, instead of these village symbols,"[75] Peirce devoted himself to developing his "high-level sign language" based on his "insight" that mathematical knowledge is innate, if *silent*, and identical with the activity of "Imagination," participating through its "mimetic logic" in the celestial pantomime as much as in the "wisdom of bees." "Nature offers all her creatures ... as a picture-language,"[76] Emerson observed, and Peirce realized that this language required transcription. "We know that the secret of the world is profound, but who or what shall be our interpreter," asked Emerson.[77] Peirce responded with his system of signs. A sign, Peirce offered, "is something by knowing which we know something more." As Joseph Brent explains, a sign "constitutes a *pragmatic instruction to interpret*" (emphasis added). Brent recounts that "between about 1900 and 1912, Peirce transfigured his entire architectonic on the basis of a transcendental doctrine of signs that had been present in kernel in 1867," and goes on to note that it was his system of signs, his *semeiosis* – "the activity of using signs" – that marked his "pragmaticism," a "cosmologically oriented" and "synechistic" practice in contrast to the "individualist pragmatism of James and others."[78] His early internalization of his father's reverent lessons in "Pythagorean prayer" had attuned him to the changing shapes of number patterns, of ratios, harmonics and transpositions, the aural forms of the continuous morphing of space-time that Peirce realized even before Einstein. This visionary understanding had been fostered by all he learned from Henry James, Sr., like his dear friend Emerson, furthering the Swedenborgian project to dissolve "all mean egotism" by cultivating "habits of conversation with nature" to uncover, more and more, our "bond to all that dust." His stated concern, in this following Emerson specifically, was with "the conduct of life" in the face of the accumulating information after Darwin of our being nothing more than "golden averages, volitant stabilities, compensated or periodic errors, houses founded on the sea,"[79] adrift in the cosmic weather: "For Peirce, all reasoning – and especially mathematical reasoning – turn upon the idea that if one exerts certain kinds of volition, one will undergo in return certain complementary perceptions.

Now this sort of consideration, namely, that certain lines of conduct will entail certain kinds of inevitable experiences is what is called a 'practical consideration.'"[80]

In 1936, Alfred North Whitehead described America as the developing center of worthwhile philosophy and identified Peirce and William James as the founders of the American renaissance. "Of these men," Whitehead wrote in a letter to his student Charles Hartshorne, "W. J. is the analogue to Plato and C. P. to Aristotle."[81] Peirce's student, John Dewey, would continue the scene of instruction.

CHAPTER 4

Purpose: John Dewey, The conduct of life

I have sometimes thought of the phenomenon called 'total reflexion' in optics as a good symbol of the relation between abstract ideas and concrete realities, as pragmatism conceives it. Hold a tumbler of water a little above your eyes and look up through the water at its surface – or better still look similarly through the flat wall of an aquarium. You will then see an extraordinarily brilliant reflected image say of a candle-flame, or any other clear object, situated on the opposite side of the vessel. No candle-ray, under these circumstances gets beyond the water's surface: every ray is totally reflected back into the depths again. Now let the water represent the world of sensible facts, and let the air above it represent the world of abstract ideas. Both worlds are real, of course, and interact; but they interact only at their bound- ary, and the locus of everything that lives, and happens to us, so far as full experience goes, is the water. We are like fishes swimming in the sea of sense, bounded above by the superior element, but unable to breathe it pure or penetrate it. We get our oxygen from it, how- ever, we touch it incessantly, now in this part, now in that, and every time we touch it we are reflected back into the water with our course re-determined and re-energized. The abstract ideas of which the air consists are indispensable for life, but irrespirable by themselves, as it were, and only active in their re-directing function.

WILLIAM JAMES, Pragmatism

TRUTH OR CONSEQUENCES

In preparing to write this chapter about John Dewey's way of looking at prag- matism, I returned, of course, to the texts I had read and studied at earlier moments in my career before I went on to consider as much of the remain- ing body of his work I could manage to take into careful account without spending the years required to make me a "Dewey scholar," in the way I am a scholar of Emerson, of William James, of Wallace Stevens, of Stanley Cavell,

95

and to lesser but adequate extents, of C. S. Peirce and of Jonathan Edwards. (Edwards's generally overlooked contribution to pragmatism is his having animated the thinking of both Emerson and James.[1]) What I found in these excursions startled and delighted me. I recognized how pervasively Dewey had colored my experience as I realized at the same time that his significance had been gradually obscured over the years I devoted to other practition-ers and inheritors of pragmatism, figures whose stylistic exuberance and/or deliberate difficulty called for repeated attention to the forms as much as to the content of their perceptions. But reading Dewey now revealed – to para-phrase Stevens – what was always seen but never seen before.

Dewey's persistent and varied articulations over the course of his life of what we need to look at, reflect on, and practice as "live creatures" inhabiting what his teacher Peirce called "a universe of chance" have been so interwoven into our habit of mind that he has "succeeded in render-ing back to [us our] consciousness." His "statements" are not those of a "separated philosophy," but "natural transcripts of the course of events and of the rights of man." These last descriptions are borrowed from what Dewey himself wrote about Emerson in his 1903 essay, "Emerson – The Philosopher of Democracy," a concisely powerful voicing of his debt to the one he was the first to recognize and name a "philosopher." Dewey points out with subtle grace how Emerson's enlarged understanding of "logic" was a necessary recalibration of this most basic instrument of thought, more adequate to "this new yet unapproachable America" – "America" realized *un*exceptionally, not as a "place," but as an "event," an idea unfolding in time, an "extended duration" (in Whitehead's phrase), a new name for an old idea: democracy. "The fact is that all structure is structure of some-thing; anything defined as structure is a character of *events*, not some-thing intrinsic and *per se*," Dewey observed later, in *Experience and Nature* (1929; his emphases).[2] More than any other pragmatist, Dewey translated the method, a "method" extrapolated most specifically from the proce-dures of seventeenth-century science adapted to the Darwinian informa-tion, into all areas of human engagement: psychology, education, ethics, politics, and esthetics.[3] He was, moreover, the most explicitly political of the first-generation pragmatists, the one from whom Stanley Cavell and Richard Rorty learned to further this aspect, in their different dispensa-tions extending the ramifications of this philosophical method into all areas of individual and collective societal experience. Again, what Dewey observed of Emerson – that "he takes the distinctions and classifications which to most philosophers are true in and of and because of their systems, and makes them true to life, of the common experience of the everyday man"[4] – can be said equally of Dewey. It is not, to my mind, accidental that it is from this essay that Cavell took the phrase that titles his own early acknowledgment of Emerson's profound significance, "Thinking of Emerson." Here is the passage from Dewey:

> But at least, *thinking of Emerson* [emphasis added] as the one citizen of the New World fit to have his name uttered in the same breath with that of Plato, one may without presumption believe that even if Emerson has no system, none the less, he is the prophet and herald of any system which democracy may henceforth construct and hold by, and that when democracy has articulated itself, it will have no difficulty in finding itself already proposed in Emerson.[5]

There are several things to note especially in thinking, in turn, of Dewey that together illuminate what is distinctive about his contribution. I list them here as topics, with illustrations as appropriate from Dewey's texts, and go on later to discuss them in themselves and in their interrelatedness. The order is not hierarchical, but rather moves from background into detail, from panning shots to close-ups. Dewey was the first of the pragmatists self-consciously to adapt the method of nature that Darwin had uncovered to writing and teaching; he called this adaptation, his approach, *selective emphasis*. He chose the traits he wanted to breed from lived experience and from recognizing the truth of his experience in others' texts. From these elements he drew the terms of the sets of operations his philosophy would perform. It is, therefore, useful to have these elements at hand, imagining them somewhat as the integers that Dewey set to work in what he called his "operational thinking." Here, then, is the list:

- Dewey's preparation in psychology and as a psychologist enabled him to integrate that experience into all his analyses: Dewey foregrounds the significance of this integration in his Preface to *Studies in Logical Theory* (1903), a collection of eleven essays on logic, including four of his own on "Thought and its Subject-Matter." Dewey dedicated the volume to William James, who broadly acknowledged the tribute, noting that these pieces of Dewey's were "splendid stuff" that corrected his earlier misprision of Dewey's work, now naming him "a hero" for having given his own "radical empiricism" "a dynamics and a method."[6] The following passage from Dewey's Preface highlights the salient elements of his contribution; I have italicized key words and phrases:

  > [J]udgment is the central *function* of knowing, and hence affords the central problem of logic; that since the act of knowing is intimately and

indissolubly connected with the like yet diverse *functions of affection, appreciation, and practice*, it only distorts results reached to treat knowing as a self-inclosed [*sic*] and self-explanatory whole – *hence the intimate connections of logical theory with functional psychology*; that since *knowledge appears as a function within experience,* and yet passes judgment upon both the processes and contents of other functions, its work and aim must be distinctively reconstructive or transformatory; that since *Reality must be defined in terms of experience,* judgment appears accordingly as the medium through which the consciously effected *evolution of Reality* goes on; that there is no reasonable standard of truth (or of success of the knowing function) in general, except upon *the postulate that Reality is thus dynamic or self-evolving.*[7]

- His "narrative of Western culture's coming to maturity" being rooted, as Ross Posnock has observed (following John McDowell's tracing the influence of the famous early pragmatist on Rorty) in Dewey's personal struggle to shake off the sense of sin inculcated in him by his God-fearing mother,[8] while preserving, I would add, scriptural elements and phrasings from his early experience naturalized into secular "sacraments of praise,"[9] as in "The process of art in production is related to the esthetic in perception organically – as the Lord God in creation surveyed his work and found it good"[10] or,

  > Even the Almighty took seven days to create heaven and earth, and, if the record were complete, we should also learn that it was only at the end of that period that he was aware of just what He set out to do with the raw material of chaos that confronted Him. Only an emasculated subjective metaphysics has transformed the eloquent myth of Genesis into the conception of a Creator creating without any unformed matter to work upon.[11]

Complementarily, Dewey used scientific language to describe what during an earlier period would have been restricted to religious or mystical experience, as here in one of the extended discussions of his use of "energy" to explicate the "esthetic" – "...esthetic effect is due to art's unique transcript of the energy of things of the world":

> An English writer, Galsworthy I think, has somewhere defined art "as the imaginative expression of energy which, through technical concretion of feeling and perception, tends to reconcile the individual with the universal by exciting in him impersonal emotion." Energies that constitute the objects and events of the world and hence determine our experience are the "universal." "Reconciliation" is the attaining, in immediate unargumentative

form, of periods of harmonious cooperation of man and the world in experiences that are complete. The resultant emotion is "impersonal" because it is attached not to personal fortune but to the object to the construction of which *the self has surrendered itself in devotion* [emphasis added].[12]

- Dewey's internalization of the Darwinian information and his understanding of the development and method of science as itself Darwinian:

  The nature of experience is determined by the essential conditions of life. While man is other than bird or beast, he shares basic vital functions with them and has to make the same basal adjustments if he is to continue the process of living. Having the same vital needs, man derives the means by which he breathes, moves, looks and listens, the very brain with which he coordinates his senses and his movements from his animal forbears. The organs with which he maintains himself in being are not of himself alone, but by the grace of struggles and achievements of a long line of animal ancestry.

  ... The first great consideration is that life goes on in an environment; not merely *in* it but because of it, through interaction with it [Dewey's emphasis].[13]

- His persistent and varied rephrasings of both Emerson and William James, their echoes heard as leitmotifs throughout his work and inflecting particularly the centrality of the following:

  – of *experience* ("Things interacting in a certain way *are* experience [Dewey's emphasis]; they are what is experienced.... Experience reaches down into nature; it has depth. It also has breadth and to an indefinitely elastic extent. It *stretches. That stretch constitutes inference*"[14] [emphasis added]; "Experience in the degree in which it *is* experience is heightened vitality" [Dewey's emphasis][15]; "An experience is a product, one might almost say a by-product, of continuous and cumulative interaction of an organic self with the world"[16]);

  – of the *ordinary* or *common*, of the *transitory*, of *interest* ("A sensitive and vital mental career ... depends upon being awake to questions and problems; consciousness stagnates and becomes restricted and dull when this *interest* wanes"[17]; "convert emotion into interest"[18]);

  – of *feeling* ("William James ... pointed out that there are direct feelings of such relations as 'if,' 'then,' 'and,' 'but,' 'from,' 'with.'.... We cannot grasp any idea, any organ of mediation, we cannot possess it in its full force, until we have felt and sensed it, as much as if it were an odor or a color.... Different ideas have their different 'feels,' the immediate qualitative aspects just as much as anything else"[19]), of consistently regarding the human as "part or particle" of nature;

  – of *process* ("the role of organic acts in all mental processes"[20]).

- His comprehensive and thorough knowledge of philosophy and preparation in forms of argument, especially dialectical, reflecting his early indebtedness to Hegel. His characteristic manner of presentation moves through repeated analyses to syntheses to further analyses to effect course corrections in navigating the stream of Western thought, necessary to accommodate the change, in light of the Darwinian event, from mechanism to organism as the basis of thinking:

> We live in a world in which there is an immense amount of organization, but it is an external organization, not one of the ordering of a growing experience, one that involves, moreover, the whole of the live creature, toward a fulfilling conclusion.[21]

- His attention to and study of natural history and science, including developments in relativity and quantum theory, and his conversion of this information into available forms of reflective description and definition of human experience. (It is important to remember that Dewey's daughter Jane was a physicist – beginning with a specialization in physical chemistry, later extending into quantum theory and mechanics – who began her professional life working with Niels Bohr and Werner Heisenberg; she lived with her father for years at a time during the middle period of her career.)
- Dewey's deep familiarity, as well, with art, the history of art, and esthetic theory – sharpened through years of conversation with A. C. Barnes (many of the conversations, as Dewey noted, "in the presence of the unrivaled collection of pictures he … assembled")[22] – and equally with literature and poetics.
- His experience as a teacher and his ongoing interactions with other prominent educators including, notably, early on, Jane Addams and W. E. B. Du Bois.
- His American-ness understood as intrinsically connected to the *idea* of America as experiment:

> A … significant change that would issue from carrying over experimental method from physics to man concerns the import of standards, principles, rules. With the transfer, these, and all tenets and creeds about good and goods, would be recognized to be hypotheses. Instead of being rigidly fixed, they would be treated as intellectual instruments to be tested and confirmed – and altered – through consequences effected by acting upon them. They would lose all pretense of finality – the ulterior source of dogmatism.[23] (We recall Emerson: "It is very unhappy, but too late to be helped, the discovery we have made, that we exist. That discovery is called the Fall of Man. Ever afterwards, we suspect our instruments."[24])

- His progressivism, consistently evidenced in his explicit commitment to breaking down hierarchies of all kinds, and particularly in relation to the continuing American experiment, the break down of class systems:

  > The conception that contemplative thought is *the* [Dewey's emphasis] end in itself was at once a compensation for inability to make reason effective in practice, and a means for perpetuating a division of social classes. A local and temporal polity [that of ancient Greece] became a metaphysics of everlasting being [once translated through Platonism into the basis of the Christian West]. Thought when it achieves truth may, indeed, be said to fulfill the regularities and universalities of nature; to be their natural end. But its incarnation as an end in some, not others, does not partake of any universality. It is contingent, accidental; its achievement is a rational fulfillment only when it is the product of deliberate arts of politics and education.

  > Since nothing in nature is exclusively final, rationality is always means as well as end. The doctrine of the universality and necessity of rational ends can be validated only when those in whom the good is actualized employ it as a means to modify conditions so that others may also participate in it, and its universality exists in the course of affairs.[25]

- Having realized "that the problems which constitute modern epistemology ... have a single origin in the dogma which denies temporal quality to reality as such,"[26] his primary focus on *temporality* in its various manifestations including –

  > *event* ("A bare event is no event at all; *something* happens,"[27] Dewey here emphasizing pragmatism's core; "Every existence is an event.... The important thing is measure, relation, ration, knowledge of the comparative tempos of change"[28]);

  > *rhythm* ("There are ideas that would be destroyed if they were spaced by means of spondees instead of trochees"[29]; "Rhythm is rationality among qualities"[30]);

  > *pulsing, oscillation, alternation, wave/amplification* ("an act of perception proceeds by waves that extend serially throughout the entire organism"[31]);

  > *dynamics*

  – all illustrating the continuity of life forms, including, most importantly, thought:

  > As an organism increases in complexity, the rhythms of struggle and consummation in its relation to its environment are varied and prolonged, and they come to include within themselves an endless variety of sub-rhythms. The designs of living are widened and enriched. Fulfillment is more massive and more subtly shaded.

> Space thus becomes something more than a void.... It becomes a comprehensive and enclosed scene within which are ordered the multiplicity of doings and undergoings which man engages. Time ceases to be either the endless and uniform flow or the succession of instantaneous points which some philosophers have asserted it to be. It, too, is the organized and organizing medium of the rhythmic ebb and flow of expectant impulse, forward and retracted movement, resistance and suspense.... It is an ordering of growth and maturations – as James said, we learn to skate in summer after having commenced in winter. Time as organization in change is growth, and growth signifies that a varied series of change enters upon intervals of pause and rest; of completions that become initial points of new processes of development. Like the soil, mind is fertilized while it lies fallow, until a new burst of bloom ensues.[32]

Additionally, in pointing out his continuity with the Jamesian project, Dewey revealed the pragmatist method itself to be an esthetic exercise, having always an end, an aim, in mind in plotting thought. In this unfolding, he "transform[ed]" what he had learned from "the eloquent myth of Genesis" into explaining pragmatism's practice of reflecting on intention (the end in mind) as projected into action in order to measure, to *see*, its *good*, its meaning:

> In every integral experience there is a form because there is dynamic organization. I call the organization dynamic because it takes time to complete it, because it is a growth. There is inception, development, fulfillment. Material is ingested and digested through interaction with that vital organization of the results of *prior experience that constitutes the mind* [Dewey's emphasis] of the worker.... That which distinguishes an experience as esthetic is conversion of resistance and tensions, of excitations that in themselves are temptations to diversion, into a movement toward an inclusive and fulfilling close.

> Experiencing like breathing is a rhythm of intakings and outgivings. Their succession is punctuated and made a rhythm by the existence of intervals, periods in which one phase is ceasing and the other is inchoate and preparing. William James aptly compared the course of a conscious experience to the alternate flights and perchings of a bird. The flights and perchings are intimately connected with one another; they are not so many unrelated lightings succeeded by a number of unrelated hoppings. Each resting place in experience is an undergoing in which is absorbed and taken home the consequence of prior doing, and, unless the doing is that of utter caprice or sheer routine, each doing carries in itself meaning that has been extracted and conserved.[33]

> These funded and retained meanings become a part of the self. They constitute the capital with which the self notes, cares for, attends, and purposes.[34]

- His intimate understanding of what it means to be embodied – the actuality of what he called the "live creature" whose integrity is broken when knowing is separated from feeling and acting:

> When real objects are identified, point for point, with knowledge-objects, all affectional and volitional objects are inevitably excluded from the 'real' world, and are compelled to find refuge in the privacy of an experiencing subject or mind.... The self become not merely a pilgrim but an unnaturalized and unnaturalizable alien in the world.[35]

Dewey's still largely ignored solution to this situation, the "mind-body problem" that is so much at the center of current discussion, goes back to Peirce's *synechism* (a term, as noted earlier, meaning "continuity") to re-present it as a lucid narrative:

> In the history of mankind ... the individual characteristics of mind were regarded as deviations from the normal, and as dangers against which society had to protect itself. Hence the long rule of custom, the rigid conservatism, and the still existing regime of conformity and intellectual standardization. The development of modern science began when there was recognized in certain technical fields a power to *utilize variations as the starting points of new observations, hypotheses and experiments.* The growth of the experimental as distinct from the dogmatic habit of mind is due to increased ability to utilize variations instead of suppressing them. Life, as a trait of natural organisms, was incidentally treated in connection with the development of tools, of language and of individual variations. Its consideration as the link between physical nature and experience forms the topic of the *mind-body problem....* *The isolation of nature and experience from each other has rendered the undeniable connection of thought and effectiveness of knowledge and purposive action, with the body, an insoluble mystery. Restoration of continuity is shown to do away with the mind-body problem. It leaves us with an organism in which events have those qualities, usually called feelings, not realized in events that form inanimate things, and which, when living creatures communicate with one another, so as to share in common, and hence universalized, objects, take on distinctively mental properties* [emphases added].[36]

- His reminders of the limitations of language, of knowledge – that experience exceeds the boundaries of both – and the consequent necessity of attending, as "live creatures," to the excesses, to what James called the "fringe" and the "vague" ("About every explicit and focal object there is a recession into the implicit which is not intellectually grasped. In reflection we call it dim and vague"[37]) and George Santayana termed "hushed reverberations"[38]:

> Illusions are illusions, but the occurrence of illusions is not an illusion, but a genuine reality. What is really 'in' experience extends much further

than that which at any time is *known*. From the standpoint of knowledge, objects must be distinct; their traits must be explicit; the vague and unrevealed is a limitation. Hence whenever the habit of identifying reality with the object as such prevails, the obscure and the vague are explained away. It is important for philosophic theory to be aware that the distinct and evident are prized and why they are. *But it is equally important to note that the dark and twilight abound. For any object of primary experience there are always potentialities which are not explicit; any object that is overt is charged with possible consequences that are hidden; the most overt act has factors which are not explicit....*

The assumption of 'intellectualism' goes contrary to the facts of what is primarily experienced. *For things are objects to be treated, used, acted upon and with, enjoyed and endured, even more than things to be known. They are things had before they are things cognized* ['*known*' and '*had*' Dewey's emphases; others added].[39]

- His reinvigoration of the proverbial and homiletic, exemplifying the vitality of the ordinary, as epitomized in these particularly "homely" examples: "Through habits formed in intercourse with the world, we also in-habit the world. It becomes a home and the home is part of our every experience"[40]; "It [knowledge] signifies events understood, events so discriminately penetrated by thought that mind is literally at home in them;"[41] "Space is room, *Raum,* and room is roominess, a chance to be, live and move. The very word 'breathing-space' suggests the choking, the opposition that results when things are constricted. Anger appears to be a reaction in protest against fixed limitation of movement"[42]; and, finally,

  fear, whether an instinct or an acquisition, is a function of the environment. Man fears because he exists in a fearful, an awful world. The *world* is precarious and perilous.... Everything that man achieves and possesses is got by actions that may involve him in other and obnoxious consequences in addition to those wanted and enjoyed. *His acts are trespasses upon the domain of the unknown.* [This last sentence, emphasis added; '*world*' Dewey's][43]

- His stress on the centrality of the *esthetic* – "That esthetic and moral experience reveal traits of real things as truly as does intellectual experience..."[44]: the esthetic's basic connection to "ordinary experience," its products "enhancements of the processes of everyday life," markers of "all the rhythmic crises that punctuate the stream of life"[45]; the esthetic's actualizing of *feeling-tone,* of *quality* – "The *intrinsic* nature of events is revealed in experience as the immediately felt qualities of things"[46](Dewey's emphasis) – making, as it were, the invisible visible;

and, his signally important reminder that this aspect belongs to our earliest beginnings: "To grasp the sources of esthetic experience it is ... necessary to have recourse to animal life below the human scale" where reside "resonances of dispositions acquired in primitive relationships of the living being to its surroundings, and irrecoverable in distinct or intellectual consciousness."[47]

THE SIGN'S SOUL[48]

Dewey's profound understanding of process in all aspects of nature, on every level of experience, translated into the way he understood himself and his work. His own experience embodied the actuality Emerson described poetically and prophetically in opening *Nature*; the transcendentalists' scripture became a script for Dewey's adaptation and performance of Jamesian pragmatism.[49] We recall Emerson's breathtakingly surreal hymnic passage as it settles into lesson:

> Standing on the bare ground, – my head bathed in the blithe air, and uplifted into infinite space, – all mean egotism vanishes. I become a transparent eye-ball; I am nothing; I see all; the currents of the Universal Being circulate through me; I am part or particle of God.... In the tranquil landscape, and especially in the distant line of the horizon, man beholds somewhat as beautiful as his own nature.
>
> The greatest delight which the fields and woods minister, is the suggestion of an occult relation between man and the vegetable.... The waving of the boughs in the storm, is new to me and old. It takes me by surprise, and yet is not unknown. Its effect is like that of a higher thought or a better emotion coming over me, when I deemed I was thinking justly or doing right.
>
> Yet it is certain that the power to produce this delight, does not reside in nature but in man, or in a harmony of both.[50]

Dewey was inhabited by and inhabited this passage. Its reverberations are felt everywhere throughout his work, animating the tissue of his perceptions. Emerson's thought precipitated into Dewey's idiom, a language formed out of the reciprocal relation between the nature of nature as it was disclosing itself to be in his time and Dewey's complex response: the arc of his experience. Over the course of his study of the Darwinian information, he realized the activity of his own intelligence as the backward and forward movement that characterizes evolution itself and that characterizes pragmatism as well, the method devised to approximate thinking's accommodation of process – "to establish working connections between old and new subject-matters"[51] –, backstitching to reinforce the stressed seam of the present in the habit of mind we wear as we step with every moment into the future. The Sage of Concord's studious ghost was presiding spirit for Dewey who "regard[ed] . . . Emerson's whole work as a hymn to intelligence, a paean to the all-creating, all-disturbing power of thought."[52] In his praise, Dewey repeated Oliver Wendell Holmes's insight, as noted here earlier, into Emerson's stunning originality in having anticipated evolution even before Robert Chambers's 1844 *Vestiges of Creation*.[53] Completing the arc of this recognition into the next generation, Oliver Wendell Holmes, Jr. would observe of Dewey: "His insights into the movements of the universe as it shows itself to man goes [*sic*] to as high a point as has ever been reached by articulate speech."[54]

Drawing out, *ab-stracting*, from evolution its motive action, and complementing and extending William James's emphases on *interest* and *attention* as the primary constituents of consciousness, Dewey denoted *selection* and *selective emphasis* as the terms he would use to foreground the identity between the larger natural function and individual perception: "Selective emphasis, with accompanying omission and rejection, is the heart-beat of mental life."[55] This focus belonged to Dewey's grand purpose. Again continuing the Emersonian project, he borrowed Emerson's language to announce his own intention: *to annul the divorce between* intellect and action. As noted in Chapter 2, in "The Method of Nature," Emerson described his aspiration "to annul that adulterous divorce which the superstition of many ages has effected between the intellect and holiness," this repair to be achieved through "discovery and performance."[56] Once the "occult relation between man and the vegetable," a relation extending through "the currents of Universal Being" is perceived, *felt* – as Emerson, Darwin, James, and Dewey each actively reported – "all mean egotism vanishes": "Where egotism is not made the measure of reality and value, we are citizens of this vast world beyond ourselves, and any intense realization of its presence with and in us brings a peculiarly satisfying sense of unity in itself and with ourselves."[57] This transcending of ego's limit comes not as a result of intellectual exercise, but in these acutely felt, immediate if fleeting, recognitions of our co-extension with the universe. Emerson, stitching onto the fraying religious fabric of his culture, described his realization as an experience of "holiness," while Dewey, in his more secularized moment, described it as an activity of the imagination, recuperating, as Richard Rorty pointed out, Shelley's view, which Dewey quoted with approval, that "the imagination is the chief instrument of the good."[58] "Consciousness," Dewey particularizes, "so far as it is not a dull ache and torpid comfort is a thing of the imagination"[59]; and more, that the work of imagination is intrinsically involved in communication – "communication is a condition of consciousness."[60] (It is worthwhile to recall in this context and remembering Dewey's religious upbringing, Jonathan Edwards's exquisite description, "God is a communicating being."[61]) In a brilliant yet stylistically uninflected passage that goes back to recuperate John Milton's opening phrasing of his epic purpose "to justify the ways of God to men" in "Paradise Lost" (a foundational text for American culture), as much as it does Emerson's aspiration and, significantly, William James's framing in *Pragmatism* of the challenge the newly named method takes up – "The really vital question for us all is, What is this world going to be? What is life eventually to make of itself?"[62] – Dewey offers the following in closing the explicitly titled second chapter of *Experience and Nature*, "Existence as Precarious and as Stable":

> While metaphysics may stop short with noting and registering these traits [the existential conditions of nature], man is not contemplatively detached from them. They involve him in his perplexities and troubles, and are the source of his joys and achievements. The situation is not indifferent to man because *it forms man as a desiring, striving, thinking, feeling creature. It is not egotism that leads man from contemplative registration of these traits to interest in managing them, to intelligence and purposive art. Interest, thinking, planning, striving, consummation and frustration are a drama enacted by these forces and conditions.* A particular choice may be arbitrary; this is only to say that it does not approve itself to reflection. *But choice is not arbitrary, not in a universe like this one, a world which is not finished and which has not consistently made up its mind where it is going and what it is going to do.* Or, if we call it arbitrary, the arbitrariness is not ours but that of existence itself. And to call existence arbitrary or by any moral name, whether disparaging or honorific, is to patronize nature. To assume an attitude of condescension toward existence is perhaps a natural human compensation for the straits of life. But it is an ultimate source of the covert, uncandid and cheap in philosophy.... *A true wisdom, devoted to the ... task [of opening and enlarging of the ways of nature in man], discovers in thoughtful observation and experiment the method of administering the unfinished processes of existence so that frail goods shall be substantiated, secure goods extended, and the precarious promises of good that haunt experienced things be more liberally fulfilled.* (Emphases added)[63]

This combination of a radical and urgent message phrased in uninflected, limpid – one could say, instead, *transparent* – prose is characteristic of Dewey's manner throughout his work. While style is, certainly, a matter of temperament, I would suggest that in Dewey's case, this transparency resulted from deliberate and disciplined *selection* and reflects a formal achievement suited to an understanding of his self-appointed role as a second Melancthon in the continuing Reformation project that William James understood pragmatism to be. We recall James – himself Melancthon to Peirce's Luther – describing, both in his eponymous text and in letters: "It will be an alteration in 'the seat of authority' that reminds one almost of the protestant reformation."[64] Dewey – echoing James in titling the seventh chapter of *The Quest for Certainty*, "The Seat of Intellectual Authority" – perceived his own particular value in the ongoing effort to be in his having internalized the impersonal procedures of both scientific method and dialectic while sustaining, through his preparation and practice in psychology, as constant, like a *basso continuo*, the sense of the human as animal. His resultant habit of mind produced his variety of pragmatism's method, which he called "the empirical method":

> The empirical method is the only method which can do justice to this inclusive integrity of [Jamesian] 'experience' [an integrity that recognizes no division between act and material, subject and object, but contains them both in an unanalyzed totality].... The problem is ... to get together again what has been sundered....
>
> The pursuance of an empirical method is ... the only way to secure execution of *candid* [emphasis added] intent. Whatever enters into choice, determining its need and giving it guidance, an empirical method frankly indicates what it is for; and the fact of choice with its workings and consequences, an empirical method points out when and where and how things of a designated description have been arrived at. It places before others a map of the road that has been travelled [as the first chapter of *Genesis* provides the map of God's translation of his celestial intention into word and act]; they may accordingly, if they will, re-travel the road to inspect the landscape for themselves. Thus the finding of one may be rectified and extended by the findings of others, with as much assurance as is humanly possible of confirmation, extension and rectification. The adopting of empirical method thus procures for philosophic reflection something of that cooperative tendency toward consensus – which marks inquiry in the natural sciences.[65]

Following this method, Dewey moves through thought with the step-by-step precision of Newton in his *Opticks* while at the same time exercising the muscles of reflection and projection – flexing in technical description, relaxing into colloquial phrasing – thus capturing the systole and diastole of mind's activity:

> we recognize a certain rhythm of direct practice and derived theory; of primary construction and of secondary criticism; of living appreciation and of

abstract description; of active endeavor and of pale reflection. We find that every more direct primary attitude passes upon occasion into its secondary deliberative and discursive counterpart. We find that when the latter has done its work it passes away and passes on. From the naïve standpoint such rhythm is taken as a matter of course.[66]

It is, informingly, also the case that Dewey's manner represents a solution he found and successfully applied as a "live creature" to a problem he experienced beginning in childhood and continuing into his maturity: stammering, which he came to recognize as "psychiatric and not [due to] any trouble with [his] vocal organs."[67] Exercising deliberation in all aspects – thinking ahead to what was to be said, rehearsing words and phrases, moving carefully backwards and forwards from intention through expression in his rehearsed sentences, and especially to be noted, attending to his breathing ("Experiencing like breathing...") – became a deeply ingrained set of habits: "psychological considerations are not subsidiary incidents, but of essential importance so far as they enable us to trace the generation of the thought-situation."[68] It is also instructive to note here, particularly in connection with Dewey's address to the "mind-body problem," that he found practical corroboration of his insights, as his biographer Jay Martin records, in the breathing and posture treatments of F. M. Alexander that he underwent during 1916–17, finding them effective and important in relation to his own psychology. "For inclusion in the brief biography of Dewey officially composed by [his daughter] Jane, John wrote: 'My theories of mind-body, of the coordination of the active elements of the self and of the place of ideas in inhibition and control of overt action required [for confirmation] contact with the work of F. M. Alexander.'"[69] Through his condition and corrective practice, Dewey came to know all the more keenly the space between experience and language. "Language does not equal experience – it points to it," as Richard Serra, another drawing from the Emersonian source, whom Dewey would have both recognized as a kindred spirit and celebrated as an artist, put it in an early interview.[70] "The abiding struggle of art is then to convert materials that are stammering or dumb in ordinary experience into eloquent media." This last Dewey observed in *Art as Experience*, the 1934 volume composed from the lectures on esthetics he delivered as the first William James Lecturer at Harvard in 1932. (The 1990 reissue of *Art as Experience* as part of *The Collected Works of John Dewey* features an Introduction by Abraham Kaplan, the one from whom Stanley Cavell came to appreciate Dewey and his abiding value. We shall have occasion to return to and cross the bridge Kaplan provides from Dewey to Cavell in the following chapter, offering for the moment, as enticement, that Cavell still refers to Kaplan as his "beloved teacher."[71])

"Convert materials that are stammering or dumb in ordinary experience into eloquent media": while Dewey did not regard himself as an "artist" and would reserve the adjective "eloquent" to describe work that stirs feeling, he did strive in carefully crafting a contemporary version of his Puritan forbears' "plain style" to extricate and reveal from ordinary experience its extraordinary substrate of perception. I quoted Richard Serra not only for the aptness of his observation concerning language's limits, but also because I hoped to bring to the reader's mind an image of one of Serra's unsettlingly simple monuments to the unseen, as it is, in fact, gravity rather than shaped steel that is the actual material of his work – the invisible common space of our experience revealed in its mystery by the steel interruptions in and around which he has us move. (Indeed, Serra has remarked about the intended experience of some of his pieces that those moving in and around them would find themselves in spaces they could never before have known.) "The visible is set in the invisible; and in the end what is unseen decides what happens in the seen; the tangible rests precariously upon the untouched and ungrasped," Dewey wrote in *Experience and Nature*; he might have been writing a catalogue description of Serra's works. Dewey's prose, like Serra's sculpture, is a modern, secular exercise in "making the invisible visible." Dewey converted the figure of Emerson's mystical "transparent eyeball" into the everyday transparency of his prose. In the clarity of his presentation, the concept of philosophy itself is deconstructed to reveal it – in its *ordinariness* – as, simply, a set of operations, his method and manner producing somewhat the inverse of Ludwig Wittgenstein's oblique, gnomic utterances. While Wittgenstein's sentences keep us going round and round like the gnomon's shadow, Dewey's offer secure perches for reflection.

In *The Quest for Certainty: A Study of the Relation Between Knowledge and Action* (1929) – one of the texts informing my early experience, the text in which Dewey writes of *annulling the divorce between* knowing and doing – he follows his characteristic pattern of looking back to recuperate what is valuable from the past and looking ahead to project the possible consequences for the future of this capture in its present form. He invokes Charles Sanders Peirce, with whom he studied mathematical logic during his second year at Johns Hopkins, noting (as others had) that Peirce's 1878 essay, "How to Make Our Ideas Clear," set the stage for pragmatist method.[72] Dewey goes on to name Albert Einstein and Arthur Eddington as prime exemplifiers of the existence of the "operational thinking" earlier outlined by Peirce and codified by James. The method practiced by all – restated and illustrated by Dewey – underscores that "we mean by any concept nothing more than a set of operations; *the concept is synonymous with the corresponding set of operations … operations define and test the validity of the meanings by which we state natural happenings*" (emphasis added). There is, in other words, no metaphysical essence or "quantity of matter," but only endlessly changing shapes, sizes, and weights of space-time – *space-time* being, as Dewey was careful to explain, one of the required course corrections in terminology necessary to align our perception with the axis of things as they were coming to be revealed: "When … the scientific inquirer was obliged to take the consequences of the act of perception into account with his subject-matter, he passed from space *and* time to a unity which he could describe only as space-time. He thus came upon a fact that is exemplified in every ordinary perception."[73] Dewey cites Eddington speaking of Einstein, observing that Einstein's theory "insists that each physical quantity should be defined as a result of certain operations of measurement and calculation."[74]

In the neutral way in which Dewey presents what is, effectively, earth-shattering information about the nature of reality here and throughout *The Quest for Certainty*, his own sentences proceeding as an ongoing series of set operations (what is on one side of the equation in an illustration perfectly balanced in its translation to the other side, as in his moving backwards and forwards from Peirce to Einstein) *he* is simply a *function*, a *transformer*, or, more properly, a *transducer* – the accidental consciousness through which the information passes: *all mean egotism vanished* in this witnessing and recording of the extraordinary mystery of experience. We recall Dewey's observing in the passage quoted earlier from *Experience and Nature* – "It is not egotism that leads man from contemplative registration of these traits [the existential conditions of nature] to interest in managing them, to intelligence and purposive art. Interest, thinking, planning, striving, consummation and frustration are a drama enacted by these forms and conditions."[75] We remember William James in the famous "Stream of Thought" chapter from *The Principles of Psychology* observing of the human condition of finding ourselves *in* language, *in* thought, that it would be more accurate to say "it thinks" rather than "I think" or "he thinks," "she thinks." Dewey echoes: "it is not exact or relevant to say 'I experience' or 'I think.' 'It' experiences or is experienced, 'it' thinks or is thought is a juster phrase."[76] We recall as well from Dewey's essay on Emerson, his quoting that most exaltingly humbling passage: "Emerson says 'We lie in the lap of an immense intelligence which makes us organs of its activity and receivers of its truth'." It is after this quotation that Dewey continues: "such things, as we read Emerson, cease to be statements of separated philosophy and become natural transcripts of the course of events and of the rights of man."[77]

The level of human activity engaged and exemplified by Dewey is Emerson's "reception" – "All I know is reception" – secular, naturalized grace, "which makes us organs of its activity and receivers of its truth."[78] Dewey realized perception as common property extended through space-time. We dip into its stream. The descriptions we spin out from this collective experience are filaments of the great web of being, the operations we devise to get from here to there – our intentions, the ends we have in mind: "Connection is instituted through operations which define ideas, and operations are as much matters of experience as are sensory qualities." "'Thought' is not a property of something termed intellect or reason apart from nature. It is a mode of directed overt action."[79] The implicit figure I have offered of the spider casting its silk to the next branch or purchase – for all practical purposes its *intention* – gives body to the notion animating James's radical empiricism: that relations and feelings of relation are no less real than physical objects. The habitat ensuring nourishment to the spider is its web, the structure formed out of its need for sustenance meeting the accidents of situation. Human intentions are no less real than the filaments of the spider's web; they take the shape of our necessity meeting the accidents of our more extended experience in space-time. Recording the shape of this meeting, reflecting on it, gives pleasure, stimulates wonder – the product as beautiful as a web glinting in the sunlight: "the power to produce this delight, does not reside in nature but in man, or in a harmony of both"; "reflective thinkers have taken the way to truth for their truth; *the method of life for the conduct of life*" (emphasis added).[80] The particular shape of an individual's web of relations is the pattern of that person's interaction with the universe, a record of the event each individual is, as Alfred North Whitehead, also taking cues from James and Dewey, later described in a passage partially cited earlier:

> [I]n the language of physics, the aspects of a primate are merely its contributions to the electro-magnetic field. This is in fact exactly what we know of electrons and protons. An electron for us is merely the pattern of its aspects in its environment, so far as those aspects are relevant to the electromagnetic field....
>
> [A] pattern need not endure in undifferentiated sameness through time. The pattern may be essentially one of aesthetic contrasts requiring a lapse of

time for its unfolding ... when we translate this notion into the abstractions of physics, it at once becomes the technical notion of "vibration."[81]

Or, as Emerson, recalled by Dewey, offered: "*the individual man is only a method*, a plan of arrangement"[82] (emphasis added), a web of consciousness, as Henry James – another of Emerson's spiritual heirs – described, vibrating in the currents of Universal Being.

MIND THE GAP

In the eighth chapter of *The Quest for Certainty*, titled "The Naturalization of Intelligence," Dewey observes, "the value of any cognitive conclusion depends upon the *method* [Dewey's emphasis] by which it is reached, so that the perfecting of method, the perfecting of intelligence, is the thing of supreme value." Contextualizing this observation against a background contrasting the Newtonian worldview with the then recently emergent fields of Einstein's relativity and quantum theory, he continues:

> Viewed in this connection, the conception just advanced involves hardly less than a revolutionary transformation of many of our most cherished convictions. The essential difference is that between a mind which beholds or grasps objects from outside the world of things, physical and social, and one which is participant, interacting with other things and knowing them provided the interaction is regulated in a definable way [*Conditions Handsome and Unhandsome* in Cavell's later phrasing].... The principle of indeterminacy thus presents itself as the final step in the dislodgment of the old spectator theory of knowledge. [We see here, as will be discussed more fully in Chapter 6 of this volume, the point from which Richard Rorty would begin in *Philosophy and the Mirror of Nature*.] It marks the acknowledgement, within scientific procedure itself, of the fact that knowing is one kind of interaction which goes on within the world. Knowing marks the conversion of undirected changes into changes directed toward an intended conclusion.... The change from intrinsic rationality in the traditional sense to an intelligibility to be realized by human action places responsibility upon human beings.[83]

Human beings are as intrinsically implicated in creating intelligence as spiders in creating their webs, with the difference that – so to speak – time is on our side; that instead of being completely subject to the brute facts of existential conditions, we have, in language, frozen or stored thought and so can slow or impede responses – *time-release action*, as it were. Through intention, our invisible element, we create the *architectonic* of our continuing being through a kind of "mindsight," to borrow a term

from the contemporary vocabulary of cognition and consciousness studies. But, as Dewey reminds us, "While instinctive need is impatient and
hurries to its discharge (as a spider whose spinning is interfered with will
spin itself to death), impulse that has become conscious of itself tarries
to amass, incorporate, and digest congenial objective material."[84] I have
used "architectonic" rather than "architecture" or "structure" because in
carefully articulating his method, Dewey was implementing to the full-
est all he had come to learn from Peirce, whose lessons concerning "The
Architectonic of Theories" and so much else, he, at first – like William
James – had had difficulty apprehending. Indeed, one could describe
his understanding in relation to Peirce as itself a *time-release activity*, as
Jay Martin has discussed. Through his own deliberately repeated efforts
to understand, and with the help of James's explications, Dewey came to
experience what Peirce described so that finally he was able to provide
an anatomy – or, more accurately, a flowchart – of pragmatism. Without
naming its parts, he illustrated its movements from inside out – like a
spider repeatedly moving back to the center of its web before setting out
again to spin the next strand – while also following the different paces of
the mind's life: "The process of organic life *is* variation," Dewey writes (his
emphasis) and goes on: "In words which William James often quoted,
it marks an instance of 'ever, not quite.'... Every movement of experience in completing itself recurs to its beginning, since it is a satisfaction of
the prompting initial need. But the recurrence is with a difference."[85] Or,
again, calling attention to the value of ordinary language, the idiomatic,
for philosophy, Dewey offers:

> It seems to me ... that the idiomatic use of the word "mind" gives a much
> more truly scientific, and philosophic, approach to the actual facts.... For
> in its non-technical use, "mind" denotes every mode and variety of interest
> in, and concern for, things: practical, intellectual, and emotional. It never
> denotes anything self-contained, isolated from the world of persons and
> things, but is always used with respect to situations, events, objects, per-
> sons and groups. Consider its inclusiveness. It signifies memory. We are
> reminded of this and that. Mind also signifies attention. We not only keep
> things in mind, but we bring mind to bear on our problems and perplex-
> ities. Mind also signifies purpose; we have a mind to do this or that. Nor is
> mind in these operations something purely intellectual. The mother minds
> her baby; she cares for it with affection. Mind is care in the sense of solici-
> tude, anxiety, as well as of active looking after things that need to be tended;
> we mind our step, our course of action, emotionally as well as thoughtfully.
> From giving heed to acts and objects, mind also comes to signify, to obey –
> as children are told to mind their parents. In short "to mind" denotes an

activity that is intellectual, to *note* something; affectional, as caring and lik-
ing, and volitional, practical, acting in a purposive way.

Mind is primarily a verb.[86]

And further:

> Only action, interaction, can change or remake objects.... "Thought," rea-
> son, intelligence, whatever word we choose to use, is existentially an adjec-
> tive (or better an adverb), not a noun. It is disposition of activity, a quality
> of that conduct which foresees consequences of existing events, and which
> uses what is foreseen as a plan and method of administering affairs.[87]

Indeed, it was in recognition of Dewey's beginning his patient spelling
out of pragmatism's ambit and ambition in *Studies in Logical Theory* that
Peirce acknowledged his old student's achievement. Reviewing the volume
in *The Nation*, Peirce wrote "that the book exhibited 'an impressive decade's work,' offering 'conclusive proof' that Dewey's efforts to ally mind
with experience was leading to the fruitful conclusion that logic could
become 'a natural history of thought.'" (It is worth noting in this connection that Emerson's *Natural History of the Intellect* – published post-
humously in 1893 from lectures worked on over the years and given again
during a Harvard course in 1870–1 – was "most admired" by Dewey.[88])
"From this time on," as Jay Martin notes, "Peirce started to claim Dewey
as 'a pupil of mine, & one of the shining lights of the philosophy of
today, – and highly original as most of my pupils have turned out'."[89]

From this time on, having come to realize the import of Peirce's contribution and translating it into his own plain style, Dewey returned to reading his teacher's work; a habit he continued to cultivate for the next forty
years, putting the pragmatist method into practice in his lived experience – "establish[ing] working conditions between old and new subject
matters," now concentrating particularly on developing Peirce's "logic of
use." Having measured Peirce's specific gravity, Dewey recommended that
the Carnegie Institution help publish "the contributions of ... Peirce to
the logic of the sciences."[90] As discussed in Chapter 3, the beating heart
of Peirce's contribution to logic belonged, in fact, to his having himself
devoted many years of his young life to the measure of the universe's
pulse, as an employee of the United States Coast and Geodetic Survey
using an astrophotometer and swinging pendulums to detect variations
in the earth's position in relation to other bodies in the solar system, as
well as measuring the scales of star-magnitudes in order, finally, "to determine the form of the cluster in which our sun is situated."[91] This experience combined in the crucible of his spirit with his studious reading and

was catalyzed by his keen grasp of the centrality of statistical method for understanding the various aspects of the "universe of chance." The precipitate, his *synechism*, inseminated Kant's "theory of the architectonic," animating it with the evolutionary information he had come to imagine in its fullness. While the Copernican revolution was a prerequisite for Kant's particular understanding of architectonic,[92] the Darwinian revolution, revealing every aspect of nature to be in constant change at infinitely varying rhythms, was prerequisite for Peirce's. As noted in Chapter 3 as well, he first read *On the Origin of Species* shortly after its publication while he was still a student at Harvard; he reread it several times throughout his life. He was particularly attentive to Darwin's observations concerning the nature of mind and thought: "we can thus trace causation of thought...obeys [the] same laws as other parts of structure."[93] By the time of writing "The Architectonic of Theories," Peirce was able to delineate *his* architectonic – uniting cosmos, mind, and signs – to explain the commonality of physical, psychical, and semiotic phenomena. *Synechism* was the term he used to describe the common continuing process characteristic of everything in the universe, visible and invisible.

CHANGED SUSPENSE

In moving toward this chapter's closing, I want to underscore certain characteristic features of Dewey's manner and method that he recuperatively selected, pondered, and cultivated from his eccentrically brilliant teacher. Perhaps the most important element of Peirce's contribution – itself an elaboration of an aspect foregrounded poetically, although not articulated analytically by Emerson as it was by Darwin – is the realization that everything in the universe exists on a spectrum of some kind; that there is nothing fixed, nothing still. To recall Emerson in "Circles," "Permanence is but a word of degrees." And Darwin demonstrated the same realization throughout his work, cataloguing the variations that account for endlessly evolving forms; noting, too, that even human madness is simply a matter of degree, as each night we experience that range of wild being in dreams. Peirce extracted from his careful and repeated readings of Darwin what Dewey would select to propagate in various forms: the new kind of logic that came under Peirce's heading of *synechism* that Dewey pursued as the "logic of use." As Peirce had specified in his 1878 paper, "The Doctrine of Chances," Darwin's method embodied this new logic as "the idea of continuity" using imagined probabilities – fictions, as it were – to fill in retrospectively the gaps in the record of the past, thereby creating an historical calculus.[94]

Converting the idea of continuity to practical use, in deliberately and persistently blurring the boundaries of the areas of study and application he engaged in over the course of his career, Dewey heralded what today comes under the description of "interdisciplinarity." As he was careful to point out in different ways throughout his work, in order to become aware of our actual condition – being always in "changed suspense,"[95] constantly moving and being moved – we need to break down all fixed categories and realize every aspect of experience to consist of wavelengths and band-widths vibrating in a spectrum: "The terminal of tendencies are bands not lines, and the qualities that characterize them form a spectrum instead of being capable of distribution in separate pigeonholes"; "we are in the presence ... of a spectrum and not separate classes."[96]

With this description in place, realizing all things to be constituted by the different periodicities of their various elements, Dewey recognized habits as corrugations on the skin of experience, repetitions that define character – the shape of an individual's movement in space-time – a parallel on the human scale to the shape of the star clusters that Peirce began investigating early in his career. And within a particular disturbance of the electromagnetic field on the human scale, repeated uses of certain words, certain expressions, define an individual as specifically as the lines of the hand and face or the lines of a spectrometer reveal the composition of a distant star. In Dewey's case, among the words used most often and in various contexts – in addition to those listed earlier, such as *experience, feeling,* and *ordinary,* indicating his areas of shared interest with Emerson and William James – are: *candor/candid/uncandid, potential/potentiality/ potentialities, predicament, organ/organic/organism, energy/energies, action/ activity,* and *experiment.* Remembering Dewey's stress on the centrality of "selection and selective emphasis" – and taking into account as well his pragmatist understanding of habit as determinant of belief – we would, to my mind, be right to think that Dewey chose and deliberately set these words in the stream of thought. (We remember James's famous advice: "You must bring out of each word its practical cash-value, set it at work within the stream of your experience.") Words deliberately chosen and set, as motifs in a musical score, create eddies disturbing the flow and pools for reflection. Navigating the stream with its changed contours requires corrections to the routes recommended on earlier charts, these words functioning like marker buoys or beacons.

Stretching attention across the spectrum of a concept, a word, is a practice cultivated by philosophers as well as by poets. A word is as much of an experience, an event in time, as the pyramids of Egypt – as Whitehead observed when elaborating William James's lessons about "if," "of," "then," and "between." A concept, a word "reaches down into nature; it has depth. It also has breadth and to an indefinitely elastic extent. It stretches. That stretch constitutes inference." Dewey realized that the major course correction necessary to get us out of the predicament that Western thinking had settled into was to turn 180 degrees back to Aristotle, modifying the Kantian project at the same time by drawing on the currents uncovered by modern science. Dewey energized the categories – also known as *predicaments* (derived from the Latin literal translation of the Greek *kategoria*) – into which experience had been confined by Aristotelian logic and by what Dewey described as Kant's mastery in "drawing distinctions" but then "erecting them into compartmental divisions"[97]:

> With slight exaggeration, it may be said that the thoroughgoing way in which Aristotle defined, distinguished and classified rest and movement, the finished and the incomplete, the actual and the potential, did more to fix tradition, *the* [Dewey's emphasis] genteel tradition one is tempted to add, which identifies the fixed and regular with the reality of Being and the changing and hazardous with deficiency of Being than ever was accomplished by those who took the shorter path of asserting that change is illusory.
>
> His philosophy was closer to empirical facts than most modern philosophers, in that it was neither monistic nor dualistic but openly pluralistic. *His plurals fall, however, within a grammatical system, to each portion of which a cosmic status is allotted* [emphasis added]. Thus his pluralism solved the problem of how to have your cake and eat it too, for a classified and hierarchically ordered set of pluralities, of variants, has none of the sting of the miscellaneous and uncoordinated plurals of our actual world.[98]

And further:

> Thus a discovery which is the greatest single discovery of man, putting man in potential possession of liberation and of order, became the source of an artificial physics of nature, the basis of a science, philosophy and theology in which the universe was an incarnate grammatical order constructed after the model of discourse.[99]

Dewey carefully explained the consequences of the Greeks having taken "the structure of discourse for the structure of things, instead of for the forms which things assume under the pressure and opportunity of social cooperation and exchange":

Failure to recognize that [the] world of inner experience is dependent upon an extension of language which is a social product and operation led to the subjectivist, solipsistic and egotistical strain in modern thought. If the classic thinkers created a cosmos after the model of the dialectic, giving rational distinctions power to constitute and regulate, modern thinkers composed nature after the model of personal soliloquizing.[100]

But, as Dewey offered and illustrated abundantly throughout his work – charging his explanations with words that had accumulated force by their repeated deployment in his idiolect – "Language considered as an *experienced event* [Dewey's emphasis]" provides the solution:

Language is ... not a mere agency for economizing energy in the interaction of human beings. It is a release and amplification of energies that enter into it, conferring upon them the added quality of meaning. The quality of meaning thus introduced is extended and transferred, actually and potentially, from sounds, gestures and marks, to all other things in nature. Natural events become messages to be enjoyed and administered....Thus events come to possess characters; they are demarcated, and noted. For character is general and distinguished.

When events have communicable meaning, they have marks, notations, and are capable of con-notation and de-notation. They are more than mere occurrences; they have implications. Hence inference and reasoning are possible; these operations are reading the message of things, which things utter because they are involved in human associations.[101]

Especially to be remarked in these excerpts and throughout his writing is the frequency of his use of *potential* and its variants for, as Dewey realized – and to recall Stevens's beautiful observation once more, "the imperfect is our paradise" – the condition of ongoing possibility, *not* the perfect Being of Aristotle's *actual*. (We recall from a passage quoted earlier: *"For any object of primary experience there are always potentialities which are not explicit; any object that is overt is charged with possible consequences that are hidden."*) The more often Dewey could bring this fact of experience to mind, the greater the potential of each of his individual readers and listeners to pay closer attention to the "fringes" of experience and experiment, take chances with the possibilities endlessly emerging during a lifetime. "The organism is a force, not a transparency"[102] through which the meanings of a fixed grammar pass unchanged. As Dewey reminded his audiences:

Experience is a matter of the interaction of organism with its environment, an environment that is human as well as physical, that includes the materials of traditions and institutions as well as local surroundings. The organism brings with it through its own structure, native and acquired, forces that play a part in the interaction. The self acts as well as under-goes, and its undergoings are not impressions stamped upon inert wax but depend upon the way the organism reacts and responds. There is no experi-ence in which the human contribution is not a factor in determining what actually happens.[103]

It is in these conditions that "[t]ruth … *happens* to an idea," as William James offered in what has become the thumbnail description of pragma-tism. This grounding of pragmatism in the accidental reality of organ-ism underpins its also having been called "humanism" as it is a method designed to enable the human organism to recognize the provisional nature of its individual and collective experience, taking into full account the responsibility and risks thereby enjoined on and entailed by each one of us. "Every thinker puts some portion of an apparently stable world in peril and no one can wholly predict what will emerge in its place," as Dewey put it.[104] And, in another phrasing masterfully blending the nature of the American experiment with an echo of James's subtitle for *Pragmatism – A New Name for Some Old Ways of Thinking*:

> The individual, the self, centred in a settled world which owns and spon-sors it, and which in turn it owns and enjoys, is finished, closed. Surrender of what is possessed, disowning of what supports one in secure ease, is involved in all inquiry and discovery; the latter implicate an individual still to make, with all the risks implied therein. For to arrive at new truth and vision is to alter. The old self is put off and the new self is only forming, and the form it finally takes will depend upon the unforeseeable result of an adventure. No one discovers a new world without forsaking an old one; and no one discovers a new world who exacts guarantee in advance for what it shall be, or who puts the act of discovery under bonds with respect to what the new world shall do to him when it comes into vision.[105]

The idea of "this new yet unapproachable America" once more – Stanley Cavell's pointed recuperation of this phrase from Emerson to title one of his own volumes incorporated into his project all he had learned from Dewey, as well as his quarrels with him. He has responsively and respon-sibly reminded us that one of the meanings of *experience* is to explore *peril, adventure*.

"In the beginning all the world was America," John Locke famously observed. It was because of the conditions in which the inhabitants of the Old World found themselves in their new one, perforce stripped of their inherited habits of mind, "face to face" with what William Bradford called "this howling wilderness" that Emerson could ask the "vital question" that hangs still in the heavenly night air: "Why should not we also enjoy an original relation to the universe?" As noted in Chapter 2, Ross Posnock has recently unfolded the implications of James's rephrasing of Emerson's question in closing the third lecture/chapter of *Pragmatism* – portions of which have been quoted earlier:

> The really vital question for us all is, What is this world going to be? What is life eventually to make of itself? The centre of gravity of philosophy must therefore alter its place. The earth of things, long thrown into shadow by the glories of the upper ether, must resume its rights.... It will be an alteration in the "seat of authority" that reminds one almost of the protestant reformation.[106]

As discussed, Posnock perspicaciously and patiently focuses attention on the shift from verticality to horizontality as "the earth of things ... resume[s] its rights," altering the "centre of gravity" and "seat of authority." This horizontal plane is, of course, the imaginative space inhabited by Dewey's "live creature." As Peirce had spelled out in the lessons Dewey took in and reinflected, in this reformed dispensation, authority no longer comes from *above*, from an Unmoved Mover, from dogma – "a fixed form and final cause," as he described in his 1909 lecture/essay, "The Influences of Darwinism on Philosophy"[107] – but from the shared, ongoing common sense of the individuals standing side by side, *face to face*, in a community, *communi*cating back and forth about *how to make ideas clear* to one another:

> The idea of an activity proceeding in only one direction, of an unmoved mover, is a survival of Greek physics. It has been banished from science, but remains to haunt philosophy. The vague and mysterious properties assigned to mind and matter, the very conceptions of mind and matter in traditional thought are ghosts walking underground.[108]

Philosophy in this new environment of fact, Dewey observed, "will not be a study of philosophy but a study, by means of philosophy, of life experience." This experience entails banishing the "ghosts" – stripping away the "absorbed borrowings" haunting our thought: "An empirical philosophy is ... a kind of intellectual disrobing ... there is attainable a cultivated naïveté of eye, ear and thought, one that can be acquired only through *the discipline of severe thought* [emphasis added]."[109] This would be "candid intent."

We should remember that more or less contemporary with Dewey's beginning his task of cleaning philosophy's stable with his *Studies in Logical Theory*, John Ruskin was also teaching in his *Elements of Drawing* (1904) the necessity of unlearning the lessons of the past in order to recover "the innocence of the eye" and look at nature again with "infantine" vision. His emphasis on "live" and direct experience, becoming intimate with details we might see while lying on the ground, "the squirming facts exceed[ing] the squamous mind" – to borrow once more from Stevens[110] – parallels Dewey's stress on our creatureliness. These instances mark, finally, the naturalization of the "transcendental" – stripping it of any remaining residue of the sublime and hieratic, permitting it to move freely among us as common sense:

> O thin men of Haddam
> Why do you imagine golden birds?
> Do you not see how the blackbird
> Walks around the feet
> Of the women about you?

Again, this stanza from Stevens "Thirteen Ways of Looking at a Blackbird" (quoted fully in Chapter 1) captures the descent into the ordinary that characterizes this naturalization of the transcendental accomplished by pragmatism's "severe discipline of thought."

As offered earlier, it was not accidental that Peirce borrowed from Kant the word *pragmatisch* that he would use to name his method; for Kant, *pragmatisch* indicated whatever is necessary to take into consideration in order to achieve happiness – importantly including understanding the nature of nature. Nor is it accidental that Cavell, in his endeavor to align Anglo-American and Continental philosophies and in his concern with "moral perfectionism," has continued to be involved with Kant. As Arnaud Maillet has pointed out in his study of the Claude Glass – a device that in its different applications illustrates the movement from eighteenth-century neoclassicism into nineteenth-century romanticism as emblematized by Kant's Copernican revolution in philosophy – Kant's "transcendental" had already shifted understanding to "a transcendence that is horizontal." As Gilles Deleuze has pointed out, Kant "did away with the harmony between the subject and object, together with the theological principle that guaranteed this finality, replacing it with the principle of the object's necessary submission to the subject." This is the principle he calls "transcendental."[111] Peirce, James, and Dewey understood the profound significance of Kant's contribution, but also realized and variously pointed out that the very structure of Kant's language – the grammar in which his ideas were confined – did not permit the potential of his revolutionary insight to be released; Dewey, in his discussion of Kant's *Critique of Judgment* even noting: "The effect upon German thought of Capitalization has hardly received proper attention."[112] (It is worth comment in this context that J. L. Austin – whose teaching was the catalyst for Cavell's concentration on the importance of ordinary language philosophy – had been drafted from his study of philosophy at university during World War II to work in Intelligence on German code-breaking. He came to realize that the grammar structuring the German propaganda statements was the same as that structuring the arguments of the analytic philosophy he had been pursuing. This experience prompted his sharp turn away into exploring performatives and further developing ordinary language philosophy.)

Dewey was amply primed to translate the "transcendental" into ordinary language. He had been Peirce's student, gleaning his value after a period of gestation – "Like the soil, mind is fertilized while it lies fallow, until a new burst of bloom ensues"[113] – to then continue studying him for the rest of his life in the full realization that the logic and semiotic Peirce had devoted himself to shaping was required by the Darwinian information. Dewey had also been deeply affected by the work of James Marsh, the "American Coleridge," whose 1825 edition of *Aids to Reflection*, he noted, had served him as his "first Bible." (Marsh, leader of the Vermont branch of the Transcendental Movement, had been president from 1826–33 of the University of Vermont, Dewey's alma mater. He is thought to be the first American to study Kant; Coleridge thought Marsh the greatest disseminator of his own thought in the United States. Marsh reorganized the curriculum of the University of Vermont along the lines of Coleridge's thought.[114] Jay Martin, as indicated in a note to this chapter, thinks Marsh was Dewey's primary conduit to the transcendentalists.) Dewey observed late in his life – on the occasion of his birthday party at Columbia University when he was presented with a copy of the Marsh edition – that the volume had provided "our spiritual emancipation in Vermont." He added that Coleridge's "idea of the spirit came to us as a real relief, because we could be both liberal and pious."[115] Summing up the effect of this early influence on his thinking, Dewey went on:

> My ideas on religion have not changed since then; I still believe that a religious life is one that takes the continuity of the ideal and the real, of spirit and life, seriously, not necessarily piously. Such "common faith" became a commonplace for me. But I soon discovered that nobody had much interest either in Coleridge or in my ideas of religion, so I kept quiet about it.[116]

Finally, sparking these currents and transforming the energy of Dewey's thinking into white heat was what he learned from his daughter Jane, who could describe to him in ordinary language the extraordinary intricacies of the quantum universe we inhabit and inhabiting us. As we have come to understand today through the work of quantum physicists and mechanical engineers such as Richard Feynman, Alan Guth, Roger Penrose, Lisa Randall, and Seth Lloyd, graced as they are with the ability to give nonspecialists some access to the scintillant intricacies of our universe, "Physical systems speak a language whose grammar consists of the laws of physics."[117] In this grammar – as Dewey, following Peirce, recognized – "transcendental" is not a predicate, not a condition, not simply the Kantian "horizontal" plane, but ongoing sets of interactive operations; wave functions fluctuating, endlessly moving, the celestial ancientness in which we are suspended, hissing and spinning like every other body in space-time.

ECSTASY OF CLARITY

A last word: I had thought at a certain moment as I composed this chapter that I might call it "The Candor of Dewey," and attentive readers might have noted that in a passage quoted early on I italicized the word "candid" without then taking up the reason for my emphasis, though I did later indicate "candid" and its variants as among the words reemerging with periodicity throughout Dewey's work. I have been aware of this incomplete thought throughout the experience of writing these pages. Returning to me with regularity as well has been Emerson's "the rapt saint is found to be the only logician." In closing now, I realize the reason for both the open thought and the echo.

   Because of Dewey's repeated use, I was prompted somewhere along the line in thinking about his way of looking at pragmatism to take the etymology of "candid" into account, and so images of whiteness – as in "the whiteness of the Whale" – and so of the spectrum, and of white containing all colors, and of "candid" as "white hot, incandescent," played constantly in my imagination, as well as, of course, "candid" as "sincere," evoking Dewey's various expressions of "the necessity of sincerity."[118] The echo of "the rapt saint is found to be the only logician," in turn, brought to mind Jonathan Edwards's emphasis throughout his career on giving "close attention of the mind in thinking." This echo further reverberated as I reflected on the central experiences of Dewey and Peirce as logicians and on the devout attention they gave to developing a new logic capable of approximating a description of the complexity added by the Darwinian information into the calculus of thinking. Dewey's use of "candid" and its variants is consistently in the context of his pointing out the necessity in practicing pragmatism's "empirical method" of specifying the motive activating a particular train of thought. Revealing this motive has the effect of stripping away everything inessential and/or false to the end at hand; to leave shining, as it were, in its white heat, intention – *the invisible made visible* – a secular form of religious experience achieved through "the severe discipline of thought." (It is worth remarking, coincidentally, that studies beginning as early as 1867 and recorded by William James, have shown brain activity to be accompanied by a local discharge of heat: the more intense the activity, the greater the heat.[119]) "What William James wrote about religious experience," Dewey noted, "might well have been written about the antecedents of acts of expression," and he continues, quoting from James:

> A man's conscious wit and will are aiming at something only dimly and inaccurately imagined. Yet all the while the forces of mere organic ripening within him are going on to their own prefigured result, and his conscious strainings are letting loose subconscious allies behind the scenes which in their way work toward rearrangement, and the rearrangement toward which all these deeper forces tend is pretty surely definite, and definitely different from what he consciously conceives and determines. . . . When the new center of energy has been subconsciously incubated so long as to be ready to burst into flower, "hands off" is the only word for us – [120]

It is, in other words, white hot.

I came to realize that I had not completed the thought opened by my emphasizing "candid" early on because I only recognized it as motive later, in process. Completing its trajectory, coming to *its* end required me to include in my experience of Dewey's significance all I have described along the way, my path, following pragmatism's empirical method. It reminds me, once more and finally, that the Greek root of the word "empirical" means *experience*.

CHAPTER 5

Effects 1: Stanley Cavell, Squaring the circle: transcendentalist pragmatism

We must summon energy and *pitch* it at a responsive key in order to *take* in.

JOHN DEWEY, Art and Experience

The difficulty is to know one's way about among the concepts of "psychological phenomena".... one has got to master the kinships and differences of our concepts. As someone is master of the transition from any key to any other one, modulates from one to the other.

LUDWIG WITTGENSTEIN, Remarks on the Philosophy of Psychology

The paradox of reading – namely, that to understand from a work of a certain ambition how to read it is already to have understood how to read it – occurs in Emerson as the paradox of writing such a work, namely, that to find how to write a work of a certain ambition is already to have found it written; all its words are the words of others.

STANLEY CAVELL, Emerson's Transcendental Etudes

FOR IF I SHOULD DIE, I COULD NOT MAKE THE ACCOUNT SQUARE[1]

Before taking up in this chapter what I call Stanley Cavell's "transcendentalist strain" of pragmatism,[2] a note about spatio-temporal sequencing is in order. While the chapter concerning Charles Sanders Peirce precedes that given to John Dewey, I composed the latter before the former, and on coming to its end, found myself wanting to write the chapters on Peirce and Cavell at the same time, so clearly had Dewey's singular mediate significance in relation to both – rather like a hinge – in the story of the story of pragmatism shown itself. In the case of Peirce, it was my realizing how profoundly Dewey had internalized his teacher's project for a new tripartite logic of naturalism – though unlike his teacher, he could not implement, but only describe this logic in the ordering of his prose. (Interestingly, in view of what will be considered in discussing Cavell, Peirce's aspiration was, like William James's and Ludwig Wittgenstein's – one of Cavell's heroes – to counter the impulse of philosophers "to sublime the logic of our language."[3] This notion will be developed as the chapter unfolds.) Reversing my temporal order of composition, to have the Dewey chapter follow immediately that on Peirce, has, I trust, made their affiliation clear.

In the case of Cavell, it is the devotion of his "beloved teacher" Abraham Kaplan to the work of Dewey that, by Cavell's account, informed everything he "[has had] to say about American pragmatism,"[4] which – having focused him on what he found to be lacking in its "sound" – limited, until more recently, his view of its scope and possibilities while at the same time sharpening his sense of the centrality of the aesthetic in any philosophical enterprise.[5] And, again by his own account, Cavell, having come to the study of philosophy during the period of dominance of "tough-minded linguistic analytic philosophy,"[6] never came to have an extensive involvement with the work of William James, nor with that of Peirce.[7] As Richard Bernstein has noted, in the United States after the Second World War, in "respectable" graduate philosophy departments, "the American pragmatists were marginalized, relegated to the dustbin of history."[8] Kaplan's rescuing Dewey from the dustbin provided Cavell an access he would not otherwise have had not only to Dewey, but through Dewey to Emerson – though it was only after achieving tenure at Harvard that Cavell felt safe enough to indulge in what he described a few years ago as the "pleasure" of Emerson's texts.[9] And, had Cavell engaged Peirce and James in the same way he did Kant and Wittgenstein, he would clearly have understood the "use of calling Emerson a pragmatist"[10] – a use and claiming articulated by Richard Poirier, among others, that, following Richard Rorty's publication of *Philosophy and the Mirror of Nature* in 1979, led to the revival of pragmatism as a field of inquiry and as a culture-critical tool during the last decades of the twentieth century.[11] And yet, following Dewey's lead – as noted earlier, Dewey was the first to name Emerson a philosopher – Cavell found himself effectively drawing from the same spring as had James, who continued in his reverence for "the divine Emerson"[12] throughout his life. And by way of a parallel engagement with Kant, Cavell began on the same page as had Peirce: addressing and countering that proclivity of philosophers "to sublime the logic of our language," though Cavell identified his own

motive in Martin Heidegger and the later Wittgenstein – who, it should
not be forgotten, was himself deeply affected by the work of James.[13]
Russell Goodman has importantly considered "the question of James's
presence (and hence an American presence) in Cavell's 'inheritance' of
Wittgenstein," since, as he observes, "James is referred to more than almost
any other philosopher in the *Investigations*, and Wittgenstein, late in life,
anxiously considered his own relation to pragmatism."[14]

There will be more to say about these recuperative relations further on.
For now, to set the stage for this chapter, it is enough to remark again that
Cavell drew the title of one of his first soundings of Emerson, "Thinking
of Emerson," from Dewey's 1903 paean of praise, "Emerson – The
Philosopher of Democracy," where it is Emerson's ability to make "the dis-
tinctions and classifications ... of ... systems ... true to life, of the com-
mon experience of the everyday man," that Dewey extols as his supreme
gift. Amplifying Dewey's appreciation, Cavell would find in Emerson an
American grounding for what would later emerge in the "ordinary language philosophy" of Wittgenstein and of Cavell's other esteemed teacher,
J. L. Austin – though, as Ian Hacking has pointed out, Wittgenstein's and
Austin's practices as ordinary language philosophers were quite distinct.[15]
Acknowledging Poirier's uncovering of the stream of thought leading from
Emerson to Nietzsche, Cavell continued to make a significant part of his
own project squaring the circle, aligning the developments in Continental
and Anglo-American philosophy by establishing Emerson retrospectively
as the reigning spirit animating both strains. (Richard Rorty, of course,
also had as his aim the alignment of Anglo-American and Continental
philosophy, albeit without invoking Emerson as source for the Europeans.
Discussion of Rorty's schema, where Dewey is placed in company with
Wittgenstein and Heidegger –that would prompt Cavell's thinking again
about Dewey[16] – will follow in the next chapter.) Along the way of Cavell's
recuperation of Emerson, setting him as standard, Dewey was weighed
in the balances and found wanting. As Cavell observes in his sixth meditation on Emerson, "Finding as Founding: Taking Steps in Emerson's
'Experience'" (a lecture delivered in 1987):

> For Emerson, as for Kant, putting the philosophical intellect into prac-
> tice remains a question for philosophy. For a thinker such as John Dewey
> it becomes, as I might put it, merely a problem. That is, Dewey assumes
> that science shows what intelligence is and that what intelligent practice
> is pretty much follows from that; the mission of philosophy is to get the
> Enlightenment to happen. For Emerson the mission is, rather, or as much,
> to awaken us to why it is happening as it is, negatively not affirmatively.
> "For skepticisms are not gratuitous or lawless, but are limitations of the

affirmative statement, and the new philosophy must take them in and make affirmations outside of them, just as it must include the oldest beliefs." In a new world everything is to be lost and everything is to be found.[17]

It was remarked in Chapter 4 that Dewey's prose style aspired to and achieved a kind of transparency, moving step-by-step in the manner of scientific exposition, providing each of the details necessary for others to repeat "crucial experiments" in thought: a paradigm, as pointed out, deployed so effectively by Newton in the *Opticks*.[18] In cultivating this practice, Dewey not surprisingly followed what he had learned from Peirce, "the first American to list his profession as that of logician."[19] As Peirce observed, "It is necessary to reduce all our actions to logical processes so that to do anything is but to take another step in the chain of inference."[20] For the pragmatists concerned above all with "how to make our ideas clear" against and within the vicissitudes of the "cosmic weather," the virtues of this approach are apparent. But for those like William James (recalling here the discussion of the differences in temperament and preparation of James and Peirce), adhering to the procedures of mathematical calculation translated into sentential equations would, understandably, be found limiting in dealing with religious experience and psychic weather – "the darker, blinder strata of character," James described, where "we catch real fact in the making."[21] While pragmatism evolved as a response by its framers to the Darwinian information, in its Peircean dispensation – applying scientific method and mathematical logic to the processes of thought – pragmatism remains rooted in what Reinhold Niebuhr, himself an heir to the Jamesian strain, characterizes as a "naïve belief, widely held particularly in America ... which has found classic expression in the philosophy of John Dewey," an implicit faith in progress following the "reason" of scientists. As Niebuhr continues,

> Underlying this whole view of history is the assumption that the realm of history is only slightly distinguished from the realm of nature. All the complexities arising in human history from *the fact that human agents, who are a part of the process of history, are also its creators, is obscured* [emphasis added]. The historical character of man as both agent in, and creature of history is not recognized.[22]

At issue, once again, is the Kantian distinction between *praktisch* and *pragmatisch* and, in consequence, how philosophy itself is to be understood and used.

Cavell, navigating his own way through the seas of thought about thinking, helps greatly in charting passages and suggesting course corrections to keep us from foundering on the shoals of one *or* the other, *either*

the *praktische* or the *pragmatische* model. Rather than adhere to one way
or the other, Cavell not only addresses but takes up residence in *both/
and* – the territory of the excluded middle where choice is suspended in
duck-rabbit flickering, the territory forbidden entry by most academic philosophers in the West since the Enlightenment, especially those trained in
the analytic tradition – in Cavell's words, "I have said that I have seemed
to myself fated to take what appear as eccentric perspectives, as it were,
to remain between, to refuse sides."[23] Like Peirce, Cavell explores the productive atmosphere of ambivalence, voyaging into unsettling currents and
turbulent vortices, enlarging, at his professional risk, the ambit of philosophic ex-*peri*-ence – a word that, he reminds us (as noted earlier), shares
its root with *peril*. But unlike Peirce, Cavell remains all the while acutely
attentive to bringing back home to ordinary ethical consideration – to the
praktisch – what this amplifying understanding of experience means to
what he calls, variously, *moral perfectionism* or *Emersonian perfectionism*:

> (... I might say that the question whether morality has a foundation in
> reason is given the following slant of answer in Emerson: Perfectionism
> has its foundation in rethinking.) In Emerson's teaching – ... the moral is
> not a separate realm or a separate branch of philosophical study, but one in
> which each assertion is a moral act....
>
> Moral Perfectionism's contribution to thinking about the moral necessity
> of making oneself intelligible (one's actions, one's sufferings, one's position)
> is, I think it can be said, its emphasis before all on becoming intelligible
> to oneself, as if the threat to one's moral coherence comes most insistently
> from that quarter, from one's sense of obscurity to oneself, as if we are sub-
> ject to demands we cannot formulate, leaving us unjustified, as if our lives
> condemn themselves.[24]

And, more comprehensively,

> Perfectionism, as I think of it, is not a competing theory of the moral life,
> but something like a dimension or tradition of the moral life that spans the
> course of Western thought and concerns what used to be called the state of
> one's soul, a dimension that places tremendous burdens on personal rela-
> tionships and on the possibility or necessity of the transforming of oneself
> and of one's society.[25]

Of course, William James (self-acknowledged spiritual heir of Emerson)
also had "thinking as the only morality" as the focus of his work, but he
did not, like Peirce and Cavell, take his lead from Kant. This is, perhaps, another reason that Cavell – together with the majority of the
twentieth-century Anglo-American philosophical community – chose,

until the revival of pragmatism, to leave James out of their conversations. In *This New Yet Unapproachable America: Lectures after Emerson after Wittgenstein*, Cavell takes up the quarrel with that wish of philosophers, as described by Wittgenstein, "to sublime the logic of our language": a wish "to find super-strong connections between consciousness and its objects ... a super-order between super-concepts." Following Wittgenstein, Cavell locates this concept of *subliming* in Kant:

> A pertinent formula of Kant's for the sublime is as "the straining of the imagination to use nature as a schema for ideas [as it were to picture the unconditioned] ... [which is] forbidding [or terrible] to sensibility, but which, for all that, has attraction for us, arising from the fact of its being a dominion which reason exercises over sensibility with a view to extending it to the requirements of its own realm (the practical) and letting it look out beyond itself into that infinite, which for it is an abyss." [Cavell's bracketed additions to Kant's translated text.][26]

Usefully for our discussion, this description captures almost perfectly Peirce's understanding of the value and activity of Kant's *pragmatisch*. And, as was observed in Chapter 3 here devoted to Peirce, his ability to project his imagination far out beyond the then-observable limits of space-time, into the "abyss," enabled him to provide through his diagrammatic logic what he called "existential graphs" of the invisible motives animating variations in voice and mood in language, and to establish a system of signs, his *semeiotic*, that has only in recent years begun to be appreciated. Nonetheless, it is the case that his language, his style – by his own account, "a mere table of contents, so abstract, a very snarl of twine" – deflects rather than fosters taking steps toward "moral perfectionism." (Bernstein describes Peirce's writing as "brilliant, extremely dense, and occasionally cryptic,"[27] echoing William James's initial reaction to hearing Peirce lecture, as described in a letter to his sister Alice.[28]) The focus of Peirce's address was, indeed, to the "unconditioned" rather than to our ineluctable paradoxical condition as "human agents, who are," as Niebuhr points out, "a part of the process of history, [and] also its creators." Heeding Emerson – "Permanence is but a word of degrees" – Peirce understood that in a universe with chance as an operator, "[r]ather than statements being either true or false, what is needed is a logic based on degrees of truth, ranging from zero to 100% certainty,"[29] and it was to this new logic that he devoted his energies. But logic is not the form in which human agents create and describe their condition; this happens in natural or ordinary language: "Natural languages – as opposed to the formal languages that are used in logic and computing – are full of imprecision and ambiguity."[30] It is to this perplexing ordinary and "unhandsome" condition that both William James and Stanley Cavell, also following the pluripotent Emerson, turn attention – each using language in strikingly different ways, having all to do, I would offer, with the differences in both their respective historical moments and their familial and cultural inheritances; significant factors to consider in the context of establishing philosophy as a field in its own right in America's ever-unsettled landscape.

THE RESPONSE TO AN INFINITE OBJECT . . .[31]

Further along in his "Finding as Founding: Taking Steps in Emerson's 'Experience'," pursuing the issue of "America's search for philosophy," Cavell observes:

> Every European philosopher since Hegel has felt he must inherit this edifice ["the completed edifice of philosophy as system and as necessary, unified foundation"] and/or destroy it; no American philosopher has such a relation to the history of philosophy. In the generation after Hegel has announced the completion of philosophy, American writers must be free to discover whether the edifice of Western philosophy is as such European or whether it has an American inflection. (Here is where Emerson's and Thoreau's attraction to Eastern philosophy is crucial, as an experiment can be crucial, a crossroads past where there is no return. [Cavell is here himself playing on the meaning of "crucial experiment," *experimentum crucis*.] America's search for philosophy continues, by indirection, Columbus's great voyage of indirection, refinding the West by persisting to the East.)[32]

In a later volume, *A Pitch of Philosophy: Autobiographical Exercises* – comprised of three lectures delivered in Jerusalem in 1992, revised and somewhat expanded for publication (1994) – Cavell expresses his hope, in closing the last of the lectures/chapters, for "some eventual international philosophical culture that will include both America (both hemispheres) and Israel." In this pursuit, Cavell follows, by his own account, Emerson and Thoreau, nominating them as this philosophy's "belated founders," their voices expressing "devotion to philosophy reaching beyond Christendom, beyond the West; and their problematic of what Thoreau calls 'repeopling the woods,' which is to say, making new people of these strange newcomers to this land, which proved not to be empty"[33] – immigrancy, in other words, as unavoidable national condition.

It is helpful in tracing a path "reaching beyond Christendom" to turn once more to Pierre Hadot to consider what he recuperated concerning the manner of Stoic philosophical practice, a practice understood (as noted earlier) to be identical with "spiritual exercises." Cavell admires Hadot's work, particularly in connection with his own therapeutic ambition for philosophy. Of the notations of the ancients – long thought to be imperfect, fragmentary remains – Hadot observes, rather, that "the written work is a reflection of pedagogical, psychagogic, and methodological preoccupations" ("psychagogy" being "the art of seducing souls").[34] He continues:

> Although every written work is a monologue, the philosophical work is always implicitly a dialogue. The dimension of the possible interlocutor is always present within it.... In philosophical works such as these, thought cannot be expressed according to the pure, absolute necessity of a systematic order. Rather it must take into account the level of the interlocutor, and *the concrete tempo of the logos in which it is expressed.* [Emphasis added][35]

Though so different in style, the writing of both William James and Stanley Cavell works therapeutically in the manner Hadot describes – as does that of Emerson – to offer a cure, a *mindcure*, a method to disentangle the individual from the collective neurosis of an inherited Western history embodied in language that has ignored the predicament of being "*both* agent in *and* creature of [that] history": a history complicated by the Darwinian information that Emerson had anticipated and which required, as indicated in Chapter 3, a complete reset of the linguistic system. "The ideas of philosophy as turning itself, and us, around, and as returning words from fixations" is the way Cavell puts it.[36] As Perry Miller observed in 1954 during the period he was establishing the field of American Studies and locating pragmatism's central place in it:

> Peirce and James, we must perceive, would not have been so ready to confront the problem of belief in these vital terms [of developing a linguistic method to alter outworn habits of mind], to rescue ideas from the imprimatur of a system, and to give them a chance to discover their meanings in action, had not Darwin supplied them with a technique for appreciating the logic of life rather than that of the syllogism. Primarily because of him – although they were anything but meek Darwinians – they could formulate this logic in a language utterly different from that of [traditional] logicians.[37]

As detailed earlier, Peirce effected this reset with his system of signs, but could not translate it into a grammar that could accommodate ordinary language; he could not because he did not, for the most part – unless specifically directed to do so – take into account "the dimension of the possible interlocutor" in the "concrete tempo of the logos" of a shared contemporary moment. Rather, as has been remarked variously in these chapters, his "thought [was] expressed according to the pure, absolute necessity of a systematic order" – though that order, the order of our universe, is ever-moving, approximate, and quantitative; his interlocutors were earlier and later investigators of this order, like Ptolemy in the second century, Tycho Brahe in the seventeenth, and those he projected far in the future. Significantly, these imagined exchanges were, perforce, always silent; conducted, in fact, in sign language, translating what I have called *startalk* into mathematical notation. In contrast, William James, perhaps because so rigorously prepared by his father to attend to the society that Henry James, Sr. hoped would become "the redeemed form of man" – *Society, the Redeemed Form of Man* is the title of James Sr.'s 1879 tract demonstrating God's spiritual incarnation in human natures where, following Emerson, "all mean egotism vanishes"[38] – was particularly careful always to imagine his actual possible interlocutors as he wrote. Indeed, all of his major works began as lectures, and those comprising what would become the published volume of *Pragmatism* (1907) were designated more specifically as "*Popular* Lectures on Philosophy" (emphasis added). The pitch of his philosophy was aimed, very much like Shakespeare's plays with their multiple registers of metaphor and diction, to reach as many as possible. Near the end of his life in 1908, suffering from persistent vertigo and insomnia as he composed the Hibbert Lectures that would be published the following year as *A Pluralistic Universe*, James became uncertain about continuing to write in his "picturesque and popular style."[39] He had taken on the charge of minister to the Emersonian gospel, preparing the way for its larger and later reception, in an academic climate already chilled by positivist winds. Offering in available terms all he had learned about mind and matter would provide the menstrum for Emerson's pigments. It would take time, James realized, for Emerson's vision to materialize on the canvas of American experience. James was indeed taking account of the "concrete tempo of the logos" of his moment: a moment, notably, still dominated by the Protestant work ethic with its appreciation of the "cash-value" of ideas and innocent of what the catastrophe of World War I would mean to all aspects of Western culture, particularly to language and belief systems, as Paul Fussell powerfully documented in *The Great War and Modern Memory* (1975). As James Conant has observed in a related context, a particular "economy of exchange prevails between the culture at large and those who attempt to speak philosophically in it."[40]

In "What's the Use of Calling Emerson a Pragmatist," a lecture first delivered in 1995 and later collected in two different volumes (1998, 2003),[41] Cavell has the following to say about James and Dewey in their relationship to Emerson:

> To my mind, to understand Emerson as essentially the forerunner of pragmatism is perhaps to consider pragmatism as representing more effectively or rationally what Emerson had undertaken to bring to these shores. This is the latest in the sequence of repressions of Emerson's thought by the culture he helped to found, of what is distinctive in that thought. Such a repression has punctuated Emerson's reputation from the very first moment he could be said to have acquired one. So my question becomes: What is lost if Emerson's voice is lost?
>
> ... To repress Emerson's difference is to deny that *America is as transcendentalist as it is pragmatist, that it is in struggle with itself at a level not articulated by what we understand as the political* [emphasis added].... What Emerson calls for is something we do not want to hear, something about the necessity of patience or suffering in allowing ourselves to change.[42]

More recently, in a chapter of *Philosophy the Day After Tomorrow* (2005), expanding on a 1998 talk, Cavell voices his point about Emerson once again with urgency, noting that he does not "quite *believe*" in the "particular brand of pragmatism called Emersonian" because, for example, while Dewey and James "both testified to their love and admiration of Emerson, neither ... could *put Emerson's writing to sufficient use* [emphasis added] to express this love and admiration." "This is controversial," he adds, and then continues:

> There is something that is currently called Emersonian pragmatism.... The identification of Emerson in terms of pragmatism (a tendency associated also with the writing of Cornel West and Richard Rorty) is, to my mind, yet one more form in which the distinctiveness of Emerson's writing is repressed. Of course I do not deny that Emerson, standing at the source of American thought, is an influence on the pragmatists. What I deny is that an insistence on this influence does justice to what is distinctive either in Emerson or in pragmatism.[43]

There is much to remark about these critical passages, not the least observing what might be called a territorial imperative inflecting Cavell's repeatedly staking the claim for Emerson's difference: "the recent revivals of pragmatism have taken place, for some reason, at the cost of underestimating (in my view) John Dewey's and William James's differences from Emerson."[44] It is clearly important for Cavell to emphasize the difference of *his* project from those of West and Rorty as philosophers, as well as from Poirier's earlier tracing of the Emersonian dispensation of pragmatism. ("How many candidates are there in a generation for the role of representing a present of philosophy?" Cavell asks in *This New Yet Unapproachable America*.[45]) Moreover, having identified whatever he understands American pragmatism to be with the work of Dewey and its privileging of scientific method as model, Cavell effectively ignores for the moment what is "distinctive" in the Jamesian variety, though he will later acknowledge James's pragmatism as "mediating." He does not, however, recognize that James had taken his interlocutors into account, but that the "concrete tempo of the logos" in which James expressed himself belongs, simply, to a very different moment in the evolution of the nature and function of philosophy in America. As James's student Gertrude Stein would observe in "Composition as Explanation" (1926), having learned her lessons well, here capturing in her prose the riffs and syncopation of the jazz age: "The composition is the thing seen by every one living in the living they are doing, they are the composing of the composition that at the time they are living is the composition of the time in which they are living."[46] Given this framing, it could be said that Emerson at the moment he came onto the American scene was speaking broken English, feeling himself an immigrant, his words halting, in this vast "land which proved not to be empty"; or, perhaps, that he found himself, following one of his own examples, *infans*, without words, just learning to speak in the new environment of fact so abundantly evidenced by ongoing discoveries in the western continents, a strange new world indeed – its strangeness brought into even sharper relief by the accumulating evolutionary information. Cavell, the son of an immigrant father and sensitive from childhood to the tension between what can and cannot be spoken (for a variety of reasons) would, of course, recognize and want to emulate (again, for a variety of reasons) this aspect of what he calls Emerson's "passionate utterance": "this need for a change in the hearing of language, toward sensitivity to its voices." This last characterization belongs to Sandra Laugier's reading of Cavell; she continues: "Our words, like our lives, have lost their senses, and we must learn to get them back."[47] There will be more to say about immigrancy and voices further along.

As noted earlier, James, like Emerson, was keenly aware of the various "levels" of his interlocutors, careful always to accommodate his "picturesque and popular style" to the greatest number of present and future readers, exercising his "art [in] seducing souls" to convert them to the Emersonian faith in transience: "Nothing solid is secure, every thing tilts and rocks"; "There are no fixtures in nature. The universe is fluid and volatile"; "this surface on which we now stand is not fixed, but sliding"; and again, "People wish to be settled; only as far as they are unsettled is there any hope for them."[48] James's directions and observations to readers in his Preface to *The Principles of Psychology* speak to the catholicity of his intention and to his understanding of thinking as an open system:

> The man must indeed be sanguine who, in this crowded age, can hope to have many readers for fourteen hundred continuous pages from his pen. But *wer vieles bringt, wird manchem etwas bringen*; and by judiciously skipping according to their several needs, I am sure that many sorts of readers, even those who are just beginning the study of the subject, will find my book of use. Since the beginners are most in need of guidance, I suggest for their behoof that they omit altogether on a first reading chapters 6, 7, 8, 10 (from page 314 to 350), 12, 13, 15, 17, 20, 21, and 28. The better to awaken the neophyte's interest, it is possible that the wise order would be to pass directly from chapter 4 to chapters 23, 24, 25, and 26, and thence to return to the first volume again....
>
> I have ... treated our passing thoughts as integers, and regarded the mere laws of their existence with brain-states as the ultimate laws for our science. The reader will in vain seek for any closed system in the book. It is mainly a mass of descriptive details, running out into queries which only a metaphysics alive to the weight of her task can hope successfully to deal with. That will perhaps be centuries hence; and meanwhile the best mark of health that a science can show is this unfinished-seeming front.[49]

James's mapping of possible directions follows what he had observed from having given careful attention over many years to the activity of mind thinking, in this following Emerson in the central "Language" chapter of *Nature* – we recall:

> The moment our discourse rises above the ground line of familiar facts, and is inflamed with passion or exalted by thought, it clothes itself in images. A man conversing in earnest, *if he watch his intellectual processes* [emphasis added], will find that a material image, more or less luminous, arises in his mind, cotemporaneous with every thought, which furnishes the vestment of the thought.... This imagery is spontaneous. It is the blending of experience with the present action of the mind.[50]

Minds move not linearly, but radiantly and idiosyncratically, obedient to the experience and needs of different individuals. In a response to the 1903 publication of John Dewey's *Studies in Logical Theory*, the collection of work by Dewey and his disciples at "The Chicago School" that Peirce praised in reclaiming Dewey as his student, James commends the "system" they outline, noting its parallel concerns with the "pragmatism" or "humanism" set up quite independently at Oxford by F. S. C. Schiller. James comments particularly that, "the nucleus of the *Studies in Logical Theory* becomes ... an account of the judging process," and observes:

> Consciousness is functionally active in readjustment.... Only where there is hesitation, only where past habit will not run, do we find that the situation awakens explicit thought. Thought is thus incidental to change in experience, to conflict between the old and new. The situation must be reconstructed if activity is to be resumed, and the rejudging of it mentally is the reconstruction's first stage.[51]

James's manner of composition, as he describes it in the Preface to *Principles* – aggregating "a mass of descriptive details, running out into queries" that will remain open for "perhaps ... centuries hence" – is synchronized to the slow tempo of evolving speculation punctuated as it is by periodic findings in the sciences. The places of hesitation for James – the spaces of *in-between*, of turning words, dressing thoughts in this vestment or that – occur at the level of the paragraph and chapter. For Emerson and Cavell, in contrast, closely following as they do the fugitive and superpositioned activity of mind in its present process, as activity, these spaces are at the level of the words in a sentence – "the manifesting of the reverses of thought in the refiguration or defiguration of word"[52] – and of the sentences themselves. Of this use of words, Cavell has importantly noted:

> (Overcoming Kant's idea of thinking as conceptualizing – say analyzing and synthesizing concepts – is coded into Emerson's idea that our most unhandsome part belongs to our condition ... that Emerson is transfiguring Kant's key term "condition" so that it speaks not alone of deducing twelve categories of the understanding but of deriving – say schematizing – every word in which we speak together (speaking together is what the word condition says); so that the conditions or terms of every term in our language stand to be derived philosophically, deduced.)[53]

And just further along, Cavell observes of the sentences composed of words so deployed that, "essentially every Emersonian sentence can be taken as the topic of the essay in which it finds itself." Emerson's prose then takes on, Cavell adds, the character of "a kind of conversation with itself, as a dialogue"[54] concerning the difficulty of coming to "terms" with our condition. What is the use of such "agonized prose"?[55]

THE POSTURE OF THINKING

Emerson and Cavell disrupt ordinary habits of reading, impede forward movement through sentences, making us acutely attentive to the process of mind itself: the stream of thought agitated to a sharp chop by the heavy weather of syntactic and grammatical turbulence as words attempt to clothe, to capture, what is going on in the *in-between* – in the charged synaptic spaces of the still *unthought*, those processes too quick to be recognized as thinking that yet are truly where thinking goes on.[56] It is also worth comment in connection with Cavell's stress on the "sound" of philosophy that "impedance" in physics is the measure of resistance to an alternating effect, as the resistance to vibration of the medium necessary in sound transmission. Emerson's and Cavell's resistance, *aversiveness*, to conformity produces the distinctive sound of their voices. As Cavell remarks of the "agonized prose of Emerson's essays.... What is it ... that motivates the prose?"

> [W]hen Emerson says he will "hazard the contradiction, – freedom is necessary," he is announcing a metaphysical proposition demonstrated not in this paradox alone but in principle in every sentence of his writing, which I would like to describe as a continuous resistance to dictation, an aversiveness to conformity, not an acceptance but an exploration of, or experimenting with, the conditions and contradictions of speech. "The revelation of Thought [that] takes man out of servitude into freedom." (... But why and how has *that* calamity happened, that we have become unhappy with language as such?) Put otherwise, the paradox that freedom is necessary is an instance of the injunction in "Self-Reliance" to speak with necessity ("to sink darts in their ears"). Call this the discovery of free speech. No wonder Emerson's writing can set sensible people's teeth on edge.[57]

It is abundantly clear from this reading of Emerson's style why Cavell's criticism of the pragmatists focuses on their not having grappled with the "political" ground of America in their writing (Dewey's *Democracy and Education* and other political writing notwithstanding): they have not "s[u]nk darts in [the] ears" of their audiences. America, in its aspiration to bring "forth on this continent a new nation" and to "enjoy an original relation with the universe," as Emerson so poignantly recognized, is, indeed, "in struggle with itself at a level not articulated by what we understand as the political." As Cavell notes, in full recognition of our condition, Emerson, like Wittgenstein later, "is in struggle with the threat of skepticism":

> In contrast, neither James nor Dewey seems to take the threat of skepticism seriously. This is hasty. James's treatment of the "sick soul" intersects with something I mean to capture in the concept of skepticism. But on James's account, it does not seem imaginable that *everyone* might be subject to this condition. That is, James perceives the condition as being of a particular temperament, not as something coincident with the human as

such, as if, as with the skeptical threat that concerns me, it is the necessary
consequence of the gift of speech.... Pragmatism seems designed to refuse
to take skepticism seriously, as it refuses – in Dewey's, if not always James's
case – to take metaphysical distinctions seriously.[58]

At the same time as Emerson and Cavell sabotage the forward movement through sentences, they foreground the sound and rhythm of words,
as though reminding us with each breath that, as Emerson observed,
"Every word was once a poem."[59] In consequence, we are persistently
turned back to beginnings, to the condition of our *firstness* in language,
to the original, as it were, innocent or naïve skeptical position: *infans*, just
learning words, how to speak – an appropriate, perhaps the *only*, "posture"
in which to "enjoy an original relation with the universe." When Cavell
critiques James and Dewey for not having followed and implemented, as
he has, the lessons of the master as part of "putting the philosophical intellect into practice," it is hard not to agree with him. And yet, had not James
and Dewey prepared the way for the reception of Emerson by describing
and continuing, each in his own manner, the scientific and cultural revolution provoking Emerson's distinctive voice and style, it would not have
been possible for Cavell to pitch his voice to those many like me, already
converted, with the help of James and Dewey, to habits of conversation
with Emerson. And, indeed, while Cavell, like James, always takes the
interlocutor into account, the "level" to which he aims his pitch is consistently to those who have already learned to speak "Emersonian." So, for
example, while Emerson in "Circles" observes, "The field cannot be well
seen from within the field"[60] – prompting us immediately to fly up out of
the labyrinth of lines of sentences confining us to the page – Cavell offers
the following, which serves as an extended gloss on Emerson's piquant
observation. In these remarks, Cavell draws his own circles around the
"patience or suffering" belonging to our condition in language that he
identifies with the "transcendentalist" strain in Emerson's writing not
found in that of the pragmatists:

> Emerson's emphatic call to patience [in closing "Experience": "Patience
> and patience, we shall win at the last"] should threaten a familiar idea of
> Emersonian power.... I would like to say that it is the philosophical power
> of passiveness that Emerson characteristically treats in considering what he
> calls attraction, as important to him as gravity is to Newton. Since in the
> figure of Waldo [Cavell is speaking of Emerson's famous invocation of his
> dead son in opening "Experience"] the power of passiveness, say passion,
> is shown as mourning, Waldo means: Philosophy begins in loss, in finding
> yourself at a loss, as Wittgenstein more or less says. Philosophy that does

not so begin is so much talk ("this talking America" is how "Experience" puts it).... The recovery from loss is, in Emerson, as in Freud and in Wittgenstein, a finding of the world, a returning of it, to it. The price is necessarily to give something up, to let go of something, to suffer one's poverty. Emerson is describing this procedure in saying: "Life itself is a mixture of power and form.... To finish the moment, [to live in wisdom, is {Cavell's addition}] to find the journey's end in every step of the road." A finding in every step is the description of a series, perhaps in the form of a proof, or a sentence.

And here we reach our momentary end, since we are beginning again at our beginning. "The *last*," at which we shall win, if we are patient, is an instruction about philosophical patience or suffering or reception or passion or power. It speaks of lasting as enduring, and specifically of enduring as on a track, of following on, as a succession of steps (which bears on why a shoemaker's form is a last). Hence it speaks of a succession as a leaving of something, a walking away, as the new world is a leaving of the old, as following your genius is leaving or shunning something. *Is this pragmatic?* [emphasis added; others, except where indicated, Cavell's] (Is this walking, knowing how to *go* on, philosophizing without leaps? But suppose the leaps are uses of the feet to dance (not, say, to march) – as when one uses the hands to clap (not to clutch). But Nietzsche's leaping and dancing, like Emerson's dancing and standing and sitting, and like Thoreau's sitting long enough in some attractive spot, pose further questions of *the posture of thinking* [emphasis added]. Following, succeeding; in particular questions of *starting* to think.[61]

This passage provides an excellent example of what I observed earlier about Cavell's occupying the territory of the excluded middle – as does Emerson – where contradictions exist side by side and where it is not judgment but perception that is called on to be exercised since, as we recall Emerson's warning to us, "Our life is not so much threatened as our perception." Here, the contradictions involve "leaping and dancing" or "following, succeeding" as the modality of "*starting* to think." We must, indeed, fly up and out of these twisting, turning sentences, stop following the words on the page with our eyes. Instead, with a *start*, we begin to understand, "to think," when we *hear* Cavell's voice *performing* the parts of a dialogue – an *agon* – he has, as it were, choreographed, putting "to use" all he has learned from Emerson's "somersaulting"[62] style, recuperating his master's voice, but modulating it to the "concrete tempo of the logos" of his time. We recall that Cavell has repeatedly observed, "in philosophy it is the sound which makes all the difference."[63] And, further, it is not insignificant that Cavell mentions Freud in the same breath as Emerson and Wittgenstein; it is a tip-off concerning the tempo of his moment and a hint about how to read his mind and his difference from Dewey. As he describes his moment:

> I remember, when first beginning to read what other people called philosophy, my growing feelings about Dewey's work, as I went through what seemed countless of his books, that Dewey was remembering something philosophy should be, but that the world he was responding to and responding from missed the worlds I seemed mostly to live in, missing the heights of modernism in the arts, the depths of psychoanalytic discovery, the ravages of the century's politics, the wild intelligence of American popular culture. Above all, missing the question, and the irony in philosophy's question, whether philosophy, however reconstructed, was any longer possible, and necessary, in this world.[64]

Already knowing Wittgenstein to be as significant as Emerson for Cavell, we prick up our ears at the mention of Freud in their company in the previous passage. It does not take too long, once the question of why Freud has been included is posed, to realize that, in fact, Cavell's manner of composing in these paragraphs – particularly the second – is highly inflected by what we can recognize as free association – his interlocutor/analysand variously playing rebus-like word games (on "last") and sliding across the metonymic floor into an implicit consideration of Old World and New, generating questions about "pragmatic" and "philosophizing," fantasizing Nietzsche in the Old World "leaping and dancing" and Emerson "dancing and sitting and standing," before remembering Thoreau "sitting long enough in some attractive spot." And then we recall, too, that before turning to the study of philosophy, Cavell had pursued training to become an analyst, having himself had extensive experience in two Freudian analyses and having spent, by his own account, from ten to twelve hours a day reading Freud during a period of nervous collapse after he gave up his first career in music – he had hoped to compose – a forgoing and "undoing [he came] to understand in connection with the work of mourning,"[65] a strong connection to his reading "Experience" as Emerson's work of mourning.[66]

When, finally, we recall, as well, Cavell's periodic recuperation in his writing of observations from Thoreau's *Walden* – a seminal text for him – it does not take much longer before we imagine the "attractive spot" where Thoreau is sitting in Cavell's fantasy as the one described in the "Solitude" chapter of *Walden*: "In those driving north-east rains, which tried the village houses so ... I sat behind my door in my little house, which was all entry and thoroughly enjoyed its protection." It is in this setting, having recounted how he has explained to others why he does not feel lonely in his solitude, sharing as he does Confucius's sense of being surrounded always by studious ghosts, "an ocean of subtile [*sic*] intelligences," "the subtle powers of Heaven and Earth," that Thoreau famously observes, "With thinking we may be beside ourselves in a sane sense" – which Cavell uses as epigraph for his first venture into autobiography, *A Pitch of Philosophy*. Thoreau continues in the passage recalled in Chapter 1 of this volume:

> By a conscious effort of the mind we can stand aloof from actions and their consequences; and all things good and bad, go by us like a torrent. We are not wholly involved in Nature.... I only know myself as a human entity; the scene, so to speak, of thoughts and affections; and am sensible of a certain doubleness by which I can stand as remote from myself as from another. However intense my experience, I am conscious of the presence and criticism of a part of me, which, as it were, is not a part of me, but spectator, sharing no experience, but taking note of it; and that is no more I than it is you.[67]

Here is psychoanalysis *avant la lettre*,[68] complete with note-taking analyst and observing ego, but, more significantly, the process described is simply that of *thinking* itself. Is it any wonder that Cavell wants to claim Thoreau, and Emerson before him, who gave the direction – "a man conversing in earnest, *if he watch his intellectual processes*" – as philosophers, advancing, with their instructions for setting and method (solitude, watching one's intellectual processes) for the inhabitants of "the nervous, rocky West"[69] the kind of introspection offered by Augustine, Montaigne, and Rousseau?

Important to note here in connection with the *praktisch/pragmatisch* distinction that underpins the issue of how philosophy is to be understood and used – a distinction implicit as well in Niebuhr's criticism of Dewey's variety of pragmatism – is Thoreau's already having realized the problem Niebuhr locates, "the assumption that the realm of history is only slightly distinguished from the realm of nature." Thoreau is emphatic when he writes, "We are not wholly involved in Nature," underscoring a point that might be elided or missed in Emerson if one does not follow him out of *Nature* into the unsettled terrain of "Experience," where we find:

> It is very unhappy, but too late to be helped, the discovery we have made, that we exist. That discovery is called the Fall of Man. Ever afterwards, we suspect our instruments. We have learned that we do not see directly, but mediately, and that we have no means of correcting these colored and distorting lenses which we are, or of computing the amount of their errors.[70]

Cavell takes on this knowledge with the power of Emerson's and Thoreau's voices and uses it – the grounding of skepticism in our condition – to chastise Dewey and James for seeming to have followed too closely the method of nature in their scientifically informed use of words, and so ignoring in their practice the most fundamental aspect of our existence: that language and thinking not only bring us the knowledge that we will die but also, at the same time, separate us from pure being. "Life itself is a bubble and a skepticism," Emerson announced.[71] All we have, finally, is our history in the descriptions of things, not the thing itself. Yet, this is our condition: "I do not know which to prefer,/ The beauty of inflections/ Or the beauty of innuendoes,/ The blackbird whistling/ Or just after." Skepticism *is* the human condition: "The imperfect is our paradise." In that paradise we do what we do, what we must, remembering that skepticism's root is a verb meaning "to look about, look carefully at, look after, watch" (*skopeo* in Greek), before it comes to be used to describe what the mind does, "to look to, view, examine, consider" (*skeptomai*).[72] We recall Emerson once more:

> Words are signs of natural facts.... Every word which is used to express a moral or intellectual fact, if traced to its root, is found to be borrowed from some material appearance.... We say the *heart* to express emotion, the *head* to denote thought; and *thought* and *emotion* are words borrowed from sensible things, and now appropriated to spiritual nature. [Emerson's emphases][73]

Cavell is specific about Emerson's acceptance of skepticism in "Aversive Thinking: Emersonian Representations in Heidegger and Nietzsche," one of the Carus Lectures he delivered in 1988:

> Domestication in Emerson is the issue, or urgency of the *day*, today, one among others, an achievement of the everyday, the ordinary, now, here, again, never again. In Wittgenstein's *Philosophical Investigations* the issue of the everyday is the issue of the siting of skepticism not as something to be overcome, as if to be refuted, as if it is a *conclusion* about human knowledge (which is skepticism's self-interpretation), but to be placed as a mark of what Emerson calls "human condition," a further interpretation of finitude, a mode, as said, of inhabiting our investment in words, in the world. [Cavell's emphases][74]

Cavell understands and himself experiences the agony, the unavoidable struggle – from the Greek *agonia* – like Jacob wrestling the angel, to find and compose words into prose quick and vast, delicate and urgent enough to capture all we see and feel when trying to put a sentence together. In other words, "agonized prose" captures the feeling of skepticism, of William James's "ever, not quite … ever not quite," of Emerson's and James's and Stevens's "And yet … and yet … and yet."

To illustrate the pragmatists' distance from this understanding, Cavell quotes Dewey (notably excepting James here, whom he will present almost sympathetically a bit further on in his lecture):

> The following sentence from Dewey's *Experience and Education* is, I assume, characteristic of what makes him Dewey: "Scientific method is the only authentic means at our command for getting at the significance of our everyday experiences of the world in which we live." Perhaps Emerson was wrong to identify mourning as a pervasive character of what we know as experience, and perhaps, in any case, philosophy need not regard it as part of "the significance of our everyday experiences." Yet Emerson finds a work of what he understands as mourning to be the path to human objectivity with the world, to separating the world from ourselves, from our private interests in it. That understanding offers the possibility of moral relationship. According to Wittgenstein, "Concepts … are the expression of our interest, and direct our interest."… Does science have anything different to say about mourning? Is it supposed to? Might one say that science has its own understanding of objectivity, call that "intersubjectivity"? It is an understanding that neither Emerson nor Wittgenstein can assume to be in effect; the human subject has first to be discovered, as something strange to itself.[75]

Cavell continues his critique to lead up to what is, effectively, a gloss on his own practice. (It is, once more, necessary to quote Cavell extensively since to paraphrase him, in the same way as to paraphrase Emerson, James, or Dewey is to miss the point of the exercise, seeing and hearing what is "distinctive" in their voices.) And so, then:

> Dewey's remark about scientific method being the authentic means for getting at the significance of our everyday experiences in effect insists that the works of men, requiring human intelligence, are part of this everyday. Of some of these works Emerson writes: "In every work of genius we recognize our own rejected thoughts; they come back to us with a certain alienated majesty." Do not be put off by Emerson's liberal use of "genius." For him genius is, as with Plato, something each person has, not something certain people are. Emerson's remark about genius is a kind of definition of the term: If you find the return of your thoughts to be caused by a work in this way, then you are apt, and in a sense justified, to attribute this return to the genius of the work. You might even say that this kind of reading requires what Emerson calls "experimenting," something Thoreau calls "trying" people. Does what you might call "science," or its

philosophy, have an understanding of this use of experimentation, experimentation as provocation? Is this use less important than the understanding science requires?

Dewey writes that pragmatism "is the formation of a faith in intelligence, as the one and indispensable belief necessary to moral and social life." Compare this with Emerson: "To believe your own thought, to believe that what is true for you in your private heart is true for all men – that is genius." Emerson expresses what he calls the ground of his hope that man is one, that we are capable of achieving our commonness, by saying that "the deeper [the scholar] dives into his privatest, secretest presentiment, to his wonder he finds, this is the most acceptable, most public, and universally true." Is this route to the universal compatible with what Dewey means by science and its method?[76]

THE FREE WINDS OF HEAVEN[77]

It is important to recall in the context of "experimentation" and "experimentation as provocation," that in addition to the voices of Emerson, Thoreau, and Wittgenstein, Cavell is also provoked by the call of another powerful voice equally reminding him and us of the necessity of "patience or suffering" in facing our all-too-human condition and working to improve ourselves nonetheless, if only by a half-step. Most explicitly, Cavell, again by his own account, has often found himself "taken back or taken to a text of Nietzsche's," and he adds, "for some years it has become familiar to me that, however I get there, what I find eventually takes me further back to Emerson."[78] Of course, for one whose project it is to draw the circle of Continental and Anglo-American philosophy, "Nietzsche is," in Cavell's words, "the pivot." As Cavell observes, "Nietzsche was one of Emerson's two great readers of the nineteenth century (the other being Thoreau) – a most ambitious heritage ... since Heidegger, in 1942, especially singles out early Nietzsche at his most purely Emersonian, as the greatest Nietzsche."[79] Further, Cavell offers,

> It is in Nietzsche, wherever else, that some explanation must be sought for the inner connection between such a writer (such as Heidegger) who calls for thinking knowing the completed presence of European philosophy or, say, facing its aftermath, as if needing to disinherit it, and a writer (such as Emerson) who calls for thinking not knowing whether the absence of philosophical edifice for America means that it is too late for a certain form of thinking here or whether his errand just is to inherit remains of the edifice. Nietzsche is the pivot here because of his early and late devotion to Emerson's writing together with his decisive presence in Heidegger's *What*

is Called Thinking? But no matter how often this connection of Nietzsche to Emerson is stated, no matter how obvious to anyone who cares to verify it, it stays incredible, it is always in a forgotten state. This interests me almost as much as the connection itself does, since the incredibility must be grounded in a fixed conviction that Emerson is not a philosopher, that he cannot be up to the pitch of reason in European philosophy. The conviction is variously useful to American as well as to European philosophers as well as to literary theorists. When one mind finds itself or loses itself in another, time and place seem to fall away – not as if history is transcended but as if it has not yet begun.[80]

Complementarily, Gilles Deleuze, from the Continental side, observes, "it goes without saying that modern philosophy has for the most part lived off and still lives off Nietzsche."[81] While Deleuze does not draw the line to Emerson, recent scholarship has demonstrated the closeness of Deleuze's own thinking to Emerson's: Gregg Lambert by way of Nietzsche and Paul Grimstad by way of William James.[82] In any case, Cavell correctly finds the European bridge to Emerson in Nietzsche, who took to heart and translated into his own style the declaration from Emerson's "Divinity School Address" that Cavell uses as the epigraph to *The Claim of Reason* (1979): "Truly speaking, it is not instruction, but provocation, that I can receive from another soul."

In connection with *The Claim of Reason* and the provocation offered by what Cavell recalls as "Nietzsche's leaping and dancing" – a figure drawn from *The Gay Science*, from which Cavell also draws the title of his last collection, *Philosophy the Day after Tomorrow*[83] – it is informing of his relation to the "concrete tempo of [his own] logos" that in composing *The Claim of Reason* he offers readers concrete examples of the difference in his "frame of mind" between the time he wrote what comprises the greater part of the text, his doctoral dissertation sixteen years earlier (Parts One, Two, and Three), and the later time when he added opening paragraphs (up to about the middle of page six) and Part Four, which, in Cavell's words, "can seem simply and suddenly to wrench itself away from the moment in Part One from which it takes its cue, and begin[s] again, in, as it were, a different frame of mind." He adds, significantly, "I wonder how I might defend my conviction that the parts could not exist, or, say, would not be what they are, apart from each other, *that they call for each other*" (emphasis added)[84] – his earlier voice *provoking* his later one. The "cue" to which he refers is his realization in writing the dissertation, particularly at the conclusions of chapters 4 and 5 of Part One, that the "writing periodically, almost chronically, would threaten to bend the constraints of academic exposition too far, or as I sometimes felt, *leap out of its skin*" (emphasis added).[85]

What does it mean, or feel like, for writing to "leap out of its skin"? And what do we make of Cavell's returning, in the passage quoted earlier, to Nietzsche's "leaping and dancing" and Emerson's "dancing"? It is useful in thinking about these figures to consider them, as one would in a psychoanalytic or therapeutic setting, as overdetermined. There are, of course, as noted, Nietzsche's particular evocations connecting leaping and dancing to the restoration of the health of the soul. There is, too, also mentioned earlier, Emerson's "somersaulting" that we find in "The Uses of Great Men" in his description of "the transmutings of the imagination … [that] expose the invisible organs and members of the mind … the summersaults [*sic*], spells, and resurrections, wrought by the imagination. When this wakes, a man seems to multiply ten times or a thousand times his force" – as though he were leaping out of his skin, we could say. Emerson continues,

> a sentence in a book, or a word dropped in conversation, sets free our fancy, and instantly our heads are bathed with galaxies, and our feet tread the floor of the Pit [*sic* uppercase]. And this benefit is real, because we are entitled to these enlargements, and once having passed the bounds, shall never again be quite the miserable pedants we were.[86]

"The moment our discourse rises above the ground line of familiar facts, and is inflamed with passion or exalted by thought…" – "With thinking we may be beside ourselves in a sane sense" – "I wonder how I might defend my conviction that the parts could not exist, or, say, would not be what they are, apart from each other, that they call for each other" – "The field cannot be well seen from within the field" – "I fear we are not getting rid of God because we still believe in grammar." With the last observation here from Nietzsche's *Twilight of the Idols*, this constellation of quotations represents some of the echoes I find resonating in Cavell's use of "leap" and "leaping." In "The Avoidance of Stanley Cavell," Garrett Stewart remarks on Cavell's conception of philosophy as "a textual process" and comments on his "ability to produce in his writing a form of 'prose flight,'" noting also that "[f]or Cavell, the reader is as much read by, as she is reader of, the text."[87] "There is no wing like meaning," Wallace Stevens observes in one of his *Adagia*, his collection of aphorisms. Being "read by" a text is being transported by it up into the radiant atmosphere of imagination as Emerson describes in the passage just quoted, flying up and out of the rules of grammar – "Every sentence is a prison," Emerson elsewhere observes – to become god-like oneself: "[I]t is the blending of experience with the present action of the mind. It is proper creation. It is the working of the Original Cause through the instruments he has already made." Of course, creating the possibility for such flights – a version of what Zennists call *satori* – does not come easily, but requires patience and/ or suffering. It is not surprising that D. T. Suzuki was a deep reader of Emerson.

In "Old and New in Emerson and Nietzsche," first published in 2003 in *Emerson's Transcendental Etudes*, Cavell shows his hand – and his thinking – in the language game he has been playing against the pragmatists, placing patience and suffering, his pair of aces, on the table for all to see. He locates them in Nietzsche's new Preface to *Human, All Too Human* (1886), where Cavell also notes that Nietzsche "invokes the image of turning, as in Emerson's 'aversion [to the demand for conformity],' challenging his reader to a 'reversal [*Umkehrung*] of one's habitual estimation and esteemed habits.'" Cavell continues:

> As early as "The American Scholar," Emerson had identified thinking as being turned, turned around or turning something toward something else – the two characteristics of thinking he names there as "conversion" and "transfiguration," conversion suggesting disorientation, being reversed, and transfiguration (incorporating figuration as a term of rhetoric) suggesting the manifesting of the reverses of thought in the refiguration or defiguration of words. I have taken the idea of turning in Emerson's linking of self-reliance and aversion (taking "self-reliance" as the title of an essay of his, hence as a representative title for his writing as such), to characterize something of his manner with words (as duplicitous as Nietzsche's), as when he turns our attention to the hand in *unhandsome* (to characterize a violence in our grasp of concepts), or to the partiality of thinking (to capture both the incompleteness and the desire in what thinking should be), or to the sound of casualty in *casualness* (to emphasize the fatality of the everyday). *I need this* [emphasis added; others Cavell's] in order to make plausible hearing Nietzsche's idea of linking the philosopher with the wanderer (at the close of *Human, All Too Human*) as a response to Emerson's linking of thinking with walking in the essay "Experience," as when he says, in the essay's concluding paragraph, "Patience and patience, we shall win at the last," a form of words about which I claim that "last" contains both its sense of enduring, bearing up, and at the same time its sense of the shoemaker's form, implying that our task is to last as on a long path (an image featured in the new Preface to *Human, All Too Human*). Patience and suffering [*Geduld* and *leidend* (this Cavell's bracketed addition)] occur explicitly, in paragraph 5 of that Preface, as necessary "steps onward" of the free spirit in its journey of convalescence, following on an

event Nietzsche calls "the great separation" [as from the past, requiring a reconception of time].

Cavell goes on, drawing additional parallels between Nietzsche's and Emerson's texts – Nietzsche's image of the "long ladder on whose rungs we have sat and climbed.... Here is a Higher, as Deeper, a Below-us, an enormous long ordering, a hierarchy which we *see*" – echoing the famous opening of Emerson's "Experience," for example, where "we find ourselves on a stair; there are stairs below us, which we seem to have ascended; there are stairs above us, many a one, which go upward and out of sight."[88] And he offers others, all illustrating a central point he is making about thinking: that it means or is "having another 'in mind.'" And with this, in this "intuition," as he calls it, echoing Emerson, there is another voice Cavell does not mention, but one he clearly has somewhere in mind, even if he claims he does not or cannot hear it. Consider this passage from Dewey's *Experience and Nature*, no doubt among the "countless" Dewey texts that Cavell had read. Here, then:

Upon the whole, professed transcendentalists have been more aware than have professed empiricists of the fact that language makes the difference between brute and man. The trouble is that they have lacked naturalistic conception of its origin and status. Logos has been correctly identified with mind; but logos and hence mind was conceived supernaturally. Logic was thereby supposed to have its basis in what is beyond human conduct and relationships, and in consequence the separation of the physical and the rational, the actual and the ideal, received its traditional formulation.

In protest against this view empirical thinkers have rarely ventured in discussion of language beyond reference to some peculiarity of brain structure, or some psychic peculiarity, such as tendency to "outer expression" of "inner" states.... The office of signs in creating reflection, foresight and recollection is passed by....

It is safe to say that psychic events, such as are anything more than reactions of a creature susceptible to pain and diffuse comfort, have language for one of their conditions. It is altogether likely that the "ideas" which Hume found in constant flux whenever he looked within himself were a succession of words silently uttered.... When the introspectionist thinks he has withdrawn into a wholly private realm of events disparate in kind from other events, made out of mental stuff, he is only turning his attention to his own soliloquy. And soliloquy is the product and reflex of converse with others; social communication not an effect of soliloquy. If we had not talked with others and they with us, we should never talk to and with ourselves.... Through speech a person dramatically identifies himself with potential acts and deeds; he plays many roles, not in successive stages of life but in a contemporaneously enacted drama. Thus mind emerges.[89]

"What is lost if Emerson's voice is lost?" From this passage we see that it was Dewey who seeded Cavell's offering that "America is as transcendentalist as it is pragmatist" and that Dewey had also elaborated around the all-important fact of conversation Thoreau's observation that "With thinking we may be beside ourselves in a sane sense." Returning to Cavell's passage, then, to follow him in his struggle with his studious ghosts and with words, to sound his own voice, we have:

> But suppose that the intelligible world is "the city of words," say Utopia; and suppose that the world of that city is not a "something" that is "outside" ... but is, as it says, "no place," which perhaps suggests no place *else* [Cavell's emphasis], but this place transfigured. (*Walden* is the instance I know best, this pure pool of words, which not everyone sees, but anyone might see, at Walden Pond, and hence where not?) Then all that thinking needs to be an incentive for is thinking itself, in particular for stopping to think (say not for action but for passion), as if to let our needs recognize what they need. This is a reasonable sense of intelligence – not the sense of applying it but that of receiving it. The incentive to the world I think is ... the world. Reason does not need to make anything happen ... what happens in the world ... is always happening.[90]

In Section 5 of the new Preface to *Human, All Too Human*, to which Cavell has pointed his readers, we find the words "suffering" and "patience" "in their site,"[91] describing the return to health of the "free spirit" in words echoing Thoreau's illustration of "thinking":

> He has been *beside himself* [emphasis added], there is no doubt. He now sees himself for the first time, – and what surprises he feels thereby! What thrills unexperienced hitherto! What joy even in the weariness, in the old illness, in the relapses of the convalescent! How he likes to sit still and suffer, to practice patience, to lie in the sun![92]

"Then all that thinking needs to be an incentive for is thinking itself, in particular for stopping to think (say not for action but for passion), as if to let our needs recognize what they need" – here the heart of Cavell's fear of losing "Emerson's voice." Straining in silence, stopping to hear, to receive passively – remembering the common root of "passion" and "patience" – "Nothing that is not there and the nothing that is" makes voice sound. A passage describing one of the Buddhist aspects of mind is helpful here as a reminder of Cavell's following Wittgenstein in the ambition to lead words back home from their metaphysical use:

> In China the Taoists have always spoken of "the activity of heaven"; for us to speak of the "activity of the enlightenment is in no way far-fetched. This is in fact the function of grace, namely *to condition men's homecoming to the center from start to finish* [emphasis added]. It is the very attraction of the center itself, revealed to us by various means, which provides the incentive to start on the way and the energy to face and overcome its many and various obstacles. Likewise grace is the welcoming hand into the center when man finds himself standing at long last on the brink of the great divide where all familiar human landmarks have disappeared.[93]

WHAT'S THE USE OF CALLING CAVELL A PRAGMATIST?

In bringing Nietzsche back into conversation with Emerson in the particular way he has, pointing to words and passages that send us back to the texts to replace them "in their sites," Cavell enjoins us to reexperience their distinctive difficulty and varying moods. Rereading Emerson and Nietzsche in the context of discussing pragmatism, it is impossible not to hear the difference between their voices and those of the self-proclaimed "pragmatists." The voices of Emerson and Nietzsche are, indeed, characterized by what Cavell calls "passionate utterance," patience and suffering straining to prophecy. Most importantly, Cavell's pointers to Nietzsche reveal the subtext of his own project, of what he means by saying:

> American writers must be free to discover whether the edifice of Western philosophy is as such European.... Here is where Emerson's and Thoreau's attraction for Eastern philosophy is crucial.... America's search for philosophy continues, by indirection, Columbus's great voyage of indirection, refinding the West by persisting to the East.

Nietzsche made no secret of the fact that the illness from which he figured the "free spirit" only beginning to convalesce was Christianity, but that the "Philosophy of the Future," of "such free spirits will be possible someday ... to-morrow and the day after to-morrow"[94]:

> If we could look upon Christian doctrines and church-history in a free and impartial way, we would have to express several views that oppose those that are generally accepted. But confined as we are from our earliest days under the yoke of custom and prejudice and inhibited in the natural development of our spirit, determined in the formation of our temperament by the impressions of our childhood, we believe ourselves compelled to view it virtually as a transgression if we adopt a freer standpoint from which to make a judgment on religion and Christianity that is impartial and approximate to our time.

Such an attempt is not the work of a few weeks, but of a lifetime.

How could one destroy the authority of two millennia and the security of the most perceptive men of all time as a consequence of youthful pondering? How could one dismiss all the sorrows and blessings of a religious development so deeply influential on world history by means of fantasies and immature ideas?[95]

Cavell, son of immigrant Jews, has had to be considerably more circumspect in expressing his aspirations for American philosophy, particularly as he began his career in a profession still dominated by WASPs (White Anglo-Saxon Protestants). At Harvard, where he was appointed in 1963, the third and last year of Kennedy's presidency, a period only just emerging from the lingering shadow of the House Un-American Activities Committee witch hunts, while there had been in respect to McCarthyism a more liberal attitude under the presidency of Nathan Marsh Pusey, as a conservative Episcopalian, Pusey nonetheless favored Christian values. (As late as 2012, as I composed this paragraph, the Christian credentials of both President Obama and the Republican candidate running against him – Mitt Romney – continued to be a political issue.)

The use of calling Cavell a pragmatist is, on the one hand, to put "God" back in the equation, but God reconceived for a pluralist democracy, recalling William James's announcement: "Pragmatism ... she widens the field of search for God." This new dispensation offers, as it were, a field concept of God. As James suggested in closing *The Varieties of Religious Experience,* not only is polytheism better suited to a pluralist society, but God might be imagined as even a slightly better version of oneself: "It might conceivably even be only a larger and more godlike self"[96] – in Cavell's terms, borrowing from Emerson, a "crescive self,"[97] having advanced if only by a half-step toward "moral perfection." In his "Overture" to *A Pitch of Philosophy* (the Jerusalem Lectures), Cavell, once again in his oblique, circuitous manner – "Tell all the truth but tell it slant-/ Success in Circuit lies."[98] – in accounting for having borrowed the subheadings for the volume's sections from the Jewish mystic, Gershom Scholem, has the following to say in connection with being a Jew himself, but "not being in Jerusalem," (having chosen, after the establishment of the Jewish state in 1948, to remain in America). I have excerpted the salient passages, emphasizing segments to foreground what might otherwise remain between the lines, so to speak. Here, then:

I relate this progress [in the movement of the three Jerusalem texts/lectures] to the importance, always decisive for me, of the *Eastern longings,*

that is, the non-European longing in the writing of Emerson and Thoreau....
Without knowing much, one could know that Scholem had devoted his
life to reclaiming the mystical tradition in Judaism, a tradition to which
he attributed *the power to regenerate fixed religious institutions....* Having
spent much of my last decade and a half trying to show something like the
present usefulness, even *potential regenerativeness, of Emerson and Thoreau
as thinkers,* I held out some hope for myself that that persistence, somehow, could be found to bear, however lightly, on the way that Scholem ...
thought of the Kabbalah....

[Quoting Scholem:] "The symbols of the kabbalists ... did not speak only
to the private individual, they displayed a symbolic dimension in the whole
world. *The question is whether in the reality in which today's secular person
lives this dimension will be revealed again.* I was strongly criticized when
I dared to say that Walt Whitman's writings contain something like this.
Walt Whitman revealed in an utterly naturalistic world what kabbalists and
other mystics revealed in their world." *That is the Emersonian connection I
wanted....*

Scholem had been asked about Oriental influences on Jewish mysticism.
He mentions Ramakrishna and describes the book of conversations with
him written down by his disciples as "an authentic document – one of
the most interesting religious documents I know." He then mentions that
Romain Rolland wrote a famous book about Ramakrishna.... It happens
that Rolland wrote a companion book about Ramakrishna's greatest dis-
ciple, Vivekananda, who, unlike his master, visited the United States. In
that book Rolland cites Whitman as the genuine if flawed embodiment of
*America's advanced spiritual state, ready to receive Vedantism, and sees Emerson
as something like the facilitator and intellectualizer of that role ...* In Rolland's
account Emerson is unable to appear as a thinker with his own relation to
establish between philosophy and religion. It is a mission, roughly simultaneous with Marx's claim that the philosophical critique of religion is
completed, that shows Marx's claim to be premature. *I assume this mission
provides a reasonable ground for Nietzsche's undying debt to Emerson....*

Whitman tapped a stratum of nineteenth-century America that might
equally be taken to characterize *an utterly transcendental world, in its breath-
less quest for itself, its desperation to work out, to imagine, to express itself....
I am putting myself in the way of a certain validation from the direction of
Jerusalem, however indirect ... for my investment in the Emersonian event.*[99]

We must not forget that pragmatism is not a dogma or platform, but
was conceived to be and was called by James a *method* for finding one's
way along the road. (We recall Cavell: "[O]ur task is to last as on a long
path. Patience and suffering...." And additionally: "I have insisted that
philosophy is interested in questions in its own way – call it a way in
which the answer is not in the future *but in the way the future is approached*

[emphasis added], or seen to be approachable, in which *the journey to the answer, or path, or tread, or the trades for it* [emphasis added], are the goal of it."[100]) It is a practice designed for and perfectly suited to the experience of being human after the news of the Darwinian event has registered, and particularly well suited to a nation of immigrancy: "[E]ach one here has a story," Cavell writes, "to begin with, the story of his or her path here, as if to make credible to oneself the sheer fact that one is here."[101] Pragmatists always address *where* we *happen* to *find ourselves* – I am here intentionally braiding the echo of Emerson's famous opening to "Experience" and William James's famous description of "truth" as what "*happens* to an idea." As Cheryl Misak has recently put it, rephrasing what Peirce and Dewey stressed, pragmatists concern themselves "where the decision to be made is a decision about what to believe from here, not what to believe were we able to start from scratch – from certain infallible foundations."[102]

Cavell's temperamental aversion to science and his justified criticism of reductionist descriptions of human nature and behavior have obscured for him the use and value of admitting scientific information appropriately. It was, after all, as we recall, Emerson who wholeheartedly approved the mission "to put science and the soul, long estranged from each other, at one again."[103] And not only Emerson, Nietzsche in *The Gay Science* also looked ahead to a moment when science would inform a secularized spirituality. Nonetheless, in his indirect way, like Columbus on his "great voyage of indirection, finding the West by going East," Cavell has importantly brought the soul, redeemed from Christian coinage into universal currency, back into circulation in the conversation of philosophy. It is especially to be noted that since James's and Peirce's clear and direct attempts to present and preserve the value of religious experience, ideas of God, the soul, and religious experience distinct from metaphysical explanations of being, have (with the exception of Cornel West, as noted in Chapter 1) been starkly absent from the vocabularies of those who call themselves pragmatists and claim their inheritance from Peirce and/or James. As Jeffrey Stout has pointed out in his contribution to Misak's 2007 *New Pragmatists* reader, elaborating Richard Rorty's focus on different "vocabularies":

> The vocabularies in which we claim this or that about something or other –
> thus raising to salience the things, properties, events, and relations with
> which we have come to be concerned – are products of our social practices.
> Change the vocabularies enough by using terms differently, and you will
> end up talking about somewhat different things, properties, events, and
> relations. As a result, you will be entertaining somewhat different candidates

for truth and falsity, and using those conceptual vehicles to make different claims. For a descriptive act, an application of a concept, to succeed in answering to what is being talked about, for it to have conceptual content at all, it needs to have a place in a broader, socially interactive activity in which individuals give and ask for reasons and keep track of commitments and entitlements. No such social practice, then no conceptual content, no conceptual norms, no subjects holding each other responsible.[104]

Cavell has recuperated into the vocabulary of American philosophy both the terms and the tempo of religious experience, but religious experience naturalized as it was for Emerson and in the way Scholem, following Rolland, described Whitman's world: *transcendental* and *transcendentalist*, *mystic* and *mystical, advanced spiritual states*, allowing suspension in unknowing. As I have observed elsewhere, Cavell's voice, no less than Emerson's, though quite distinct in its pitch and cadence, transports us and returns us to an Indic/Hellenic/Hellenistic/Hebraic space – the "eastern transcendental" from which Peirce as a young man wanted to separate himself, but that, he acknowledged later in his life, had touched him nonetheless. These are the "Eastern longings" Cavell hears in Emerson and Thoreau, the strains he experiences and follows.[105] In doing so, Cavell imports the "posture of thinking" – of being patient, still, stopping, turning – into the shapes and sound of his sentences. "The plain fact" is, as Cavell sharply reminds us, that the inherited languages of philosophy and science, " the measures which soak up knowledge of the world leave us dryly ignorant of ourselves,"[106] measures recently called "semiocentrism" by cultural critic Mark Bartlett.[107] In contrast, the plaintive strains of Eastern modes, *longings*, orienting us to the limits of our knowledge, to our all-too-human condition, and ultimately to our finitude, express what Hadot has described as the "mysterious connection between language and death."[108] This sound, embodying pain and loss, is foreign to the oom-pah-pah rhythm and major-scale tonalities associated with Christian soldiers marching off to war, well-suited accompaniments to the meliorism and progressivism of American Protestantism inflecting the language of the classical pragmatists. Cavell's writing, like Emerson's, syncopates this "Onward Christian Soldier" tempo in which "the self is concealed in assertion and action,"[109] the temper of pragmatism's projection of belief as a platform for action. As noted earlier, Emerson's and Cavell's aversive use of words – turning backwards, folding back recursively, exemplifying in these movements the recognition of our historical character – purposely impedes and sabotages progress. Practicing their exercises, we learn, with patience and suffering, to attend to more than what can be said, to move in all the dimensions of our experience; this is experience in language as adventure, peril, risk – experience as the pragmatists understand it. It hurts to read Emerson and Cavell. Muscles tear as they grow; reading Emerson and Cavell tears old habits of mind.

In one of his latest reminders of the centrality of the Emersonian project, Cavell, still focused on "patience" and "suffering" after all these years, presents "Emerson's calling for patience (the closing paragraph of ... "Experience") ... [as] a demand for the kind of waiting, or, say, suffering, necessary to achieve a new future. It is a future I imagine characterized by Emersonian ideas of 'unsettling all things' – a remark directed at those who claim to have 'settled' America."[110] Cavell's American experience, conditioned by his familial situation in all aspects of Jewish immigrancy and "settlement" from the late-nineteenth century and into the present, keenly sharpened his sense, as he has put it, "of the ways my Jewishness and my Americanness inflect each other." He continues:

> I am moved to say ... that I can understand certain forms taken by my devotion to Thoreau and to Emerson as expressions of that issue, particularly, I suppose, my perception that they provide in philosophizing for and against America, a philosophy of immigrancy, of the human as stranger, and so take an interest in strangeness, beginning no doubt with the strangeness of oneself. Some will see this as a clinical issue, with more bearing on myself than on those I claim to perceive. I will, I trust, be excused for seeing it also as a critical issue, enabling genuine perceptions that might otherwise go unwon.[111]

Not forgetting Cavell's desire to restore a therapeutic function to philosophical practice, it is useful to consider recent findings in medical research concerning oncologists and patient loss.[112] Oncologists are not – or, at least, have not been until recently – trained to deal with their own grief. In consequence, there is a troubling relationship between their discomfort with death and how they react in their personal lives and with grieving families. The conclusion drawn by the researchers is that in addition to providing training for doctors in facing loss, it is necessary to normalize death and grief as natural parts of life. Cavell's pragmatist project, addressing where America finds itself – as Emerson pointed out, just beginning on the path to achieve a more perfect union between aspiration and actuality – has been to normalize the patience and suffering attendant on continuing to pursue our errand into the wilderness of mere being; an errand not limited by national agendas, but by what happens to the idea of democracy. We need to normalize the fact of our condition and understand the use of pragmatism as a tool, a method that takes into full account where we are, still struggling within the rules of a language game that occludes the actual and accidental nature of experience. As Cavell has recently voiced, reiterating his concern:

> ...in my mind is Locke's unforgettable remark that in the beginning all the world was America. The form the thought releases in me is one begun in Emerson's suggestion that America does not exist, or is not inhabited, that it has not been approached and arrived at. The thought, panic-struck, is that there may be no longer an America, not because of its global dispersion, but because the idea of democracy, of inclusive, equitable, mutual legislation, cannot be mocked indefinitely without threatening to disappear. My characterization of Emerson and Thoreau as philosophers of immigrancy ... includes the sense that it is apt to be in memories of oppression that freedom remains heart's blood. Yet some are capable of imagining oppression as if they are remembering suffering it.[113]

It will take time.

CHAPTER 6

Effects 2: Richard Rorty, Sea change and/or ironic scraping

The opinion that is fated to be ultimately agreed to by all who investigate the truth in any depth is now what we mean by truth, and the object represented in this opinion is the most real. Logicality requires that our interests shall not stop at our own fate, but must extend to all races of beings with whom we can come into immediate or mediate intellectual relations.

CHARLES SANDERS PEIRCE, *Collected Papers,*
Volume 5, Paragraph 654

And they said then, "But play, you must,
A tune beyond us, yet ourselves . . . ."

WALLACE STEVENS, "The Man With the Blue Guitar"

In every work of genius we recognize our own rejected thoughts; they come back to us with a certain alienated majesty.

RALPH WALDO EMERSON, "Self-Reliance"

[O]ur Glassy Essence is something we share with the angels, even though they weep for our ignorance of its nature.

RICHARD RORTY, *Philosophy and the Mirror of Nature*

IN PRAISE OF THERAPEUTIC PHILOSOPHY AND AGAINST SYSTEM BUILDING[1]

So effective was Richard Rorty's *Philosophy and the Mirror of Nature* (1979) for me when I first read it in 1981 (the 1980, second corrected edition) that long before I came to inhabit and be inhabited by James's *Pragmatism* and later coming to identify myself as a pragmatist, I felt comfortable, safe, after moving through Rorty's mirror, in setting aside the thornier problems troubling hundreds of years of thinking about thinking contained in the canonic texts I had studied as a student of philosophy. One could say that Rorty liberated me, primed me to become self-reliant, Emersonian.[2] I reread Rorty's volume during the summer of 1998 in West Cork, Ireland in the shadow of Mount Gabriel, and appropriately recalled its annunciation as I prepared readings for the graduate seminar I was to offer that fall in "American Aesthetics," one in a series I give every year at The Graduate Center, CUNY exploring and cultivating the field whose yield includes *A Natural History of Pragmatism* and now – having gone through Rorty's *Mirror* a third time – the chapters of this text. This last reading, coming after my wrestling with the other necessary angels who are the subjects of this volume, particularly my grappling with Peirce, has been provocative in ways I could not have anticipated, ways spinning around Stevens's observation of "disillusion as the last illusion."[3] Let me explain.

Stanley Cavell somewhere offers the model of thinking as reading, reminding us of reading's radical connection (from the Old English root *redan*) with "explaining, ruling, advising." This model takes fully into account all the ways possible, all the ways available to a reader, of thinking about the object under consideration – *thirteen ways of looking at a blackbird*, one might say. All aspects of the terrain are examined as one moves backward, forward, up, down, and around (somewhat in the manner of quarks).[4] Reading this way is to "reconceive reason," in Cavell's words, and is at the heart of pragmatism as James and Peirce understood and practiced the method. Pragmatism, as we know, is not meant – as literature is not meant – to convey information, but to teach us how to live, what to do, or better, perhaps, how to read the signs to learn what to do wherever it is we happen to find ourselves. In James's rephrasing of what has come to be referred to as the "pragmatist maxim," the form this guidance takes is to understand that "our beliefs are really rules for action," and so,

> to develop a thought's meaning, we need only determine what conduct it is fitted to produce: that conduct is for us its sole significance. And the tangible fact at the root of all our thought-distinctions, however subtle, is that there is no one of them so fine as to consist in anything but a possible difference in practice. To attain perfect clearness in our thought of an object, then, we need only consider what conceivable effects of a practical kind the object may involve – what sensations we are to expect from it, and what reactions we must prepare. Our conception of these effects, whether immediate or remote, is then for us the whole of our conception of the object, so far as that conception has positive significance at all.

> This is the principle of Peirce, the principle of pragmatism. It lay entirely unnoticed by anyone for twenty years, until I ... brought it forward again

and made a special application of it to religion. By that date [1898] the time seemed ripe for its reception. The word 'pragmatism' spread, and at present it fairly spots the pages of the philosophic journals.[5]

I would like to recall here the chapter epigraph from Emerson: "In every work of genius we recognize our own rejected thoughts; they come back to us with a certain alienated majesty." I want to play this note of Emerson's – sound it – in relation to Rorty's arrogation of voice in using the figure of "man's glassy essence" to acknowledge Peirce and at the same time dismiss him; this sounding will have as its *basso continuo* the "pragmatist maxim" concerning the "conduct" that developing a thought's meaning has as its aim. Rorty quotes from Isabella's "ape and essence" speech in *Measure for Measure* in "The Invention of the Mind," the first chapter of Part One of *Philosophy and the Mirror of Nature*, titled "Our Glassy Essence" – the phrase inflected for him, as he notes, by Peirce as well as by Francis Bacon in the *Advancement of Learning* and, all the way back, by Anaxagoras. Here are the lines from Shakespeare that he quotes:

> But man, proud man
> Dressed in a little brief authority
> Most ignorant of what he's most assured –
> His glassy essence – like an angry ape,
> Plays such fantastic tricks before high Heaven
> As make the angels weep – who, with our spleen,
> Would all laugh themselves mortal.

Rorty's footnote to the lines closes with this sentence:

> The phrase *man's glassy essence* was first invoked in philosophy by C. S. Peirce in an 1892 essay of that title on the "molecular theory of protoplasm," which Peirce strangely thought important in confirming the view that "a person is nothing but a symbol involving a general idea" and in establishing the existence of "group minds."[6]

Rorty does not note that before using the phrase "man's glassy essence" to title his 1892 essay, Peirce had used three lines from Isabella's speech quite pointedly in closing "Some Consequences of Four Incapacities," the second of his three celebrated anti-Cartesian papers of 1868, which, as Richard Bernstein and others have argued, together comprise "the origin of American pragmatism."[7] In the first, "Questions Concerning Certain Capacities Claimed for Man," Peirce concluded that "every cognition is determined by previous cognitions; that we have no power of thinking without signs; that we have no conception of the absolutely incognizable"[8] – a sounding that clearly forecasts Rorty. These two papers are generally considered Peirce's two "strongest philosophical works."⁹ The second paper concludes by making the case for the identity of man as sign pointedly using Isabella's lines:

[313.] … In fact, therefore, men and words reciprocally educate each other; each increase of a man's information involves and is involved by a corresponding increase of a word's information.

[314.] Without fatiguing the reader by stretching this parallelism too far, it is sufficient to say that there is no element whatever of man's consciousness which has not something corresponding to it in the word; and the reason is obvious that the word or sign which man uses *is* the man himself. For, as the fact that every thought is a sign, taken in conjunction with the fact that life is a train of thought, proves that man is a sign; so, that every thought is an *external* sign, proves that man is an external sign. That is to say, the man and the external sign are identical. Thus my language is the sum total of myself; for the man is the thought. [This last sentence echoes Emerson's "this thought which is called I" from "The Transcendentalist"¹⁰ and could also be honestly mistaken for Rorty.]

[315.] It is hard for man to understand this, because he persists in identifying himself with his will, his power over the animal organism, with brute force. Now the organism is only an instrument of thought. But the identity of a man consists in the *consistency* of what he does and thinks, and consistency is the intellectual character of a thing; that is, is its expressing something.

[316.] Finally, as what anything really is, is what it may finally come to be known to be is the ideal state of complete information, so that reality depends on the ultimate decision of the community; so thought is what it is, only by virtue of its addressing a future thought which is in its value as thought identical with it, though more developed. In this way, the existence of thought now depends on what is to be hereafter; so that it has only a potential existence, dependent on future thought of the community. [We think of Rorty's *Contingency … Solidarity* and of his argument concerning different "vocabularies"; his Masters thesis and his dissertation had "potentiality" as their subject.¹¹]

[317.] The individual man, since his separate existence is manifested only by ignorance and error, so far as he is anything apart from his fellows, and from what he and they are to be, is only a negation. This is man,

> …proud man,
> Most ignorant of what he's most assured,
> His glassy essence. [Peirce's emphases]¹²

Understood in the way that Peirce uses *man's glassy essence* to point a reflection on these paragraphs – as *a potential existence, dependent on future thought of the community* – Shakespeare's figure is the "room of the idea"[13] where Rorty's *cognition* of Peirce's loaded gun lies – hidden, forgotten, repressed – as, clearly, as *face to face in a glass*, Peirce had already taken aim and shattered the mirror Rorty sets himself to shatter again. The "'idea' idea"[14] was already deconstructed, lying in pieces, Peirce's fait accompli in these anti-Cartesian papers that began his career. Indeed, Rorty opens a late essay, "Pragmatism and Romanticism" (2003), with a thumbnail description of pragmatism that identifies it with this deconstruction: "At the heart of pragmatism is the refusal to accept the correspondence theory of truth and the idea that true beliefs are accurate representations of reality."[15] If the work that *Philosophy and the Mirror of Nature* aimed to accomplish had already been done 100 years before, why would Rorty set out to do it again? One could answer that just as with *The Principles of Psychology* William James aimed, with that volume's scope and tone, to legitimize to an academic audience the findings of the nascent field of psychology informed, as he put it, by "the darwinian facts," *Philosophy and the Mirror of Nature* was intended to bring the professional field up-to-date, temporarily aligning "the linguistic turn" with what Richard Bernstein has called "the pragmatic turn," tracing their common swerve away from the history of dualism – their *clinamen* from what Wilfrid Sellars called the "Myth of the Given." (*Clinamen* is a technical term from Harold Bloom's vocabulary, recently redeemed into currency by Steven Greenblatt's ingeniously titling his story of the serendipitous Renaissance finding of a manuscript of *De Rerum Natura*, Lucretius's great poem, *The Swerve*.) But in the story Rorty tells, Peirce – leader of the pack, the modern moment's Luther – is relegated to a smugly dismissive footnote: "Peirce strangely thought important." Why?

Rorty's failure to take Peirce into account in his own later work has been pointed out recently by Bernstein in *The Pragmatic Turn* (2010) as well as in his commemoration of Rorty's achievement in "Richard Rorty's Deep Humanism," published in *New Literary History* in 2008.[16] Vincent Colapietro has also more recently and extensively focused on Rorty's ambivalence toward and occlusion of Peirce in his superb essay, "Richard Rorty as Peircean Pragmatist: An Ironic Portrait and Sincere Expression of Philosophical Friendship," where he, like Bernstein, reminds us that

> despite Peirce's prominence in the history of pragmatism, Rorty virtually denied the title of pragmatist to the figure who is generally recognized as the father of this movement. In his [Rorty's] Presidential Address to the Eastern Division of the APA [1979], he said ... Peirce's contribution to

pragmatism was merely to have given it a name, and to have stimulated James.[17]

In the same vein, Susan Haack, described by some as a "neo-classical pragmatist," had noted already in 1998 "that Rorty's version of pragmatism is at odds with that offered by Charles Peirce, and hence inauthentic."[18] Similarly, Jeffrey Stout in commenting on Rorty's elevation of James and Dewey (but not Peirce) to "heroic status" has noted that "some latter-day pragmatists" have similarly observed "that Rorty's neglect of Peirce is exactly what gets him into trouble in the first place"; the "trouble" being his version of pragmatism construed by some as a kind of "narcissism"[19] in its not doing "justice simultaneously to the objective and social-practical dimensions of inquiry."[20] In other words, the *pragmatisch* and *praktisch* are at issue once more.

In the article entitled "What Pragmatism Is," published in the *Monist* in 1905, Peirce reclaimed and renamed his "pragmatism" *pragmaticism*, "to serve the precise purpose of expressing the original definition" – "pragmatism," as James notes in the aforementioned passage, having caught on and "spread" wildly after he reintroduced it in his 1898 talk at Berkeley. (See also the earlier discussion in this volume in connection with this and the following arguments.) In "announc[ing] the birth of the word 'pragmaticism,'" Peirce commented that he hoped the new word was "ugly enough to be safe from kidnappers." He continued to explain his intention in adopting the original term "pragmatism" in the specific context of the distinction between *pragmatisch* and *praktisch*, especially useful to consider once again in relation to Rorty's equivocation with regard to Peirce in the "man's glassy essence" footnote. In this piece, referring to himself in the third person, Peirce offers:

> Endeavoring, as a man of that type [an experimentalist] naturally would, to formulate what he so approved, he framed the theory that a *conception* [Peirce's emphasis], that is, the rational purport of a word or other expression, lies exclusively in its conceivable bearing upon *the conduct of life* [emphasis added; that all-important phrase borrowed from Emerson and used by James and Dewey as well]; so that, since obviously nothing that might not result from experiment can have any direct bearing upon conduct, if one can define accurately all the conceivable experimental phenomena which the affirmation or the denial of a concept could imply, one will have therein a complete definition of the concept, and *there is absolutely nothing more in it*. For this doctrine he invented the name *pragmatism* [Peirce's emphases]. Some of his friends wished him to call it practicism or practicalism.... But for one who had learned philosophy out of Kant, as

the writer, along with nineteen out of every twenty experimentalists who have turned to philosophy, had done, and who still thought in Kantian terms most readily, *practisch* and *pragmatisch* were as far apart as two poles, the former belonging to the region of thought where no mind of the experimentalist type can ever make use of solid ground under his feet, the latter expressing relation to some definite human purpose. *Now quite the most striking feature of the new theory was its recognition of an inseparable connection between rational cognition and rational purpose, and that consideration it was which determined the preference for the name pragmatism* [emphasis added, except for "pragmatism"].[21]

Richard Bernstein, who first came to know Rorty when they were both students at the Hutchins College at the University of Chicago ("the institution described by A. J. Liebling [as] the biggest collection of juvenile neurotics since the Childrens' Crusade,"[22] as Rorty noted in his 1992 autobiographical essay, "Trotsky and the Wild Orchids") and who then followed Rorty's suggestion to join him in pursuing graduate study in philosophy at Yale, has also cited this passage from Peirce (though imprecisely) in a note commenting on the various meanings of pragmatism – "the metamorphoses of so protean an entity," as A. O. Lovejoy described in his "Thirteen Pragmatisms" of 1908. (Bernstein adds: "I suspect that today, a hundred years after Lovejoy wrote these words, many philosophers may want to suggest that Lovejoy was far too conservative in discriminating *only* thirteen pragmatisms."[23]) In connection with Rorty's ambivalent relation to Peirce, Bernstein reminds us of an early "stunning article" of Rorty's, "Pragmatism, Categories, and Language" (1961), where Rorty points to pragmatism's becoming "relevant again" after the "linguistic turn" occasioned in Anglo-American philosophy by the virtual takeover of the profession first by the influx to the United States of refugees affiliated with the Vienna Circle during and after the Second World War, then intensified by the flocking to Cambridge and Oxford – "where young American philosophers made their intellectual pilgrimage after the Second World War."[24] In that article, Rorty names "Charles S. Peirce ... the most up-to-date pragmatist." But by the time of writing *Philosophy and the Mirror of Nature*, "he dismissed the importance of Peirce, and claimed that the true progenitors of pragmatism were William James and John Dewey." Bernstein continues to detail Rorty's earlier perception in "Pragmatism, Categories, and Language" of Peirce and his value:

> But in 1961, Dick [Bernstein and Rorty were close personal friends for more than fifty years in addition to their professional affiliation] wrote: "Peirce's thought envisaged, and repudiated in advance, the stages in the

development of empiricism which logical positivists [Rorty wrote "positivism"] represented, and that it came to rest in a group of insights and a philosophical mood much like those we find in the *Philosophical Investigations* and in the writings of philosophers influenced by the later Wittgenstein." In his aloof metaphilosophical stance, he makes it clear that he is not trying to show that "Peirce saw through a glass darkly what Wittgenstein saw face to face, nor the reverse.... What I am trying to show is that the closer one brings pragmatism to the writings of the later Wittgenstein and of those influenced by him, the more light they shed on each other."[25]

"Man's glassy essence" stands as the emblem of Rorty's anxiety of influence: if reading is a form or model of thinking, then, as we have learned to entertain as a working hypothesis from Bloom, misreading is a form or model of repression. "Man's glassy essence" serves as a perfect figure for "disillusion as the last illusion," of *both/and* – of, at the same time, the idea of a Platonic essence, the "'idea' idea," *and* of the icy surface of language that Emerson taught we must learn to skate on. The one was an ideal Rorty began with as a self-described "reactionary metaphysician ... trying to stop the positivist invasion"[26]:

> When Rorty discovered philosophy at Chicago, he was initially attracted by the Platonic idea of holding "reality and justice in a single vision." He thought that reaching the top of Plato's divided line – the place "beyond hypotheses" – would enable him to find a grand synthesis of public justice and private pleasures.[27]

The other was a realization Peirce had come to through practice as a celestial observer, through which practice he learned to negotiate the slippery slope of "hypotheses" that he developed into his various descriptions of the ongoing conversation that constitutes community and truth. Peirce realized and expressed long before Rorty that in language, there is no place "beyond hypotheses." While Rorty would come to this realization as well, he seems to have forgotten somewhere along the way to acknowledge what he had learned and valued early on in Peirce. As Bernstein goes on to observe, sometimes indicating his quotations from Rorty's "Trotsky and the Wild Orchids," sometimes not:

> But by the time he left Chicago, Rorty was disillusioned with whether the study of philosophy would make one genuinely wise and virtuous. "Since [my] initial disillusion (which climaxed about the time I left Chicago to get a PhD in philosophy at Yale), I have spent 40 years looking for a coherent and convincing way of formulating my worries about what, if anything, philosophy is good for." Eventually, Rorty came to the conclusion that the

project of seeking a synthesis between public justice and private interests is a misguided endeavor – one that had led Plato astray.[28]

Reflecting for a moment on Peirce's paragraph closing with the lines from Isabella's speech will allow us in the next section of this chapter to "consider what conceivable effects of a practical kind" Peirce's paragraph might have had on Rorty that could have led to his early "disillusion" and to his later ambivalence about Peirce. In glossing Isabella's speech, Rorty offers the scholarly history of the "intellectual soul" as "glassy essence," summing up with:

> Our Glassy Essence was not a philosophical doctrine, but a picture which literate men found presupposed by every page they read. It is glassy – mirror-like – for two reasons. First, it takes on new forms without being changed – but intellectual forms, rather than sensible ones as material mirrors do. Second, mirrors are made of a substance which is purer, finer grained, more subtle, and more delicate than most. Unlike our spleen, which, in combination with other equally gross and visible organs, accounted for the bulk of our behavior, our Glassy Essence is something we share with the angels, even though they weep for our ignorance of its nature. The supernatural world, for sixteenth-century intellectuals, was modeled upon Plato's world of Ideas, just as our contact with it was modeled upon his metaphor of vision.[29]

In Peirce's paragraph –

> The individual man, since his separate existence is manifested only by ignorance and error, so far as he is anything apart from his fellows, and from what he and they are to be, is only a negation. This is man,
> 　　　... proud man,
> 　　Most ignorant of what he's most assured,
> 　　His glassy essence –

it is man's "separate existence ... manifested only by ignorance and error," that would make angels weep. For Peirce, man's "glassy essence" belongs, as noted earlier, to an ongoing continuity of the individual in and through time with "his fellows, what he and they are to be" – in other words, *synechism*, the key informing the father of pragmatism's understanding of the human relation to the cosmos within which individual potentiality can be realized, a condition that "proud man" (his "mean egotism" not yet vanished) ignores. We recall from Chapter 2, the discussion of Peirce's analogy between the "I" and zero, a cipher around and through which new aspects encountered are drawn as by the gravitational pull of earlier experiences turning and returning; William James's figure of the "I" as a "storm-centre" derives from this same perception. All is in constant activity and changing relation. There is no *separate* Cartesian "I" that thinks. We shall have occasion to follow Peirce dissolving this "I" into its "glassy essence" further on in considering his 1892 essay concerning the "molecular theory of protoplasm" that Rorty so rudely dismisses in his footnote.

ANOTHER ORCHID, ANOTHER BIRD[30]

Before getting to that discussion, it should be noted in moving away from what has already been offered that Rorty was intimate with Peirce's foundational anti-Cartesian papers; he had, after all, studied with and written his Masters thesis at Chicago under the direction of Charles Hartshorne,[31] a preeminent scholar of Peirce as well as of Alfred North Whitehead. (Hartshorne as a post-doctoral fellow at Harvard assisted Paul Weiss between 1925 and 1928 in editing the *Collected Papers of Charles Sanders Peirce*, in six volumes – the first collection of the philosopher's work.) Hartshorne would eventually come to be identified with translating Whitehead's "process philosophy" into "process theology." In addition, Rorty at Yale wrote his doctoral dissertation on "The Concept of Potentiality" under the direction of Weiss – "a metaphysician of the grand style"[32] – to whom he had been guided by Hartshorne; Weiss (whose entry on Peirce in the 1934 *Dictionary of American Biography* was required reading for anyone interested in pragmatism) was even more purely a Peircean than Hartshorne. Also while still a graduate student at Chicago, Rorty studied with Manley Thompson, like Hartshorne and Weiss, another of the "country's leading scholars of Charles Peirce." And, in fact, in the "stunning article" to which Bernstein refers, Rorty recuperates "Peirce's master argument against Cartesian intuitionism,"[33] citing chapters and verses from the two seminal 1868 papers in the text and footnotes of his own paper.

It is worth remarking, as well, in texturing this account of Rorty's complex responsiveness to philosophical forebears, the detail that Hartshorne had a passion for birdsong and became an internationally known published expert in the field. The *Stanford Encyclopedia of Philosophy* describes Hartshorne as,

> the first philosopher since Aristotle to be an expert in both metaphysics and ornithology. He writes specifically of the aesthetic categories required to explain why birds sing outside of mating season and when territory is not threatened – two occasions for bird song that are crucial to the behaviorists' accounts. Birds *like* [author's emphasis] to sing, he concludes.

And Richard Hocking observes that "Charles Hartshorne's gifted avoca-
tion in ornithology is altogether becoming to his philosophy of nature's
innovative process."[34] It is not difficult to imagine the sympathy the still
adolescent Rorty – he began at Hutchins College at fifteen and completed his M. A. at twenty – whose interest in birds had begun in childhood (later to develop, at a crucial juncture in his life, into a passion
as well) would have felt for Hartshorne. Nor is it a stretch to suggest
that Rorty's coming in his later work to justify so absolutely the place
and value of aesthetic pursuits, separate from any moral or practical concern, was in part seeded by Hartshorne's idea about birdsong extended
to human parallels. Indeed, as Rorty's biographer Neil Gross observes,
"Hartshorne was ... much influenced by Peirce," and while he "did not
accept [Peirce's] categorical scheme in its entirety ... he did agree that
triadic, semiotic relationships extend beyond the domain of human consciousness to form part of the world itself."[35] (Indeed, Peirce observed in
"The Simplest Mathematics," a manuscript piece written in 1902 – which
Hartshorne as editor of his papers would have known – "Thought is not
necessarily connected with a brain. It appears in the work of bees, of
crystals, and throughout the purely physical world; and we can no more
deny that it is truly there, than that the colors, the shapes, etc. of objects
are really there."[36])

In any case, it is significant to me, one of whose vocabularies is that of
a biographer as well, that Rorty became an avid birdwatcher only during
"the second half of [his] life," as he describes in a revealing and poign-
ant Dutch television interview first broadcast in 2000 entitled "Of Beauty
and Consolation." Regular and systematic birdwatching began during
the period when Rorty was putting together *The Linguistic Turn*, his first
published book, and also undergoing a five-to-six-year psychoanalysis, a
period during which his father, who had long battled bouts of depression
and mental illness – some episodes severe enough to have required hospi-
talization – suffered two serious nervous breakdowns, the second of which
"included claims to divine prescience."[37] It was this last episode, by Rorty's
account, that occasioned his beginning analysis:

> I was in treatment with Dr. Ellen Simon for obsessional neurosis from the
> time my father went psychotic in late 1962 or so, with some follow-up visits
> in the late sixties and early seventies. Full-fledged analysis began sometime
> in 1963 and ended about five years later.[38]

In addition, during this extended moment, Rorty's marriage to the philosopher Amelie Oksenberg Rorty was stressed. Their relationship had

begun while they were graduate students in the philosophy program at Yale; by the mid-sixties they had a young son, and, as Rorty's mother wrote to a friend in late 1966, both were "climbing that ladder, career-wise.... Also, they are both changing ... Amelie took a semester off and got a grant to do a study in anthropology.... Dick has stopped being a metaphysician."[39] The marriage ended in divorce in 1972. During the same year he, "a strict atheist," married Mary Varney, a bioethicist and "practicing Mormon."[40]

In the Dutch television interview, Rorty talks about his childhood interest in birds, noting that by twelve he had pored through *Audubon's Birds*, matching the local specimens he knew from the northwestern New Jersey countryside against the exquisite renderings of Audubon's plates, but that because there were "no binoculars" in the household – one wonders why he didn't ask his parents for a set – he "could not watch birds carefully," and so he switched his interest to the many varieties of wild orchids hiding in the wooded and mountainous landscape. In "Trotsky and the Wild Orchids," Rorty describes somewhat differently the reason for switching his interest to wild orchids, adding more detail:

> A few years later [when he would have been ten or eleven], when my parents began dividing their time between the Chelsea Hotel and the mountains of northwest New Jersey, these interests ["I ... had private, weird, snobbish, incommunicable interests." Another of these had been in Tibet: "I had sent the newly enthroned Dalai Lama a present accompanied by warm congratulations to a fellow eight-year-old who had made good."] switched to orchids. Some forty species of wild orchid occur in those mountains, and I eventually found seventeen of them. Wild orchids are uncommon and rather hard to spot. I prided myself enormously on being the only person around who knew where they grew, their Latin names, and their blossoming times. When in New York, I would go to the 42nd Street Public Library to reread a nineteenth-century volume of the botany of the orchids of the eastern U.S.
>
> I was not quite sure why those orchids were so important, but I was convinced that they were. I was sure that our noble, chaste North American wild orchids were morally superior to the showy, hybridized, tropical orchids displayed in florists' shops. I was also convinced there was a deep significance in the fact that the orchids are the latest and most complex plants to be developed in the course of evolution. Looking back, I suspect that there was a lot of sublimated sexuality involved (orchids being a notoriously sexy sort of flower), and that my desire to learn all there was to know about orchids was linked to my desire to understand all the hard words in Krafft-Ebing.

I was uneasily aware, however, that there was something a bit dubious about this esotericism – this interest in socially useless flowers. I had read (in the vast amount of spare time given to a clever, snotty, nerdy only child) bits of *Marius the Epicurean* and also bits of Marxist criticisms of Pater's aestheticism. I was afraid that Trotsky (whose *Literature and Revolution* I had nibbled at) would not have approved of my interest in orchids.[41]

Rorty spoke to the Dutch interviewer about his pleasure in knowing the places where the different kinds of orchids grew: "the hidden nodes of one's life," as he described, a secret world that he did not talk about with others, thinking others "wouldn't understand or would laugh." He collected and catalogued his specimens – channeling what was even in boyhood a "rage for order" into an exquisite habit. The passion for birds remained, however, to be reanimated during that critical passage in mid-life, as though Rorty, in witnessing his father's disappearance into delusions of "divine prescience," took up the activity through which he could internalize Hartshorne, at least in part to fill the emptied paternal psychic space. It also seems that it was during this period that Rorty's estimation of Peirce's value changed or began to change, or, at least, that his prominence receded, as reflected in diminishing to absent references to him. Rorty's announced turn away came later, beginning by his own account in 1981 and focusing on what he described as "Peirce's unfortunate attempt ... to define truth in terms of 'the end of inquiry'."[42] We shall have occasion further along to consider this moment and its consequences.

Looking more closely at "Pragmatism, Categories, and Language," Rorty's 1961 paper previously quoted by Bernstein, will provide a concrete sense of what a radical change this was. Before turning to that reading, however, some background context is called for: on the one hand, concerning how the paper has been regarded; on the other hand, providing additional details about Rorty's involvement with Peirce and the climate in which his "disillusion" was precipitated.

In terms of past treatments, what has not received comment by Bernstein or others, as far as I have been able to determine, is that this paper turns out to be not only one of the most lucid explications of the central aspect of Peirce's contribution – *Thirdness* – but also exhibits a level of engagement with Peirce's work that reflects the same kind of scrupulous attention Rorty gave to wild orchids and birds. In other words, Peirce's work too was, or had been, a passion for Rorty. Neil Gross has astutely framed Rorty's aim in offering this paper "to bring attention to himself within the philosophical community" by "mak[ing] a case for pragmatism's centrality for the analytic project" within the double development from the mid-1950s on of the "increasing pragmatic temper of analytic philosophy and the growing interest in Wittgenstein" – the publication of *Philosophical Investigations* in 1953 having been "a major event."[43] (Even today humanities instructors in the academy need only name Wittgenstein in the title of a course to have the class over-tallied on the first day of registration.) It is abundantly clear from the footnotes and internal references citing volumes and paragraph numbers throughout Rorty's paper that he was at least as fluent in Peirce as he was in Wittgenstein, and had given even closer attention to Peirce's mind thinking than he had to Plato's – "I read through Plato during my fifteenth summer," another of his "weird, snobbish ... interests": "I wanted a way to be both an intellectual and spiritual snob and a friend of humanity – a nerdy recluse and a fighter for justice."[44]

In terms of Rorty's involvement with Peirce, in New Haven he had greatly deepened this relationship, begun at Chicago under Hartshorne's guidance – Gross comments that at Yale he was "immersed in Peirce."[45] In addition to studying with Weiss and serving as a teaching assistant for a course on pragmatism taught by John E. Smith – as keenly interested in Peirce as he was in James and Dewey; Colapietro comments that Smith was "a (if not *the*) major interpreter of the pragmatic tradition"[46] – Rorty was taught by Rulon Wells, another specialist in Peirce. (Wells also had a strong background in linguistics, originally a Sanskritist.[47] After his arrival at Yale, where he was appointed to the faculty in philosophy in 1945, he emerged as one of the leading linguists of the country.) Wells's obituary in the *Yale News* (July 2008) notes: "The mind of 19th-century logician Charles S. Peirce held a special fascination for him." This fascination is reflected in his pointing the students in his course on Peirce (offered during the 1952–3 academic year, in which Rorty was enrolled) to Weiss's *Dictionary of American Biography* entry, where the young Peirce is described as having been even more solitary, snobbish, precocious, and odd in his interests than Rorty felt himself to have been in his childhood and youth. While Rorty had read through all of Plato by fifteen, Peirce by fifteen had read through Kant and by sixteen knew "almost by heart" (by his own account) the *Critique of Pure Reason* – in German. While Rorty had begun at Hutchins at fifteen, Peirce had begun Yale at sixteen. As Gross documents, Rorty took fourteen pages of detailed notes recording the contents of Wells's lectures, which provide "at least some indication of the background against which Rorty's own views of Peirce might have been forged."[48] Wells's take on Peirce is reflected even in the title of an essay he contributed to a 1965 volume edited by Richard Bernstein commemorating the fiftieth anniversary of Peirce's death: "Charles S. Peirce as an American." As remarked by Donald Gustafson reviewing the commemorative volume, Wells emphasizes variously "the respects in which Peirce's philosophy embodies American traits." Gustafson continues:

> Wells contends that Peirce's account of the good or end of his evolutionism is insufficiently drawn and that a satisfactory account of it (as something other than hope) cannot be given in terms of the categories Peirce employs. Peirce's "great hope" about the fated truth is only one trait in his philosophy that is writ large in the American character. Wells also has interesting things to say about Peirce's practical and theoretical views.[49]

Wells's sensitivity to Peirce's "American-ness" is to be especially remarked in the context of Rorty's family history grounded in the life and death of a Civil War hero, in his parents' social activism – aspects to be described in more detail a bit further on – and in his childhood feeling about the wild orchids in the western New Jersey countryside:

> that our noble, chaste North American wild orchids were morally superior to the showy, hybridized, tropical orchids displayed in florists' shops. I was also deeply convinced there was a deep significance in the fact that the orchids are the latest and most complex plants to be developed in the course of evolution.

Just like us, in other words. It is my guess that Rorty was strongly influenced by Wells's sense of Peirce, and that his settling on "categories" as the mediating term between "pragmatism" and "language" in his 1961 paper followed a direction pointed to by Wells. We shall have occasion to consider this point during the discussion of "Pragmatism, Categories, and Language."

There was also one more ingredient essential to Rorty's giving his attention to Peirce and valuing him as he did in the 1961 paper. Wilfrid Sellars joined the Yale faculty after Rorty finished his work there, but they established nonetheless a productive relationship. Even before the time Rorty completed his dissertation under Paul Weiss's direction in 1956 and the time he published "Pragmatism, Categories, and Language," conversations with Sellars, actual and in thought, had begun. As Richard Bernstein recounts:

> Dick started reading analytic philosophy when he was completing his dissertation. Wilfrid Sellars was the philosopher who initially had the greatest influence on Dick. I vividly recall discussing Sellars with Dick in those early days. We both felt that Sellars represented the best of the analytic tradition because he was leading the way in showing how the linguistic

turn with its subtle analytic techniques could be used to clarify and further the discussion of many traditional philosophical issues.[50]

Sellars, in addition to being identified as an analytic philosopher, was also a philosopher of science with a strong background in mathematics; given this preparation, he was exceptionally involved with Peirce and drew on his work, extending Peircean ideas with his own contributions in favor of what has been called his "pragmatic realism" to transcend the dualism of the *praktisch* and *pragmatisch* – in his vocabulary, between "manifest images" and "scientific images."[51] Of Sellars, Robert Brandom – one of Rorty's most distinguished students and one of our most distinguished currently practicing philosophers – observes:

> Wilfrid Sellars is the greatest American philosopher since Charles Sanders Peirce. He is the most profound and systematic epistemological thinker of the 20th Century. When intellectual historians look back at the progress of philosophy, our century will appear as a time when, after three hundred and fifty years, we finally saw through Descartes. It is in our time that the collection of puzzles and problems that have collected around Cartesian dualism of body and mind has been supplanted by those associated with what now appears to be the most fundamental Humean-Kantian dualism of fact and norm. Heading the list of names they will associate with that conceptual sea-change are Wittgenstein and Sellars.[52]

Attending to all Sellars had to say about Peirce, Rorty followed the founder of pragmatism's difficult texts rigorously. As noted earlier, it is patent from his references in "Pragmatism, Categories, and Language" that just as Peirce knew an important part of Kant "by heart," so did Rorty know an equally important part of Peirce by heart.

To report on the climate of Rorty's intellectual and spiritual development during the time of his deepening involvement with Peirce, it is useful to turn once more to "Trotsky and the Wild Orchids" where we can revisit more extensively than Bernstein does Rorty's reflection on the moment of "that initial disillusion (which climaxed about the time I left Chicago [and Hartshorne] to get a Ph.D. in philosophy at Yale)" since which time, as Rorty went on to recount, he "spent forty years looking for a coherent and convincing way of formulating [his] worries about what, if anything, philosophy is good for." Rorty continues, recollecting the intermediate period, twenty years after the "initial disillusion" and the time of writing this 1992 autobiographical piece:

> As I tried to figure out what had gone wrong, I gradually decided that the whole idea of holding reality and justice in a single vision had been

a mistake – that a pursuit of such a vision had been precisely what led Plato astray. More specifically, I decided that only religion – only a nonargumentative *faith in a surrogate parent who, unlike any real parent, embodied love, power, and justice in equal measure* [emphasis added] – could do the trick Plato wanted done. Since I couldn't imagine becoming religious, and indeed had gotten more and more raucously secularist, I decided that the hope of achieving a single vision by becoming a philosopher had been a self-deceptive atheist's way out. So I decided to try to write a book about what intellectual life would be like if one could manage to give up the Platonic attempt to hold reality and justice in a single vision.[53]

That book would be *Contingency, Irony, and Solidarity*, published in 1989. "I desperately wanted to be a Platonist," Rorty remembered, "to become one with the One, to fuse myself with Christ or God or the Platonic form of the Good or something like that." In *Contingency*, as James Ryerson has noted, "Rorty rebuked that objective."[54] But before arriving at that moment, Rorty had already sparked the revival of pragmatism and established himself as its new, if controversial, champion, having, at least for a while, completely internalized Peirce's mode and "philosophic mood."

In the Dutch television interview, Rorty talks about how his childhood shyness and bookishness and his odd interests developed in part as a consequence of his having attended seven or eight different schools as a boy and early adolescent; the only feature common to these various educational experiences having been that he was taunted and bullied in all of them. He speaks touchingly and reticently of the fantasies he entertained about getting back by becoming superior intellectually – "dominating." In "Trotsky and the Wild Orchids," he writes of the transitional period, as he was about to move to Chicago:

> At fifteen I escaped from the bullies who regularly beat me up on the playground of my high school (bullies who, I assumed, would somehow wither away once capitalism had been overcome) by going off to the so-called "Hutchins College" of the University of Chicago.... Insofar as I had any project in mind, it was to reconcile Trotsky and the orchids. [Earlier Rorty noted, "I grew up knowing that all decent people were, if not Trotskyites, at least socialists."] I wanted to find some intellectual or aesthetic framework that would let me – in a thrilling phrase I came across in Yeats – "hold reality and justice in a single vision." By "reality" I meant, more or less, the Wordsworthian moments in which, in the woods around Flatbrookville (and especially in the presence of certain coralroot orchids, and of the smaller yellow lady-slipper), I had felt touched by something numinous, something of ineffable importance, something *really* real. By "justice" I

meant what Norman Thomas and Trotsky both stood for, the liberation of the weak from the strong.[55]

The course that most intrigued him after he began at Hutchins – that he most valued at sixteen, as he told the Dutch interviewer – was a philosophy course because the "order" it provided appealed to his "need to be in control," to "dominate." He found philosophical ideas, at least those then on offer at Chicago in 1946 advanced by the neo-Thomists and Leo Strauss and his cohort, fit the bill; they were "cold, hard, non-sensuous": "Only an appeal to something eternal, absolute, and good," Rorty writes in "Trotsky and the Wild Orchids," – "like the God of St. Thomas or the nature of human beings, as described by Aristotle – would permit one to answer the Nazis, to justify one's choice of social democracy over fascism."[56]

Rorty's parents were both deeply committed socialists. His mother, Winifred, continued in her own way the Social Gospel work of her father, the theologian Walter Rauschenbusch; and his father, James – named for his Civil War-hero uncle killed at Gettysburg, James McKay Rorty (through whose efforts the Rorty family was brought to America) – was always politically active, even "almost … accompan[ying] John Dewey to Mexico as P.R. man for the Commission of Inquiry [into the Moscow Trials] that Dewey chaired." Sidney Hook, Lionel Trilling, and the Italian anarchist Carlo Tresca were, like Dewey, frequent guests in the Rorty home; John Frank (Trotsky's secretary) even lived for a period with the Rortys under an assumed name.[57] One of the shapes Rorty's adolescent rebellion assumed, once he was at Hutchins, was to "sneer," along with Robert Hutchins himself and his friends Mortimer Adler and Richard McKeon, at their "most frequent target": John Dewey and his pragmatism. "All of them [together with the "revered" Leo Strauss] seemed to agree," Rorty continues,

> that something deeper and weightier than Dewey was needed if one was to explain why it would be better to be dead than to be a Nazi. This sounded pretty good to my fifteen-year-old ears. For moral and philosophical absolutes sounded a bit like my beloved orchids – numinous, hard to find, known only to a chosen few. Further, since Dewey was a hero to all the people among whom I had grown up, scorning Dewey was a convenient form of adolescent revolt.[58]

What he does not write about in "Trotsky and the Wild Orchids," nor say anything about during the Dutch interview, is his long immersion in Peirce.

About halfway through the Dutch interview, Rorty speaks of the momentary "consolations" that the beauty of "birds, flowers, landscapes – not people" offer him, and that these moments are "connected with other states of being where … ecstasy … is the norm." The interviewer pushes Rorty to express in more detail what he sees and feels in these moments of experiencing the "numinous," and asks if perhaps, instead, he observes and learns as a naturalist would. Rorty responds that he cannot look at a bird or flower for longer than five minutes – rather, for him it is off to "another orchid, another bird." Rorty's naturalism, in other words, remained confined to listing, classification – a necessary step in our knowledge of nature, as Emerson pointed out, but only as *preliminary* to imagining, to abstracting from the particulars, allowing the "esemplastic power" of the imagination to make "a guess at the riddle"[59] of being, as Peirce did repeatedly. For Rorty, having witnessed his father's repeated breakdowns, letting go of reason's claim to order was far too threatening; his aversion to what Emerson called "reception" connected to a fear of losing himself into what he perceived as the "psychotic" state of his father, with all it entailed of "divine" overtones. In Peirce's far-ranging speculations and emotional volatility, Rorty would have recognized something akin. With his over-arching need "to be in control," continuing to follow Peirce into his projections back into protoplasm's organizing itself into incipient mind or forward into possibilities of multiple universes would have been too much of a danger – better to split the aesthetic pleasure of participation in the celestial pantomime into five-minute fixes, taking in controlled doses the beauty of the precipitates of the cosmic weather in the shape of a yellow lady-slipper or the tail feather of a cedar waxwing. So, unlike Darwin with his finches or Nabokov with his butterflies – Nabokov was another whose work Rorty had much of "by heart," nourished by the "aesthetic bliss" captured in his periods – Rorty did not allow himself to *see through* his wild orchids and birds to what they could reveal about the greater order. Taking on Peirce's knowledge, but not his visionary power, Rorty assuaged his abandonment of the seer by taking on, as a kind of protective coloration, the bird-watching habit of Peirce's mild-mannered avatar, Charles Hartshorne.

VAGUENESS IS REAL[60]

"Pragmatism, Categories, and Language" should be read by anyone wanting to get under the skin of what is at issue, finally and crucially, for pragmatists and for the later Wittgenstein, the Wittgenstein of *Philosophical*

Investigations, as what is at issue requires an experienced guide like Rorty to lead the way: the issue is the troubling nature of our human condition in language. Emerson pointedly described our predicament in "Experience," one of pragmatism's sacred texts, as "the Fall of Man"; we recall once more: "It is very unhappy, but too late to be helped, the discovery we have made, that we exist. That discovery is called the Fall of Man. Ever afterwards, we suspect our instruments."[61] Without language, we would not know that we exist, and, that we will die. Without God or a divine authority as the guarantor of language's correspondence to things as they are, language – the only instrument we have to translate what we know – becomes "suspect." The Darwinian event, which, as noted here earlier in different contexts, Emerson had anticipated by 1836, left those paying attention to the news in free-fall – like Milton's angels cast headlong – out of any possibility of certainty. It was the full realization of this situation that was, as discussed variously in these chapters, the occasion of pragmatism's emergence. Pragmatism's eclipse by analytic and Continental schools during the period surrounding World War II did not diminish the urgency of its address. As Rorty came to realize, the hottest thing off the philosophical press since *Pragmatism* itself, the *Philosophical Investigations*, was as urgently concerned with the self–same issue: the nature and use of language in our brave, new world vacated by transcendental guardians. Rorty recognized moreover that it was Peirce among the pragmatists with whom Wittgenstein's investigations were in conversation. Rorty made this connection explicit in one of the forty illuminating footnotes enriching the thirty-five pages of his already rich-format text exploring their imagined exchanges; the note comments on his purpose in this paper; it is indicated at the end of the following sentence already quoted by Bernstein (who does not reproduce Rorty's emphasis), "What I *am* trying to show is that the closer one brings pragmatism to the writings of the later Wittgenstein and of those influenced by him, the more light they shed on the other":

> In particular, Peirce and Wittgenstein complement each other especially well; one presents you with a bewildering and wonderfully abstract apparatus of categories; the other shoves you into very particular puzzles. Peirce's odd numerological categories, just because they are so abstract and so far from the clichés of the history of philosophy, are perhaps the best handles for grasping what one learns from Wittgenstein. Conversely, Wittgenstein's riddles and aphorisms, just because they are so fresh and fragmentary, let one see the point of some of Peirce's darker sayings.[62]

The clarity with which Rorty encapsulates the reciprocal relationship between Peirce and Wittgenstein in this note is characteristic of the piece as a whole. Equally characteristic is the unqualified appreciation of Peirce's work: "My purpose in this paper is to try to show that the point Peirce is making [about 'the irreducibility of Thirdness' grounding both 'the validity of the pragmatic maxim' and 'Scotistic Realism' – a commonality Rorty will explain] in this identification is sound and important"; Peirce "can direct us toward the crucial insights which generate master strategies"; and "Peirce's odd numerological categories ... are perhaps the best handles for grasping what one learns from Wittgenstein." Additionally, in opening Section I of his text, Rorty, in his characteristic homely "shoot from the hip" style,[63] deftly presents Peirce's argument about "Thirds," distinguishing his position from that of nominalists of any stripe:

> Peirce liked to refer to any doctrine he disagreed with as "nominalistic." One of the dozens of different ways in which he tried to formulate the common error of all nominalists was by calling nominalism the doctrine that vagueness is not real.*[Rorty's footnote here, reflecting his fluency in Peirce's corpus, refers readers to paragraphs in three volumes of his papers detailing various aspects of "vagueness," "nominalism," and "scholastic realism."] Nominalists thought, that is, that whatever was real had sharp edges (like a sense datum or an atomic fact), and that whatever did not have sharp edges could be "reduced" to things that did. Most of Peirce's work was devoted to showing that this reduction could not be performed. Among the vague things which, he thought, nominalists could not reduce (and hence could not account for consistently with their assumptions) were Intelligence, Intention, Signs, Continuity, Potentiality, Meaning, Rules, and Habits. All of these he blithely baptized – to the perpetual delight of neo-Pythagorean hedgehogs among his readers and the confusion of all foxes – "Thirds." The point of his baptism was his claim that phenomena which exhibit features referred to by some or all of these capitalized terms have in common a certain peculiarity: their adequate characterization requires a language which contains, as primitive predicates, the names of triadic relations.**[64]

It could be said without exaggeration that this paragraph is the handle for grasping what one needs to know about Peirce in order to begin understanding his singular contribution. In opening Chapter 3, it was remarked that Peirce recognized the fundamental aspect of three/thirds to our experience of this universe. It was also noted that the triadic is the particular realm where humans reside, what Peirce called "Thirdness," which includes all manner of description; "Thirdness" contains, for example, what happens when one person tells another about something. Joseph

Brent provides a succinct account of the relations of Peirce's categories, offering first Peirce's definitions:

> First is the conception of being or existing independent of anything else. Second is the conception of being relative to, the conception of reaction with, something else. Third is the conception of mediation, whereby a first and second are brought into relation.

Brent then offers as partial gloss:

> Firstness is the chaos of sense experience before it is thought about. It is original, fresh, immediate, spontaneous, and it cannot be articulately thought or asserted, since articulation implies otherness and assertion implies negation of something else.

He then quotes additionally from Peirce on Firstness in a passage reverberating with Emerson's lesson about "the Fall of Man" from, as it were, innocence (Firstness) into experience (language and description):

> Stop to think of it, and it has flown! ["The blackbird whistling/ Or just after."] What the world was to Adam on the day he opened his eyes to it, before he had drawn any distinctions, or had become conscious of his own existence – that is first, present, immediate, fresh, new, initiative, original, spontaneous, free, vivid, [un]conscious, evanescent. Only, remember that every description of it must be false to it.

"Secondness," Brent continues in his glossing, "is existence independent of oneself, otherness, opposite, the dyad; it is the necessary quality in existence which brings about struggle. Peirce called it 'Brute Actuality'." He then goes on to quote once more from Peirce:

> We find secondness in occurrence, because an occurrence is something whose existence consists in our knocking up against it. A hard fact is of the same sort; that is to say, it is something which is there, and which I cannot think away, but am forced to acknowledge as an object or second beside myself, the subject or the number one, and which forms material for the exercise of my will.

Summing up, Brent offers this most useful outline:

> While the monadic quality of Firstness is mere potentiality of what could be and is without existence, the dyadic quality of Secondness is mere individual fact which has no generality. Thirdness gives generality by mediating between a first and a second. It is the category which gives meaning and is meaning itself. For the pragmaticist, the meaning of a first and a second is constituted as Thirdness. Meaning is, therefore, purposive because something *will* [Brent's emphasis] happen when a first meets a second. Words

to describe Thirdness are *mediation, purpose, generality, order, interpretation, representation,* and *hypothesis.*[65]

Rorty, as though having imagined the full import of Peirce learning his "Pythagorean prayers" at his father's knee, understood the profound accuracy of the mature philosopher's having extended the triadic schema to all aspects of experience, *including*, most importantly, language. In his footnote to the last sentence of his aforementioned paper (marked by two asterisks), Rorty underscores the centrality of "Thirds" as explicated by Peirce in relation to *meaning*, explaining that even "tetradic, pentadic, etc. relations could be analyzed into triadic ones, but that no triadic relation could be built up out of monadic or dyadic relations." In other words, any aspect of experience that comes under the headings of intelligence, intention, signs, continuity, potentiality, meaning, rules, and habits – headings that cover the full range of the *vagueness* out of which mental life is fabricated – "cannot be made intelligible in language which lacks names for triadic relationships." (We recall William James's stated intention in composing *The Principles of Psychology*: "the reinstatement of the vague to its proper place in mental life.") Rorty rehearses Peirce's example of the act of giving to illustrate:

> If I give you a book, can you describe my action "adequately" in terms which avoid the prima-facie triadic character of the situation? Can you replace the three-place predicate "giving" with a set of two-place or one-place predicates? The obvious move is to try some such pair of dyads as "You shoved it toward me and I picked it up." But something is missing.... What is missing is ... the kind of thing people mean when they talk of the "meaning" of the action or of the "intention" behind it.... To put it loosely, if something passes from my hand to yours we are, in so far forth, just two things bumping into one another in a somewhat complicated way. The situation thus does not differ in any essential way from the collision of two billiard balls (which is one of Peirce's examples of pure Secondness).[66]

Rorty goes on to contextualize Peirce's formulation of his architectonic of categories, built up out of three into a ten-point schema – like the points comprising Pythagoras's equilateral triangle – within Peirce's comprehensive study of medieval logic out of which the contribution of Duns Scotus held particular weight; hence, his intention to align the "pragmatist maxim" and "Scotistic Realism." "But what illumination does Peirce's Thirdness offer us? And why must he call his doctrine of the reality of Thirdness 'Scotistic Realism?'" Rorty asks. He provides the answer by quoting Peirce, after explaining that the intent of realism is *not* the notion that universals are "things," instead:

> The intent of realism is the opposite; rather than adding new determinate entities to the world, it was intended precisely to get rid of "the Ockhamite prejudice ... that in thought, in being, and in development the indefinite is due to a degeneration from a primary state of perfect definiteness.... The truth is rather on the side of the scholastic realists that *the unsettled is the primal state* [emphasis added], and that definiteness and determinateness ... are, in the large, approximations, developmentally, epistemologically, and metaphysically."[67]

Rorty goes on to clarify:

> For Peirce, it is the nominalist and the reductionist who succumb to belief in metaphysical figments – namely the belief that beneath all the evident fuzziness, vagueness, and generality which we encounter in language (and therefore in all thought* [This footnote cross-references two extensive passages in Peirce, again demonstrating Rorty's intimacy with his papers.]) there are nonfuzzy, particular, clearly intuitable reals (Compare 6.492, 5.312 [two additional sites]).[68]

It is informing to know that during the period when Peirce was composing the anti-Cartesian papers that, as has been noted, marked the beginning of what was to become "pragmatism," he was particularly involved with the history of logic and with Duns Scotus. As Max Fisch offers:

> Through 1867 (and on beyond) Peirce made frequent additions to his library in the history of logic. In March and April he acquired early editions of Duns Scotus. On 1 January 1868 he compiled a "Catalogue of Books on Mediaeval Logic which are available in Cambridge" – more of them in his own library than at Harvard's or anywhere else.[69]

Rorty seems intuitively to have realized about this complicated history that "Peirce was in advance of the positivism of his day ... and [able to] repudiate in advance the stages in the development of empiricism which logical positivism represented" *because* he had expertly trained himself in the history of logic *and* was also expert in actual, physical measurement, calculation, and imaginative projection –that it was this combination of skills that permitted the "group of insights and a philosophical mood" that linked him to Wittgenstein.

Wittgenstein was, of course, as Rorty and the philosophical community in 1961 knew of the man who "by 1939 was recognized as the foremost philosophical genius of his time," also superbly trained in logic, having by the age of twenty-four superseded his teacher, Bertrand Russell, to become the "wearer of Russell's mantle in logic."[70] Moreover, also like Peirce, Wittgenstein had practical experience of the physical world, having by age nineteen earned a certificate in engineering in Berlin and then continuing on to Manchester to further his studies by concentrating in aeronautics. Among his explorations, Wittgenstein "experimented with the design of kites by trial and error in hopes of someday constructing and flying his own airplane."[71] It was while enrolled "in the Engineering Department at Manchester University that he began to develop an interest in pure mathematics" and "pursued research in the logical foundations of mathematics."[72] It has been observed of Wittgenstein's preparation in engineering that it both "influenced [his] conception of the solutions to philosophical problems" and "also seemed to significantly affect his philosophical style."[73] A passage discussing force from Heinrich Hertz's *Principles of Mechanics* that the young Wittgenstein committed to memory offers a clear instance of the importance of this training to his later manner of thinking: "When these painful contradictions are removed, the question as to the nature of force will not have been answered; but our minds, no longer vexed, will cease to ask illegitimate questions."[74] One can hear the echo of this passage in Wittgenstein's 1939 argument with Alan Turing about contradiction; their exchange is recorded by Ray Monk, who closes his account with:

> "You seem to be saying," suggested Turing, "that if one uses a little common sense, one will not get into trouble." "No," thundered Wittgenstein, "that is NOT what I meant at all." His point was rather that a contradiction cannot lead one astray because it leads nowhere at all. One cannot calculate wrongly with a contradiction, because one simply cannot use it to calculate. One can do nothing with contradictions, except waste time puzzling over them.[75]

Putting two and two together, Rorty writes, in closing the second introductory paragraph of "Pragmatism, Categories, and Language" from which Bernstein and others have quoted (without, however, including these sentences):

> A little empiricism, plus a passion for rigor, will make a man a nominalist. Thinking about the antinomies created by the mutual repugnance of experience and rigor will drive him, if he thinks as long and as hard as Peirce and Wittgenstein did, to something quite different. In trying to show that this "something different" was pretty much the same for both men, I shall argue ... .[76]

Rorty goes on to list the points of commonality that he will elaborate painstakingly in the three sections of the paper, revealing throughout that he was, as it were, in on the ground floor of Peirce's perceptions, beginning with the premise that "language is incurably vague, but perfectly real and utterly inescapable."[77] And, most curiously in light of his dismissive footnote in *Philosophy and the Mirror of Nature* concerning Peirce's odd theories about protoplasm in his 1892 "Man's Glassy Essence," the conceptual framework Rorty draws from Peirce to illustrate his own argument in "Pragmatism, Categories, and Language" about the significance of Peirce's contribution is only extended and more fully elaborated in "Man's Glassy Essence"; yet this paper is not referred to at all by Rorty either in passing or in a note. That conceptual framework derives from Peirce's brilliant realization that what nominalists, Platonists, and other believers in eternal forms call "universals" are, in fact, nothing more than *habits* of the behavior of matter and mind acquired over eons. In other words, Peirce naturalized universals, demonstrating through his protoplasm example that they are habits that last because they *work*, are *useful*. As Rorty explains:

> Peirce, looking at the universe as perfused with habits as well as with signs, explains the convenience of naming certain batches – of slicing up nature in certain ways, and thereby developing certain habits of expectation – by reference to the fact that nature has already sliced itself up by developing habits on its own.*

The asterisk here indicates Rorty's exceedingly important footnote that ties this Peircean realization to how Peirce understands "belief" and to work, developing this understanding by Wilfrid Sellars – to whom, as noted earlier, Rorty was directly indebted – as well as to Wittgenstein. Rorty continues in the note to observe that

> the thesis that nature has habits ... the starting point of Peirce's solution to the problem of induction (cf. 5.170, 5.457) ... is ... too large a topic to enter on here; suffice it to say that he is here putting in metaphysical language the conclusion at which present-day inquiry is now gradually arriving: that the control which nature exercises over our inductive inferences appears not only in the results of experiment and observation but in the construction of frameworks within which we observe and experiment, and that this latter sort of control is not reducible to the former.

Rorty ends this footnote referencing both Nelson Goodman and Michael Polanyi and continues in his text to complete his paragraph with a passage that serves as a perfect gloss to one of Peirce's "darker," more inscrutable passages in the 1905 *Monist* paper quoted earlier in this chapter in which he reclaimed his pragmatism to rename it "pragmaticism." Here then the passage from Rorty following "developing habits on its own" in the lines quoted above:

Thus his [Peirce's] realism can be seen as the thesis that the "reasoned choice of usage which is naming *is* [Rorty's emphasis] rational, in part, because of its respect for the rationality in nature. [We recall Emerson's enjoining us to "habits of conversation with nature."[78]] But for nature to be rational in this sense does not mean that it "recognizes the same universals" as does the mind, but simply that it contains the sort of determinate indeterminations that our mind does.[79]

And here the passage from Peirce, reconnecting his understanding of the manner and scope of his method to Kant's *pragmatisch*:

> [[T]he *pragmatisch*] express[es] relation to some definite human purpose [thereby including the *praktisch*]. Now quite the most striking feature of the new theory [Peirce's "pragmatism" rechristened "pragmaticism" with this paper] was its recognition of an inseparable connection between rational cognition and rational purpose, and that consideration it was which determined the preference for the name pragmatism.

In other words, since we belong to the larger order, recognizing the connection between that order and human purposes is recognizing, as it were, our own "thoughts come back to us with a certain alienated majesty."

Time and space constraints forbid a comprehensive interlineated reading of Rorty's paper and Peirce's source texts. Instead, I offer an excerpt from "Man's Glassy Essence" as a "frontier instance"[80] of what Rorty came to have as the necessary background to understand and explain, as he does in "Pragmatism, Categories, and Language," Peirce's central notions of "the reality of Thirdness," of *synechism*, of a "picture of the universe as perfused by signs," and "of a man's mind being itself a sign ... and 'nature' (the sum of objects of knowledge) being an utterer of signs which we interpret."[81] Here, then, is the passage from Peirce – the extended quotation clearly necessary to capture Peirce's intricate exposition; I have added relevant comments in brackets. After detailing the many extraordinary properties discovered about protoplasm, he continues:

> Another physical property of protoplasm is that of taking habits.... But the [property] which has next to be mentioned, while equally undeniable, is infinitely more wonderful. It is that protoplasm feels. We have no direct evidence that this is true of protoplasm universally, and certainly some kinds feel far more than others. But there is fair analogical inference that all protoplasm feels. It not only feels but exercises all the functions of mind....
>
> If consciousness belongs to all protoplasm, by what mechanical constitution is this to be accounted for? The slime is nothing but a chemical compound.... [Recent work on slime molds investigates the means whereby

slime mold cells communicate and move as one organism.] Protoplasm certainly does feel; and unless we are to accept a weak dualism, the property must be shown to arise from some peculiarity of the mechanical system. Yet the attempt to deduce from it the three laws of mechanics, applied to never so ingenious a mechanical contrivance, would be obviously futile. It can never be explained, unless we admit that physical events are but degraded or undeveloped forms of psychical events....

It remains to consider the physical relations of general ideas. It may be well here to reflect that if matter has no existence except as a specialization of the mind, it follows that whatever affects matter according to regular laws is itself matter. [Here we can overhear both the ongoing conversation with William James that issued in James's focus on "habit" in *The Principles of Psychology* and later in his "radical empiricism" as well as the lingering strains of Emerson's "Spirit is matter reduced to an extreme thinness – O *so* thin!"] But all mind is directly or indirectly connected with all matter, and acts in a more or less regular way, so that all mind more or less partakes of the nature of all matter. Hence, it would be a mistake to conceive of the psychical and the physical aspects of matter as two aspects absolutely distinct. Viewing a thing from the outside, considering its relations of action and reaction with other things, it appears as matter. Viewing it from the inside, looking at its immediate character as feeling, it appears as consciousness. [These two sentences echo almost to the word James's observation in *Principles* that were later rephrased by Niels Bohr.] These two views are combined when we remember that mechanical laws are nothing but acquired habits, like all the regularities of mind, including the tendency to take habits, itself; and that this action of habit is nothing but generalisation [*sic* spelling], and generalisation is nothing but the spreading of feeling. But the question is, how do general ideas appear in the molecular theory of protoplasm?

... if habit be a primary property of mind, it must be equally so of matter, as a kind of mind ... a general idea is a certain modification of consciousness which accompanies any regularity or general relation between chance actions.

The consciousness of a general idea has a certain "unity of the ego" in it, which is identical when it passes from one mind to another. It is, therefore, quite analogous to a person; and, indeed, a person is only a particular kind of general idea. Long ago, in the *Journal of Speculative Philosophy* (Vol. II, p. 156) [This, "Some Consequences of Four Incapacities," which Rorty certainly knew, is the 1868 paper quoted earlier that has been recognized by many as marking, even before "How to Make Our Ideas Clear," the beginning of American pragmatism. It is in this paper where Peirce quotes from Isabella's "Man's Glassy Essence" speech; Peirce's sustained attention to developing this thought over thirty-four years – *carried far enough* – is especially to be noted.], I pointed out that a person is nothing but a symbol involving a general idea; but my views were, then, too nominalistic to enable me to see that every general idea has the unified feeling of a person.[82]

"Nature is mind precipitate," Emerson observed in *Nature*; "The mind feels when it thinks," Jonathan Edwards observed about a century earlier, the first in the line of America's feeling thinkers, or thinking feelers, who would shape the method of pragmatism. Peirce was, so to speak, only following directions.

THE RIVALRY OF THE PATTERNS IS THE HISTORY OF THE WORLD[83]

In his biography of Peirce, Joseph Brent points out that in "Man's Glassy Essence" and in his speculative writing generally, Peirce anticipated the late twentieth-century work of theoretical physicists working with quantum mechanics, such as Freeman Dyson, Richard Feynman, John A. Wheeler, and David Bohm. As Brent observes, Bohm, never having read Peirce, came to the same understanding of the order of things as Peirce had so much earlier. (In addition, Bohm, of course, like the other noted quantum physicists of his moment, had the benefit of having observed and tracked subatomic particles in cloud chambers and with later devices such as bubble and spark chambers.) Bohm writes in his noted 1980 volume, *Wholeness and the Implicate Order*:

> Throughout this book the central underlying theme has been the unbroken wholeness of the totality of existence as an undivided flowing movement without border.
>
> It seems clear ... that the implicate order is particularly suitable for the understanding of such unbroken wholeness in flowing movement, for in the implicate order the totality of existence is enfolded within each region of space (and time). So whatever part, element, or aspect we may abstract in thought, this still enfolds the whole and is therefore intrinsically related to the totality from which it has been abstracted. Thus, wholeness permeated all that is being discussed, from the very outset.[84]

This "undivided flowing movement without border" is Peirce's *synechism*; it is, also, of course, William James's *vague*, from the French word for "wave"; a quantum wave is itself composed of particles only visible when observed. (It is instructive to remember here Emerson's prehension: "Society is a wave. The wave moves onward, but the water of which it is composed does not. The same particle does not rise from the valley to the ridge. Its unity is only phenomenal. The persons who make up a nation to-day, next year die, and their experience with them."[85]) As noted earlier, *synechism*, Peirce's coinage, derives from the Greek verb *synecho*, meaning "continuing and holding together," originally describing the moving together in rhythm of tiers of rowers on a bireme or trireme, propelling their archaic craft through the wine-dark sea. Peirce experienced this sense of continuity, and of participating with others to propel ideas into the dark future because of the very high sort of seeing into invisible time that he had learned from childhood to make his habit of mind. Rorty, for whatever combination of constraints, could not or would not follow Peirce into this "high sort of seeing" that Emerson describes, though he did speak and write *about* it:

> This insight [into "the symmetry and truth" which accounts, for example, for the "iterated nodes of a seashell" or the "habits" of protoplasm], which expresses itself by what is called Imagination, is a very high sort of seeing, which does not come by study, but by the intellect being where and what it sees, by sharing the path, or circuit of things through forms ["all mean egotism vanishe[d]"], and so making them translucid to others. The path of things is silent.[86]

In his last published piece before his death, "The Fire of Life," composed for *Poetry* magazine, Rorty, knowing that he would soon succumb to an inoperable pancreatic cancer, reflected that his "ambivalent relation to poetry" was most probably "a result of Oedipal complications by having had a poet for a father." "See James Rorty, *Children of the Sun* (Macmillan, 1926)" he added in parentheses and continued,

> However that may be, I now wish that I had spent more of my life with verse. This is not because I fear having missed out on truths that are incapable of statement in prose. There are no such truths; there is nothing about death that Swinburne and Landor knew but Epicurus and Heidegger failed to grasp. Rather it is because I would have lived more fully if I had been able to rattle off more old chestnuts – just as I would have if I had made more close friends. Cultures with richer vocabularies are more fully human – farther removed from the beasts – than those with poorer ones.[87]

Rorty opened the piece by framing his reflection with a reference to his 2003 essay, "Pragmatism and Romanticism," in which he restated the argument of Shelley's "Defense of Poetry":

> At the heart of Romanticism, I said, was the claim that reason can only follow paths that the imagination has first broken. No words, no reasoning. No imagination, no new words. No such words, no moral or intellectual progress.

He went on, summarizing his own argument:

> I ended the essay by contrasting the poet's ability to give us a richer language with the philosopher's attempt to acquire non-linguistic access to the really real. Plato's dream of such access was itself a great poetic achievement. But by Shelley's time, I argued, it had been dreamt out. We are now more able than Plato was to acknowledge our finitude – to admit that we shall never be in touch with something greater than ourselves. We hope instead that human life here on earth will become richer as the centuries go by because the language used by our remote descendants will have more resources than ours did. Our vocabulary will stand to theirs as that of our primitive ancestors stands to ours.
>
> In that essay, as in previous writings, I used "poetry" in an extended sense. I stretched Harold Bloom's term "strong poet" to cover prose writers who had invented new language games for us to play – people like Plato, Newton, Marx, Darwin and Freud as well as versifiers like Milton and Blake. These games might involve mathematical equations, or inductive arguments, or dramatic narratives, or (in the case of the versifiers) prosodic innovation. But the distinction between prose and verse was irrelevant to my philosophical purposes.

Rorty then relates that it was shortly after finishing "Pragmatism and Romanticism" that he was diagnosed with the inoperable cancer. Some months after that, in conversation with his elder son and a visiting cousin, a Baptist minister, he was asked by his cousin whether he had found his thoughts turning toward religious topics; he replied that he had not. His son then asked, "Well, what about philosophy?" Again, he replied "No." His son persisted, "Hasn't *anything* you've read been of any use?" "Yes, I found myself blurting out, 'poetry.'" "Which poems?" his son asked:

> I quoted two old chestnuts that I had recently dredged up from memory and been oddly cheered by, the most quoted lines of Swinburne's "Garden of Proserpine":
>
> > We thank with brief thanksgiving
> > > Whatever gods may be
> > That no life lives for ever;
> > That dead men rise up never:
> > That even the weariest river
> > > Winds somewhere safe to sea.
>
> and Landor's "On His Seventy-Fifth Birthday":
>
> > Nature I loved, and next to Nature, Art;
> > I warmed both hands before the fire of life,
> > It sinks, and I am ready to depart.

I found comfort in those slow meanders and those stuttering embers. I suspect that no comparable effect could have been produced by prose. Not just imagery, but also rhyme and rhythm were needed to do the job. In lines such as these, all three conspire to produce a degree of compression, and thus of impact, that only verse can achieve. Compared to the shaped charges contrived by versifiers, even the best prose is scattershot.

Rorty was defensively arrogant, even in the face of "[d]eath's ironic scraping"[88] – "This is not because I fear having missed out on truths that are incapable of statement in prose. There are no such truths"; even though he *felt* the *truth* of comfort ("Truth is what *happens* to an idea"), he was blinded by what he feared. Given the experience of his father's last psychotic breakdown, Rorty, becoming by his own account ever more "raucously secularist," and in spite of his having felt in his youth, like Emerson, "in the woods ... touched by something numinous, something of ineffable importance, something *really* real," turned away from exploring that indeed it might be possible to continue to "be in touch with something greater than ourselves," though there might not ever be, a "vocabulary" adequate to describe it. (As Stevens voiced, without giving up on the attempt, nor gainsaying vision, "...Where shall I find/Bravura adequate to this great hymn?"[89]) Rather than continue to entertain this possibility, Rorty chose disillusion as his last illusion: "Our only cognitive access to beavers, trees, stars, our own subjectivity, or the transcendental ego lies in our ability to wield such expressions as 'beaver,' 'tree,' 'star,' 'subjectivity,' and 'transcendental ego.'"[90] But of course, as we recall Emerson detailed: "Imagination ... does not come by study, but by *the intellect being where and what it sees*, by sharing the path, or circuit of things through forms," allowing the ego to dissolve into "the NOT ME."[91] Rorty could not afford such dissolution; better, then, disillusion. But why not, at least, allow for others in our pluralistic universe that we include among our working vocabularies hypotheses, expressions of, as Stevens called them "supreme fictions"? Indeed, in "Pragmatism and Romanticism" and elsewhere, Rorty celebrated the good of these imaginings. But in his own quotidian experience, rather than having pursued visionary poetry – whether in poems of "high seeing," or in following Peirce into his "high seeing" of the solar galaxy and the imagined community of minds – Rorty offered instead his story that "Plato's dream" of "access to the really real" was by Shelley's time "dreamt out," in this following Nietzsche, patron saint of *uber*-philosophers:

> When he used the figure of the divided line to symbolize the ascent from opinion to knowledge, and when he used the metaphor of the cave for the

same purpose, Plato was implicitly recognizing that the only way to escape from redescription was to attain a kind of knowledge that was not discursive – a kind that did not rely on choice of a particular linguistic formulation. To reach truth that one cannot be argued out of is to escape from the linguistically expressible to the ineffable. Only the ineffable – what is not describable at all – cannot be described differently. [We think again of Stevens's famous line closing "The Snow Man": "Nothing that is not there and the nothing that is."]

When Nietzsche says that a thing conceived apart from its relationships would not be a thing, he should be read as saying that since all language is a matter of relating some things to other things, what is not so related cannot be talked of. Language establishes relationships, by, for example, tying blood in with sunsets and full moon with tree trunks. Lack of describability means lack of relations, so our only access to the indescribable must be the sort of direct awareness that the empiricist has of redness and that the mystic has of God. Much of the history of Western philosophy, from Plotinus to Meister Eckhart down to Husserl and Russell, is the history of the quest for such direct awareness. . . .

Nietzsche viewed this quest as a symptom of cowardice – of inability to bear the thought that we shall always live and move and have our being within a cloud of words.[92]

It is, of course, understandable, if sadly ironic, that Rorty internalized Nietzsche's view of this quest as a symptom of cowardice. In the opening paragraph of "Derrida and the Philosophical Tradition," an essay collected in the 1998 volume of his *Philosophical Papers*, Rorty characterized Nietzsche in this way:

In the actual world Nietzsche was a twitchy, irresolute, nomadic nerd who never got a life outside of literature. . . . Could he have written so well against resentment if he had experienced it less often? Could he have written The Will to Power if he had gotten some?[93]

Clearly no longer himself the "nerd" he described himself to be in his youth, and clearly having used his own will to power to become one of philosophy's "heavy hitters," Rorty did not externally inhabit a spiritual environment anything like Nietzsche's – and yet. The effects of the repeated bullying in childhood and adolescence lingered in the compensating feeling-tone of his writing, so often characterized by pugnacity, brashness, almost abusive dismissiveness – as when, for example, he refers to Peirce "as just one more whacked-out triadomaniac" – we shall return to this remark and its context just a bit further on. It is also important to register – as Neil Gross has underscored in his sociologically inflected biography, and as Rorty himself recounted in the very last piece he wrote before his death, an "intellectual autobiography"[94] – that the choices he made of which figures to wrestle or to ignore were determined as much, if not more, by the intellectual fashions of the culture and the profession as they were by what Emerson would have called his temperament and Jonathan Edwards, his heart.

Temperamentally, Rorty, like Nietzsche, was a pessimist – clinically a depressive, if not a manic-depressive like Nietzsche. In this context, it is informing to consider the following description of Rorty's manner in speaking:

> Diffidence, surely, is rarely audible in Rorty ... he is more likely to give the impression of self-assurance (his harshest critics would say "brashness") than timidity or reserve. Interestingly, his colleagues have always drawn attention to the curious disparity between his spoken and written tone. Rorty's voice, as Daniel Dennett notes, "is sort of striking – those firebrand views delivered in the manner of Eeyore". Of Rorty's mode of presentation, the British philosopher Jonathan Ree says, "There's a tremendous kind of melancholy about it. He tries to be a gay Nietzschean, but it's an effort for him." For [James] Conant, hearing Rorty speak for the first time was something of a revelation. "It's easy to read his writings in a register of excitement and a heightened breathless voice," he explains. "But the note that I heard when he was reading these sentences in his own cadence and rhythm was – for want of a better word – depression. I thought, this is the voice of a man who feels as if he's been let down or betrayed by philosophy." Jurgen Habermas similarly concurs that Rorty's antiphilosophy "seems to spring from the melancholy of a disappointed metaphysician."[95]

In contrast, Emerson, James, Dewey – all three of whom Rorty conflates with Nietzsche in focusing our energies on the creation of better vocabularies – and Peirce, as well, *converted* themselves to optimism, almost as a form or residue of religion, of faith, and left open the possibility of there being a greater order. (For Peirce, James, and Dewey, of course, this conversion was directly connected to what they knew of the physiology of habit.) Rorty – the "strict atheist" and witness of his father "gone psychotic" – clearly refused conversion. In arguing for more and richer vocabularies, however, he was, if in a limited way and in spite of himself, sharing in Peirce's vision of an ever-perfecting human community, persevering despite knowing that "the imperfect is our paradise."

Abandoning the quest for "something greater than ourselves," forgetting Emerson's reminder from Proverbs that "Where there is no vision, the people perish"[96] – while nonetheless claiming his "metaphor of endlessly expanding circles" as the model Nietzsche and Wittgenstein used to supersede "Plato's metaphor of ascent to the indubitable" – Rorty chose to shape his poetic habit of mind from snippets of "old chestnuts," the equivalents of his five-minute fixes of "certain coralroot orchids" and red-wing blackbirds. We recall that Darwin found in the supreme fiction conjured in Milton's *Paradise Lost* the key to his theory of evolution and that Niels Bohr found in Lucretius's *On Nature* the clue he needed to imagine atomic theory; Darwin and Bohr lost themselves in the "high seeing" of these poets, carried by their words beyond the limits of words. But for Rorty, who so powerfully talked *about* our primary debt to "strong poets," what was most necessary in his own economy, as he disclosed so ingenuously in the Dutch television interview, was "being in control." Where Peirce was able to perceive that even in the absence of a divinely guided order or a world of eternal forms "something greater than ourselves" *was itself the continuity* that links our being back not only to monocellular protoplasm, but also to the matter of the stars and ahead to generations beyond counting, Rorty split infinity: "We are now more able than Plato was to acknowledge our finitude – to admit that we shall never be in touch with something greater than ourselves. We hope *instead* that human life here on earth will become richer as the centuries go by." For Peirce it was *both/and*, as we recall from Chapter 3:

> And then, after the universe is dead (according to the prediction of some scientists), and all life has ceased forever, will not the shock of atoms continue though there will be no mind to know it? To this I reply that, though in no possible state of knowledge can any number be great enough to express the relation between the amount of what rests unknown to the amount of the known, yet it is unphilosophical to suppose that, with regard to any given question (which has any clear meaning), investigation would not bring forth a solution to it, if it were carried far enough. Who would have said, a few years ago, that we could ever know of what substances stars are made whose light may have been longer in reaching us than the human race has existed? Who can be sure of what we shall not know in a few hundred years? Who can guess what would be the result of continuing the pursuit of science for ten thousand years, with the activity of the last hundred? And if it were to go on for a million, or a billion, or any number of years you please, how is it possible to say that there is any question which might not ultimately be solved?
>
> But it may be objected, "Why make so much of these remote considerations, especially when it is your principle that only practical distinctions have a meaning?" Well, I must confess that it makes very little difference whether we say that a stone on the bottom of the ocean, in complete darkness, is brilliant or not – that is to say, that it *probably* makes no difference, remembering always that that stone *may* be fished up to-morrow. But that there are gems at the bottom of the sea, flowers in the untraveled desert,

etc., are propositions which, like that about a diamond being hard when it is not pressed, concern much more the arrangement of our language than they do the meaning of our ideas.

Rorty would have done well in his aspiration for many and richer vocabularies, to have remained in open conversation with Peirce. He would also have done well to attend *practically* to "Plato's dream" as the "poetic achievement" he recognized it to be: the myth of an ascent beyond hypotheses, simply a figure for our continuing process, *not* its end – like the myth of the Messiah, a metaphor for striving, patience, abiding aspiration, a particularly useful story to tell the inhabitants of "this new yet unapproachable America." As Rorty, invoking Hilary Putnam, reminded his readers in *Achieving Our Country* (1998), the "primacy of the practical over the theoretical" is "the defining essence of pragmatism," asking, "What can philosophy do for the United States?"[97]

DECONSTRUCTING RORTY

Instead of continuing his conversation with Peirce in the pages of his writing, from having been intimate with his thinking and imagining as he put together "Pragmatism, Categories, and Language," and translating what was useful for him from Peirce's vocabulary into his own *lingua franca* to become the new champion of pragmatism in *Philosophy and the Mirror of Nature*, Rorty went on not only to repress him – that is, apart from what may or may not have been the case psychologically, he did, in fact, increasingly efface Peirce's influence – but also, eventually, to revile him as he unwove and rewove a different narrative of himself in "The Pragmatist's Progress" (one of the 1990 Tanner Lectures, given in response to the work of Umberto Eco). In this context and before looking at that piece, it is informing to read the first paragraph of Rorty's 1988 paper, "Inquiry as Recontextualization: An Anti-Dualist Account of Interpretation":

> Think of human minds as webs of beliefs and desires, of sentential attitudes – webs which continually reweave themselves so as to accommodate new sentential attitudes. Do not ask where the new beliefs and desires come from. Forget, for the moment, about the external world, as well as about the dubious interface between self and world called "perceptual experience." Just assume that new ones keep popping up, and that some of them put strains on old beliefs and desires. We call some of these strains "contradictions" and others "tensions." We alleviate both by various techniques. For example, we may simply drop an old belief or desire. Or we may create a whole host of new beliefs and desires in order to encapsulate the disturbing

intruder, reducing the strain which the old beliefs and desires put on it and which it puts on them. Or we may just unstitch, and thus erase, a whole range of beliefs and desires – we may stop *having* [Rorty's emphasis] attitudes toward sentences which use a certain word (the word "God," or "phlogiston," for example).[98]

In "The Pragmatist's Progress," Rorty begins by describing his reading of *Foucault's Pendulum* as "a send-up of structuralism" before coming to realize that "By interpreting *Foucault's Pendulum* in this way I was doing the same kind of thing as is done by all those monomaniacal taxonomists who whirl round the pendulum." He then offers an initially disarming and consistently disclosive account of himself that ends with an interpretation of his own earlier engagement with Peirce that would certainly send all but the most dogged of scholars off the scent of what he had learned from his close encounter with Peirce and the *Third* kind[99]:

> My own equivalent of the secret history of the Templars – the grid which I impose on any book I come across – is a semi-autobiographical narrative of the Pragmatist's Progress. At the beginning of this particular quest romance, it dawns on the Seeker after Enlightenment that all the great dualisms of Western Philosophy – reality and appearance, pure radiance and diffuse reflection, mind and body, intellectual rigour and sensual sloppiness, orderly semiotics and rambling semiosis – can be dispensed with. They are not to be synthesized into higher unities, not *aufgehoben* [merged, overridden, repealed, redescribed], but rather actively forgotten. An early stage of Enlightenment comes when one reads Nietzsche and begins thinking of all these dualisms as just so many metaphors for the contrast between an imagined state of total power, mastery and control and one's own present impotence. A further state is reached when, upon rereading *Thus Spake Zarathustra*, one comes down with the giggles. At that point, with a bit of help from Freud, one begins to hear talk about the Will to Power as just a high-faluting euphemism for the male's hope of bullying the females into submission or the child's hope of getting back at Mummy and Daddy.

> The final stage of the Pragmatist's Progress comes when one begins to see one's previous peripeties not as stages in the ascent toward Enlightenment, but simply as the contingent results of encounters with various books which happened to fall into one's hands. This stage is pretty hard to reach, for one is always being distracted by daydreams: daydreams in which the heroic pragmatist plays a Walter Mitty-like role in the immanent teleology of world history. But if the pragmatist can escape from such daydreams, he or she will eventually come to think of himself or herself as, like everyone else, capable of as many descriptions as there are purposes to be served. There are as many descriptions as there are uses to which the pragmatist might be put, by his or her self or by others. This is the stage in which all

descriptions (including one's self-description as a pragmatist) are evaluated according to their efficacy as instruments for purposes, rather than by their fidelity to the object described.

So much for the Pragmatist's Progress – a narrative I often use for purposes of self-dramatization, and one into which I was charmed to find myself being able to fit Professor Eco. Doing so enabled me to see both of us having overcome our earlier ambitions to be code-crackers. This ambition led me to waste my twenty-seventh and twenty-eighth years trying to discover the secret of Charles Sanders Peirce's esoteric doctrine of "the reality of Thirdness" and thus of his fantastically elaborate semiotico-metaphysical "System." I imagined that a similar urge must have led the young Eco to the study of that infuriating philosopher, and that a similar reaction must have enabled him to see Peirce as just one more whacked-out triadomaniac. In short, by using this narrative as a grid, I was able to think of Eco as a fellow pragmatist.[100]

One would have thought that as one of the masters of the contemporary universe, among the first crop of MacArthur "geniuses," Rorty could have afforded to be accurate and generous in his acknowledgments rather than to keep secret the places he found some of his most valuable treasures, like keeping secret the places where he had found his wild orchids.

What's the use of making a fuss about this repression? Of spending time and space tracing Rorty's appropriation and misappropriation of Peirce? Why not simply remark on yet another instance of the anxiety of influence and leave it at that? Because the real question is a somewhat inverted form of the one Cavell asks in connection with claiming Emerson as a pragmatist, "What is lost if Emerson's voice is lost?" In this case, "What is lost if Peirce's voice is lost?"

Rorty's public announcement of his rejection of Peirce came in a footnote to the Introduction to *Consequences of Pragmatism*, published in 1982; Rorty indicates this in another footnote to a 1986 piece, "Pragmatism, Davidson and Truth," where he writes, "I started retracting this Peirceanism ["Peirce's unfortunate attempt ... to define truth in terms of 'the end of inquiry'"] in the Introduction to that book (e.g., p. xlv, written in 1981) and am still at it." (A study of Rorty's footnotes would provide an illuminating *under-study*, so to speak, of both his influences and anxieties.) Rorty continues in this later footnote to observe that he was "persuaded of the untenability of [the] Peircean view" by an article published by Michael Williams in a 1980 issue of the *Review of Metaphysics*, "in particular by his claim ... 'that we have no idea what it would be for a theory to be ideally complete and comprehensive ... or of what it would be for an inquiry to have an end'."[101] In the earlier recanting footnote,

Rorty indicates how he was led to escape from the "trap" of Peirce's "end of inquiry" *definition* of truth:

> Many pragmatists (including myself) have not, in fact, always been wise enough to avoid this trap. Peirce's definition of truth as that to which inquiry will converge has often seemed a good way for the pragmatist to capture the realists' intuition that Truth is One. But he should not try to capture it. There is no more reason for the pragmatist to try to assimilate this intuition than for him to accept the intuition that there is always One Morally Best Thing To Do in every situation. Nor is there any reason for him to think that a science in which, as in poetry, new vocabularies proliferate without end, would be inferior to one in which all inquiries communicated in the Language of Unified Science. (I am grateful to discussions with [Hilary] Putnam for persuading me to reject the seduction of Peirce's definition – although, of course, Putnam's reasons for doing so are not mine.[102] I am also grateful to a recent article by Simon Blackburn, "Truth, Realism, and the Regulation of Theory" ... which makes the point that "It may be that the notion of improvement [in our theories] is sufficient to interpret remarks to the effect that my favorite theory may be wrong, but not itself sufficient to justify the notion of a limit of investigation).[103]

It is clear from the terms of the claims against the Peircean view that Rorty takes up here that what has happened is that Rorty has fallen into a different trap, one that his signature argument about the good of proliferating vocabularies is designed to avoid: he argues, that is, that inventing a new vocabulary allows one to escape the trap of attempting to frame a vision, or "a guess at the riddle," in terms of an already existing vocabulary, an inappropriate or outworn language game whose rules outlaw the moves of the newly invented game. In the case of Peirce's "end of inquiry," Rorty et al. here have fallen into the trap of arguing *in analytic terms* against Peirce's *pragmatist option*. As Rorty elsewhere offers, "revolutionary achievements in the arts, in the sciences, and in moral and political thought typically occur when somebody realizes that two or more of our vocabularies are interfering with each other, and proceeds to invent a new vocabulary to replace both."[104] As is evident in the passage quoted again from "How to Make Our Ideas Clear," Peirce was not offering a *definition* of truth as what will be agreed upon "at the end of inquiry," but – like Plato with his allegory of the cave or myth of the ascent – a fable, a figure of capable imagination. As Cheryl Misak has recently noted, Peirce "did not want to *define* truth as that which satisfies our aims in inquiry. A dispute in definition, he says, is usually a 'profitless discussion.'"[105] *Figures of the quest for truth* are *not*, in terms that Rorty borrows from Ian Hacking, "truth-value candidates"[106]; *definitions of truth* are.

But what this scholastic nit-picking allowed Rorty to do was to justify unstitching the shadow of Peirce from his equipage. ("'Merely philosophical' questions," Rorty notes in "The Contingency of Language," "are attempts to stir up a factitious theoretical quarrel between vocabularies which have proved capable of peaceful coexistence ... all cases in which philosophers have given their subject a bad name by seeing difficulties nobody else sees."[107]) What is lost, however, in Rorty's occulting Peirce's presence is not so much his voice – since Rorty so masterfully arrogates it into his own down-home idiom that while it seems as though he is speaking another language, he is, in fact, channeling Peirce – but rather, the "irrational element,"[108] the "transcendentalist strain" entailed by Peirce's "end of inquiry" figure. As Misak observes, "There is something at which we aim that goes beyond what seems right to us here and now. The Peircean pragmatist calls that truth."[109] Misak's view is shared by James Conant and John McDowell, although they do not specify that it is only "the Peircean pragmatist" who calls this truth.[110]

Rorty's extraordinary facility in learning new language games combined with the polished Irish barroom charm of the non-technical writing style he uses to address non-specialists made him one of the most persuasive and important public intellectuals of his time. His profound commitment to the possibilities offered by a liberal democracy and his unflagging commitment to education and social reform exemplified, in the manner of Dewey, his recuperated hero, what philosophy can do in the United States. Rorty added to the varieties of pragmatism what he called "cultural politics" at its best. Because of his stature as a public figure, even if a controversial figure within the restricted arena of the academy, it is all the more necessary to reenter into his account of the Pragmatist's Progress his debt to Peirce concerning the nature of hope and the use of philosophy. As Vincent Colapietro offers:

> Richard Rorty spoke more persuasively to a contemporary audience than any other pragmatist of his generation.... So we might turn (or perhaps return) to the question, What *use* [Colapietro's emphasis] may I (and I precisely as a Peircean) make of Rorty? Was Rorty rejecting the possibility of painstaking, honest inquiry of the kind championed by Peirce or rather was he (precisely in his role as ironist) questioning the actuality of philosophy being an instance of such inquiry?[111]

Along the way to an answer to Colapietro's question, it is *useful* to look at *Achieving Our Country* (1998), where Rorty addresses the vexed issue of political responsibility and national pride and writes:

I think the Dewey-Whitman answer is that there are many things that should chasten and temper such pride, but that nothing a nation has done should make it impossible for a constitutional democracy to regain self-respect. To say that certain acts *do* [Rorty's emphasis] make this impossible is to abandon the secular, antiauthoritarian vocabulary of shared social hope in favor of the vocabulary which Whitman and Dewey abhorred: a vocabulary built around the notion of sin.

He goes on to invoke Andrew Delbanco, saying that Delbanco "gets Dewey exactly right when he says that for him,

> 'evil was the failure of imagination to reach beyond itself, the human fail-
> ure to open oneself to a spirit that both chastises one for confidence in
> one's own righteousness and promises the enduring comfort of reciprocal
> love. There is a sense in which all of Dewey's thought was an extended
> commentary on Emerson's remark, "the only sin is limitation."'[112]

It is deeply ironic that in the same set of notes to the Introduction to *Consequences of Pragmatism* in which Rorty made his first public announcement of his rejection of Peirce's "end of inquiry" *definition* of truth, there is also this note:

> Peirce said that "the first rule of reason" was "Do not block the way of
> inquiry" (*Collected Papers*, 1.135). But he did not mean that one should
> always go down any road one saw – a point that comes out in his emphasis
> on "logical self-control" as a corollary of "ethical self-control." (See, e.g.,
> *Collected Papers*, 1.606). What he was getting at in his "rule of reason"
> was the same point as he makes about the ubiquity of language – that we
> should never think that the regress of interpretation can be stopped once
> and for all, but rather realize that there may be always a vocabulary, a set of
> descriptions around the corner which will throw everything into question
> once again. To say that obedience to criteria is a good thing *in itself* would
> be like saying that self-control is a good in itself. It would be a species of
> Philosophical puritanism.[113]

"Do not block the way of inquiry." "The only sin is limitation." Peirce's "emphasis on 'logical self-control' as a corollary of 'ethical self-control'" belonged to *his* "redescription" of Kant's transcendental strain: that is, for Peirce, the *praktisch* and the *pragmatisch* are *complementary processes*. For him, the central notion about pragmatism to keep in mind is that it is, to borrow James's words, "a go-between" moving between the ethical and the scientific, imagination and reason, the activities of both reciprocally informing each other. It is not that Peirce saw philosophy *as* a science but he understood that practice in logic, in mathematics, in extended imaginary moves in the cosmic game plan – these exercises in mental agility – are useful in expanding our skill sets ("tool boxes" in Wittgenstein's vocabulary) for practical considerations and performance. Complementarily, as Rorty himself indicates in the note just quoted, ethical habits inform the applications or uses of reason. Both/and *not* either/or. Both processes are necessary if we hope to align human history, as Reinhold Niebuhr described, in its difference from natural history. This alignment can be facilitated by understanding Peirce's *pragmatische* efforts as exercises in stretching imagination's boundaries. These enlarged spaces permit consideration of the human beyond the human. When we recall that "consideration" means, literally, "with the stars," Emerson's seemingly simple homily, "Hitch your wagon to a star" reminds us that language is itself a life form embodying the history of the human "bond to all that dust": "The only sin is limitation." To exclude Peirce's *pragmatische* practice from how pragmatism is understood is to preserve a very dangerous dualism. Peirce's idea of "useful" involves a purpose beyond us yet ourselves. If at least some of us do not, as he did, investigate and imagine the planet itself as a life form in the neighborhood of stars, then the practical, ethical choices on offer in our liberal democracy will be severely restricted. Moreover, the "failure of imagination to reach beyond itself," to keep aiming at transcending the current limits of the human, entails another kind of political danger. The triangulation of attention required to locate ourselves on this planet by measuring the axis of vision between us and even our most local star is a necessary corrective to believing language to have no relation to extra-human realities. As Misak points out,

> What Rorty finds when he looks at our practices is that the transcendental account of truth, which has beliefs or sentences corresponding to something nonhuman, plays no role whatsoever.... Once you give up on aiming at truth – once you give up aiming at something that goes beyond the standards of your own community – then you give up the wherewithal to argue against the might-is-right view.[114]

Circling back, I offer the speculation that had Rorty dealt more directly than he did with "Man's Glassy Essence" as imagined and explored by Peirce, it could have given him – as he attempted to "de-divinize"[115] our account of the world – the naturalized version of a transcendental argument that he needed to support the notion that liberal democracy is the best and most hopeful social arrangement yet devised, since what Peirce provided in the 1891–2 series concluding with "Man's Glassy Essence" is the grounding of the transcendentalist strain in evolutionary process – a *curve ... its direction constantly chang[ing]* – our beginning and extending, with *consistency*, "the molecular theory of protoplasm," circling out, spiralling.... Instead, Rorty "spent 40 years looking for a coherent and convincing way of formulating [his] worries about what, if anything, philosophy is good for," abandoning the hope to "hold reality and justice in a single vision."

Rorty's last bird sighting was of a condor, its flight marking the edge of one of many circles, over the Grand Canyon in February 2007, four months before he died – a strong mind in the mountains.[116]

CODA

Finally, the choice is about what kind of practice we, as pragmatists, choose to engage in our conduct of life as we consider placing a stake in the future: that of a cranky "radical deflationist," a "syncretist hack" regretting at the end of his life not having read more poetry, or that of one who allows "that in the planetary scene" we might glimpse extensions of being "more truly and more strange."[117] While Rorty did on the surface grant the same "ontological status" to the *praktisch* and the *pragmatisch* – his examples are human rights and quarks respectively – he understood them both, following his particular construals of Thomas Kuhn and Bruno Latour, as "social constructions." This casting, together with his "reject[ing] the suggestion that natural science should serve as a paradigm for the rest of culture,"[118] indeed "erase[s] a whole range of beliefs and desires" we might very well do better to keep in play, keeping in mind James's singularly important offering: "will and belief, in short, meaning a certain relation between objects and the self, are two names for one and the same psychological phenomenon.... Our beliefs and attention are the same fact."[119] "If you ask the questions properly, she [the earth] answers. It's a dialogue."[120] It matters what you pay attention to.

Notes

Preface

1 William James, "Is Life Worth Living," in *The Will to Believe* collected in *Writings 1878–1899*, ed. Gerald E. Myers (New York: The Library of America, 1992), p. 501; opening passage, p. 502. (Quotations in this Preface without endnote indications appear again in the main body of the text where they are noted and referenced.)

2 Ralph Waldo Emerson, *Essays and Lectures*, ed. Joel Porte (New York: The Library of America, 1983), p. 471. This volume hereafter cited as *EL*.

3 Arthur O. Lovejoy, "The Thirteen Pragmatisms," *The Journal of Philosophy, Psychology, and Scientific Methods*, vol. 5, no. 1 (January 2, 1908), 11.

4 Joan Richardson, "*Deadwood*: Unalterable Vibrations," *The Hopkins Review*, vol. 3, no. 3 (Summer 2010; New Series), 376–405.

1. Introduction: Thirteen ways of looking at pragmatism

1 As Harvey Cormier reminded readers of *The New York Times* Opinionator blog a few weeks before the last election on October 14, 2012, the December 29, 2008 issue of *The Nation* magazine even proclaimed in all caps on the cover: "Barack Obama, Pragmatist" at http://opinionator.blogs.nytimes.com/2012/10/14/reconsidering-obama-the-pragmatist/?pagewanted=print. The title of his posting is "Reconsidering Obama the Pragmatist."

2 David Brooks, "Obama, Gospel and Verse," *New York Times*, April 26, 2007, A25. The echo of this "take-away" reverberates near the closing of Obama's Second Inaugural Address:

> Our actions will not prevent every senseless act of violence in this country. Indeed, no laws, no initiatives, no administrative acts will perfectly solve all the challenges I've outlined tonight. But we were never sent here to be perfect. We were sent here to make what difference we can.

3 In *Reading Obama: Dreams, Hopes and the American Political Tradition* (Princeton: Princeton University Press, 2012), James T. Kloppenberg notes additionally that "Some commentators understood Obama's Nobel Speech as a

species of Niebuhr's Christian realism, others as a Deweyan pragmatist's chastened realism" (p. 243–4).

4 Cass Sunstein, "The Empiricist Strikes Back: Obama's Pragmatism Explained," *The New Republic,* September 10, 2008.

5 There are some notable exceptions to this take: Cass Sunstein's various articles on Obama's pragmatism and its relation to his administration; James Kloppenberg in his *Reading Obama* (2010) locates – as Harvey Cormier notes in his "Reconsidering Obama the Pragmatist" posting (see note 1 to this chapter) – "Obama's writings and speeches in this historical pragmatic philosophical tradition that originates with Charles Peirce and William James"; and Cormier himself who sees Obama as directly continuing the Jamesian project: "William James and President Obama have the same realistic view of belief and how it works. They both believe that we can and should develop shared beliefs and use them in our fight to make our social world better."

6 *EL,* p. 471.

7 William James, "What Pragmatism Means," Lecture II in *Pragmatism, A New Name for Some Old Ways of Thinking* in *Writings 1902–1910,* ed. Bruce Kuklick (New York: The Library of America, 1987), p. 522.

8 A collection published by Oxford University Press in 2007 under the title of *New Pragmatists,* edited by Cheryl Misak, is comprised of contributions by Jeffrey Stout, Ian Hacking, Arthur Fine, David Macarthur and Huw Price, David Bakhurst, Terry Pinkard, Danielle Macbeth, and the editor herself. Misak notes that "[t]he best of Peirce, James, and Dewey has … resurfaced in deep, interesting, and fruitful ways" in the work of the new pragmatists, but, again, the aspect of what remains "beyond us yet ourselves" – in the phrasing of Wallace Stevens – is of central concern to the first-generation pragmatists, but is notably absent for these thinkers. Only Stanley Cavell and Cornel West, of the previous generation, have addressed, albeit in very different ways, what I call the "residues of God."

9 James, *Pragmatism,* p. 492.

10 "Redescription" and "renarration" are terms derived from second-generation pragmatists and following the direction pointed by John Edwin Smith at the conclusion of his presidential address to the Eastern Division of the American Philosophical Association in 1981; that is, to abandon the claim that any single approach to philosophical inquiry is the legitimate one. Richard Rorty's call for different "vocabularies" belongs to this reframing of philosophy's use. See also Vincent Colapietro, "Richard Rorty as Peircean Pragmatist: An Ironic Portrait and Sincere Expression of Philosophical Friendship," *Pragmatism Today: The Journal of the Central-European Pragmatist Forum,* Special Issue: The Roots of Rorty's Philosophy, vol. 2, issue 1 (Summer 2011), 31–50.

11 David Brooks, "Mirror on America," *New York Times,* Sunday Book Review, May 24, 2009, 6.

12 Martin Heidegger, *Sojourns, the Journey to Greece,* tr. John Panteleimon Manoussakis (Albany: State University of New York Press, 2005), p. 60.

13 James, *Pragmatism,* p. 513.

14 Anonymous review of Philip J. van der Eijk, ed. *Hippocrates in Context. Papers Read at the XIth International Hippocrates Colloquium*, University of Newcastle upon Tyne, 27–31 August 2002: *Studies in Ancient Medicine* 31 (Leiden: Brill, 2005) in *Bryn Mawr Classical Review* July 14, 2006.

15 Goetz Richter, "Is Philosophy the Greatest Kind of Music? Reflections on Plato's *Phaedo* 61a" at www.goetzrichter.com/pages/Writings/Phaedo%20 61a.pdf. It is worth remarking that *stochasmos* informs a current Web-based platform called "CoReflect," a learning and teaching platform that offers digital support for inquiry, collaboration, and reflection on socio-scientific debates. *Stochasmos* will be used to develop and host the inquiry-learning environments. "Such environments can couple data-rich scientific rigor with the flexibility and modifiability that is needed for wide-spread adoption and use."

16 In Misak, *New Pragmatists*, pp. 20–1.

17 Donald Davidson did not call himself a pragmatist; Richard Rorty insisted that he was, and the designation has remained in place for many people. As noted by Colapietro in "Richard Rorty as Peircean Pragmatist": "He [Rorty] would repeatedly call Davidson a pragmatist while Davidson himself would vehemently reject this characterization. Despite Davidson's protest-ation, Rorty took himself to be justified in applying this appellation to this thinker." And in the accompanying footnote referring to a signally import-ant lecture/essay by Alasdair MacIntyre ("On Not Knowing Where One is Going," his 2010 John Dewey Lecture to the Central Division of the APA) suggesting ways the relationship between Peirce and Rorty might be rede-scribed, Colapietro offers:

> In the essay on which I have been drawing, MacIntyre notes that he is indebted to Rorty for not only their conversations but also introducing him to Davidson, "both the man and the work": "But the Davidson to whom Rorty introduced me turned out to have a *Doppelganger*, that subtle and imaginative fiction, Rorty's Davidson. And Rorty's Davidson became one of the major *dramatis personae* in a story that Rorty developed of how 'analytic philosophy culminates in Quine, the later Wittgenstein, Sellars, and Davidson – which is to say that it transcends and cancels itself'" [2010, 71]). MacIntyre is here quoting Rorty himself. (*London Review of Books*, January 20, 2005)

18 Jeffrey Stout, "On Our Interest in Getting Things Right: Pragmatism with-out Narcissism" in Misak, *New Pragmatists*, p. 19, and quoting Davidson and Rorty.

19 James, *Pragmatism*, p. 509.

20 *Nature* (1836), *EL*, p. 23.

21 Henry David Thoreau, *Walden* in *A Week on the Concord and Merrimack Rivers, Walden; or, Life in the Woods, The Maine Woods, Cape Cod*, ed. Robert F. Sayre (New York: The Library of America, 1985), p. 429.

22 Christopher Bollas, *The Evocative Object World* (East Sussex and New York: Routledge, 2009), p. 59.

23 James, *Pragmatism*, p. 510.

24 Noted by Anne Freadman, *The Machinery of Talk: Charles Peirce and the Sign Hypothesis* (Stanford, CA: Stanford University Press, 2004), p. xv: as Freadman describes, "in a touching draft for the introduction of one of his unwritten books, Peirce writes. . . ."

25 For readers interested in Stevens's biography, see Joan Richardson, *Wallace Stevens: The Early Years, 1879–1923* and *Wallace Stevens: The Later Years, 1923–1955* (New York: Beech Tree Books/William Morrow, 1986 and 1988).

26 Joseph Brent, *Charles Sanders Peirce: A Life* (Bloomington and Indianapolis: Indiana University Press, 1993), p. 138.

27 Wallace Stevens, "Le Monocle de Mon Oncle" in *Wallace Stevens: Collected Poetry and Prose*, ed. Frank Kermode and Joan Richardson (New York: The Library of America, 1997), p. 12; this volume hereafter cited as *CPP*.

28 James Longenbach, "A Music of Austerity," *The Nation*, September 14, 2009, 25–30.

29 William James, *Talks to Teachers and Students* in *Writings 1878–1899*, ed. Gerald E. Myers (New York: The Library of America, 1992), p. 708.

30 Russell Goodman in his *Wittgenstein and William James* (Cambridge: Cambridge University Press, 2002) provides an excellent, carefully textured account of Wittgenstein's relation to James.

31 Charles Sanders Peirce, "How to Make Our Ideas Clear" in *The Essential Peirce: Selected Philosophical Writings*, Volume 1 (1867–1893), ed. Nathan Houser and Christian Kloesel (Bloomington and Indianapolis: Indiana University Press, 1992), p. 129.

32 Freadman, *Machinery of Talk*, p. xiv.

33 "Circles," *EL*, p. 408.

34 Joan Richardson, *A Natural History of Pragmatism: The Fact of Feeling from Jonathan Edwards to Gertrude Stein* (Cambridge: Cambridge University Press, 2007), p. 122.

35 *CPP*, p. 904.

36 "The Poet," *EL*, p. 463.

37 Ian Hacking, "On Not Being a Pragmatist" in Misak, *New Pragmatists*, p. 43.

38 Paul Jerome Croce, *Science and Religion in the Era of William James*, vol. 1: *Eclipse of Certainty, 1820–1880* (Chapel Hill: University of North Carolina Press, 1995), p. 205.

39 MS 678, *The Charles S. Peirce Papers* [microform]. Houghton Library, Harvard University, Cambridge, MA: Harvard University Photographic Department, Widener Library, 1966. Manuscript sources.

40 James, *Pragmatism*, p. 574.

41 *The Collected Papers of Charles Sanders Peirce*, vols. 1–6, ed. Charles Hartshorne and Paul Weiss; vols. 7–8, ed. Arthur W. Burks (Cambridge, MA: Harvard University Press 1931–5 and 1958), vol. 8, par. 112.

42 James, *Pragmatism*, pp. 559–60.

43 There is renewed general interest in America's relation to Vedanta. See Philip Goldberg, *American Veda: From Emerson and the Beatles to Yoga and*

Meditation, How Indian Spirituality Changed the West (New York: Harmony, 2010). Ann Louise Bardach, a writer at large for *Newsweek*, is at work on a new biography of Vivekananda. See her "How Yoga Won the West," *New York Times*, October 1, 2011.

44 Romain Rolland, *The Life of Vivekananda and The Universal Gospel: A Study of Mysticism and Action in Living India*, tr. E. F. Malcolm-Smith (Kolkata[India]: Advaita Ashrama, 2010 [1931]), pp. 48, 37.

45 Ibid., p. 40.

46 Joan Richardson, "Thinking in Cavell: The Transcendentalist Strain," in *Stanley Cavell: Philosophy, Literature and Criticism*, ed. James Loxley and Andrew Taylor (Manchester and New York: Manchester University Press, 2011), pp. 199–224.

47 James, *Pragmatism*, p. 606.

48 William James, "The Energies of Men," *The American Magazine* (1907) reprinted by Moffat, Yard and Company in New York (1914), pp. 29, 27, 34–5. James delivered under the same title a slightly different version of this piece as the Presidential Address before the American Philosophical Society at Columbia University in December 1906; this version was reprinted in *The Philosophical Review* in January 1907 and is collected in *Writings 1902–1910*, pp. 1223–41.

49 Ibid., pp. 34, 30.

50 William James, *The Varieties of Religious Experience*, Lecture XVIII, in *Writings 1902–1910*, p. 388.

51 James, "Mysticism," Lectures XVI and XVII, *Varieties*, p. 385.

52 James, *Pragmatism*, p. 522.

53 Bardach, "How Yoga Won the West."

54 Rolland, *Life of Vivekananda*, p. 71.

55 Margaret Elizabeth Noble, *The Master as I Saw Him: Being Pages from the Life of the Swami Vivekananda* (Elibron Classics, 2005), pp. 24–5. www.elibron.com.

56 Rolland, *Life of Viveknanda*, p. 102.

57 Ibid., p. 92, quoting Vivekananda's *My Plan of Campaign*.

58 Noble, *Master*, p. 28.

59 James, *Pragmatism*, p. 548.

60 Alfred North Whitehead, *Science and the Modern World* (New York: The Free Press, 1967 [1925]), pp. 132, 154.

61 James, *Pragmatism*, p. 612.

62 Ibid., p. 613.

63 David Brooks, "Where Obama Shines," *New York Times*, July 19, 2012.

64 *CPP*, p. 179.

65 John Milton, "Paradise Lost," Book VII.

66 James, *Pragmatism*, p. 619.

67 James, *Varieties*, p. 401.

68 James, *Pragmatism*, pp. 618–19.

69 Noble, *Master*, pp. 300–1.

70 Ibid., pp. 266–8.
71 I have for several years in teaching and writing referred to Cavell's strain of philosophical practice in this way. In searching for the source of a particular gloss on the difference between Peirce's and James's understanding of "pragmatism," having to do with Immanuel Kant's distinction between the *praktisch* and the *pragmatisch*, I came across Sami Pihlstrom's references to "transcendental pragmatism"; see, for example, his "The Prospects of Transcendental Pragmatism: Reconciling Kant and James," *Philosophy Today*, vol. 41 (1997), 383–93. My own usage is drawn specifically from Cavell's central claim that Emerson's voice "is as transcendentalist as it is pragmatist."
72 From the *Adagia*, in *CPP*, p. 909.
73 Richard Rorty, *Philosophy and the Mirror of Nature* (Princeton, NJ: Princeton University Press, 1980 [1979]), p. 7.
74 "Experience," *EL*, p. 473.
75 In addition, recent issues of *Contemporary Pragmatism*, particularly the issues of June 2009 and December 2011 edited by Mitchell Aboulafia and John R. Shook, are especially useful in foregrounding current debates.
76 *The Recovery of Philosophy in America: Essays in Honor of John Edwin Smith*, ed. Thomas P. Kasulis and Robert Cummings Neville (Albany: State University of New York Press, 1997), p. 11.
77 Robert Cummings Neville, "Reflections on Philosophic Recovery" in *Recovery of Philosophy*, p. 4.
78 Arthur Lothstein, "'No Eros, No Buds': Teaching as Nectaring," in *Experience as Philosophy: On the Work of John J. McDermott*, ed. James Campbell and Robert E. Hart (New York: Fordham University Press, 2006), pp. 188–9.
79 James, *Pragmatism*, p. 527.

2. Context: William James, Into the cosmic weather

1 For "I will be a naturalist," see Ralph Waldo Emerson, *Selected Journals 1820–1842*, ed. Lawrence Rosenwald (New York: The Library of America, 2010), p. 276. For "to annul that adulterous divorce…," see "The Method of Nature," an oration delivered in 1841 before the Society of the Adelphi at Waterville College, Maine, *EL*, p. 130.
2 The famous image of "the transparent eyeball" comes from the first chapter of *Nature*, *EL*, p. 10; "Man thinking" and "man inhabited by thought" from "The American Scholar," *EL*, pp. 53–71; "an original relation to the universe," from the opening of *Nature*, p. 7.
3 For a full discussion of this background and of Emerson's seminal place in the development of pragmatism, see Richardson, *Natural History of Pragmatism*, esp. chapter 3, "Emerson's Moving Pictures," pp. 62–94.
4 Henry James, *Notes of a Son and Brother* in *Autobiography*, ed. Frederick W. Dupee (Princeton: Princeton University Press, 1983), p. 359.
5 *The Correspondence of William James*, vol. 1: *William and Henry 1861–1884*, ed. Ignas K. Skrupskelis and Elizabeth M. Berkeley (Charlottesville: University

Press of Virginia, 1992), p. 188. See also Richardson, *Natural History of Pragmatism*, pp. 98–9.

6 William James, *Varieties*, pp. 448–9.

7 As John Diggins reminded us in *The Promise of Pragmatism: Modernism and the Crisis of Knowledge and Authority* (Chicago: University of Chicago Press, 1994), in the context of William James's "liberating modern religion from … Calvinist determinism," James sought to take religion away from the theologians and deliver it to the people as though it were a long-lost passion. In "The Will to Believe," James begins by telling his audience that "I have brought with me tonight something like a religious sermon on justification by faith to read to you." That James saw himself delivering a hopeful sermon rather than a rigorous philosophical treatise may have had something to do with his emotional relationship with his father. For James's long interest in the psychology of religious experience was also bound up not only with his therapeutic concerns, but also with the "voice" of his "father's cry" – "that religion is real." (p. 130; last quotations from Ralph Barton Perry's *The Thought and Character of William James: Briefer Version* [New York, 1964])

8 *CPP*, p. 902.

9 James, *Varieties*, pp. 467–9.

10 James, *Pragmatism*, pp. 540, 522.

11 *CPP*, p. 786.

12 I have borrowed here from Ezra Pound's "Cantico del Sole" (From *Instigations*, 1920).

13 Henry James, *A Small Boy and Others* in *Autobiography*, pp. 122–3.

14 *Correspondence of William James*, vol. 1, p. xxix. For discussion in *Natural History of Pragmatism*, see pp. 103–18.

15 "Circles," *EL*, p. 413.

16 Michael Wood, "Understanding Forwards," a review of *William James: In the Maelstrom of American Modernism* by Robert D. Richardson, *London Review of Books*, September 20, 2007, 22–3.

17 "The Necessary Angel" is the title of Stevens's collection of essays and a line from his poem "Angel Surrounded by Paysans"; "believe,/Believe…" lines from "The Man with the Blue Guitar," *CPP*, pp. 637–751, 423, 144.

18 *CPP*, p. 903.

19 James, *Pragmatism*, p. 535 (see also p. 517).

20 William James described the difficulty of framing his sentences adequately against "the stubborn facts" of scientific findings. See letter of March 10, 1887 to Henry James (brother), *The Correspondence of William James*, vol. 2: *William and Henry 1885–1896*, eds. Ignas K. Skrupskelis and Elizabeth M. Berkeley (Charlottesville: University Press of Virginia, 1993), p. 59.

21 Pierre Hadot, *Philosophy as a Way of Life: Spiritual Exercises from Socrates to Foucault*, ed. Arnold I. Davidson (Malden, MA and Oxford, UK: Blackwell, 1995), pp. 85, 65. I have reversed the order of the original passage for ease of transition here; in the original, the bracketed segment precedes the first sentence quoted here.

22 James, *Varieties*, pp. 88–9.

23 Ibid., pp. 56–7.

24 Alfred North Whitehead, *Modes of Thought* (New York: The Free Press, 1968 [1938]), p. 2.

25 The more complete reference is as follows: "In 1962 Bohr ... remembered definitely having read James before 1912., i.e., long before complementarity appeared in 1927.... Harald Hoffding [the Danish philosopher, a vigorous admirer of James, and one of Bohr's preceptors] had visited William James in America in 1904, during which time Bohr was Hoffding's immediate student." In addition, "Bohr explicitly link[ed] his remembrance of reading James with Edgar Rubin, a psychology student and member of the Ekliptika Circle. The reputation of James's *Principles of Psychology* was ... immense at this time (especially in Europe).... We know that at this time in the discussions of the Ekliptika Circle and on his own the young Bohr was struggling to come to grips with the problems of describing the contents of psychological processes, an interest common to both his father [Christian Bohr, a prominent psychologist] and Hoffding as well." From Peter Mutnick, "Bohr on EPR [electron paramagnetic resonance, also known as electron spin resonance] as Influenced by James and Kant, Part I," first quoting Henry Folse, *The Philosophy of Niels Bohr* (p. 49); second quotation Mutnick, http://www.geocities.com/saint7peter/BohronEPRI.html?200820.

26 Ibid. I am indebted to Ross Posnock for alerting me, originally, to Bohr's crediting William James with having stimulated his thinking about complementarity.

27 William James, *The Principles of Psychology* (rpt. Cambridge, MA: Harvard University Press, 1983 [1890]), pp. 277, 204.

28 Niels Bohr, *The Philosophical Writings of Niels Bohr*, vol. I: *Atomic Theory and the Description of Nature* (Woodbridge, CT: Ox Bow Press, 1987), p. 96; also quoted by Mutnick in "Bohr on EPR."

29 James, *Principles*, pp. 226, 238.

30 Bohr, *Atomic Theory*, p. 98; also quoted in Mutnick.

31 Ibid., p. 119, closing in "The Atomic Theory and the Fundamental Principles underlying the Description of Nature" (1929), Bohr observes: "Besides, the fact that consciousness, as we know it, is inseparably connected with life ought to prepare us for finding that the very problem of the distinction between the living and the dead escapes comprehension in the ordinary sense of the word. That a physicist touches upon such questions may perhaps be excused on the ground that the new situation in physics has so forcibly reminded us of the old truth that we are both onlookers and actors in the great drama of existence."

32 Gillian Beer, *Open Fields: Studies in Cultural Encounter* (Oxford: Clarendon/Oxford University Press, 1996), pp. 247–8.

33 Mutnick, "Bohr on EPR."

34 "Experience," *EL*, p. 475.

35 For a full discussion of Edward's incorporation of Newton's description of the nature and behavior of light into his description of the activity of grace, see my chapter on Edwards in *A Natural History of Pragmatism*, pp. 24–61.
36 Jonathan Edwards, "Of Being" in *The Works of Jonathan Edwards*, vol. 6: *Scientific and Philosophical Writings*, ed. Wallace E. Anderson (New Haven and London: Yale University Press, 1980), p. 206.
37 Bohr, *Atomic Theory*, pp. 34–5.
38 James, *Principles*, p. 236.
39 Richard Rorty, "Matter and Event" (1963) in *Explorations of Whitehead's Philosophy*, ed. Lewis Ford and George Kline (New York: Fordham University Press, 1983), pp. 68–103. The passage referred to is: "time cannot be taken seriously until one ceases to think of the present as a knife-edge and begins to think of it as an extended duration." This essay was a comparison of Whitehead and Aristotle, the subject of Rorty's dissertation.
40 Stuart Hampshire, *Spinoza and Spinozism* (Oxford and New York: Oxford University Press, 2005), p. 147, cited by Meyer.
41 In Samuel Alexander, *Spinoza and Time* (London: G. Allen and Unwin, 1921), p. 349, as cited by Meyer.
42 As cited in Stephen J. Meyer in an unpublished paper. [p. 13]
43 As cited in Meyer, same unpublished paper. [p. 13]
44 The last three phrases here are taken from Donna Haraway, *When Species Meet* (Minneapolis: University of Minnesota Press, 2008), pp. 241–2, to which Meyer refers in his paper.
45 "The imperfect is our paradise" is a line from Stevens's poem, "The Poems of Our Climate," *CPP*, p. 179.
46 Ross Posnock, "The Earth Must Resume Its Rights: A Jamesian Genealogy of Immaturity," in John J. Stuhr, ed., *100 Years of Pragmatism: William James's Revolutionary Philosophy* (Bloomington and Indianapolis: Indiana University Press, 2010), p. 65.
47 James, *Pragmatism*, pp. 531–2.
48 See also Richardson, *Natural History of Pragmatism*, p. 122.
49 Posnock, "Earth," p. 64, quoting Hadot, *Philosophy*, p. 265.
50 Posnock, "Earth," pp. 64–5.
51 As quoted by Emily Wilson in "Stoicism and Us," *The New Republic*, vol. 241, no. 4,880 (April 8, 2010), pp. 32–6.
52 Passages from William James's letter to Alice Gibbens James quoted in Robert D. Richardson, *William James: In the Maelstrom of American Modernism* (Boston and New York: Houghton Mifflin Company, 2006), pp. 374–5. "Convert, convert, convert ..." from Henry James, *Autobiography*, p. 123.
53 "History," *EL*, p. 251.
54 James, *Pragmatism*, pp. 588–9.
55 James's brother Wilky (named for James John Garth Wilkinson, Swedenborgian scholar and writer, friend of Henry James, Sr.), having enlisted in 1862 at the age of seventeen in the 44th Massachusetts Regiment,

212 *Notes to pages 49–51*

in 1863 was recommended and accepted to serve as one of the thirty white officers for the newly forming black regiment, the 54th Massachusetts, under the command of the twenty-five-year-old Colonel Robert Gould Shaw, and composed of 1,000 black soldiers, including the sons of Frederick Douglass. As Robert Richardson notes, "In April, as William was working on Jonathan Edwards and Epictetus, his own name appeared on the certified enrollment list for the state militia for Ward 5 in Newport." Henry James, Sr. had, it seems, bought the service of substitutes to serve in the places of both William and Henry. In any case, William James was in the crowd in Boston as the 54th regiment arrived at South Station from Camp Meigs on its way to war and Richardson offers that just as Charles Russell Lowell, one of the 54th's new officers, was passing on his horse, Lowell's fiancée – Colonel Shaw's nineteen-year-old sister, Josephine – came "whirling up on horseback" and reined in beside Lowell, just behind where William was standing. William knew Josephine; he had met her in Newport. As he described the scene many years later to Josephine's daughter, William wrote, "I looked back and saw their faces and figures against the evening sky, and they looked so young and victorious, that I, much gnawed by questions as to my own duty of enlisting or not, shrank back – they had not seen me – from being recognized...." Richardson, *William James*, pp. 54–5.

56 Richardson, *William James*, pp. 52–3, 55.

57 Ibid., p. 65.

58 In connection with James's fluency as well as his stylistic versatility and early nomadic intellectual training, Robert Richardson observes, "John Dewey would ... remark that James's lack of formal education was one of his greatest assets, 'since it protected his mind against academic deadening'" (*William James*, p. 51).

59 As noted earlier, in "Circles," *EL*, p. 413.

60 Gillian Beer, "Four Bodies on the *Beagle*: Touch, Sight, and Writing in a Darwin Letter," in *Open Fields*, pp. 13–30.

61 *The Correspondence of William James*, vol. 3: *William and Henry 1897–1910*, ed. Ignas K. Skrupskelis and Elizabeth M. Berkeley (Charlottesville: University Press of Virginia, 1994), p. 234, from a letter dated May 3, 1903.

62 It is significant that James revealed in *The Varieties of Religious Experience*, in the guise of an anonymous French correspondent, that it was his internalization of Biblical texts that saved him from growing "really insane" during his most serious nervous collapse: "I mean that the fear was so invasive and powerful that if I had not clung to scripture-texts like 'The eternal God is my refuge,' etc., 'Come unto me, all ye that labor and are heavy-laden,' etc., 'I am the resurrection and the life,' etc., I think I should have grown really insane" (in *Writings 1902–1910*, p. 151). For a detailed analysis of James's experience of "vastation," see "William James's Feeling of *If*" in Richardson, *Natural History of Pragmatism*, pp. 98–136. Emerson quotation, *EL*, pp. 122–3.

63 *EL*, p. 117.

64 James, *Pragmatism*, p. 535.

65 In "The Comedian as the Letter C," Wallace Stevens describes the experience of his mock-hero Crispin at sea in this way; *CPP*, p. 28.

66 "Fate," *EL*, 964–5. The larger context is worth having at hand: "Nature and Thought ... matter and mind are in perpetual tilt and balance.... The whole world is the flux of matter over the wires of thought to the poles or points where it would build.... Certain ideas are in the air. We are all impressionable, for we are made of them.... The truth is in the air, and the most impressionable brain will announce it first, but all will announce it a few minutes later. So women, as most susceptible, are the best index of the coming hour. So the great man, that is, the man most imbued with the spirit of the time, is the impressionable man, – of fibre irritable and delicate, like iodine to light. He feels the infinitesimal attractions."

67 An epithet from "The Comedian as the Letter C," *CPP*, p. 23.

68 Richardson, *William James*, p. 79.

69 Ibid., p. 375.

70 *The Correspondence of William James*, vol. 8: *1895–June 1899*, ed. Ignas K. Skrupskelis and Elizabeth M. Berkeley (Charlottesville: University Press of Virginia, 2000), pp. 460, 539, quoted in Richardson, *William James*, p. 382.

71 William James, "Philosophical Conceptions and Practical Results" in *Writings 1878–1899*, pp. 1077–9.

72 Ibid., p. 1079.

73 Ibid., p. 1091.

74 "Self-Reliance," *EL*, p. 269.

75 "Habits of conversation with nature" from "History," *EL*, p. 251; the fuller context: "Man is the broken giant, and, in all his weakness, both his body and his mind are invigorated by habits of conversation with nature."

76 Quoted in Nolan Pliny Jacobson, *Understanding Buddhism* (Carbondale: Southern Illinois University Press, 2010), p. 94.

77 James's notebook records the following: Hallam, Fergusson, Orbigny, Siebold, Milnes, Edwards, Villon, Rabelais, Sir Thomas Browne, Mill, Butler, Browning, Pascal, Carlyle, Confucius, Zoroaster, Epictetus, the *Imitation of Christ*, Persian poetry, *Gulistan* of Saadi, Heine, Goethe, *Vishnu Purana*, fragments of the *Mahabarata* and several other Indic texts, Plato, Aristotle, Bacon, Descartes, Locke, Jeremy Taylor's *Holy Living and Holy Dying*; and in French editions, Vico's *Science Nouvelle*, Condorcet's *Eloge* of Haller, and Plotinus's *Enneades* (Richardson, *William James*, p. 287).

78 Ibid., p. 288.

79 Ian T. Ramsey, *Religious Language: An Empirical Placing of Theological Phrases* (New York: The Macmillan Company, 1963), p. 6.

80 For a full discussion, see James, "The Stream of Thought" in *Principles*, pp. 219–78; James also refers to this "fringe" as "psychic overtone" or "suffusion." This seminal chapter of *Principles* should be required reading for anyone interested in the processes of mind, language, thought/thinking, and consciousness.

81 Ramsey, *Religious Language,* pp. 15–16.
82 Ibid., p. 17.
83 Ibid., p. 19.
84 Ibid., p. 22.
85 Ibid., p. 25.
86 "The Transcendentalist," *EL,* p. 196
87 "Prospects" in *Nature, EL,* p. 47.
88 *Collected Papers of Charles Sanders Peirce,* vol. 5, par. 462 and vol. 7, pars. 538–40: quoted in Nolan Pliny Jacobson, *The Heart of Buddhist Philosophy* (Carbondale: Southern Illinois University Press, 2010 [1988]), p. 71.
89 *The Essential Peirce,* vol. 1: *1867–1893,* p. xx.
90 John Locke, *An Essay Concerning Human Understanding,* ed. Peter H. Nidditch (Oxford: Clarendon/Oxford University Press, 1991), pp. 720–1, 405.
91 See Gregory Bateson, *Steps to an Ecology of Mind* (Chicago and London: University of Chicago Press, 2000 [1972]), esp. "Double Bind, 1969" and all of Part III, "Form and Pathology in Relationship," pp. 271–8, 159–342; and *Mind and Nature: A Necessary Unity* (Creskill, NJ: Hampton Press, 2002 [1979]).
92 Jacobson, *Heart,* pp. 71–7; asterisks refer to his notes, in order: *Milton Singer, *Man's Glassy Essence: Explorations in Semiotic Anthropology* (Bloomington: Indiana University Press, 1984), pp. 3, 494, 501; **Gilbert Ryle, *The Concept of Mind* (New York: Barnes and Noble, 1949); ***Peirce, *Collected Papers,* vol. 6, par. 134; vol. 5, pars. 549–604 and from Peirce's famous letter to Lady Welby of December 23, 1908 and also see Charles S. Hardwick, ed. *Semiotic and Significs: The Correspondence Between Charles S. Peirce and Victoria Lady Welby* (Bloomington: Indiana University Press, 1977), p. 73; ****Peirce, *Collected Papers,* vol. 5, pars. 549–604.
93 James, *Principles,* p. 949.
94 Ibid., pp. 948–9.
95 "The Method of Nature," *EL,* p. 123.
96 William James, *Essays in Radical Empiricism* (New York: Dover Publications, 2003), p. 94. This address with a revised opening was later incorporated as "Appendix B" in *A Pluralistic Universe,* in *Writings 1902–1910,* where the sentence appears on p. 807.
97 James, *Radical Empiricism,* pp. 81–2.
98 Ibid., p. 84 (in *Writings 1902–1910,* p. 799).
99 The closing line of "The Snow Man," arguably the earliest of Stevens's most Vedantic poems; *CPP,* p. 8.
100 "Circles," *EL,* p. 401.
101 James, *Radical Empiricism,* pp. 89–90 (in *Writings 1902–1910,* pp. 803–4).
102 From the penultimate paragraph of "The Place of Affectional Facts in a World of Pure Experience," the article preceding "The Experience of Activity" in James, *Radical Empiricism,* p. 80; in *Writings 1902–1910,* p. 1213.

103 Jacobson, *Understanding Buddhism*, p. 129, quoting Charles Hartshorne, *Creative Synthesis and Philosophic Method* (La Salle: Open Court Publishing, 1970), p. 177.
104 James, *Radical Empiricism*, pp. 95–6 (in *Writings 1902–1910*, pp. 808–10).
105 Northrop Frye, *The Great Code: The Bible and Literature* (New York and London: Harcourt Brace Jovanovich, 1981), p. 86. See Joan Richardson, "Pragmatism ... she widens the field of search for God," in *Revisiting Pragmatism: William James in the New Millennium*, ed. Susanne Rohr and Miriam Strube, (Heidelberg: Universitatsverlag Winter, 2012), pp. 27–42 for a full elaboration of James's figuring pragmatism as female, very much in the shape of "a young bride about to be instructed in her duties."
106 Frye, *Great Code*, p. 168.
107 Ibid., pp. 86–7, 100–01.
108 Ibid., pp. 17–18.
109 Henry Corbin, *Spiritual Body and Celestial Earth: From Mazdean Iran to Shi'ite Iran*, tr. Nancy Pearson, Bollingen Series XCI:2, (Princeton: Princeton University Press: 1977), p. xii.
110 Ludwig Wittgenstein, *Philosophical Investigations*, tr. G. E. M. Anscombe (New York: Macmillan Publishing, 1968 [1953]), §116 and §109, pp. 48e, 47e.

3. Method: Charles Sanders Peirce, The call of the wild

1 Charles Sanders Peirce, *Photometric Researches in the Years 1872–1875* (Leipzig: Wilhelm Engelman, 1878), p. 93.
2 The details concerning Peirce's work for the Harvard Observatory, which when he began was under the direction of Joseph G. Winlock and supervised by the United States Coast and Geodetic Survey, are complicated primarily by issues of personality and power between Benjamin Peirce (Charles's father and at the time head of the Coast Survey) and Charles William Eliot (who had once been a student of Benjamin Peirce's) and between President Eliot and Charles Peirce himself. For a complete discussion, see Joseph Brent, *Charles Sanders Peirce: A Life* (Bloomington and Indianapolis: Indiana University Press, 1993), pp. 106–11.
3 Brent, *A Life*, p. 106. Brent continues: "Peirce placed considerable importance on the publication of this, his first major entry into the front ranks of scientific research, an effort which had already been noticed favorably by William Kingdon Clifford," in the *Fortnightly Review* 23 (1878): 788–9. (Brent mistakenly gives 1875 instead of 1878 for the year of the review issue.)
4 Ian Hacking was perhaps the first (1965) to note Peirce's invocation of "John the Evangelist's *three* cardinal virtues of faith, hope, and charity" as underpinning his understanding of the logical foundation of science. "'Charity' ... not the charitable donations to the poor that Peirce mocked" – in this following Ralph Waldo Emerson, I would add – "but the classical rendering of *caritas*, often translated as disinterested love," and which Hilary Putnam and

Hacking translate as the "altruism" that "probable reasoning requires, among other things ... in order to be sound." See Ian Hacking, "On Not Being a Pragmatist" in Misak, *New Pragmatists*, p. 43. Brent remarks that it was from Peirce's discussions with his first wife, Harriet Melusina Fay (Zina), that Peirce came to include the Christian virtues in his triadic relations. Zina at age twenty-three, in 1859, had experienced a religious conversion; they married in 1862. She became an active feminist who believed in a "true trinity of Father, Mother, and Only Son," the feminine principle in the place of the Holy Spirit. In his text, Brent notes that he believes "that their discussions of the Trinity and community influenced his [Peirce's] thinking about categories of being and the nature of validity in science." As Brent observes, in his last Lowell Institute Lecture in the fall of 1866, Peirce in closing offers: "Here, therefore, we have a divine trinity of the object, interpretant, and ground.... In many respects, this trinity agrees with the Christian trinity; indeed I am not aware that there are any points of disagreement. The interpretant is evidently the Divine *Logos* or word; and if our former guess that a Reference to an interpretant is Paternity be right, this would be also the *Son of God*. The *ground*, being that partaking of which is requisite to any communication with the Symbol, corresponds in its function to the Holy Spirit." (Peirce's capitalizations and italics) See Brent, *A Life*, pp. 62–7 for further details, including Zina's relationships to such literary figures as Emerson, James Russell Lowell, and George Eliot.

5 Peirce, *Collected Papers*, vol. 6, p. 332.

6 John F. Sowa, "Signs, Processes, and Language Games: Foundations for Ontology" (October 2006), http://www.jfsowa.com/pubs/signproc.htm, p. 14.

7 This student was Charles Eliot, later to become president of Harvard, who in that capacity was to project onto Charles Sanders Peirce his resistance to Benjamin Peirce's ideas and his resentment toward him for his not having given Eliot "first place in the [last] class" he took with him. See Brent, *A Life*, pp. 108–9.

8 *CPP*, p. 904.

9 Rivka Galchen, "Dream Machine: The Mind-Expanding World of Quantum Computing," *New Yorker* (May 2, 2011), 35.

10 Ibid., 39.

11 Charles Sanders Peirce, "Training in Reasoning," Lecture 5, *Reasoning and the Logic of Things: The Cambridge Conference Lectures of 1898*, ed. Kenneth Laine Ketner, with an Introduction by Ketner and Hilary Putnam (Cambridge, MA and London: Harvard University Press, 1992), pp. 192–3. An illustration of the practical yield of this kind of imaginative projection is Peirce's 1879 Quincuncial Projection map of the planet's surface where the whole sphere is represented on repeated squares; tessellations showing the connection of all parts of the earth's surface and superior to other kinds of maps, including the Mercator projection, in having the least distortion, with the angular relation of meridians and parallels strictly preserved. Peirce's Quincuncial Projection

continues to be used for meteorological, magnetological, and other purposes. Googling "Charles S. Peirce's Quincuncial Projection Map" will provide samples.

12 Charles Sanders Peirce, "Some Consequences of Four Incapacities," originally published in the *Journal of Speculative Philosophy* (1868), reprinted in *The Essential Peirce*, vol. 1, pp. 28–55.

13 Charles Sanders Peirce, "How to Make Our Ideas Clear" in *The Essential Peirce*, vol. 1, pp. 139–40.

14 Seth Lloyd, *Programming the Universe* (New York: Vintage Books, 2007), p. 164.

15 Peirce, "Training in Reasoning," *Reasoning and the Logic of Things*, p. 192.

16 *Nature, EL,* p. 7. This passage seems to echo Section 10 of Emanuel Swedenborg's *The Economy of the Animal Kingdom* (full bibliographic details in note 49 here following), where we find: "Whether a statement be true or not, is easily ascertained. If it be true, all experience spontaneously evidences and favors it, and likewise all the rules of true philosophy: and what I have often wondered at, various hypotheses, in proportion as they are founded on some common notion, either coincide with it, or else indicate particular points of contact or approximation; much as the shadowy appearances of the morning are shewn in their connexion with real objects by the rising sun. When the truth is present everything yields a suffrage in its favor; and therefore it immediately declares itself and wins belief; or, as the saying is, displays itself naked." While Emerson would not have had access before 1845 to an English translation of this text, he was deeply familiar with Sampson Reed's *Notes on the Observation of the Mind* – a pure Swedenborgian work.

17 From "Swedenborg; or, The Mystic" in *Representative Men, EL,* p. 671.

18 From another letter to William James (perhaps not sent) concerning the lectures that will comprise *Reasoning and the Logic of Things*, partially quoted in that volume, p. 24.

19 Kenneth Laine Ketner and Hilary Putnam, "Introduction: The Consequences of Mathematics," *Reasoning and the Logic of Things*, p. 2.

20 Charles Sanders Peirce, Lecture 2, "Types of Reasoning," in *Reasoning and the Logic of Things*, pp. 140–2.

21 James, *Writings 1878–1899*, p. 1079.

22 Peirce reviewed James Sr.'s *The Secret of Swedenborg: Being an Elucidation of His Doctrine of the Divine Natural Humanity* in the *North American Review* 110 (April 1870): 463–8. In 1863, the same year that James Sr. published *Substance and Shadow or, Morality and Religion in their Relation to Life: An Essay Upon the Physics of Creation*, Peirce for the first time in print referred to Swedenborg in an essay entitled, "Analysis of the Ego."

23 "Swedenborg; or, the Mystic," *EL*, pp. 677, 671.

24 Eugene Taylor, "Peirce and Swedenborg," *Studia Swedenborgiana*, vol. 6, no.1 (June 1986), online version at: www.baysidechurch.org/studia/default. asp?AuthorID=45. Taylor notes that it is likely that William's talk of his father to Peirce spurred his interest in Swedenborg while at the same time, James

Sr.'s "gift to Harvard around this time of some forty original editions of Swedenborg must have attracted Peirce's attention" as well. Peirce was primed to pursue reading Swedenborg because of his own earlier preparation under his father's guidance in studying Immanuel Kant, who had himself early in his career, in 1763, begun reading and investigating Swedenborg. Kant was particularly intrigued by Swedenborg's *Dreams of a Spirit-Seer* (1766) and at one point even tried to contact him.

25 Charles Sanders Peirce, "The First Rule of Logic," Lecture 4, *Reasoning and the Logic of Things*, p. 177.

26 Brent, *A Life*, p. 33.

27 Peirce, *Reasoning and the Logic of Things*, p. 19.

28 Brent, *A Life*, p. 269.

29 "Nature," *EL*, p. 9.

30 As noted in Chapter 2 as well, from "History," *EL*, p. 251.

31 Lloyd, *Programming the Universe*, p. 50.

32 From Charles Sanders Peirce's manuscript, *MS* 891, Houghton Library at Harvard University and quoted in Kenneth Laine Ketner, *His Glassy Essence: An Autobiography of Charles Sanders Peirce* (Nashville and London: Vanderbilt University Press, 1998), p. 191.

33 Ketner, *Glasssy Essence*, pp. 196–7.

34 Freadman, *Machinery of Talk*, pp. xxiii–xxiv. The parenthetical references are to the Fisch edition mentioned in the text here: *Writings of Charles S. Peirce: A Chronological Edition*. 6 vols. ed. Max H. Fisch (Bloomington: Indiana University Press, 1982). Missing from Freadman's account is that Peirce was not alone in foregrounding the importance of conversation. Not only had Emerson pointed the direction, but Peirce's friend and colleague, Chauncey Wright (also a mathematician, a logician, and constant member of "The Metaphysical Club") defined philosophy, following the practice of Socrates, *as* conversation; see earlier discussion in "Conversation is a game of circles" section of Chapter 1 in this volume.

35 Charles Sanders Peirce's manuscript, *MS* 672, Houghton Library, and quoted in Freadman, *Machinery of Talk*, p. xii.

36 "Nature," *EL*, p. 15.

37 Charles Sanders Peirce, "Philosophy and the Conduct of Life," Lecture 1, *Reasoning and the Logic of Things*, p. 105.

38 Ketner and Putnam, "Introduction," *Reasoning and the Logic of Things*, p. 4.

39 John P. Murphy, *From Peirce to Davidson* (Boulder, San Francisco and London: Westview Press, 1990), p. 8. Murphy adds: "While reading Kant, Peirce sometimes 'came upon strains of thought that recalled the ways of thinking of the laboratory.' So he felt he might 'trust to' Kant. As a consequence of this, his industry, and his genius, the teenage Peirce became so deeply imbued with many of Kant's ways of thinking that he was never able to free himself of them. 'When I was a babe in philosophy my bottle was filled from the udders of Kant,' he wrote in 1860."

40 Ketner and Putnam, "Introduction," *Reasoning and the Logic of Things*, p. 19.

41 Hilary Putnam, "Comments on the Lectures," *Reasoning and the Logic of Things*, pp. 94, 96–7.

42 Sami Pihlstrom, "Peirce's Place in the Pragmatist Tradition," *The Cambridge Companion to Peirce*, ed. Cheryl Misak (Cambridge: Cambridge University Press, 2004), p. 41.

43 The title of one of Stevens's poems is "Of the Manner of Addressing Clouds," *CPP*, p. 44.

44 Ralph Barton Perry, *The Thought and Character of William James* (Nashville and London: Vanderbilt University Press, 1996 [1947 one-volume edition]), pp. 131–2.

45 From "A Sketch of Logical Criticism," *Collected Papers of Charles Sanders Peirce*, vol. 6, as quoted in Perry, p. 132.

46 Taylor, "Peirce and Swedenborg," *Studia Swedenborgiana*, last paragraph.

47 William James's phrase describing his brother Henry after his long residence in England: "He's really ... a native of the James family, and has no other country," as quoted by F. O. Matthiessen, *The James Family: A Group Biography* (New York: Vintage Books, 1980 [1947]), p. 69.

48 Henry James, *A Small Boy and Others* in *Autobiography*, pp. 123–4.

49 "In 1908 and 1909 ... Peirce published [in the *Monist*] the 'amazing mazes' series. These were a development of his 1903 Lowell Lectures and had the same purpose, to expose to a popular audience the visible skeleton of logical form – 'a moving picture of thought'" (Brent, *A Life*, p. 311).

50 Emanuel Swedenborg, *The Economy of the Animal Kingdom, Considered Anatomically, Physically, and Philosophically*, vol. I, tr. Rev. Augustus Clissold (London: W. Newbery, 1845), pp. 8–10. Charles G. Gross in "Emanuel Swedenborg: A Neuroscientist Before His Time" has reminded us that this text published as *Oeconomia Regni Animalis* in 1740 was Swedenborg's first published writing on the brain: "By 'regni animali' he meant kingdom of the anima or soul; he considered this kingdom or realm to be the human body and, particularly, the brain. By 'oeconomia' he meant organization. Thus a better translation of his title might be *Organization of the Body*, or, less literally, *The Biological Bases of the Soul*. He also dealt with the brain and sense organs in his second major biological work, *Regnum Animale*, published a few years later. Again, 'animale' here means pertaining to the soul." See Charles G. Gross, *Brain, Vision, Memory: Tales in the History of Neuroscience* (Cambridge, MA: MIT Press, 1999), p. 123. It is to be especially remarked again here that the translator of *Regnum Animale* into English, in two volumes as *The Animal Kingdom* (1843–44) was James John Garth Wilkinson, a close friend and correspondent of Henry James, Sr., and for whom, as noted in Chapter 2 as well, the third James son, Garth Wilkinson (1845–83, known as "Wilky") was named.

51 From a letter of William James to C. S. Peirce in early 1898 concerning the lectures Peirce was to begin delivering in February and drafts of which he had sent to James to preview; in *Reasoning and the Logic of Things*, p. 32. In the same letter, James asked Peirce to change the order of the lectures or perhaps

reconsider even offering one that seemed to James overly full of "paradoxical irradiations."

52 Ketner and Putnam, "Introduction," *Reasoning and the Logic of Things*, p. 36.

53 Ross Posnock, *The Trial of Curiosity: Henry James, William James, and the Challenge of Modernity* (New York and Oxford: Oxford University Press, 1991), p. 155.

54 The research and literature on this subject are vast, occupying the attention of those most active in the fields of cognitive neuroscience, consciousness studies, and philosophy of mind: in addition to Edelman, Daniel Dennett, Ray Jackendoff, the late Francis Crick, Christof Koch, Mark Solms, Paul and Patricia Churchland, David Marr, David Chalmers, Roger Penrose, Andy Clark, and John Searle. A comprehensive yet accessible survey is offered by Crick and Koch in "The Unconscious Homunculus" in *The Neuronal Correlates of Consciousness*, ed. Thomas Metzinger (Cambridge, MA: MIT Press, 2000), pp. 103–10. There are also several recent titles by Jackendoff, who is also, as indicated in the text here, a performing musician, that provide excellent examples and explanations of the mental processes being explored.

55 Leonie Welberg, "Turning Neural Activity into Words," *Nature Reviews Neuroscience* 13, 150 (March 2012), doi:10.1038/nrn3206.

56 Ralph Waldo Emerson, *The Collected Works of Ralph Waldo Emerson*, vol. 6, ed. Alfred R. Ferguson et al. (Cambridge MA: Harvard University Press, The Belknap Press, 1971–2003), p. 2.

57 Francis Crick and Christof Koch, "The Unconscious Homunculus" in *The Neuronal Correlates of Consciousness*, ed. T. Metzinger (Cambridge, MA: MIT Press, 2000), pp. 103–10, online version at: www.klab.caltech.edu/~koch/unconscious-homunculus.html, including discussion of Ray Jackendoff, *Consciousness and the Computational Mind* (Cambridge, MA: MIT Press, 1987).

58 Quoted in Crick and Koch, "Unconscious Homunculus."

59 John Banville, "The Most Entertaining Philosopher," *New York Review of Books*, vol. LVIII, no. 16 (October 27, 2011), 40–2; a review of Robert Richardson, *The Heart of William James* (Cambridge, MA: Harvard University Press, 2011). As observed in an earlier note, William James cloaked his identity in describing his "vastation," attributing the experience to an anonymous French correspondent. For a full discussion of this experience and James's account, see my chapter, "William James's feeling of *if*" in *Natural History of Pragmatism*, pp. 98–136.

60 It is worth remarking in this context the story of Bernard Moitessier, one of the entrants in the famous *Sunday Times* Golden Globe single-handed round-the-world sailing race in 1968. As he neared completion and about to win (one of the two successful competitors – nine had set out, the other still in the race was Robin Knox-Johnston), knowing that his wife and children were waiting to greet him on the dock at Plymouth, Moitessier, whose "conversation" over

the preceding eight months had been with the elements, with sea creatures and with his craft, turned around to set off for another circumnavigation. Knox-Johnston won by default.

61 Ralph Waldo Emerson, *Journals and Miscellaneous Notebooks*, vol. 3, ed. Linda Allardt et al. (Cambridge, MA: Harvard University Press, 1960–82), p. 316.

62 Crick and Koch, "Unconscious Homunculus."

63 Quoted in Perry, *Thought and Character*, p. 130, from a paper (circa 1906) published for the first time in vol. 5 (1934), §12, of the *Collected Papers of Charles Sanders Peirce*.

64 Charles G. Gross, *Brain, Vision, Memory: Tales in the History of Neuroscience* (Cambridge, MA and London, England: MIT Press, 1999), p. 131.

65 *Transactions of the International Swedenborg Congress*, July 4–8, 1910 (London: The Swedenborg Society, 1911 [Second Edition]), p. 21

66 Ibid., p. 47.

67 Ibid.

68 Ibid., p. 48.

69 Ibid., p. 55.

70 *CPP*, p. 47.

71 Ricardo Nemirovsky and Francesca Ferrara, *New Avenues for the Microanalysis of Mathematics Learning; Connecting Talk, Gesture, and Eye Motion* (2004). At http://www.terc.edu/mathofchange/EyeTracking/EyeTrackerPaper.pdf.

72 Thomas Browne, *Religio Medici in Religio Medici and Other Writings* (New York: E. P. Dutton, 1951), p. 16.

73 "The Method of Nature," *EL*, p.122.

74 *EL*, pp. 456, 459.

75 Ibid., p. 464.

76 Ibid., p. 452.

77 Ibid., p. 451.

78 Brent, *A Life*, p. 308.

79 "Montaigne; or, the Skeptic," *Representative Men, EL*, p. 696.

80 Michael H. G. Hoffmann, "How To Get It: Diagrammatic Reasoning as a Tool of Knowledge Development and Its Pragmatic Dimension," *Foundations of Science* 9 (2004): 285–305: 293.

81 Introduction to *The Essential Peirce*, vol. 1, p. xx.

4. Purpose: John Dewey, The conduct of life

1 For a full discussion of Edwards's significance for Emerson and for James, see Richardson, *Natural History of Pragmatism*. To be noted as well is that John Edwin Smith, in his historicizing of pragmatism, considered Edwards a forerunner; see esp. *Jonathan Edwards: Puritan, Preacher, Philosopher* (Notre Dame, IN: Notre Dame University Press, 1993).

2 John Dewey, *Experience and Nature* (New York: Dover, 1958 [1929]), p. 72; this title hereafter cited as *EN*.

3 In this chapter, following Dewey's convention, "esthetics" is spelled without the initial "a," which I prefer both because it preserves something of the Greek original and because of the preponderant historical usage.

4 "Emerson – The Philosopher of Democracy," *International Journal of Ethics*, vol. 13, no. 4 (July 1903), 405–13; 409; a paper read at the Emerson Memorial Meeting, the University of Chicago, May 25, 1903.

5 Ibid., p. 412.

6 Jay Martin, *The Education of John Dewey: A Biography* (New York: Columbia University Press, 2002), p. 194.

7 John Dewey, *Studies in Logical Theory* (Chicago: University of Chicago Press, 1903), pp. xiv-xv.

8 Posnock, "Earth," p. 57.

9 This phrase, slightly modified, is borrowed from the closing line of Stevens's "Peter Quince at the Clavier," where memory corrects a perversion of the sacred and "makes a constant sacrament of praise"; *CPP*, p. 74.

10 John Dewey, *Art as Experience* (New York: Perigee, 1980 [1934]), p. 49; this title hereafter cited as *AE*.

11 Ibid., p. 65.

12 Ibid., pp. 185–6.

13 Ibid., p. 13.

14 *EN*, p. 4a.

15 *AE*, p. 19.

16 Ibid., p. 220.

17 *EN*, p. xv.

18 *AE*, p. 60.

19 Ibid., pp. 119–20.

20 John Dewey, *The Quest for Certainty: A Study of the Relation Between Knowledge and Action* (New York: Paragon, 1979 [1929]), p. 245.

21 *AE*, p. 81.

22 Ibid., p. viii.

23 Dewey, *Quest*, p. 277.

24 "Experience," *EL*, p. 487.

25 *EN*, pp. 119–20.

26 Ibid., p. 149.

27 Ibid., p. 1.

28 Ibid., p. 72.

29 *AE*, p. 211.

30 Ibid., p. 169.

31 Ibid., p. 53.

32 Ibid., p. 23.

33 Ibid., p. 56.

34 Ibid., p. 264.

35 *EN*, p. 24.

36 Ibid., pp. xiv–xv.

37 *AE*, p. 194.

38 Quoted by Dewey in *AE*, p. 18.

39 *EN*, pp. 20–1.

40 *AE*, p. 104.

41 *EN*, p. 161.

42 *AE*, p. 209.

43 *EN*, pp. 42–3.

44 Ibid., p. 19.

45 *AE*, pp. 6–7.

46 *EN*, p. xii.

47 *AE*, pp. 18, 29.

48 Charles Sanders Peirce's phrase from a 1909 manuscript indicating what "has its Being in its power of serving as intermediary between its Object and a Mind. Such, too, is a living constitution – a daily newspaper, a great fortune, a social 'movement'" (Peirce's capitalizations), in Brent, *A Life*, p. 311.

49 Jay Martin has a different sense of Dewey's relation to Emerson, observing that "Later in life, Dewey was often asked by those who knew little about the American transcendental movement if he had been influenced by Emerson. His answers were always a bit tepid, surprisingly so to those who inquired" (p. 42). Martin goes on to explain that "Emerson had little impact on Dewey" for two reasons: that Emerson had made a break with his Congregational background and, more importantly, that it was James Marsh, "the American Coleridge," who was for Dewey "*the* transcendentalist" (p. 43). As noted in these pages, my sense is that Dewey's estimation of Emerson is loudly and clearly proclaimed in "Emerson – The Philosopher of Democracy" and that the evidence of his profound debt to Emerson is everywhere apparent. An account of the Emersonian echoes resonating through Dewey's work would be a volume itself.

50 *Nature*, *EL*, pp. 10–11.

51 *EN*, p. viii.

52 "Emerson – The Philosopher of Democracy," p. 409.

53 Richardson, *Natural History of Pragmatism*, pp. 62–8, 268n.5.

54 From the back cover of the first (1980) Perigee printing of *AE*.

55 *EN*, p. 25.

56 *EL*, p. 130.

57 *AE*, p. 195.

58 Richard Rorty, "Pragmatism and Romanticism," *Philosophy as Cultural Politics: Philosophical Papers, Volume 4* (Cambridge: Cambridge University Press, 2007), p. 108.

59 *EN*, p. 81.

60 Ibid., p. 187.

61 *The Philosophy of Jonathan Edwards from His Private Notebooks*, ed. Harvey G. Townsend (Eugene: University of Oregon Press, 1955), p. 130.

62 James, *Pragmatism*, p. 540.

63 *EN*, pp. 76–7.

64 James, *Pragmatism*, p. 540.

65 *EN*, pp. 9, 29–30.

66 Dewey, *Studies in Logical Theory*, pp. 2–3.

67 Martin, *Education*, p. 16.

68 Dewey, *Studies in Logical Theory*, p. 7. It is to be especially noted in connection with Dewey's attention to breath and breathing and to the mind-body problem, the ongoing work of the neo-pragmatist who is perhaps Dewey's most direct heir, Richard Shusterman. In his focus on what he has called "somaesthetics," Shusterman has valuably advanced Dewey's original insights as well as his interdisciplinary approach while along the way recuperating Emerson's and Thoreau's seminal contributions to this range of experience. See, most recently, his *Thinking Through the Body: Essays in Somaesthetics* (Cambridge: Cambridge University Press, 2012).

69 Martin, *Education*, p. 286, quoting Dewey in the brief biography of him officially composed by his daughter Jane.

70 "About Drawing: An Interview," in *Richard Serra, Writings Interviews* (Chicago and London: University of Chicago Press, 1994), p. 52.

71 For a detailed description of Cavell's esteem for Kaplan, see Stanley Cavell, *Little Did I Know: Excerpts from Memory* (Stanford: Stanford University Press, 2010), pp. 242–5. Cavell referred to Kaplan this way in an extended conversation I had with him in February 2010 that was the basis for "The Transcendentalist Strain," an interview that appeared in the April/May 2010 issue of *BookForum* – only about 10% of the conversation could be printed.

72 As Martin has discussed, Dewey initially rejected Peirce, acknowledging his major influence only years later. See esp. pp. 73–4 in *Education*.

73 *AE*, p. 183.

74 Dewey, *Quest*, p. 111. It is worth adding here that in contemporary theorizing, it is specified that our universe is "a particular spacetime." As noted by Seth Lloyd, a quantum mechanical engineer working at the edge of current investigations and the designer of the first feasible quantum computer: "General relativity is a theory of space and time and their interaction with matter. Each possible configuration of space and time interacting with matter is called a spacetime. Our universe is a particular spacetime" (*Programming the Universe*, p. 171).

75 In this connection, it is informing to note Bertrand Russell's observation about Dewey in a letter to Ottoline Morrell as recorded by Martin. Dewey and Russell took a walk and continued a lunchtime conversation the day after Dewey had addressed the Harvard Philosophic Club at the invitation of T. S. Eliot, then a young Ph. D. candidate; his topic was "What Are Minds?" Russell was in Cambridge delivering the series of Lowell lectures on "Our Knowledge of the External World." "To my surprise, I liked him very much," he wrote to Morrell. "He has a large, slow-moving mind, very empirical and candid, with something of the impassivity and impartiality of a natural force." As Martin continues, "Russell noted that when he made a philosophic observation about the concept of 'I,' Dewey saw its importance at once, but Ralph Barton Perry failed to grasp the point. Dewey stayed to listen to a talk by

Russell, and Russell noted, 'the most effective criticism was from Dewey, who again impressed me very much, both as a philosopher and as a lovable man.'" (*Education*, pp. 275–6.)

76 *EN*, p. 232.
77 Dewey, "Emerson – The Philosopher of Democracy," p. 411.
78 "Experience," *EL*, p. 491.
79 Dewey, *Quest*, pp. 113, 167.
80 Dewey, "Emerson – The Philosopher of Democracy," p. 407.
81 Whitehead, *Science and the Modern World*, pp. 132–3.
82 In Dewey, "Emerson – The Philosopher of Democracy," p. 408.
83 Dewey, *Quest*, pp. 200, 204–5, 215.
84 *AE*, p. 255.
85 Ibid., p. 168. It is worth recalling that the often-quoted words of James, "ever, not quite," come from the famous 1898 Berkeley talk that announced pragmatism's birth: "Truth's fullness is elusive; ever not quite, not quite!"
86 Ibid., p. 263. It is worth recalling in this context Northrop Frye's observation that "God" should be considered a verb; see discussion at the end of Chapter 2 in this volume.
87 *EN*, pp. 158–9.
88 Martin, *Education*, p. 43.
89 Ibid., p. 195.
90 Ibid., pp. 195–6.
91 As Peirce notes in *Photometric Researches*, p. 174.
92 Kant's own first use of "architectonic" comes near the end of the Introduction to the Critique of Pure Reason and is fully elaborated in the third chapter, "The Architectonic of Pure Reason," the first paragraph of which reads: "By the term *architectonic* I mean the art of constructing a system. Without systematic unity, our knowledge cannot become science; it will be an aggregate, and not a system. Thus architectonic is the doctrine of the scientific in knowledge, and therefore necessarily forms part of our method." (Immanuel Kant, *Critique of Pure Reason*, revised and expanded translation based on Meiklejohn, ed. Vasilis Politis [London: Everyman/J. M. Dent, 1993 (1934)], p. 532). Essential to Kant's "architectonic" is having an end or purpose in mind in constructing a system; it is easy to see, then, the particular affinity with pragmatism's method as articulated by Peirce.
93 *Charles Darwin's Notebooks, 1836–1844: Geology, Transmutation of Species, Metaphysical Enquiries*, ed. Paul H. Barrett, Peter J. Gautrey, Sandra Herbert, David Kohn, and Sydney Smith (Ithaca, NY: Cornell University Press, 1987), p. 284.
94 Charles Sanders Peirce, "The Doctrine of Chances" (1878), in *The Essential Peirce*, vol. 1, p. 144.
95 *AE*, p. 169.
96 Ibid., pp. 224, 228.
97 "Kant was a past-master in first drawing distinctions and then erecting them into compartmental divisions," *AE*, p. 252. In a footnote Dewey astutely

notes, "The effect upon German thought of Capitalization has hardly received proper attention," reminding us of William James's having observed in his famous "Stream of Thought" chapter of *The Principles of Psychology* of the limitation to thinking resulting from the preponderant emphasis on substantives in Anglo-Saxon and Germanic languages.

98 *EN*, p. 49
99 Ibid., p. 172.
100 Ibid., pp. 170–1, 173.
101 Ibid., p. 174.
102 *AE*, p. 246.
103 Ibid.
104 *EN*, p. 222.
105 Ibid., pp. 245–6.
106 James, *Pragmatism*, p. 540, noted earlier as well.
107 First published in *Popular Science Monthly* 75 (1909), pp. 90–8, with the title "Darwin's Influence upon Philosophy." Revised and reprinted in John Dewey, *The Influence of Darwin on Philosophy* (New York: Henry Holt, 1910), pp. 1–19.
108 *EN*, pp. 73–4.
109 Ibid., pp. 37–8.
110 "Connoisseur of Chaos," *CPP*, p. 195.
111 Arnaud Maillet, *The Claude Glass: Use and Meaning of the Black Mirror in Western Art*, trans. Jeff Fort (New York: Zone Books, 2009), n. p. 281 and Gilles Deleuze, *Kant's Critical Philosophy*, trans. Hugh Tomlinson and Barbara Habberjam (London: Athlone, 1984), pp. 13–14 and 20, as indicated by Maillet.
112 *AE*, note p. 252.
113 Ibid., p. 23.
114 James A. Good, ed., *The Early American Reception of German Idealism* (Bristol: Thoemmes Continuum, 2002), vol. 2, Introduction, pp. v-xvii. For a fuller discussion, see also John J. Duffy, ed., *Coleridge's American Disciples: The Selected Correspondence of James Marsh* (Amherst: University of Massachusetts Press, 1973) and, more recently, Samantha C. Harvey, "Coleridge's American Revival: James Marsh, John Dewey, and the Legacy of Vermont Transcendentalism," *Symbiosis: A Journal of Anglo-American Literary Relations* 15:1 (2011), 77–103.
115 Good, *Early American Reception*, p. v.
116 Martin, *Education*, p. 43. Good reports Dewey's words somewhat differently, noting that when asked when he got over Coleridge, Dewey replied, "I never did. Coleridge represents pretty much my religious views still, but I quit talking about them because nobody else is interested in them" (p. vi).
117 Lloyd, *Programming the Universe*, p. 9.
118 As he phrased it in *AE*, p. 189.
119 See Richardson, *Natural History of Pragmatism*, pp. 29–30 for a fuller discussion.

120 *AE*, p. 72. Dewey is quoting from Lecture IX, "Conversion," in *The Varieties of Religious Experience* (in James, *Writings 1902–1910*, pp. 194–5).

5. Effects 1: Stanley Cavell, Squaring the circle: transcendentalist pragmatism

1 "Experience," *EL*, p. 491.
2 I introduced and explored this variant of the method in "Thinking in Cavell: The Transcendentalist Strain" in *Stanley Cavell*, ed. Loxley and Taylor (Manchester and New York: Manchester University Press, 2012), pp. 199–224.
3 Ludwig Wittgenstein, *Philosophical Investigations*, third edition, tr. G. E. M. Anscombe (New York: Macmillan, 1958 [1953]), §38 (as noted by Cavell, *This New Yet Unapproachable America: Lectures after Emerson after Wittgenstein* [Albuquerque: Living Batch Press, 1989], p. 56). In connection with this aspect in the case of William James, Richard Rorty has observed: "He deplored the fact that philosophers still followed Kant rather than Mill, still thought of validity as raining down upon a claim 'from some sublime dimension of being, which the moral law inhabits, much as upon the steel of the compass-needle the influence of the Pole rains down from out of the starry heavens' (*The Will to Believe*, vol. 6 [1979] of *The Works of William James*, ed. Frederick H. Burkhardt, Fredson Bowers, and Ignas K. Skrupskelis [Cambridge MA: Harvard University Press, 1975–1988])," in Rorty, "Religious Faith, Intellectual Responsibility, and Romance," *The Cambridge Companion to William James*, ed. Ruth Anna Putnam (Cambridge: Cambridge University Press, 1997), p. 84.
4 Cavell has recounted in several places his coming to understand pragmatism by way of Kaplan in his devotion to Dewey. For an analytically descriptive rendition, see his Introduction to *Conditions Handsome and Unhandsome: The Constitution of Emersonian Perfectionism*, The Carus Lectures, 1988 (Chicago and London: University of Chicago Press, 1990), pp. 13–15, where, as in other texts, Cavell refers to Footnote 31 of the "Must We Mean What We Say" chapter in the eponymous volume, where he writes: "Wittgenstein's role in combatting the idea of privacy (whether of the meaning of what is said or what is done), and in emphasizing the *functions* and *contexts* of language, scarcely needs to be mentioned. It might be worth pointing out that these teachings are fundamental to American pragmatism; but then we must keep in mind how different their arguments sound, and admit that in philosophy it is the sound which makes all the difference" (*Must We Mean What We Say? A Book of Essays* [Cambridge: Cambridge University Press, 1976 (1969)], p. 36).
5 Cavell has more recently revised his understanding of pragmatism's scope and possibilities. In response to Russell Goodman's suggestions concerning Dewey "that Cavell looks only at one side of Dewey ... the 'let's make everything scientific' side," Cavell has acknowledged, following Goodman, that he has perhaps neglected Dewey's "romantic, poetic and non-instrumental side." (See *Contending with Stanley Cavell*, ed. Russell B. Goodman [Oxford and New York: Oxford University Press, 2005], p. 8). And in the case of the

pragmatists' use of natural historical and scientific information generally, Cavell has acknowledged that at least in the case of the Darwinian event and later developments in neuroscience, taking account of this material "presents a formidable charge against [his] oppositional sense of our philosophical temperament" (as he phrased it for the "puff" for my *Natural History of Pragmatism*).

6 Richard J. Bernstein, *The Pragmatic Turn* (Cambridge, UK: Polity Press, 2010), p. 12.

7 While Cavell alludes to William James's description of the "sick soul" in *The Varieties of Religious Experience* and quotes from *Pragmatism* in at least one instance, it is not apparent that he has ever found himself "in conversation" with James's texts. As for Peirce, I am not familiar with his even mentioning him.

8 Bernstein, *Pragmatic Turn*, p. 12. Bernstein offers a very useful description of the climate in which Cavell, as well as Rorty, Hilary Putnam, George Herbert Mead, and others of their generation were trained: "From the perspective of the logical positivists [whose presence and work came to dominate American universities after World War II], the pragmatic thinkers were viewed as having seen through a glass darkly what was now seen much more clearly. The *myth* [Bernstein's emphasis] developed (and unfortunately became entrenched) that pragmatism was primarily an anticipation of logical positivism, in particular, the positivist's verifiability criterion of meaning." And, further: "To the extent that the classical pragmatists were studied, it was primarily by American intellectual historians – not by philosophers. Even though philosophers occasionally paid lip service to the [*sic*] pragmatism, there was a prevailing sense that there really wasn't much that a 'serious' philosophy student could learn from the pragmatists. From that time until today, many philosophy students at our most prestigious graduate schools do not even bother to read the works of the classical pragmatists."

9 Cavell gave this account in response to a question asked by a member of the Ralph Waldo Emerson Society on the occasion of Cavell's being presented with the 2009 Distinguished Achievement Award at the meeting of the society during the American Language Association gathering in Boston. In Ross Posnock's recent review of *American Nietzsche: A History of an Icon and His Ideas* by Jennifer Ratner-Rosenhagen in *The Nation* (November 21, 2011), he notes that Ratner-Rosenhagen claims that "Reading Nietzsche brought [Harold] Bloom and Cavell back to Emerson . . . ."

10 "What's the Use of Calling Emerson a Pragmatist?" is the title of a lecture Cavell delivered at "The Revival of Pragmatism" conference held at The Graduate Center, CUNY in November 1995, organized by The Center for the Humanities under the direction of Morris Dickstein. The idea for the conference was proposed by Charles Molesworth and planned by a committee that also included Louis Menand, John Patrick Digggins, Charles Landesman, and myself. Cavell's lecture was published together with the other proceedings in

The Revival of Pragmatism: New Essays on Social Thought, Law, and Culture, ed. Morris Dickstein (Durham, NC: Duke University Press, 1998), pp. 72–80 and in Stanley Cavell, *Emerson's Transcendental Etudes*, ed. David Justin Hodge (Stanford: Stanford University Press, 2003), pp. 215–23.

11 Louis Menand in his Introduction to *Pragmatism: A Reader* (New York: Vintage Books, 1997) dates the beginning of the revival of pragmatism to the appearance of Rorty's volume (p. xxv).

12 In a letter to his brother Henry James dated May 3, 1903, *Correspondence of William James*, vol. 3, p. 234.

13 As noted earlier, for an acute and comprehensive discussion, see Goodman, *Wittgenstein and William James*.

14 See Russell B. Goodman, "Cavell and American Philosophy" in *Contending with Stanley Cavell*, pp. 100–17.

15 Ian Hacking, "On Not Being a Pragmatist: Eight Reasons and a Cause" in Misak, *New Pragmatists*, p. 38: "[T]here is still a tendency abroad to speak of some 'linguistic philosophy' that covers both Wittgenstein and Oxford [meaning the school of ordinary language philosophy identified with J. L. Austin]. Aside from the fact that the two detested and despised each other, their instincts with respect to reality are quite different. Wittgenstein did not care a fig what we say in ordinary literate Viennese or English, and built a philosophy around imaginary possibilities."

16 See particularly Cavell's comments in the Introduction to his *Conditions Handsome and Unhandsome*, pp. 14–15.

17 Cavell, *Unapproachable America*, p. 95.

18 For a discussion of Newton's method in the *Opticks* as a linguistic analogue of the *experimentum crucis* ("crucial experiment"), see Richardson, *Natural History of Pragmatism*, pp. 24–8.

19 Susan Howe, *Pierce-Arrow* (New York: New Directions, 1997), p. 18.

20 Quoted in Brent, *A Life*, p. 59.

21 James, *Varieties*, pp. 448–9.

22 Reinhold Niebuhr, *The Irony of American History* (Chicago: University of Chicago Press, 2008), pp. 80–1.

23 Stanley Cavell, *A Pitch of Philosophy: Autobiographical Exercises* (Cambridge, MA and London: Harvard University Press, 1994) p. 13.

24 Cavell, Preface to *Conditions Handsome and Unhandsome*, p. xxix.

25 Cavell, Introduction to *Conditions Handsome and Unhandsome*, p. 2.

26 Cavell, *Unapproachable America*, pp. 57–8.

27 Bernstein, *Pragmatic Turn*, p. 17.

28 He reported to his sister late on the night of November 14, 1866: "Where have I been? 'To C. S. Peirce's lecture, which I could not understand a word of, but rather enjoyed the sensation of listening to for an hour.'" *The Correspondence of William James*, vol. 4: *1856–1877*, ed. Ignas K. Skrupskelis and Elizabeth M. Berkeley (Charlottesville: University Press of Virginia, 1995), p. 144.

29 Andrew Robinson, "The Virtue of Vagueness," a review of Kees van Deemter, *Not Exactly: In Praise of Vagueness* (Oxford: Oxford University Press, 2010) in *Nature*, vol. 463, no. 11 (February 11, 2010), p. 736.

30 Ibid.

31 Cavell, *Unapproachable America*, p. 107.

32 Ibid., pp. 108–9.

33 Cavell, *Pitch*, p. 47.

34 Hadot, "Spiritual Exercises" in *Philosophy as a Way of Life*, pp. 32, 105.

35 Ibid., p. 105.

36 Stanley Cavell, "Old and New in Emerson and Nietzsche" in *Etudes*, p. 232.

37 Perry Miller, ed., *American Thought: Civil War to World War I* (New York and Toronto: Rinehart and Co..: 1954), p. xxxv.

38 "Nature," *EL*, p. 10.

39 William James, "Chronology," *Writings 1902–1910*, p. 1347.

40 James Conant, "Cavell and the Concept of America" in Goodman, *Contending with Stanley Cavell*, p. 62.

41 See note 10 in this chapter.

42 Cavell, "What's the Use …?" in *Revival*, p. 79.

43 Stanley Cavell, *Philosophy the Day after Tomorrow* (Cambridge, MA and London, England: The Belknap Press of Harvard University Press, 2005), p. 93.

44 Ibid.

45 Cavell, *Unapproachable America*, p. 72.

46 Gertrude Stein, "Composition as Explanation" in *Writings 1903–1932*, ed. Catharine R. Stimpson and Harriet Chessman (New York: The Library of America, 1998), p. 523.

47 Sandra Laugier, "Rethinking the Ordinary: Austin *after* Cavell" in Goodman, *Contending with Stanley Cavell*, p. 85.

48 First quotation from "The Method of Nature," others from "Circles": *EL*, pp. 116, 403, 409, 413. In connection with Emerson's "art in seducing souls" and his responsiveness to audience, see Joan Richardson, "Emerson's Sound Effects," *Raritan: A Quarterly Review* vol. 16, no. 3 (Winter 1997), 83–101.

49 James, *Principles*, pp. 5, 6–7.

50 *EL*, p. 23.

51 William James, "The Chicago School," in *Writings, 1902–1910*, p. 1137.

52 Cavell, "Old and New …," *Etudes*, p. 227.

53 Cavell, "Aversive Thinking …" in *Conditions Handsome and Unhandsome*, p. 39. The embedded parentheses belong to Cavell's idiosyncratic style about which he has this to say in the Acknowledgments section of *Must We Mean What We Say? A Book of Essays* (Cambridge: Cambridge University Press, 1976 [1969]), p. x: "I can hardly excuse … a certain craving for parentheses, whose visual clarity seems to me to outweigh their oddity; for if I had found better devices [also explained are his odd use of dots of omission and the use of a dash before sentences] for helping out my meaning, there would be no excuse for not having employed them."

54 Cavell, Introduction to *Conditions Handsome and Unhandsome*, p. 8.

55 Cavell, "Old and New ...," *Etudes*, p. 230.

56 See the discussion concerning Ray Jackendoff's findings in *Consciousness and the Computational Mind* in Chapter 3.

57 Cavell, *Etudes*, pp. 230–1.

58 Cavell, "What's the Use ...," in *Etudes*, p. 221.

59 "The Poet," *EL*, p. 455.

60 "Circles," *EL*, p. 409.

61 Cavell, *Unapproachable America*, p. 115.

62 In "The Uses of Great Men" from *Representative Men*, Emerson describes one of the activities of the imagination as "somersaulting." The passage in question will be quoted further along in the main text of this chapter.

63 This observation appears first in the title essay of *Must We Mean What We Say?* p. 36, n. 31, of which essay Cavell observes, it "is the earliest essay of mine that I still use" in "What's the Use ..." in *Revival* and *Etudes*, where it is quoted and elaborated.

64 Cavell, Introduction to *Conditions Handsome and Unhandsome*, p. 13.

65 Cavell, *Little Did I Know*, p. 225.

66 Cavell is not alone in reading "Experience" in this way. Barbara Packer and Sharon Cameron are among those who also have, as Cavell has noted variously. See Sharon Cameron, "Representing Grief: Emerson's 'Experience,'" *Representations* no. 15 (Summer 1986), 15–41 and Barbara Packer, "Experience" in *Emerson's Fall: A New Interpretation of the Major Essays* (New York: Continuum, 1982); Packer's sense of mourning is more generalized – connected to disillusionment and despair – than Cameron's or Cavell's.

67 Henry David Thoreau, *A Week on the Concord and Merrimack Rivers, Walden; or, Life in the Woods, The Maine Woods, Cape Cod*, ed. Robert F. Sayre (New York: The Library of America, 1985), pp. 427–8, 429. It is worth commenting that there are more than a few moments in "Solitude" where Thoreau is drawing directly on his reading in the *Vedas*; his use of "subtle" and "subtile," for example, echo the references to the "subtle body" and "subtle world" in the Indic texts, and his characterization of the "part of me" that "is not a part of me" witnessing his being derives from the descriptions of the *Purusha*. See Swami Vivekananda, *Raja-Yoga* (New York: Ramakrishna-Vivekananda Center, 1982 [1956]). It is also worth noting that William James's use of "it" – as in "it thinks" being a more adequate description of the operation of consciousness that "he thinks" or "she thinks" – shares a similar inflection.

68 In Freud's Lecture 26, "The Libido Theory and Narcissism," of his *Introductory Lectures on Psychoanalysis*, we find: "[T]here actually exists in the ego an agency which unceasingly observes, criticizes and compares, and in that way sets itself over against the other part of the ego" (Harmondsworth, UK: The Pelican Freud Library, Penguin Books, 1976 [1973]), p. 479.

69 "The Young American," *EL*, p. 216.

70 *EL*, p. 487.

71 "Experience," *EL*, p. 481.

72 *Liddell and Scott's Greek-English Lexicon*, Abridged (Oxford: Clarendon/ Oxford, 1979), pp. 641, 638.

73 From the "Language" chapter of *Nature*, *EL*, p. 20.

74 In Cavell, *Conditions Handsome and Unhandsome*, p. 61.

75 Cavell, "What's the Use ..." in *Etudes*, pp. 216–17. An excellent and succinct gloss on "intersubjectivity" as Cavell uses it in this passage is offered by Richard Rorty: "When philosophy goes antifoundationalist, the notion of 'source of evidence' gets replaced by that of 'consensus about what would count as evidence'. So objectivity as intersubjectivity replaces objectivity as fidelity to something nonhuman." ("Religious Faith, Intellectual Responsibility, and Romance," p. 91.)

76 Cavell, "What's the Use ..." in *Etudes*, p. 217–18.

77 From the opening of Franz Kafka's *Amerika*.

78 Cavell, "Old and New ...," *Etudes*, p. 224.

79 Ibid., p. 232.

80 Cavell, "Aversive Thinking ..." in *Conditions Handsome and Unhandsome*, pp. 40–1.

81 Gilles Deleuze, *Nietzsche and Philosophy* as quoted in "On Nietzsche and the Image of Thought" in *Desert Islands and Other Texts, 1953–1974*, ed. David Lapoujade (Cambridge, MA: Semiotext(e)/ MIT Press, 2004), p. 135.

82 See Gregg Lambert, "Emerson, or *Man Thinking*," and Paul Grimstad, "Emerson's Adjacencies: Radical Empiricism in *Nature*," both in *The Other Emerson*, ed. Branca Arsic and Cary Wolfe (Minneapolis and London: University of Minnesota Press, 2010), pp. 229–50 and 251–70.

83 In the Preface for the Second Edition of *The Gay Science* (tr. Walter Kaufmann [New York: Vintage Books, 1974]) we find: "This whole book is nothing but a bit of merry-making after long privation and powerlessness, the rejoicing of strength that is returning, of a reawakened faith in a tomorrow and the day after tomorrow" (p. 32). And a bit further along: "And as the traveler knows that something is *not* asleep, that something counts the hours and will wake him up, we, too, know that the decisive moment will find us awake, and that something will leap forward then and catch the spirit *in the act*" (p. 34; emphases in original). And in §84 of Book Two, we find: "Among the Pythagoreans ... [w]hen the proper tension and harmony of the soul had been lost, one had to *dance*, following the singer's beat: that was the prescription of this therapy" (p. 139).

84 Stanley Cavell, "Responses" in Goodman, *Contending with Stanley Cavell*, p. 160.

85 Ibid., p. 164.

86 *Representative Men, EL*, p. 622.

87 In Goodman, *Contending with Stanley Cavell*, pp. 8–9.

88 Cavell, "Old and New ...," *Etudes*, pp. 227–8.

89 *EN*, pp. 168–70.

90 Cavell, Introduction to *Conditions Handsome and Unhandsome*, p. 20.

91 Ian Hacking in *Historical Ontology* (Cambridge, MA: Harvard University Press, 2002), p. 35 offers the following:

> *Words in their sites*: A concept is no more than a word or words in the sites in which it is used. Once we have considered the sentences in which the word is used, and the acts performed by uttering the sentences, and the conditions of felicity or authority for uttering those sentences, and so on, we have exhausted what there is to be said about the concept. A strict version would say we have exhausted the concept when we have considered (*per impossibile*) all the actual possible utterances of the corresponding words.

92 Friedrich Nietzsche, Preface to *Human, All Too Human*, tr. Helen Zimmern (published 1909–13, at http://www.inquiria.com/nz/hah/hah_preface.html), Section 5.

93 Marco Pallis, "Is There Room for Grace in Buddhism" in *The Sword of Gnosis: Metaphysics, Cosmology, Tradition, Symbolism*, ed. Joseph Needleman (New York and London: Penguin, 1974), pp. 275–9. It is worth remarking that Cavell is no stranger to Buddhist texts. During the interview with him that I conducted in February 2010, I asked whether he had read in this literature at any point in his career. He answered that he had during his years at Berkeley, and that one text was especially significant: *The Unborn: The Life and Teachings of Zen Master Bankei, 1622–1693*, revised edition, tr. Norman Waddell (New York: North Point Press, 2000 [1984]).

94 Nietzsche, Preface to *Human, All Too Human*, Sections 1 and 2.

95 Friedrich Nietzsche, "Fate and History: Thoughts (1862)," *The Nietzsche Reader*, ed. Keith Ansell Pearson and Duncan Large (Malden, MA and Oxford: Blackwell, 2006), p. 12.

96 James, *Varieties*, p. 468.

97 "Experience," *EL*, p. 487.

98 Emily Dickinson, Poem 1263, *The Poems of Emily Dickinson*, ed. R. W. Franklin (Cambridge, MA and London: Harvard University Press, 2005), p. 494.

99 Cavell, *Pitch*, pp. ix–xii.

100 Ibid., p. 10.

101 Ibid., pp. 11–12.

102 Misak, Introduction to *New Pragmatists*, p. 3.

103 "Swedenborg, or, The Mystic," *EL*, p. 671.

104 Stout, "On Our Interest" in Misak, *New Pragmatists*, p. 27.

105 See Richardson, "Thinking in Cavell" in *Stanley Cavell*, ed. Loxley and Taylor, pp. 199–224 for a full discussion of this aspect.

106 Cavell, *Must We Mean What We Say?* p. 68.

107 Mark Bartlett, "Synthesist Imagery and Recyclage," a catalog essay discussing the work of artist Shezad Dawood in *Piercing Brightness; Shazad Dawood* (London: Modern Art Oxford/Koenig Books, 2012), p. 60.

108 Hadot, "Spiritual Exercises" in *Philosophy as a Way of Life*, p. 93.

109 Cavell, *Must We Mean What We Say?* p. 72.
110 Cavell, "Responses" in Goodman, *Contending with Stanley Cavell,* p. 165.
111 Cavell, *Pitch,* p. xv.
112 This issue was the subject of an op-ed piece by Leeat Granek entitled "When Doctors Grieve" in *The New York Times* on Sunday, May 27, 2012.
113 Cavell, "Responses" in Goodman, *Contending with Stanley Cavell,* p. 167.

6. Effects 2: Richard Rorty, Sea change and/or ironic scraping

1 Stout, "On Our Interest" in Misak, *New Pragmatists,* p. 12.
2 In preparing this chapter, I had the great good fortune to find and read Vincent Colapietro's recent piece, "Richard Rorty as Peircean Pragmatist: An Ironic Portrait and Sincere Expression of Philosophical Friendship," where he expresses a similar consequence: "I take Rorty to have licensed me and others to turn aside in good conscience from certain technical debates in professional philosophy and to do so for the purpose of indulging more humanly worthwhile impulses and interests, aims and obsessions" (42–3). I shall draw from Colapietro's excellent offering in the pages following. I would like to note that had I met the original deadline set for this text, August 2011, this essay would not have been part of the conversation my endeavor here represents. This *happen*stance is one of several that have occurred over the course of my working on the chapters here, occasionally making me believe in angels.
3 "An Ordinary Evening in New Haven," *CPP,* p. 399.
4 It is worth noting the emergent subject of "quantum cognition." Quantum physicists have discovered that quantum mechanics enlarges our capacity to reason. As detailed in an article by George Musser in the November 2012 issue of *Scientific American,* "Quantum mechanics may be a better model for human behavior than classical logic, which fails to predict the human impulse to cooperate and act altruistically. Instead of trying to force our thinking into a rational framework, we are better off expanding the framework" (78). Musser closes by observing that the emergent field of quantum cognition takes its cue from Niels Bohr's drawing ideas about quantum activity from William James's work in psychology, as remarked in an earlier chapter of this volume.
5 James, *Pragmatism,* pp. 506–7.
6 Richard Rorty, *Philosophy and the Mirror of Nature* (Princeton: Princeton University Press, 1980 [1979]), p. 42. Rorty's footnote contains the source in Peirce: *Collected Papers,* vol. 6, pp. 270–1.
7 Bernstein, *Pragmatic Turn,* pp. 17 and 32–52.
8 As summarized by Susan Haack in introducing the second in the series, "Some Consequences" in the excellent collection she edited with Robert Lane, *Pragmatism Old and New: Selected Writings* (Amherst, NY: Prometheus Books, 2006), pp. 69–70.
9 In editors' comments introducing "Some Consequences" in *The Essential Peirce: Selected Philosophical Writings,* vol. 1, p. 28.

10 *EL*, p. 196.

11 As indicated in a note to an earlier chapter and mentioned in passing in this chapter, Rorty's M.A. thesis exploring the idea of potentiality in the work of Alfred North Whitehead was completed under the direction of Charles Hartshorne; his dissertation completed at Yale University under the direction of Paul Weiss, another prominent Peircean, was titled "The Concept of Potentiality" and compared Whitehead's to Aristotle's concept.

12 Charles Sanders Peirce, "Some Consequences of Four Incapacities" in *The Essential Pierce*, vol. 1, ed. Houser and Kloesel, pp. 54–5.

13 The "room of the idea" is a concept framed by Jonathan Edwards to describe the mental space in which an idea can be held and contemplated. For a full discussion, see "Jonathan Edwards's room of the idea" in Richardson, *Natural History of Pragmatism*, pp. 24–61.

14 Rorty carefully traces the emergence of the "'idea' idea" in the first chapter ("The Invention of the Mind") of Part One ("Man's Glassy Essence") of *Philosophy and the Mirror of Nature*; see esp. pp. 47–61.

15 Rorty, "Pragmatism and Romanticism," p. 105.

16 Bernstein, *Pragmatic Turn*, pp. 21–2; "Richard Rorty's Deep Humanism," *New Literary History*, 2008, 39: 13–27, esp. 14–15.

17 Colapietro, "Richard Rorty as Peircean Pragmatist," 38.

18 As observed by Neil Gross in his somewhat experimental intellectual biography, *Richard Rorty: The Making of an American Philosopher* (Chicago and London: University of Chicago Press, 2008), designed to make "an empirically grounded theoretical contribution to the new sociology of ideas" (p. 337). Gross draws his comment about Haack from her *Manifesto of a Passionate Moderate* (Chicago and London: University of Chicago Press, 1998). Gross notes that Donald Davidson and Hilary Putnam "resisted being read as Rorty would have them be and … charged his version of pragmatism with relativism," and that Haack also "rehearsed the same relativism charge and accused Rorty of misinterpreting and misappropriating classical pragmatism" (p. 24). In his 1986 essay, "Pragmatism, Davidson and Truth" (collected in *Objectivity, Relativism, and Truth: Philosophical Papers, Volume 1* [Cambridge: Cambridge University Press, 1991], pp. 126–50) Rorty, himself commenting on the temptation "to see Davidson as belonging to the American pragmatist tradition," notes that Davidson "has explicitly denied that his break with the empirical tradition makes him a pragmatist" (126); Rorty continues to detail the points of coincidence and difference. At the very end of a late discussion in 1997, however, Davidson, after commenting that it did not seem to him that Rorty was himself a pragmatist, asked him to explain what pragmatism meant for him at this point – after which Davidson, in closing, remarked that he guessed then that he himself was "a straightforward pragmatist … even in the Romantic sense" that Rorty had described; the discussion is available on YouTube.

19 Colapietro in "Richard Rorty as Peircean Pragmatist" observes that "the resolute refusal to acknowledge even the slightest degree of kinship" is itself "a species of narcissism" (40) in the Freudian sense.

20 Stout in Misak, *New Pragmatists*, p. 29. Gross specifies "James Conant, Simon Critchley, Terry Eagleton, [and] Nancy Fraser who took issue with aspects of [Rorty's] political and moral philosophy" (*Richard Rorty*, p. 24).

21 Charles Sanders Peirce, *The Essential Peirce: Selected Philosophical Writings*, vol. 2: *1893–1913*, ed. Nathan Houser and Christian Kloesel (Bloomington: Indiana University Press, 1998), p. 332.

22 Collected in Mark Edmundson, ed. *Wild Orchids and Trotsky: Messages from American Universities* (New York: Penguin Books, 1993), p. 36.

23 Bernstein, *Pragmatic Turn*, p. 5. Further along, Bernstein observes: "Neither Peirce nor James ever used the expression ['pragmatism'] to describe his entire philosophical orientation. Dewey preferred to describe his philosophy as 'experimentalism,' or 'instrumentalism,' and sometimes as 'instrumental experimentalism' [as discussed in Chapter 4 on Dewey in this volume]. But gradually 'pragmatism' was generalized as a convenient label to refer to this group of diverse thinkers. The expression 'pragmatism' is like an accordion; it is sometimes stretched to include a wide diversity of positions and thinkers (not just philosophers) and sometimes restricted to specific doctrines of the original American pragmatists. The truth is that ever since the origins of American pragmatism – and right up to the present – critics and champions of pragmatism have been arguing about what constitutes pragmatism and who is and is not a pragmatist" (11). Here Bernstein adds an endnote indicating the first narratives of the meaning and origins of pragmatism offered by James and Peirce and adds that Dewey relates his version in "The Development of American Pragmatism" (1925); George Herbert Mead his account in "The Philosophies of Royce, James, and Dewey in their American Setting" (1929); and his own discussion of the debates in Richard J. Bernstein, "American Pragmatism: The Conflict of Narratives" in H. J. Saatkamp, Jr., ed. *Rorty and Pragmatism* (Nashville, TN: Vanderbilt University Press, 1995), pp. 54–67.

24 Bernstein, "Richard Rorty's Deep Humanism," 14; *Pragmatic Turn*, p. 12: "They [young American philosophers] were fascinated with the new type of philosophizing initiated by G. E. Moore, Bertrand Russell, Wittgenstein (at least the Wittgenstein filtered by his Anglo-American students), Gilbert Ryle, and J. L. Austin." Gross qualifies Bernstein's account of pragmatism's place during the 1950s and 1960s:

> One of the founding myths of the recent revival of interest in American pragmatism is that the pragmatists were not discussed in major American philosophy departments in the 1950s and 1960s. An analysis of data on philosophy dissertations shows that this was not the case and that Yale was an epicenter of pragmatist activity.*

In the footnote in his text (indicated by the asterisk here) Gross points to his "Becoming a Pragmatist Philosopher: Status, Self-Concept, and Intellectual Choice," *American Sociological Review* 67 (2002): 52–76 (*Richard Rorty*, p. 140).

25 Bernstein, "Richard Rorty's Deep Humanism," 14–15; quotations from Richard Rorty, "Pragmatism, Categories, and Language," *Philosophical Review* 70, no. 2 (1961): 197–8, 198–9. Gross also quotes this passage from this early

paper and comments on it. He quotes additional passages as well, useful to have on hand for this discussion. Gross comments that "While the two philosophers [Peirce and Wittgenstein] differed in certain respects, particularly with regard to the intellectual traditions out of which they emerged, they were more alike than different," and goes on to quote from Rorty:

> Both are fighting against the "Ockhamistic" prejudice that the determinate always lurks – actually, and not merely potentially – behind the indeterminate. Both recognize the sense in which we cannot break out of the cluster of things which Peirce calls Thirds and whose workings Wittgenstein calls "logical determination" (for example, signs, words, habits, rules, meanings, games, understanding) to something more definite which will somehow replace these things.

"Rorty was convinced by both Peirce and Wittgenstein," Gross continues, "that language cannot be transcended, that the meaning of a concept lies exclusively in its use, and that reality is indefinite.

Reading Wittgenstein in light of Peirce, Rorty went on to claim, could 'help free us from preoccupation with accidents of tactics and … direct us toward the crucial insights which generate master strategies' of philosophical argumentation – strategies that, Rorty implied, lead ultimately in the direction of a rigorous ordinary language approach that could make real headway in solving or at least overcoming philosophical problems and controversies. With this argument Rorty once again positioned himself in the broadly analytic camp, seeking to transform his otherwise undervalued familiarity with alternative philosophical traditions – in this case, pragmatism – into a valuable asset." (*Richard Rorty*, p. 159)

26 Bernstein, "Richard Rorty's Deep Humanism," 21. Also see Gross, *Richard Rorty*, pp. 122–3 for details about the climate at Chicago during the period Rorty was studying there with both Rudolf Carnap and Hartshorne. Rorty's self-description as "reactionary metaphysician" comes from a letter written to his mother in December 1950, describing a term paper he had written for Carnap titled "Logical Truth, Factual Truth, and the Synthetic *A Priori*." "Someone suggested as a subtitle," Rorty writes to his mother, "'How to Square the Vienna Circle.'" I found this morsel long after using "squaring the circle" as subtitle for my chapter on Cavell and am pleased by the aptness of the coincidence given the overlapping educational experiences and later aims of Cavell and Rorty.

27 Bernstein, "Richard Rorty's Deep Humanism," 20; "reality and justice in a single vision" quoted by Bernstein from Rorty in Edmundson, *Trotsky and Wild Orchids*, p. 9.

28 Bernstein, "Richard Rorty's Deep Humanism," 20; quotation from Rorty, as Bernstein indicates, in *Trotsky and Wild Orchids*, pp. 10–11.

29 Rorty, Philosophy and the Mirror of Nature, p. 43.

30 Richard Rorty speaking to Dutch interviewer, Wim Kayzer; the interview is one (the 23rd) in a series titled "Of Beauty and Consolation" with philosophers, writers, scientists, and other intellectuals about the relationship between beauty and consolation; it can be seen on YouTube at www.youtube.com/watch?v=bTSdyxKyHrU.

31 The title of Rorty's thesis, completed in 1952, is "Whitehead's Use of the Concept of Potentiality."

32 As described by Bruce Kuklick, quoted by Gross, *Richard Rorty*, p. 132.

33 Richard Rorty, "Pragmatism, Categories, and Language," 214.

34 Richard Hocking, "Emergence and Embodiment: A Dialectic within Process" in *Recovery of Philosophy in America*, ed. Kasulis and Neville (Albany: State University of New York Press, 1997) p. 158.

35 Gross, *Richard Rorty*, p. 122.

36 Collected Papers of Charles Sanders Peirce, vol. 4 (1933), p. xx.

37 Bruce Kuklick, "Neil Gross, Richard Rorty: The Making of an American Philosopher," *Transactions of the Charles S. Peirce Society* 47.1 (2011): 36.

38 Gross, *Richard Rorty*, p. 198 n. 98.

39 Winifred Raushenbush to "MR," November 6, 1966, as quoted by Gross, who adds in his footnote, "I have reordered the last sentence for emphasis" (*Richard Rorty*, p. 189).

40 Jurgen Habermas described Rorty this way in his obituary for him that appeared on June 11, 2007 in the *Suddeutsche Zeitung*; "practicing Mormon" is from Rorty Wikipedia page.

41 Rorty in Edmundson, *Wild Orchids and Trotsky*, pp. 35–6.

42 Richard Rorty, "Pragmatism, Davidson and Truth," pp. 127, 130, 130 n.10.

43 Gross, *Richard Rorty*, pp. 152, 158, 157. Gross continues to note that Morton White, long-time head of the philosophy department at Harvard, in his 1956 *Toward Reunion in Philosophy* (Cambridge, MA: Harvard University Press) described "the present period in philosophy as an 'age of decision,' whereby 'the tradition of the analytic movement merges with that of pragmatism.'" Gross notes further, "It may have been the decisive contribution of analytic thought to show that philosophy must take the linguistic turn – White believed such a turn necessary – but the 'philosopher in the age of decision' 'does not simply ask whether words *are* used in a certain way ... [but] goes on to ask whether they *ought* to be used in a certain way.' White held that this meant no strict separation could be effected between 'describing, doing, and evaluating'" (p. 156). Gross importantly observes that White's book was the text Rorty cited in making the point in "Pragmatism, Categories, and Language" that pragmatism had come back into fashion (p. 153).

44 Rorty in Edmundson, *Wild Orchids and Trotsky*, pp. 36, 37.

45 Gross, *Richard Rorty*, p. 140.

46 Colapietro, "Richard Rorty as Peircean Pragmatist," 40, who indicates that Rorty was "trained by" Smith, Hartshorne, Weiss, and Wells.

47 Worth recalling is that F. S. C. Northrop, also prepared in Eastern texts, was a member of the faculty in philosophy at Yale during Wells's tenure.

48 Gross, *Richard Rorty*, p. 140.

49 Donald Gustafson reviewing *Perspectives on Peirce*, ed. Richard J. Bernstein (New Haven and London: Yale University Press, 1965) in the *Philosophical Review*, vol. 76, no. 3 (July 1967), 387–8.

50 Bernstein, "Richard Rorty's Deep Humanism," 15.
51 Willem deVries, "Wilfrid Sellars" entry, *Stanford Encyclopedia of Philosophy* (first published August 9, 2011) at http://plato.stanford.edu/entries/sellars/.
52 Robert Brandom at http://www.ditext.com/brandom/brandom.html p. 1.
53 Rorty in Edmundson, *Wild Orchids and Trotsky*, pp. 39, 41–2.
54 James Ryerson, "The Quest for Uncertainty: Richard Rorty's Pragmatic Pilgrimage," *Linguafranca*, vol. 10. No. 9 (December 2000/January 2001), 46.
55 Rorty in Edmundson, *Wild Orchids and Trotsky*, p. 36.
56 Ibid., p. 37.
57 Scott Holland, "The Coming Only Is Sacred: Self-Creation and Social Solidarity in Richard Rorty's Secular Eschatology," *Cross Currents*, vol. 53, no. 4 (Winter 2004), p. 2. In his 1998 volume, *Achieving Our Country: Leftist Thought in Twentieth-Century America* (Cambridge, MA: Harvard University Press), Rorty recounts: "My mother used to tell me, with great pride, that when I was seven I had the honor of serving little sandwiches to the guests at a Halloween party attended both by John Dewey and by Carlo Tresca, the Italian anarchist leader who was assassinated a few years later. That same party, I have since discovered, was attended not only by the Hooks and the Trillings, but by Whitaker Chambers. Chambers had just broken with the Communist Party and was desperately afraid of being liquidated by Stalin's hit men. Another guest was Suzanne La Follette, to whom Dewey had entrusted the files of the Commission of Inquiry into the Mocow Trials. These files disappeared when her apartment was burgled, presumably by Soviet agents" (p. 61).
58 Rorty in Edmundson, *Wild Orchids and Trotsky*, p. 37.
59 "A Guess at the Riddle" (1887–8) is the title of "perhaps Peirce's greatest and most original contribution to speculative philosophy, and it marks his deliberate turn to architectonic thought. His three categories, which he speculates are isomorphic with the three elements that are active in the universe (chance, law, and habit-taking) serve as the structure for organizing the branches of philosophy and science, and it is clear that he anticipated a complete reorganization of human knowledge around his triad of universal conceptions; for as he wrote, on a variant opening page, 'this book, if ever written, as it soon will be if I am in a situation to do it, will be one of the births of time.'" (Editors' comment preceding the thirty-five-page version of this item collected in *The Essential Peirce*, vol. 1, p. 245.)
60 Rorty, "Pragmatism, Categories, and Language," 198: "When Peirce says that 'vagueness is real,' and when Wittgenstein points to the differences between causal and logical determination, the only differences between what they are saying are verbal (or, to give the cash value of this overworked word, uninteresting)."
61 *EL*, p. 487.
62 Rorty, "Pragmatism, Categories, and Language," 199 n.5.
63 In a recent piece, "Stylists in the American Grain: Wallace Stevens, Stanley Cavell and Richard Rorty" (*European Journal of Pragmatism and American*

Philosophy, vol. II, no. 2 [2010], 211–23), Aine Kelly comments on Rorty's style:

> Rorty speaks in an informal "down home", American idiom, a self-consciously pragmatist cultivation that is intended to undercut more portentous vocabularies and return human purposes to the centre of the stage. Rorty's writing has always been accented by a pacy colloquialism, a style of address that is most pronounced in the third and fourth volumes of his *Philosophical Papers* (1997 and 2007 respectively) and in *Philosophy and Social Hope* (1998), what Rorty terms "a collection of more occasional pieces". These books are replete with Americanisms: "it didn't pan out", "put a different spin on it", "gee-whiz", "gypped", "jump-started", "pretty much", "handy ways", "pin down", "lay my cards on the table", "earn their keep", "boondoggle", "gotten some", to mention a few.
>
> Rorty's reliance on the colloquial and idiomatic highlights the importance of American vernacular in his writing, a rhetoric he sees as singularly appropriate fot the pragmatist intellectual. He writes with self-effacing charm, a quick and biting wit and a dizzying capacity for broad analogies. As his thought has changed (from analytic to non-analytic) so has his style moved increasingly from an argumentative to a narrative and "re-descriptive" mode (216).

64 Rorty, "Pragmatism, Categories, and Language," 199. The two asterisks indicate Rorty's seventh footnote – another pellucid explication – followed by references to two locations in Peirce's papers, illustrating his scrupulous attention in reading Peirce.

65 Brent, *A Life*, pp. 333–4.

66 Rorty, "Pragmatism, Categories, and Language," 200–01.

67 Ibid., 208; the quotation from Peirce is from vol. 6 of his *Collected Papers*, 348.

68 Rorty, "Pragmatism, Categories, and Language," 209.

69 Max H. Fisch, "The Decisive Year and Its Early Consequences," Introduction to vol. 2: 1867–71 in *The Writings of Charles Peirce*, in 5 volumes, ed. with a Preface by Edward C. Moore (Bloomington: University of Indiana Press, 1982–1993); online at *Peirce Edition Project*: www.iupui.edu/~peirce/

70 Ray Monk, *Ludwig Wittgenstein: The Duty of Genius* (New York: Penguin Books, 1990), pp. 415, 72, 74. It is to be remarked, following Jaime Nubiola in his "Scholarship on the Relations between Ludwig Wittgenstein and Charles S. Peirce" (in *Studies on the History of Logic. Proceedings of the iii Symposium on the History of Logic* [Berlin: Walter de Gruyter, 1996], pp. 281–94 and http://www.cspeirce.com/menu/library/aboutcsp/nubiola/scholar.htm p. 3), that "Russell in his *Principles of Mathematics* (§ 27) acknowledged the importance of Peirce's work on logic, particularly his algebra of dyadic relationships. 'I have always thought very highly of Dr. Peirce for having introduced such a method,' he wrote later to Lady Welby." It is thus possible that Wittgenstein had learned of – or even studied – Peirce's logic early on in his career. It is equally possible, as Nubiola points out, following John Passmore in his *A Hundred Years of Philosophy* (1957) – a text it is possible Rorty knew – that

the notoriously pragmatist flavor of *Philosophical Investigations* was owing to the influence of Frank P. Ramsey: according to this interpretation, it was the young Ramsey who, by awakening Wittgenstein from the dogmatic slumber of the *Tractatus*, guided Wittgenstein's reflections in a pragmatic direction (Passmore 1947: 425). However, little precise information is available as to the actual way in which American pragmatist philosophy might have helped mold the thought of the later Wittgenstein. Nubiola goes on to observe that although "The writings of Ludwig Wittgenstein do not contain a single mention of Charles S. Peirce ... Wittgenstein's scant regard for the academic practice of acknowledging intellectual property is notorious" (p. 2 in Web version as cited in note following here). Nubiola's paper is extremely valuable in tracing all the possible points of connection between Peirce and Wittgenstein as well as in bringing earlier speculative scholarship on the relation between the two into the discussion.

71 Anonymous Web Essay, "Wittgenstein: Philosophical Engineer," at www. faculty.education.illinois.edu/.../Wittgenstein_as_Engineer.html, p. 1. This essay appears to be derived from discussions in a course given by Nicholas C. Burbules and Michael A. Peters (EPS 408) at the University of Illinois at Urbana-Champaign in Fall, 1998.

72 Ibid.

73 Ibid. The essay continues on to detail the elements from Wittgenstein's formal training as an engineer that influenced his later philosophical style. There are at least five parallels that can be drawn between engineering and the writings of Wittgenstein. The examples he used, the format of the propositions, and his use of repetition with variation, are three of the tools Wittgenstein uses to get his point across that are common to engineering. The last two parallels correspond to the strategy behind the engineering curriculum in general, and implement a problem solving technique found in engineering design.

74 Quoted in "Wittgenstein: Philosophical Engineer."

75 Monk, *Ludwig Wittgenstein*, p. 421.

76 Rorty, "Pragmatism, Categories, and Language," 198.

77 Ibid., 204.

78 *EL*, p. 251.

79 Rorty, "Pragmatism, Categories, and Language," 211–12.

80 "Frontier instance" is a term borrowed from Francis Bacon by way of Charles Darwin, who in his *N Notebook* called "cases in which we are enabled to trace that general law which seems to pervade all nature – the law, as it is termed, of continuity": *Charles Darwin's Notebooks, 1836–1844: Geology, Transmutation of Species, Metaphysical Enquiries*, ed. Paul H. Barrett, Peter J. Gautrey, Sandra Herbert, David Kohn, and Sydney Smith (Ithaca: Cornell University Press, 1987), p. 577.

81 Rorty, "Pragmatism, Categories, and Language," 210.

82 "Man's Glassy Essence" in *The Essential Peirce*, vol. 1, pp. 343, 347–50.

83 William James, "Essays, Comments, and Reviews," in *The Works of William James*, ed. Frederick Burkhardt (Cambridge, MA: Harvard University Press, 1987), p. 109; quoted by Rorty in "Pragmatism and Romanticism," p. 108.

84 David Bohm, *Wholeness and the Implicate Order* (London, Boston, Melbourne, and Henley: Ark Paperbacks, 1983), p. 172 and quoted in Brent, *A Life*, p. 211.

85 "Self-Reliance," *EL*, p. 281.

86 "The Poet," *EL*, p. 459.

87 Richard Rorty, "The Fire of Life," THE VIEW FROM HERE feature, *Poetry*, November 2007.

88 "Peter Quince at the Clavier," *CPP*, p. 74.

89 "Le Monocle de Mon Oncle," *CPP*, p. 13.

90 Rorty, "Pragmatism and Romanticism," p. 116.

91 From the closing of the Introduction to *Nature*, *EL*, p. 8.

92 Rorty, "Pragmatism and Romanticism," pp. 118–19.

93 Richard Rorty, *Truth and Progress: Philosophical Papers, Volume 3* (Cambridge: Cambridge University Press, 1998), p. 327; quoted in Kelly, "Stylists in the American Grain," p. 216.

94 In *The Philosophy of Richard Rorty*, ed. Randall E. Auxler and Lewis Edwin Hahn, Volume XXXII of *The Library of Living Philosophers* (Carbondale, IL: Open Court, 2010), pp. 3–24.

95 Kelly, "Stylists in the American Grain," 219–20.

96 "The Method of Nature" in *EL*, p. 115.

97 Richard Rorty, *Achieving Our Country: Leftist Thought in Twentieth-Century America* (Cambridge, MA: Harvard University Press, 1998), p. 27.

98 In Rorty, *Objectivity, Relativism, and Truth*, p. 93.

99 It is to be especially noted that Vincent Colapietro belongs pre-eminently to this group. In "Richard Rorty as Peircean Pragmatist," he observes of "The Pragmatist's Progress":"There is, for the purpose of understanding Rorty's relationship to Peirce, arguably no more important later test by Rorty, since Eco is in both his own mind and that of Rorty, so closely associated with Peirce's efforts to circumscribe the irrepressibly wild impulses of our hermeneutic imagination" (37).

100 *Umberto Eco: Interpretation and Overinterpretation,* with Richard Rorty, Jonathan Culler, and Christine Brooke-Rose, ed. Stefan Collini, derived from the 1990 Tanner Lectures and Seminar (Cambridge: Cambridge University Press, 1992), pp. 91–3.

101 Rorty, "Pragmatism, Davidson and Truth," p. 130.

102 It is worth remarking that Putnam seems to have significantly revised this earlier take on Peirce given the evidence of what he offers in the Introduction and Comments to *Reasoning and the Logic of Things* published in 1992. For a discussion of this later valuation of Peirce's speculative writing by Putnam, see Chapter 3 in this volume.

103 Richard Rorty, *Consequences of Pragmatism (Essays: 1972–1980)* (Minneapolis: University of Minnesota Press, 1982), p. xlv.

104 Richard Rorty, "The Contingency of Language" in *Contingency, Irony, and Solidarity* (Cambridge: Cambridge University Press, 1989), p. 12. In connection with Rorty's appropriation of Davidson's work, in opening a discussion with Davidson in 1997 (available on YouTube in six parts), Rorty begins with an apology for the ways in which he had appropriated Davidson's work by being "a snapper-up of unconsidered trifles – I don't mean 'unconsidered' really or 'trifles,' but something like that – I mean to say out of your context and weaving them together with what other people have to say, and thereby, in a sense passing your project by." As an example, Rorty observes: "You have constructive projects in philosophy. I don't. I never wanted a theory of meaning – only ammunition to use against the philosophical tradition, and so I glommed onto your remarks."

105 Cheryl Misak, "Rorty's Place in the Pragmatist Pantheon" in *The Philosophy of Richard Rorty*, ed. Auxier and Hahn, *The Library of Living Philosophers*, p. 29. For an excellent extended technical discussion, see Cheryl Misak, *Truth and the End of Inquiry: A Peircean Account of Truth*, 2nd ed. (Oxford: Oxford University Press, 1991), and Misak, "Pragmatism and Deflationism" in *New Pragmatists*, pp. 68–90.

106 Rorty, "Contingency of Language," p. 18.

107 Ibid., p. 12. Similarly, Colapietro in "Richard Rorty as Peircean Pragmatist" observes "Virtually everyone actually engaged in some substantive inquiry finds the often technical debates among professional philosophers on epistemological topics of no relevance to what they are doing" (41).

108 The phrase "irrational element" belongs both to Wallace Stevens and to Niels Bohr. Bohr repeatedly referred in lectures during the 1920s and earlier to the "quantum postulate" – the alternating wave-particle duality affected as it is by the scale of observation and the observer himself – as "the irrational element." Stevens was familiar with the some of the published work of Bohr; his essay, "The Irrational Element in Poetry" describes the dithering duality between what he calls "the true subject" and "the poetry of the subject" of a poem. See Niels Bohr, "The Quantum Postulate and the Recent Development of Atomic Theory" (1927), in *Philosophical Writings*, vol. 1: *Atomic Theory and the Description of Nature* (Woodbridge, CT: Ox Bow Press, 1987) and "Introductory Survey" (1929) collected in the same volume (p. 10) that offer two such examples; for "The Irrational Element in Poetry," see *CPP*, pp. 781–92.

109 Misak, "Richard Rorty's Place," p. 38.

110 See Ryerson's discussion in "The Quest for Uncertainty," 42–51.

111 Colapietro, "Richard Rorty as Peircean Pragmatist," 42.

112 Rorty, *Achieving Our Country*, pp. 32, 33–4.

113 Rorty, *Consequences of Pragmatism*, p. xlvii, n.52.

114 Misak, "Richard Rorty's Place," p. 35

115 Rorty, "Contingency of Language," p. 21.

116 This detail is taken from Rorty's *New York Times* obituary, June 11, 2007.

117 "Radical deflationist" and "syncretist hack" are both terms Rorty used to describe himself; for the latter, see Ryerson, "The Quest for Uncertainty," p. 43. The other phrases are from "A High-Toned Old Christian Woman" and "Tea at the Palaz of Hoon" respectively, *CPP*, pp. 47, 51.

118 Rorty, Introduction to *Truth and Progress*, pp. 7–8.

119 This passage recalled here from Chapter 2, from James, *Principles*, p. 948.

120 Geophysicist Xavier Le Pichon, interviewed by Krista Tippett on National Public Radio, August 19, 2012.

Illustrations

Figure 1. *New York Times Magazine*, Cover Image, May 3, 2009. Permission, PARS International for the *New York Times*.

Figure 2. Cover of *The Irony of American History* (University of Chicago Press, 2008). Collection of the author; image permission, PARS International for *Time*, Inc.

Figure 3. Cover of *Time magazine*, "Man of the Year," March 8, 1948. Permission, PARS International for *Time*, Inc.

Bibliography

Aboulafia, Mitchell and John R. Shook. *Contemporary Pragmatism*, vol. 6, no. 1. Amsterdam and New York: Editions Rodopi, 2009.
   Contemporary Pragmatism, vol. 8, no. 2. Amsterdam and New York: Editions Rodopi, 2011.
Alexander, Samuel. *Spinoza and Time*. London: G. Allen and Unwin, 1921.
Anonymous web essay, "Wittgenstein: Philosophical Engineer" at http://www.faculty.education.illinois.edu/burbules/.../Wittgenstein_as_Engineer.html.
Anonymous review of *Hippocrates in Context: Papers Read at the 11th International Hippocrates Colloquium*, University of Newcastle upon Tyne, August 27–31, 2002, edited by Philip J. van der Eijk: *Studies in Ancient Medicine* 31. Leiden: Brill in *Bryn Mawr Classical Review* July 14, 2006.
Arsic, Branka and Cary Wolfe, eds. *The Other Emerson*. Minneapolis and London: University of Minnesota Press, 2010.
Auxier, Randall E. and Lewis Edwin Hahn, eds. *The Philosophy of Richard Rorty*, vol. XXXII of *The Library of Living Philosophers*. Carbondale, IL: Open Court, 2010.
Banville, John. "The Most Entertaining Philosopher." A review of *The Heart of William James* edited by Robert D. Richardson. *New York Review of Books*, vol. LVIII, no. 16 2011, 40–42.
Bardach, Ann Louise. "How Yoga Won the West." *New York Times*, October 11, 2011 at http://www.nytimes.com/2011/10/02/opinion/sunday/how-yoga-won-the-west.html?_r=0.
Bartlett, Mark. "Synthesist Imagery and Recyclage." Catalogue essay discussing the work of artist Shezad Dawood in *Piercing Brightness: Shezad Dawood*. London: Modern Art Oxford/Koenig Books, 2012, pp. 1–8.
Bateson, Gregory. *Mind and Nature: A Necessary Unity*. Creskill, NJ: Hampton Press, 2002.
   Steps to an Ecology of Mind. Chicago and London: University of Chicago Press, 2000 [1972].
Beer, Gillian. *Open Fields: Studies in Cultural Encounter*. Oxford: Clarendon/Oxford University Press, 1996.
Bernstein, Richard J. *The Pragmatic Turn*. Cambridge: Polity Press, 2010.
Bohm, David. *Wholeness and the Implicate Order*. London, Boston, Melbourne and Henley: Ark Paperbacks, 1983.

Bohr, Niels. *The Philosophical Writings of Niels Bohr*, vol. 1: *Atomic Theory and the Description of Nature*. Woodbridge, CT: Ox Bow Press, 1987.

Bollas, Christopher. *The Evocative Object World*. East Sussex and New York: Routledge, 2009.

Brandom, Robert, ed. *Rorty and His Critics*. Malden, MA and Oxford: Blackwell, 2000.

   Untitled piece on Wilfrid Sellars. http://www.ditext.com/brandom/brandom.html

Brent, Joseph. *Charles Sanders Peirce: A Life*. Bloomington and Indianapolis: Indiana University Press, 1993.

Brooks, David. "Mirror on America." *New York Times*, Sunday Book Review, May 24, 2009, 6.

   "Obama, Gospel and Verse." *New York Times*. April 26, 2007, A25.

   "Where Obama Shines." *New York Times*. July 19, 2012 at http://www.nytimes.com/2012/07/20/opinion/brooks-where-obama-shines.html.

Browne, Thomas. *Religio Medici and Other Writings*. New York: E. P. Dutton, 1951.

The Cambridge Companion to William James, edited by Ruth Anna Putnam. Cambridge: Cambridge University Press, 1997.

Cameron, Sharon. "Representing Grief: Emerson's 'Experience'." *Representations*, no. 15 (Summer 1986), 15–41.

Campbell, James and Richard E. Hart, eds. *On the Work of John J. McDermott*. New York: Fordham University Press, 2006.

Cavell, Stanley. *Conditions Handsome and Unhandsome: The Constitution of Emersonian Perfectionism*, The Carus Lectures, 1988. Chicago and London: University of Chicago Press, 1990.

Emerson's Transcendental Etudes, edited by David Justin Hodge. Stanford: Stanford University Press, 2003.

Little Did I Know: Excerpts from Memory. Stanford, CA: Stanford University Press, 2010.

Must We Mean What We Say? A Book of Essays. Cambridge: Cambridge University Press, 1976 [1969].

This New Yet Unapproachable America: Lectures after Emerson after Wittgenstein. Albuquerque, NM: Living Batch Press, 1989.

Philosophy the Day after Tomorrow. Cambridge, MA: Belknap/Harvard University Press, 2005.

A Pitch of Philosophy: Autobiographical Exercises. Cambridge, MA: Harvard University Press, 1994.

"What's the Use of Calling Emerson a Pragmatist?" in *The Revival of Pragmatism: New Essays on Social Thought, Law, and Culture*, edited by Morris Dickstein. Durham, NC: Duke University Press, 1998, pp. 72–80. also in Cavell, *Emerson's Transcendental Etudes*, pp. 215–23.

Colapietro, Vincent. "Richard Rorty as Peircean Pragmatist: An Ironic Portrait and Sincere Expression of Philosophical Friendship." *Pragmatism Today: The Journal of the Central-European Pragmatism Forum*, Special Issue: The Roots of Rorty's Philosophy, vol. 2, issue 1 (Summer 2011), 31–50.

Conant, James. "Cavell and the Concept of America" in *Contending*, edited by Goodman, pp. 55–81.

"Freedom, Cruelty, and Truth: Rorty versus Orwell." In Brandom, *Rorty*, pp. 268–341.

Corbin, Henry. *Spiritual Body and Celestial Earth: From Mazdean Iran to Shi'ite Iran*, translated by Nancy Pearson. Bollingen Series XCI: 2. Princeton, NJ: Princeton University Press, 1977.

Cormier, Harvey. "Reconsidering Obama the Pragmatist." *The New York Times* Opinionator, October 14, 2012 at http://opinionator.blogs.nytimes.com/2012/10/14/reconsidering-obama-the-pragmatist/?pagewanted=print.

Crick, Francis and Christof Koch. "The Unconscious Homunculus" in *The Neuronal Correlates of Consciousness*, edited by Thomas Metzinger. Cambridge, MA: MIT Press, 2000, pp. 103–10; online version at: http://www.klab.caltech.edu/~koch/unconscious-homunculus.html.

Croce, Paul Jerome. *Science and Religion in the Era of William James*, vol. 1: *Eclipse of Certainty, 1820–1880*. Chapel Hill: University of North Carolina Press, 1995.

Darwin, Charles. *Charles Darwin's Notebooks, 1836–1844: Geology, Transmutation of Species, Metaphysical Enquiries*, edited by Paul H. Barrett, Peter J. Gautrey, Sandra Herbert, David Kohn, and Sydney Smith. Ithaca: Cornell University Press, 1987.

Deleuze, Gilles. *Desert Islands and Other Texts, 1953–1974*, edited by David Lapoujade. Cambridge, MA: Semiotext(e)/MIT Press, 2004.

Kant's Critical Philosophy, translated by Hugh Tomlinson and Barbara Habberjam. London: Athlone, 1984.

Nietzsche and Philosophy, translated by Hugh Tomlinson. New York: Columbia University Press, 1983.

Dewey, John. *Art as Experience*. New York: Perigee, 1980 [1934].

"Emerson – The Philosopher of Democracy." *International Journal of Ethics*, vol. 13, no. 4 (July 1903), 405–13.

Experience and Nature. New York: Dover, 1958 [1929].

The Influence of Darwin on Philosophy. New York: Henry Holt, 1910.

"The Need for a Recovery of Philosophy" in *Creative Intelligence: Essays in the Pragmatic Attitude*, John Dewey *et al.*, eds. New York: Henry Holt, 1917, pp. 1–32.

The Quest for Certainty: A Study of the Relation Between Knowledge and Action. New York: Paragon, 1979 [1929].

Studies in Logical Theory. Chicago: University of Chicago Press, 1903.

Dickinson, Emily. *The Poems of Emily Dickinson*, edited by R. W. Franklin. Cambridge, MA and London: Harvard University Press, 2005.

Diggins, John Patrick. *The Promise of Pragmatism: Modernism and the Crisis of Knowledge and Authority*. Chicago and London: University of Chicago Press, 1994.

Duffy, John J., ed. *Coleridge's American Disciples: The Selected Correspondence of James Marsh*. Amherst: University of Massachusetts Press, 1973.

Eco, Umberto. *Interpretation and Overinterpretation*, edited by Stefan Collini. Cambridge: Cambridge University Press, 1992.

Edmundson, Mark, ed. *Wild Orchids and Trotsky: Messages from American Universities*. New York: Penguin Books, 1993.

Edwards, Jonathan. "Of Being" in *The Works of Jonathan Edwards*, vol. 6: *Scientific and Philosophical Writings*, edited by Wallace E. Anderson. New Haven and London: Yale University Press, 1980, pp. 202–7.

Emerson, Ralph Waldo. *Essays and Lectures*, edited by Joel Porte. New York: The Library of America, 1983.

   Journals and Miscellaneous Notebooks, vol. 3, edited by Linda Allardt, David W. Hill, Ruth H. Bennett. Cambridge, MA: Harvard University Press, 1960–82.

   Selected Journals 1820–1842, edited by Lawrence Rosenwald. New York: The Library of America, 2010.

Fisch, Max H. "The Decisive Year and Its Early Consequences." Introduction to vol. 2: 1867–1871 in *The Writings of Charles S. Peirce: A Chronological Edition*, in five volumes. Bloomington: University of Indiana Press, 1984 at http://www.iupui.edu/~peirce/writings/v2/v2intro.htm.

Folse, Henry J. *The Philosophy of Niels Bohr: The Framework of Complementarity*. Amsterdam: North-Holland Personal Library/Elsevier Science Ltd., 1985.

Freadman, Anne. *The Machinery of Talk: Charles Peirce and the Sign Hypothesis*. Stanford, CA: Stanford University Press, 2004.

Freud, Sigmund. *Introductory Lectures on Psychoanalysis*. Hammondsworth, UK: The Pelican Freud Library, Penguin Books, 1976 [1973].

Frye, Northrop. *The Great Code: The Bible and Literature*. New York and London: Harcourt Brace Jovanovich, 1981.

Galchen, Rivka. "Dream Machine: The Mind-Expanding World of Quantum Computing." *The New Yorker* (May 2, 2011), 34–8.

Goldberg, Philip. *American Veda: From Emerson and the Beatles to Yoga and Meditation, How Indian Spirituality Changed the West*. New York: Harmony, 2010.

Good, James A. *The Early American Reception of German Idealism*, vol. 2. Bristol: Thoemmes Continuum, 2002.

Goodman, Russell B. "Cavell and American Philosophy" in *Contending with Stanley Cavell*, edited by Russell B. Goodman. New York and Oxford: Oxford University Press, 2005.

   ed. *Contending with Stanley Cavell*. New York and Oxford: Oxford University Press, 2005, pp. 100–17.

   Wittgenstein and William James. Cambridge: Cambridge University Press, 2002.

Granek, Leeat. "When Doctors Grieve." *New York Times* Op-Ed page, May 27, 2012 at http://www.nytimes.com/2012/05/27/opinion/sunday/when-doctors-grieve.html.

Gross, Charles G. "Emanuel Swedenborg: A Neuroscientist Before His Time." In *Brain, Vision, Memory: Tales in the History of Neuroscience*. Cambridge, MA: MIT Press, 1999, pp. 119–36.

Gross, Neil. "Becoming a Pragmatist Philosopher: Status, Self-Concept, and Intellectual Choice." *American Sociological Review* 67 (2002), 52–76.

  Richard Rorty: The Making of an American Philosopher. Chicago and London: University of Chicago Press, 2008.

Gustafson, Donald. *A Review of Perspectives on Peirce*. In the *Philosophical Review*, edited by Richard J. Bernstein. New Haven and London: Yale University Press, 1965. Vol. 76, no. 3 (July 1967), 387–8.

Haack, Susan. *Manifesto of a Passionate Moderate*. Chicago and London: University of Chicago Press, 1998.

Haack, Susan and Robert Lane, eds. *Pragmatism Old and New: Selected Writings*. Amherst, NY: Prometheus Books, 2006.

Hacking, Ian. "On Not Being a Pragmatist: Eight Reasons and a Cause." In Misak, *New Pragmatists*, pp. 32–49.

Hadot, Pierre. *Philosophy as a Way of Life: Spiritual Exercises from Socrates to Foucault*, edited by Arnold I. Davidson, translated by Michael Chase. Malden, MA and Oxford: Blackwell, 1995.

Hampshire, Stuart. *Spinoza and Spinozism*. Oxford and New York: Oxford University Press, 2005.

Haraway, Donna. *When Species Meet*. Minneapolis: University of Minnesota Press, 2008.

Hardwick, Charles S., ed. *Semiotic and Significs: The Correspondence between Charles S. Peirce and Lady Welby*. Bloomington and Indianapolis: Indiana University Press, 1977.

Hartshorne, Charles. *Creative Synthesis and Philosophic Method*. La Salle, IL: Open Court Publishing, 1970.

Harvey, Samantha C. "Coleridge's American Revival: James Marsh, John Dewey, and the Legacy of Vermont Transcendentalism." *Symbiosis: A Journal of Anglo-American Literary Relations*, vol. 15., no. 1 (2011), 77–103.

Heidegger, Martin. *Sojourns: The Journey to Greece*, translated by John Panteleimon Manoussakis. Albany: State University of New York Press, 2005.

Hocking, Richard. "Emergence and Embodiment: A Dialectic within Process" in *The Recovery of Philosophy in America*, ed. Kasulis and Neville, pp. 156–66.

Hoffmann, Michael H. G. "How to Get It: Diagrammatic Reasoning as a Tool of Knowledge Development and Its Pragmatic Dimension." *Foundations of Science* 9 (2004), 285–305.

Holland, Scott. "The Coming Only is Sacred: Self-Creation and Social Solidarity in Richard Rorty's Secular Eschatology." *Cross Currents*, vol. 53, no. 4 (Winter 2004) at http://www.crosscurrents.org/hollandwinter2004.htm.

Howe, Susan. *Pierce-Arrow*. New York: New Directions, 1997.

Jackendoff, Ray. *Consciousness and the Computational Mind*. Cambridge, MA: MIT Press, 1987.

Jacobson, Nolan Pliny. *The Heart of Buddhist Philosophy*. Carbondale: Southern Illinois University Press, 2010 [1988].

Understanding Buddhism. Carbondale: Southern Illinois University Press, 2010.

James, Henry. *Autobiography*, edited by Frederick W. Dupee. Princeton, NJ: Princeton University Press, 1983.

James, Henry, Sr. *The Secret of Swedenborg: Being an Elucidation of His Doctrine of the Divine Natural Humanity*. Boston: Fields, Osgood and Co., 1869.

Substance and Shadow or, Morality and Religion in their Relation to Life: An Essay Upon the Physics of Creation. Boston: Ticknor and Fields, 1893.

James, William. "The Chicago School" in *Writings 1902–1910*, edited by Bruce Kuklick. New York: The Library of America, 1987, pp. 1136–40.

The Correspondence of William James, vol. 1: *William and Henry, 1861–1884*, edited by Ignas K. Skrupskelis and Elizabeth M. Berkeley. Charlottesville: University Press of Virginia, 1992.

The Correspondence of William James, vol. 2: *William and Henry, 1885–1896*, edited by Ignas K. Skrupskelis and Elizabeth M. Berkeley. Charlottesville: University Press of Virginia, 1993.

The Correspondence of William James, vol. 3: *William and Henry, 1897–1910*, edited by Ignas K. Skrupskelis and Elizabeth M. Berkeley. Charlottesville: University Press of Virginia, 1994.

The Correspondence of William James, vol. 4: *1856–1877*, edited by Ignas K. Skrupskelis and Elizabeth M. Berkeley. Charlottesville: University Press of Virginia, 1995.

The Correspondence of William James, vol. 8: *1895–June 1899* edited by Ignas K. Skrupskelis and Elizabeth M. Berkeley. Charlottesville: University Press of Virginia, 2000.

"The Energies of Men," *The American Magazine* (1907) rpt. New York: Moffat, Yard and Company, 1914; another version in *The Philosophical Review*, January 1907 and collected in *Writings 1902–1910*, pp. 1223–41.

"Essays, Comments, and Reviews" in *The Works of William James*, edited by Frederick Burkhardt. Cambridge, MA: Harvard University Press, 1987.

Essays in Radical Empiricism. New York: Dover, 2003.

"Philosophical Conceptions and Practical Results" in *Writings 1878–1899*, edited by Gerald E. Myers. New York: The Library of America, 1992, pp. 1077–97.

"The Place of Affectional Facts in a World of Pure Experience" in *Writings 1902–1910*, pp. 1206–14.

A Pluralistic Universe in *Writings 1902–1910*, pp. 625–819.

Pragmatism, A New Name for Some Old Ways of Thinking in *Writings 1902–1910*, pp. 479–624.

The Principles of Psychology, rpt. Cambridge, MA: Harvard University Press, 1983 [1890].

Talks to Teachers on Psychology: and to Students on Some of Life's Ideals in *Writings 1878–1899*, pp. 705–887.

The Varieties of Religious Experience: A Study in Human Nature in *Writings 1902–1910*, pp. 1–447.

The Will to Believe, vol. 6: *The Works of William James*, edited by Frederick H. Burkhardt, Fredson Bowers, and Ignas K. Skrupskelis. Cambridge, MA: Harvard University Press, 1979.

Kant, Immanuel. *Critique of Pure Reason*, revised and expanded translation based on Meiklejohn, edited by Vasilis Politis. London: Everyman/J.M. Dent, 1993 [1934].

Kasulis, Thomas P. and Robert Cummings Neville, eds. *The Recovery of Philosophy in America: Essays in Honor of John Edwin Smith*. Albany: State University of New York Press, 1997.

Kelly, Aine. "Stylists in the American Grain: Wallace Stevens, Stanley Cavell and Richard Rorty." *European Journal of Pragmatism and American Philosophy*, vol. 2, no. 2 (2010), 211–23.

Ketner, Kenneth Laine. *His Glassy Essence: An Autobiography of Charles Sanders Peirce*. Nashville and London: Vanderbilt University Press, 1998.

Kitcher, Philip. *Preludes to Pragmatism: Toward a Reconstruction of Philosophy*. Oxford and New York: Oxford University Press, 2012.

Kloppenberg, James T. *Reading Obama: Dreams, Hope, and the American Political Tradition*. New Edition. Princeton, NJ: Princeton University Press, 2012.

Kuklick, Bruce. *A History of Philosophy in America 1720–2000*. Oxford and New York; Oxford University Press, 2006 [2003].

"Neil Gross, Richard Rorty: The Making of an American Philosopher." *Transactions of the Charles S. Peirce Society*, vol. 47, no. 1 (2011), 33–7.

Laugier, Sandra. "Rethinking the Ordinary: Austin *after* Cavell" in Goodman, *Contending*, pp. 82–99.

Le Pichon, Xavier. Interview by Krista Tippett. National Public Radio. August 19, 2012.

Liddell and Scott's Greek-English Lexicon. Oxford: Clarendon/Oxford University Press, 1979.

Lloyd, Seth. *Programming the Universe*. New York: Vintage Books, 2007.

Locke, John. *An Essay Concerning Human Understanding*, edited by Peter H. Nidditch. Oxford: Clarendon/Oxford University Press, 1991.

Longenbach, James. "A Music of Austerity." *The Nation*, September 14, 2009, 25–30.

Lothstein, Arthur. "'No Eros, No Buds': Teaching as Nectaring" in Campbell and Hart, eds. *On the Work of John McDermott*, pp. 178–210.

Lovejoy, A. O. "The Thirteen Pragmatisms." *The Journal of Philosophy, Psychology, and Scientific Methods*, vol. 5, no. 1 (January 2, 1908), 5–12.

Loxley, James and Andrew Taylor, eds. *Stanley Cavell: Philosophy, Literature and Criticism*. Manchester and New York: Manchester University Press, 2011.

Maillet, Arnaud. *The Claude Glass: Use and Meaning of the Black Mirror in Western Art*, translated by Jeff Fort. New York: Zone Books, 2009.

Margolis, Joseph. *Pragmatism Ascendent, A Yard of Narrative, A Touch of Prophecy*. Stanford, CA: Stanford University Press, 2012.

Martin, Jay. *The Education of John Dewey: A Biography*. New York: Columbia University Press, 2002.

Matthiessen, F. O. *The James Family: A Group Biography*. New York: Vintage Books, 1980 [1947].

McDermott, John J. *The Culture of Experience*. New York: New York University Press, 1976.

McDowell, John. "Towards Rehabilitating Objectivity" in Brandom, *Rorty*, pp. 109–23.

Menand, Louis. *Pragmatism: A Reader*. New York: Vintage Books, 1997.

Miller, Perry, ed. *American Thought: Civil War to World War I*. New York and Toronto: Rinehart and Co., 1954.

Misak, Cheryl. *The American Pragmatists*. Oxford and New York: Oxford University Press, 2013.

    ed., *The Cambridge Companion to Peirce*. Cambridge: Cambridge University Press, 2004.

    ed., *New Pragmatists*. Oxford and New York: Oxford University Press, 2007.

    "Pragmatism and Deflationism" in *New Pragmatists*, pp. 68–90.

    "Rorty's Place in the Pragmatist Pantheon" in Auxier and Hahn, eds. *The Philosophy of Richard Rorty*, pp. 27–43.

    Truth and the End of Inquiry: A Peircean Account of Truth, Second Edition. Oxford: Oxford University Press, 1991.

Monk, Ray. *Ludwig Wittgenstein: The Duty of Genius*. New York: Penguin Books, 1990.

Murphy, John P. *From Peirce to Davidson*. Boulder, San Francisco and London: Westview Press, 1990.

Musser, George. "A New Enlightenment." *Scientific American*, vol. 307, no. 5 (November 2012), 77–81.

Mutnick, Peter. "Bohr on EPR [electron paramagnetic resonance, also known as electron spin resonance] as Influenced by James and Kant, Part I," at http://www.geocities.com/saint7peter/BohronEPRI.html?200820.

Nemirovsky, Ricardo and Francesca Ferrara. *New Avenues for the Microanalysis of Mathematics Learning: Connecting Talk, Gesture, and Eye Motion* (2004) at http://www.terc.edu/mathofchange/EyeTracking/EyeTrackerPaper.pdf.

Neville, Robert Cummings. "Reflections on Philosophic Recovery" in Kasulis and Neville, *The Recovery of Philosophy in America*, pp. 1–10.

Niebuhr, Reinhold. *The Irony of American History*. Chicago: University of Chicago Press, 2008.

Nietzsche, Friedrich. "Fate and History: Thoughts (1862)" in *The Nietzsche Reader*, edited by Keith Ansell Pearson and Duncan Large. Malden, MA and Oxford: Blackwell, 2006, pp. 12–15.

    The Gay Science, Second Edition, translated by Walter Kaufmann. New York: Vintage Books, 1974.

    Human, All Too Human, Section 5 (1909–13), translated by Helen Zimmern at http://www.inquiria.com/nz/hah/hah_preface.html).

Noble, Margaret Elizabeth. *The Master as I Saw Him: Being Pages from the Life of the Swami Vivekananda*. London and New York: Longmans, Green and Co., 1910. Facsimile reprint from Elibron Classics, 2005 at http://www.elibron. com.

Nubiola, Jaime. "Scholarship on the Relations between Ludwig Wittgenstein and Charles S. Peirce." *Studies on the History of Logic. Proceedings of the iii Symposium on the History of Logic*. Berlin: Walter de Gruyter, 1996, pp. 281– 94 and online at http://www.cspeirce.com/menu/library/aboutcsp/nubiola/ scholar.htm.

Packer, Barbara. *Emerson's Fall: A New Interpretation of the Major Essays*. New York: Continuum, 1982.

Pallis, Marco. "Is There Room for Grace in Buddhism?" in *The Sword of Gnosis: Metaphysics, Cosmology, Tradition, Symbolism*, edited by Joseph Needleman. New York and London: Penguin, 1974, pp. 275–9.

Passmore, John. *A Hundred Years of Philosophy*. New York: Penguin Books, 1978.

Peirce, Charles Sanders. *The Collected Papers of Charles Sanders Peirce*, vols. 1–6 edited by Charles Hartshorne and Paul Weiss; vols. 7–8 edited by Arthur W. Burks. Cambridge, MA: Harvard University Press 1931–5 and 1958.

    The Essential Peirce: Selected Philosophical Writings, vol. 1: *1867–1893*, edited by Nathan Houser and Christian Kloesel. Bloomington and Indianapolis: Indiana University Press, 1992.

    The Essential Peirce: Selected Philosophical Writings, vol. 2: *1893–1913*, edited by the Peirce Edition Project. Bloomington and Indianapolis: Indiana University Press, 1998.

    Photometric Researches in the Years 1972–1875. Leipzig: Wilhelm Engelman, 1878.

    Reasoning and the Logic of Things: The Cambridge Conference Lectures of 1898, edited by Kenneth Laine Ketner, with an Introduction by Ketner and Hilary Putnam. Cambridge, MA: Harvard University Press, 1992.

    The Writings of Charles S. Peirce: A Chronological Edition, 6 vols. edited by Max H. Fisch. Bloomington: Indiana University Press, 1982-).

Perry, Ralph Barton. *The Thought and Character of William James*. Nashville and London: Vanderbilt University Press, 1996 [1947 one-volume edition].

Pihlstrom, Sami. "Peirce's Place in the Pragmatist Tradition" in *The Cambridge Companion to Peirce*, edited by Cheryl Misak, pp. 27–57.

    "The Prospects of Transcendental Pragmatism: Reconciling Kant and James." *Philosophy Today*, 41 (1997), 383–93.

Poirier, Richard. *Poetry and Pragmatism*. Cambridge, MA: Harvard University Press, 1992.

Posnock, Ross. "American Idol: On Nietzsche in America," a review of *American Nietzsche: A History of an Icon and His Ideas* by Jennifer Ratner-Rosenhagen in *The Nation* (November 21, 2011) at http://www.thenation.com/ article/164321/american-idol-nietzsche-america.

    "The Earth Must Resume Its Rights: A Jamesian Geneaology of Immaturity" in John J. Stuhr, ed. *100 Years of Pragmatism: William James's Revolutionary*

Philosophy. Bloomington and Indianapolis: Indiana University Press, 2010, pp. 57–80.

The Trial of Curiosity: Henry James, William James, and the Challenge of Modernity. New York and Oxford: Oxford University Press, 1991.

Putnam, Hilary. *Pragmatism: An Open Question*. Oxford, UK and Cambridge, MA: Blackwell, 1995.

Putnam, Ruth Anna, ed. *The Cambridge Companion to William James*. Cambridge: Cambridge University Press, 1997.

Ramsey, Ian. *Religious Language: An Empirical Placing of Theological Phrases*. New York: The Macmillan Company, 1963.

Richardson, Joan. *"Deadwood*: Unalterable Vibrations." *The Hopkins Review*, vol. 3, no. 3 (Summer 2010; New Series), 376–405.

"Emerson's Sound Effects." *Raritan: A Quarterly Review*, vol. 16., no. 3 (Winter 1997), 83–101.

"It's About Time: Stanley Cavell's Memory Palace." *Raritan: A Quarterly Review*, vol. 31., no. 3 (Winter 2012), 119–37.

A Natural History of Pragmatism: The Fact of Feeling from Jonathan Edwards to Gertrude Stein. Cambridge: Cambridge University Press 2007.

"Pragmatism ... She Widens the Field of Search for God" in *Revisiting Pragmatism: William James in the New Millennium*, edited by Susanne Rohr and Miriam Strube. Heidelberg: Universitatsverlag, Winter 2012, pp. 27–42.

"Thinking in Cavell: The Transcendentalist Strain" in *Stanley Cavell: Philosophy, Literature and Criticism*, edited by James Loxley and Andrew Taylor. Manchester, UK: Manchester University Press, 2011, pp. 199–224.

Wallace Stevens: The Early Years, 1879–1923. New York: Beech Tree Books/William Morrow and Co., 1986.

Wallace Stevens: The Later Years, 1923–1955. New York: Beech Tree Books/William Morrow and Co., 1988.

Richardson, Robert D. *William James: In the Maelstrom of American Modernism*. Boston and New York: Houghton Mifflin Company, 2006.

Richter, Goetz. "Is Philosophy the Greatest Kind of Music? Reflections on Plato's *Phaedo* 61a" at http://www.goetzrichter.com/pages/Writings/Phaedo%2061a.pdf.

Robinson, Andrew. "The Virtue of Vagueness," a review of Kees van Deemter, *Not Exactly: In Praise of Vagueness*. Oxford: Oxford University Press, 2010 in *Nature*, Vol. 463, no. 11 (11 February 2010), 736.

Rolland, Romain. *The Life of Vivekananda and the Universal Gospel: A Study of Mysticism and Action in Living India*, translated by E. F. Malcolm-Smith. Kolkata, India: Advaita Ashram, 2010 [1931].

Rorty, Richard. *Achieving Our Country: Leftist Thought in Twentieth-Century America*. Cambridge, MA: Harvard University Press, 1998.

Consequences of Pragmatism (Essays: 1972–1980). Minneapolis: University of Minnesota Press, 1982.

Contingency, Irony, and Solidarity. Cambridge: Cambridge University Press, 1989.

"The Fire of Life" in *Poetry* (November 2007) at http://www.poetryfoundation.org/poetrymagazine/article/180185.

Interview by Wim Kayzer, first broadcast on Dutch television in 2000, the 23rd in a series entitled "Of Beauty and Consolation" – all interviews with philosophers, scientists, and other intellectuals about the relationship between beauty and consolation – at http://www.youtube.com/watch?v=bTSdyxKyHrU.

"Matter and Event" (1963) in *Explorations of Whitehead's Philosophy*, edited by Lewis Ford and George Kline. New York: Fordham University Press, 1983, pp. 68–103.

Philosophy and the Mirror of Nature. Princeton, NJ: Princeton University Press, 1980 [1979].

"Pragmatism, Categories, and Language." *Philosophical Review*, vol. 70, no. 2 (1961), 197–223.

"Pragmatism, Davidson and Truth" in *Objectivity, Relativism, and Truth: Philosophical Papers, Volume 1*. Cambridge: Cambridge University Press, 1991, pp. 126–50.

"Pragmatism and Romanticism" in *Philosophy as Cultural Politics: Philosophical Papers, Volume 4*. Cambridge: Cambridge University Press, 2007, pp. 105–19.

"Religious Faith, Intellectual Responsibility, and Romance" in *The Cambridge Companion to William James*, edited by Ruth Anna Putnam, pp. 84–102.

Truth and Progress: Philosophical Papers, Volume 3. Cambridge: Cambridge University Press, 1998.

Rosenbaum, Stuart, ed. *Pragmatism and Religion: Classical Sources and Original Essays*. Urbana: University of Illinois Press, 2003.

Ryerson, James. "The Quest for Uncertainty: Richard Rorty's Pragmatic Pilgrimage." *Lingua Franca*, vol, 10, no. 9 (December 2000/January 2001), 42–51.

Ryle, Gilbert. *The Concept of Mind*. New York: Barnes and Noble, 1949.

Saatkamp, Herman J. Jr., ed. *Rorty and Pragmatism: The Philosopher Responds to His Critics*. Nashville, TN: Vanderbilt University Press, 1995.

Serra, Richard. ed.,"About Drawing: An Interview" in *Richard Serra, Writings, Interviews*. Chicago and London: University of Chicago Press, 1994, pp. 51–8.

Shusterman, Richard. *Thinking through the Body: Essays in Somaesthetics*. Cambridge: Cambridge University Press, 2012.

Singer, Milton. *Man's Glassy Essence: Explorations in Semiotic Anthropology*. Bloomington and Indianapolis: Indiana University Press, 1984.

Sleeper, Ralph W. *The Necessity of Pragmatism: John Dewey's Conception of Philosophy*. New Haven: Yale University Press, 1986.

Smith, John Edwin. *Jonathan Edwards: Puritan, Preacher, Philosopher*. Notre Dame, IN: Notre Dame University Press, 1993.

Sowa, John F. "Signs, Processes, and Language Games: Foundations for Ontology" (October 2006) at http://www.jfsowa.com/pubs/signproc.htm.

Stein, Gertrude. "Composition as Explanation" in *Writings 1903–1932*, edited by Catharine R. Stimpson and Harriet Chessman. New York: The Library of America, 1998, pp. 520–9.

Stevens, Wallace. *Collected Poetry and Prose*, edited by Frank Kermode and Richardson. New York: The Library of America, 1997.

Stout, Jeffrey. "On Our Interest in Getting Things Right" in Misak, *New Pragmatists*, pp. 7–31.

Stuhr, John J., ed. *100 Years of Pragmatism: William James's Revolutionary Philosophy*. Bloomington and Indianapolis: Indiana University Press, 2010.

Pragmatism and Classical American Philosophy: Essential Readings and Interpretive Essays. Oxford and New York: Oxford University Press, 1999.

Pragmatism, Postmodernism, and the Future of Philosophy. New York and London; Routledge, 2003.

Sunstein, Cass. "The Empiricist Strikes Back: Obama's Pragmatism Explained." *The New Republic*, September 10, 2008 at http://www.newrepublic.com/article/the-empiricist-strikes-back.

Swedenborg, Emanuel. *The Economy of the Animal Kingdom, Considered Anatomically, Physically, and Philosophically*, vol. 1, translated by Augustus Clissold. London: W. Newbery, 1845.

Talisse, Robert B. *A Pragmatist Philosophy of Democracy*. New York: Routledge, 2007.

Talisse, Robert B. and Scott F. Aikin. *Pragmatism: A Guide for the Perplexed*. London and New York: Continuum, 2008.

The Pragmatism Reader: From Peirce through the Present. Princeton, NJ: Princeton University Press, 2011.

Taylor, Eugene. "Peirce and Swedenborg." *Studia Swedenborgiana*, vol. 6., no. 1 (June 1986) at: http://www.baysidechurch.org/studia/default.asp?AuthorID=45.

Thoreau, Henry David. *Walden* in *A Week on the Concord and Merrimack Rivers, Walden; or, Life in the Woods, The Maine Woods, Cape Cod*, edited by Robert F. Sayre. New York: The Library of America, 1985, pp. 321–587.

Townsend, Harvey G. ed. *The Philosophy of Jonathan Edwards from His Private Notebooks*. Eugene: University of Oregon Press, 1955.

Transactions of the International Swedenborg Congress, July 4–8, 1910. London: The Swedenborg Society, 1911 [Second Edition].

The Unborn: The Life and Teachings of Zen Master Bankei 1622–1693. Translated with an Introduction by Norman Waddell. Revised Edition. New York: North Point Press, 2000 [1984].

Vivekananda, Ramakrishna. *Raja-Yoga*. New York: Ramakrishna-Vivekananda Center, 1982 [1956].

de Vries, Willem. "Wilfrid Sellars" entry in *Stanford Encyclopedia of Philosophy* (First published August 9, 2011) at http://plato.stanford.edu/entries/sellars/.

West, Cornel. *The American Evasion of Philosophy: A Geneaology of Pragmatism.* Madison: University of Wisconsin Press, 1989.

Westbrook, Robert B. *Democratic Hope: Pragmatism and the Politics of Truth.* Ithaca, NY: Cornell University Press, 2005.

"An Uncommon Faith: Pragmatism and Religious Experience" in *Pragmatism and Religion*, edited by Rosenbaum. pp. 190–205.

White, Morton. *Toward Reunion in Philosophy.* Cambridge, MA: Harvard University Press, 1956.

Whitehead, Alfred North. *Modes of Thought.* New York: The Free Press, 1968 [1938].

Science and the Modern World. New York: The Free Press, 1967.

Wilson, Emily. "Stoicism and Us." *The New Republic*, vol. 241, no. 4,880 (April 8, 2010), 32–6.

Wittgenstein, Ludwig. *Philosophical Investigations*, Third Edition, translated by G. E. M. Anscombe. New York: Macmillan Publishing Co., 1968.

Wood, Michael. "Understanding Forwards." A review of *William James: In the Maelstrom of American Modernism* by Robert D. Richardson, *London Review of Books*, September 20, 2007, 21–4.

Index

America (*cont.*)
  and Eastern philosophy, 29
  empire of, 36
  as event, ix, 96
  and experience, 28, 157
  as experiment, 100, 101, 120
  as idea, 96, 100
  language game of, 31
  Obama's vision for, 3
  and philosophy, 29, 94, 128, 132, 136, 146
  political, 139
  pragmatism as defining philosophy of, 5, 58
  "this talking America" (Emerson), 142
  as transcendentalist, 151
  and Vedantic thought, 18, 154
  and vernacular, 239n.63
architectonic, 93, 113–14, 116, 181, 225n.92,
    239n.59
"Architectonic of Theories," 114, 116.
    See also Peirce, Charles Sanders
Aristotle
  and the actual, 119
  as analogue to C.S. Peirce, 94
  as analogue to Swedenborg, 90
  and influence of, 40
  and lists of categories, 76
  and logic, 118
  and metaphor, 8
  and nature of human beings, 176
  and ornithology, 168
  and probability, 16
  read by James, 55, 213n.77
  and thinking, 6
  and Whitehead, 211n.39, 235n.11
Art as Experience, 126. *See also* Dewey, John
assemblage/s, 40, 43
Atman, 19, 21, 23, 57
Atomic Theory and Description of Nature 41–2.
    See also Bohr, Niels
attention, 106, 118, 121, 201
  and belief (W. James), 59–60, 201
  and the body, 62
  and breath (Dewey), 224n.68
  and Darwinian event, 186
  and experience, 119
  and logic, 124
  and mind, 137
  and mind for Dewey, 114
  to the natural world, 92, 100
  and neuronal patterning, 85–6
  and Peirce, 67, 71, 73, 84
  and perception, 96
  and relaxation in thinking, 8
  and sensation, 41–2
  and therapeutic purpose, ix

and triangulation, 200
Austin, J.L., 57, 123, 128
  Sense and Sensibilia, 28

Bacon, Francis, 32, 41, 161, 213n.77, 241n.80
Bain, Alexander, 50
Banville, John, 86, 220n.59
Bartlett, Mark, 156
Barzun, Jacques, 5
Bateson, Gregory, 58
Beer, Gillian, 42, 50, 59
belief
  and "assemblages" (Whitehead and James), 43
  and attention, 59–60, 201
  and chance, 38
  communal, 37
  and correspondence theory, 163, 200
  definition of (Bain), 50
  and desires, 194–5, 201
  and doubt, 36
  and faith (Dewey), 146
  and habit, 117
  in immortality, 56
  metaphysical figments (Rorty), 182
  as "the necessary angel of reality"
    (Stevens), 37
  and Obama and James, 204n.5
  objects of (W. James), 39
  Peirce's understanding of, 184
  as platform for action, 2, 31, 156. *See also* act/
    action
  possibilities of, 24, 36, 37
  pragmatist understanding of, 2, 117
  "problem of belief" (Miller), 133
  "The Psychology of Belief," 59–60.
    See also James, William
  as rules for action, 160
  "that counts" (Stevens), 34
  and truth, 217n.16
  varieties of, 14
  Western systems of, 134
  and will, 59–60, 91, 201
Bergson, Henri, 60
  Creative Evolution, 28
Bernstein, Richard, 127, 131, 161, 165–6, 168,
    171–4, 178, 183, 228n.8, 236n.23,
    236n.24
  "pragmatist turn," 163
Berzelius, J. J., 89
Bloom, Harold, 163, 166, 189
Bohm, David, 187
Bohr, Niels, 40–2, 44, 100, 186, 193, 210n.25,
    234n.4, 243n.108
Bollas, Christopher, 9
Bolshevism, 18